More On This Day in History

ANISTATIA R MILLER & JARED M. BROWN

Prentice Hall Press

CIP Data is available from the Library of Congress.

Printed in the United States of America

10 9 8 7 6 5 4 3 2 1

ISBN 0-7352-0233-8

ATTENTION: CORPORATIONS AND SCHOOLS

Prentice Hall Press books are available at quantity discounts with bulk purchase for educational, business, or sales promotional use. For information, please write to: Prentice Hall Special Sales, 240 Frisch Court, Paramus, New Jersey 07652. Please supply: title of book, ISBN, quantity, how the book will be used, date needed.

 Paramus, NJ 07652

http://www.phpress.com

Introduction

History never ceases to be written. Just as the number of ways the news is reported has expanded since the first *On This Day in History* was written in 1997, so has the number of events that have occurred. History also tends to be revised as new facts about a given case or situation come to light thanks to improvements in technology or the disclosure of unknown documents. So you might say that history also never ceases to be rewritten.

Taking note of a timely anniversary, a notable historical event, a pertinent holiday, or an eloquent quote spoken on a particular day is always an effective way to attract an audience to your main message, whether it's conveyed in a public speech, written in an article, or posted on a web site. Why? Because the pages of history are filled with points to ponder. Events can lead the way to larger questions, providing great insights into society, human nature, and the human condition.

Every single day of the year is special from a historical point of view, marking the anniversaries of history's grand and subtle turning points. This volume is a compendium of more than 8,000 important national and international incidents, anniversaries, holidays, and other observances.

These catalogued moments range from the celebratory to the solemn, from the momentous to the humorous. The accompanying background material provides an engaging glance at the facts that surround a specific event or person. In some cases, ironically similar incidents have occurred on the same day (but in different years), a reminder that history does coincidentally repeat itself throughout time.

But history is much more than a simple series of isolated incidents. We've cross-referenced many of these events with corresponding relevant dates so that you may find related and supporting material found on other days. For example, we've traced the main chronological events that occurred throughout Elvis Presley's career so you can quickly track his first audition, the day he signed his first record deal, the day he was drafted into the army, the day he married Priscilla Beaulieu, and the day he made his triumphant comeback to the live stage.

Don't forget: Today is only the eve of the next day, and a fortnight is only two weeks away. But don't stop your search for history and its relevance here. Check the local newspapers for unusual events. Surf the Internet for a particular subject. You'll never run out of timely information to pique your interest if you supplement your reading with events that originated in your own back yard. After all, the entries here are finite—limited by this book's publication date. History never stops happening. New, noteworthy events occur daily, providing even more inspiration to learn more about what has happened around you, stimulating your own thoughts about the future. If you keep your eyes open for late-breaking news, and page through this volume, you'll never be lacking for timely information.

January

The year's first month, January, is filled with firsts. The Beatles went to their first record audition and the first Euro dollar was issued. The world's first man-made object reached the moon, while the first test-tube quadruplets were born right here on earth.

1st.

1962 The Beatles went to their first record company audition (see January 20, January 24, January 30, February 7, February 9, February 12, May 9, June 6, June 12, August 29 entries).

1978 The United States established diplomatic relations with the People's Republic of China, discontinuing relations with Taiwan.

1983 TCP and IP were established.

1996 Sweden, Finland, and Austria joined the European Economic Community (see April 10 entry).

2000 The Euro was issued.

2001 The true third millennium was celebrated.

On this day in 2000, fifteen European nations bet their economies that there really is strength in numbers, when they began to share a single unit of currency. The Euro was officially issued as the common monetary unit for the members of the European Economic Community, which includes Germany, France, Italy, the United Kingdom, Greece, Spain, Ireland, Portugal, Benelux (Belgium, the Netherlands, and Luxembourg), Denmark, Austria, Finland, and Sweden.

The system that allows servers to locate each other on the massive World Wide Web was established on this day in 1983. Undersecretary of Defense Richard DeLauer issued a military directive establishing Transmission Control Protocol (TCP) and Internet Protocol (IP) as the protocol suite for ARPANET—the forerunner to the Internet—as well as all military networks. ARPANET was originally meant to be used if all other forms of communication were to fail because of a natural disaster or a nuclear attack.

The Beatles auditioned with a record company for the first time on this day in 1962. After they performed, the jaded London record executive told their manager, Brian Epstein, "These boys won't make it. Guitar groups are out. Go back to Liverpool, Mister Epstein. You have a good business there."

The dropping of the ball had a special significance on this day in 2001, when the birth of the third millennium took place. Although most millennial celebrations took place on New Year's Eve of 2000, time experts, scientists, and navies waited, since the new millennium begins on year one, not year zero. Accordingly, the U.S. Naval Observatory's time ball—like the one in New York's Times Square—was lowered as the second millennium ended at midnight. A time ball descending a mast is actually a naval tradition, alerting ship captains to the moment they should set their chronometers. This same event took place at McMurdo Station, Antarctica; Sydney, Australia; New Delhi, India; Cape Town, South Africa; Göteborg, Sweden; Greenwich, England; Edinburgh, Scotland; and New York City.

Theodore Roosevelt wrote a letter in 1901 to the people of Colorado Springs, Colorado, in which he stated, "I hope that a century hence their descendants . . . will not lose the iron strength these pioneers and sons of pioneers had." And on this day in 2001, that letter was read for the first time, when the Colorado Springs Century Chest was opened at Colorado College's Tutt Library. The hundred-year-old, 200-pound steel trunk housed newspapers, letters, photographs, family trees, and wax-cylinder audio recordings that had been sealed since August 4, 1901. U.S. Vice President Theodore Roosevelt—who was a regular visitor to the area—had written his letter a few weeks before he became president of the United States.

2nd.

1959   *Luna 1* became the first human-made object to reach the moon.

1971   The U.S. Congress banned all cigarette-oriented radio and television advertising (see January 10, April 11, May 23, July 17, August 1, August 24, September 28, December 1 entries).

1974   U.S. President Richard Nixon made 55 mph the national maximum highway speed.

1996   Chechen rebels drove Russian troops out of Grozny.

1997   California's smoking ban was extended to bars and drinking establishments (see January 10, April 11, May 23, July 17, August 1, September 28, December 1 entries).

2001   Derrick Seaver took office.

Federal and state governments targeted smoking twice on this day in the late twentieth century. The U.S. Congress banned all cigarette-oriented radio and television advertising on this day in 1971. The state of California had already imposed a smoking ban in public places, stores, and restaurants, but on this day in 1997, the state's smoking ban was extended to bars and drinking establishments as well.

The federal government pulled into the slow lane on this day. U.S. President Richard Nixon signed a bill in 1974 requiring states to establish and enforce a nationwide maximum highway speed of 55 miles per hour. The threat of reduced oil supplies inspired the government to identify an optimal, gas-efficient speed and mandate its enforcement for over twenty years.

On this day in 2001, the youngest person ever elected to the Ohio House of Representatives took office. Eighteen-year-old Derrick Seaver was elected on November 7, 2000, winning the state's 85th District seat by 242 votes. "I'm not a spokesman for young people," Seaver explained in an interview. "I'm here to do a job for the people that elected me, and many of them are from my generation." Ohio is one of only eighteen states that allow people under thirty years old to run for public office.

Although novelist Jules Verne had written about traveling from the earth to the moon in 1865, it took almost a century before it became a reality. On this day in 1959, the first human-made object made the journey, passing within 4,750 miles of the lunar surface. The unmanned Soviet satellite, *Luna 1,* then entered a solar orbit at the end of its mission. A major discovery was made during this project. Tracking its trail of orange-hued gas emissions, the satellite's instruments documented that the moon had no magnetic field.

War is never civil. On this day in 1996, Chechen defenders drove Russian troops out of the capital city of Grozny. After the Soviet Union broke up during the early 1990s, Chechens found themselves locked in a bloody struggle for autonomy against the same Russian army that had protected them for years.

3rd.

1926   George Martin was born (see June 6 entry).

1958   The U.S. Civil Rights Commission began operations.

1973   U.S. President Richard Nixon ordered all airline passengers to be screened in an effort to curb hijackings.

1984   Navy Lieutenant Robert O. Goodman, Jr., was freed.

1987   Aretha Franklin was inducted into the Rock and Roll Hall of Fame (see March 25 entry).

1990 Manuel Noriega surrendered to U.S. forces ten days after taking refuge in the Vatican's diplomatic mission (see April 9, September 5, December 20 entries).

1993 The United States and Russia signed a nuclear limitation agreement.

1995 Wage and price controls were established in Mexico.

1999 Israeli authorities deported fourteen Americans.

1999 It was reported that the nation's murder rate fell.

2000 The seventeenth Karmapa Lama escaped Tibet (see January 16, July 6 entries).

2001 The Russian military moved nuclear weapons.

No leader is popular when his or her nation is on the rocks. Three weeks after Mexican President Ernesto Zedillo took office, the economy collapsed. On this day in 1995, Zedillo instigated an emergency plan in order to curb rapid inflation and to stabilize the peso. His scheme called for widespread government budget cuts and the establishment of major wage and price controls throughout the nation. Less than four years later his party, the PRI, which had held power for over seventy years, lost the next election.

At times the weight of diplomacy comes from the speaker more than the words. In 1984 Navy Lieutenant Robert O. Goodman, Jr., who had been shot down during a U.S. raid against Syrian anti-aircraft positions in Lebanon, was freed after a month's captivity after Rev. Jesse Jackson traveled to Syria to appeal for his release.

Civilization began to look a little more civilized on this day. A U.S. Justice Department report issued in 1999 revealed a noteworthy trend: Big cities had become safer. Statistics showed the murder rate had fallen two years earlier to its lowest level since the mid-1960s. Most surprisingly, the greatest decline occurred in large cities with million-plus populations, which had been hotbeds for homicide compared with suburbs and rural towns.

Holy places inspire reverence. Unfortunately, they also attract and incite unstable individuals. On this day in 1999, Israeli authorities apprehended and detained fourteen American visitors from Denver, Colorado who were members of a cult called Concerned. Government officials suspected that the group was plotting a number of violent events in Jerusalem, hoping to trigger the Second Coming of Jesus Christ. The group was later released and deported.

A preacher's daughter became the first female inductee into the Rock and Roll Hall of Fame in 1987. The "Queen of Soul," Aretha Franklin brought soul music into the mainstream during her five-decade-long career, singing hits like "Freeway of Love," "Respect," and "You Make Me Feel Like a Natural Woman."

Among Tibet's reincarnated spiritual guides, the Dalai Lama, Panchen Lama, and Karmapa Lama have also served as political leaders in this small Himalayan nation. Forced to flee Tibet during the Chinese invasion of the 1950s, the Dalai Lama continues to fight for his people's freedom while living in northern India. On this day in 2000, the fourteen-year-old Karmapa Lama escaped his Chinese mentors, crossing from Tibet into India to join the Dalai Lama. Guards were told that he was beginning a special prayer retreat, in which no one but his teacher and cook could see him. On December 28, 1999, he slipped out of his room at the monastery and made the eight-day journey to freedom. The ten-year-old Panchen Lama was kidnapped from Tibet in 1995 and still lives under heavy guard in China.

For the first time since the Cold War ended in 1991, the Russian military moved tactical nuclear weapons into the Baltic military base Kaliningrad on this day in 2001. The move, which directly violated the Soviets' ten-year-old pledge to the United States to reduce arsenals of tactical nuclear weapons, was in response to the North Atlantic Treaty Organization's expansion. Ironically, U.S. President George H. Bush and Russian President Boris Yeltsin had signed a historic nuclear missile reduction treaty in Moscow on this same day in 1993.

4th.

1865 The New York Stock Exchange opened its first permanent headquarters (see February 13, September 20 entries).

1887 Thomas Stevens completed the first bicycle trip around the world.

1920 The National Negro Baseball League was organized (see May 2 entry).

1946 The "Heckle and Jeckle" cartoon show made its debut.

1974 U.S. President Richard Nixon refused to hand over tapes and documents to the Senate Watergate Committee.

1979 An out-of-court settlement was awarded to victims of the Kent State shootings (see August 3 entry).

1988   *Newsweek* magazine announced that greed had gone out of style.

1989   The USS *John F. Kennedy* embarked F-14 Tomcats to down Libyan MIG-23 fighters.

1995   The 104th U.S. Congress convened.

1999   Jesse Ventura took the oath of office.

The pursuit of the almighty dollar was on people's minds on this day in 1865, when the New York Stock Exchange opened its first permanent headquarters at 10-12 Broad Street in New York City's financial district. Markets have risen and crashed more than once at the NYSE since its opening. The 1987 stock market crash, for example, burst the 1980s money-madness bubble. On this day in 1988, *Newsweek* magazine's cover announced "The '80s Are Over: Greed Goes Out of Style."

During the height of the protests against the Vietnam War, four unarmed students were killed and nine were injured at Ohio's Kent State University in 1970 by National Guardsmen sent to suppress a campus demonstration. An arduous legal battle ensued. And on this day in 1979, a $675,000 out-of-court settlement was awarded to the survivors. In January 2001, Kent State's administration sparked vocal protests when they chose to equip campus police with military-style M16 rifles.

On this day in 1887, Thomas Stevens completed the first bicycle trip around the world. Stevens had set out in 1884 from Oakland, California, after spending a few days learning how to ride a bicycle, a high-wheeler, hoping to become the first person to bicycle across North America. When he reached Boston 103 days later, the League of American Bicyclists offered him sponsorship, so he just hopped aboard a boat and kept going. On this day he arrived back in San Francisco from Japan. His epic journey is chronicled in the two-volume book *Around the World by Bicycle*.

American politics took some unusual turns on this day during the late twentieth century. In 1974 U.S. President Richard M. Nixon refused to hand over tape recordings and documents that the Senate Watergate Committee had subpoenaed. In 1995 the 104th U.S. Congress convened, marking the first Republican-controlled session since Dwight D. Eisenhower was president. And in 1999 a former World Wrestling Federation professional, Jesse Ventura, took the oath of office as Minnesota's thirty-seventh governor.

5th.

1972   U.S. President Richard Nixon signed a bill to create a series of space shuttles.

1975   *The Wiz* opened on Broadway.

1987   President Ronald Reagan produced the first trillion-dollar budget in U.S. history.

1999   Iraqi jets tested the "no-fly" zone.

2000   The U.S. Immigration and Naturalization Service decided that Eliàn Gonzalez should be sent back to Cuba.

This is a great day to look to the stars. In 1972 U.S. President Richard Nixon launched the space shuttle program. He signed a bill giving NASA the authority to develop a reusable space shuttle system.

South of the Dardanelles, a military hot zone flared up on this day in 1999. Four Iraqi MIG jets tested the designated "no-fly" zone over southern Iraq, drawing the attention of American peacekeeping forces. Four U.S. Air Force and Navy jets fired on the intruders, but they missed. It was the first time Iraqi forces had confronted peacekeepers in over six years.

6th.

1822   Heinrich Schliemann was born.

1920   Reverend Sun Myung Moon was born in Sangsa-ri, Korea (see August 25 entry).

1925   Paavo Nurmi, a Finnish runner, set two world records.

1939   The first *Superman* comic strip appeared in newspapers.

1942   A B-314 completed the first commercial flight around the world.

1952   The *Peanuts* comic strip made the first page of the Sunday funnies.

1964 The Rolling Stones began their first U.S. tour.

1984 The world's first test-tube quadruplets were born in Australia.

1993 Charles H. Keating, Jr., and his son, Charles H. Keating III, were convicted in Lincoln Savings & Loan scandal (see April 10, November 15 entries).

1993 Dizzy Gillespie died.

1995 Haitians were deported from Cuba.

"Like money in the bank" is an old expression meaning that something is assured. It nearly lost its meaning in the public mind when the Lincoln Savings & Loan scandal broke in the media, and scores of small investors discovered they'd lost their life's savings. On this day in 1993, the financial institution's former CEO, Charles H. Keating, Jr., was convicted on seventy-three counts of securities and wire fraud, racketeering, and conspiracy. His son, Charles H. Keating III, was found guilty on sixty-four similar counts.

The aeronautics industry made a major breakthrough on this day in 1942. A B-314 completed the first commercial flight around the world. The Pan-American Airways's *Pacific Clipper* landed in New York City, returning from its historic circumnavigation.

Good grief! It's truth, justice, and the American way. Two familiar comic strips debuted on this day. In 1939 the McClure Syndicate first placed Jerry Seigel and Joe Shuster's *Superman* comic in newspapers. In 1952 Charles M. Schulz's *Peanuts* comic strip made its debut in Sunday funny pages across the United States.

A great debut for rock and roll shares this day with a great loss for jazz. The Rolling Stones began their first U.S. tour on this day in 1964. The Stones' brand of rock and roll was strongly influenced by American blues and jazz stars. On this day in 1993, one of bebop's originators died in Englewood, New Jersey. Trumpeter Dizzy Gillespie had joined in the many New York jam sessions along with Charlie Parker and Thelonius Monk during the 1940s. It was from those experiments that bebop emerged, evolving into modern jazz over the next decade.

Haitian refugees had enjoyed a semblance of freedom from political oppression while they were imprisoned at the Guantanamo Bay Naval Base in Cuba during the early 1990s. But that peace ended despite public protests in the United States on this day in 1995, when U.S. military officials began to deport the refugees back to Haiti.

Early retirement does have its advantages. When Heinrich Schliemann, who was born on this day in 1822 in Neubuckow, Germany, retired after amassing a fortune in the business world by the time he was forty-six years old, he chose to live out a childhood ambition. He wanted to locate the legendary ancient Greek city of Troy. An amateur archaeologist, Schliemann was assisted by professional archaeologist Willhelm Dorpfeld as he uncovered one of the most spectacular finds of the century: nine superimposed city sites on the mound of Hisarlik in Turkey, which definitively proved the existence of Homer's epic city. After this initial success, he went on to excavate other sites found in Homeric poems: Mycenae, Ithaca, Orchomenos, and Tiryns.

On this day in 1925, the Finnish runner Paavo Nurmi set two world records in his first U.S. appearance. Nicknamed the "Flying Finn" after he won four gold medals at the 1924 Paris Olympics, Nurmi ran the mile and the 5000-meter races within an hour at Madison Square Garden. In both events it appeared that he was beaten. Then, in finishes that brought the crowds to their feet, he came up from behind and snatched the win, setting two new records.

7th.

1745 Jacques Etienne Montgolfier, co-inventor of the hot air balloon, was born.

1785 Jean-Pierre Blanchard crossed the English Channel (see January 19, July 25, August 6, August 25, September 10, December 1 entries).

1890 The fountain pen was patented (see August 17 entry).

1927 Commercial transatlantic telephone service began.

1927 The Harlem Globetrotters played their first game.

1955 Marian Anderson became the first African-American to appear in the Metropolitan Opera's production of Verdi's *Masked Ball* (see February 17, April 9 entries).

1971 Use of the pesticide DDT was outlawed.

1980 U.S. President Jimmy Carter signed the Chrysler Loan Guarantee Act (see October 1 entry).

1983 Unemployment hit 9.7 percent.

1993 Secondhand smoke was reclassified.

1999 U.S. President Bill Clinton's impeachment trial began when Chief Justice William Rehnquist was sworn in to preside along with a jury of 100 senators.

2001 The first on-line MBAs graduated.

The pen and the telephone saw great advances and a lot of use on this day, with people, business, and animals as the beneficiaries. W.B. Purvis patented the fountain pen in 1890, offering an efficient and transportable alternative to stick pens and quills, which required a separate ink source. Commercial transatlantic telephone service between New York and London was inaugurated on this day in 1927. Thirty-one calls were made on the first day. With an eye on the environment, in 1971 the pesticide DDT was outlawed by the U.S. Court of Appeals. Enough evidence had been gathered to prove that animals such as the peregrine falcon, sandhill crane, and black-footed ferret were at the brink of extinction because of DDT's widespread use by farmers and urban exterminators. In 1980 U.S. President Jimmy Carter signed the Chrysler Loan Guarantee Act, making $1.5 billion in federal support available to the troubled automaker. Unfortunately, there was also some red ink flowing. The Labor Department reported, in 1983, that unemployment had hit 9.7 percent in 1982, the highest rate since 1941.

Americans may not have breathed any easier on this day, but there was a major step in the right direction. The Environmental Protection Agency announced the results of a four-year study in 1993, stating that secondhand smoke was a Class A carcinogen, causing lung cancer and killing an estimated 3,000 nonsmokers per year. It was also implied that the symptoms of 200,000 to 1 million asthmatics under the age of 18 and 150,000 to 300,000 infant respiratory infections were caused by secondhand smoke.

School came to people who couldn't attend class as it never had before. The first Internet master's degree students graduated on this day in 2001. The six graduates of the University of Baltimore's on-line Master of Business Administration program held their commencement, meeting for the first time at a campus they'd never seen. The program was the first ever offered by a university that had been accredited by the International Association for Management Education.

Jacques Etienne Montgolfier was born on this day in 1745 in Annonay, France. The son of a paper manufacturer, Jacques and his brother Joseph were fascinated by the concept of manned flight. Together they invented and successfully launched a hot-air balloon, in 1783, that used a cauldron of burning paper as its sole energy source. Sadly, further aeronautical experiments were thwarted by the outbreak of the French Revolution. "Up, up, and away" again became the words of this day when, in 1785, Jean-Pierre Blanchard became the first balloonist to cross the English Channel. Blanchard went on to become the first person to fly an untethered balloon in North America. (George Washington was one of the spectators.) He is also alleged to be the first skydiver, as he reputedly parachuted from a balloon.

The exhibition basketball team the Harlem Globetrotters played their first game in Hinckley, Illinois, on this day in 1927. Founded the previous year by Abe Saperstein, this team of African-American players, dubbed the Ambassadors of Goodwill, performed more than 20,000 games in 114 countries over three-quarters of a century. During the late 1940s, the Globetrotters gained their stature for comic display. But don't let their antics fool you. These hard-working players also beat the nation's top team during that time—the Los Angeles Lakers.

8th.

1800	The Wild Boy of Aveyron was discovered.
1870	The U.S. mint at Carson City, Nevada, began issuing coins.
1889	The first U.S. patent for a tabulating machine was issued.
1928	Sander Vanocur was born.
1933	Charles Osgood was born.
1934	Jacques Anquetil was born.
1942	Vyacheslav D. Zudov was born.
1947	Igor Ivanov was born.
1965	The Star of India was returned.
1973	*Luna 21* was launched.
1974	Gold hit a record high in London.
1974	Silver hit a record high in New York.

1976 The Franklin Mint struck the first gold coins for the Netherlands Antilles.

1985 The *Sakigake* space probe was launched.

Precious metals made the news more than once on this day. The U.S. mint at Carson City, Nevada, issued its first coins in 1870. When the ban on private ownership of gold was lifted during the 1970s, market prices soared from an original $28-an-ounce baseline. On this day in 1974, gold hit a record $126.50 an ounce in London. On this exact same day, silver hit a record $3.40 an ounce in New York. And in 1976 the Franklin Mint struck the first gold coins issued by the Netherlands Antilles.

Personality plays a major role in the delivery of the news these days. Anchorman for the "NBC Weekend News," Sander Vanocur, who was born in 1928 in Cleveland, Ohio, provided an accessible but serious face for the news. Born in New York City in 1933, Charles Osgood took a different approach. As the anchorman for the "CBS Weekend News" and "CBS Sunday Morning Show," Osgood offered a down-to-earth delivery to the day's events.

The world sought answers to the questions posed by the vast unknown of outer space on this day. In 1942 Vyacheslav D. Zudov, one of the Soviet cosmonauts aboard *Soyuz 23,* was born in Nizniy Novgorod, Russia. The USSR launched *Luna 21* on this day in 1973, intending to land the module on the moon's surface. Japan launched the *Sakigake* space probe on this day in 1985. Its mission was to study the path and nature of Halley's Comet.

It's been said that everyone and everything has a twin in this world. Two unarguable exceptions made the news on this day. In 1800 the Wild Boy of Aveyron was discovered in southern France. In 1965 a 563-carat sapphire known as the Star of India was returned to the American Museum of Natural History in New York City. This singular gem had been stolen from the museum a few months earlier by Jack "Murf the Surf" Murphy, a surfing champion who had been inspired by the 1960s mystery movie *Topkapi* to steal the stone.

A physical champion and a mental champion were born on this day. In 1934 Jacques Anquetil, the five-time winner of the Tour de France cycle race, was born in Mont Saint-Aignan, France. In 1947 Canadian chess champion Igor Ivanov was born in Leningrad, Russia. Ivanov won international tournaments from 1981 through 1988.

9th.

1793 The first manned balloon trip in the United States took place (see January 7 entry).

1900 Richard Halliburton was born.

1923 The first successful autogyro flight took place.

1968 *Surveyor VII* landed near the lunar crater Tycho.

1969 The first Concorde trial test took place.

1984 The "Where's the beef?" commercial first appeared.

2001 The Kumbh Mela festival began in India.

In 1984 Clara Peller, a widow and former cosmetologist from Chicago, Illinois, became an instant celebrity. She appeared in Wendy's "Where's the beef?" television ads, which were first broadcast on this day.

Aeronautics reached new heights on this day. In 1793 Jean-Pierre Blanchard flew the first manned balloon trip over American land. U.S. President George Washington and other spectators paid five dollars apiece to observe the start of Blanchard's flight from Philadelphia's Independence Square to a New Jersey field. Blanchard took his accomplishment in stride, sipping wine and snacking on biscuits during the flight. In 1923 Juan de la Cierva's autogyro made its first successful flight in Madrid, Spain—the climax of four years of design and construction. And in 1969 the Concorde went through its first trial test at Bristol, England. The Franco-British supersonic commercial aircraft eventually became the fastest means of transport from Paris or London to New York, reaching speeds of Mach 2 or 1,336 miles per hour.

In 1900 Richard Halliburton was born in Brownsville, Texas, on this day. He found the love of his life in the classroom—geography. Not content to read about travel, he set out to see the world. And in the process he wrote a stack of books about his adventures, including *New Worlds to Conquer* and *The Flying Carpet,* capturing a world on the verge of globalization.

On this day, 65 million people bathed together. The 43-day religious festival called the Kumbh Mela began in Allahabad, India, on this day in 2001. Once every twelve years, devout Hindus make the pilgrimage to this city along the Ganges River to wash away their sins in the ice-cold waters that flow from the Himalayas into the nation's largest river. Hindus believe that these ablutions can speed their journey to nirvana. To handle the huge influx of devotees, twelve emergency hospitals and thirty-five temporary police stations were set up near the river banks.

10th.

1929   The *Tintin* comic book series first appeared in print.

1947   Stanford University announced that the virus that causes polio had been isolated (see February 23, August 1, October 28 entries).

1949   George Foreman was born.

1967   The Public Broadcasting System began operations.

1972   A *Washington Post* article stated that cigarette smoke potentially harmed nonsmokers (see January 2, April 11, May 23, July 17, August 1, August 24, September 28, December 1 entries).

The face of network television programming changed radically on this day in 1967. The Public Broadcasting System (PBS) began broadcasts of nature programs, news, educational programs, and children's shows over seventy stations nationwide.

Although only a handful of Americans have ever read the adventures of Tintin and his dog Milou (meaning "Snowy"), his widespread popularity has sold over 120 million copies in more than forty languages worldwide. Belgian comic artist George Remi, who worked under the pen name Hergé, published the first Tintin adventure, *Tintin in the Land of the Soviets,* on this day in 1929. He added other regular characters like the irascible Captain Haddock and the absent-minded Professor Calculus shortly thereafter. Tintin and Milou were inspired creations, fighting injustice whenever it confronted them in their comic adventures, and became role models for generations of youth.

In 1949 heavyweight boxing champion George Foreman was born in Marshall, Texas. As a troubled youth, Foreman found that boxing was a perfect outlet for his energies and interests. Foreman went from the streets of Houston to win a gold medal in the 1968 Olympics. His record as of 2001 was sixty-nine wins and three losses, with sixty-five knockouts.

11th.

1902 *Popular Mechanics* magazine was published.

1935 Amelia Earhart flew from Honolulu, Hawaii, to Oakland, California (see May 21, May 25, July 24, August 24 entries).

1943 The United States and Great Britain signed treaties relinquishing extraterritorial rights in mainland China.

1964 U.S. Surgeon General Luther Terry issued the first government report stating that smoking may be hazardous to one's health.

1978 The *Soyuz 27* docked at the *Salyut 6* space station, joining the already docked *Soyuz 26*.

1991 The U.S. Congress empowered President George H. Bush to order attacks on Iraq.

1993 Howard Stern's radio show began transmission in Buffalo, New York (see January 12 entry).

1994 The Irish government announced the end of a twenty-year broadcasting ban imposed upon the IRA.

1995 The fifth national TV network began broadcast transmission.

It was a day of mixed reception for the broadcasting world. In 1993 the notorious Manhattan talk-radio host Howard Stern began transmission of his "shock radio show" in Buffalo, New York, on station WKBW-AM. In 1994 the Irish government announced the end of a twenty-year broadcasting ban imposed upon the Irish Republican Army, which had been responsible for militant terrorist activities for over a century. On this same day in 1995, the fifth national TV network began broadcast transmission. Warner Brothers' WB channel began transmission in New York City as station WPIX-TV.

12th.

1879 The Zulu War began.

1951 Rush Limbaugh was born.

1954 Howard Stern was born (see January 11 entry).

1964 A revolution took place in Zanzibar.

1971 "All in the Family" aired on national television.

1984 U.S. President Ronald Reagan endorsed the Space Station Freedom Act.

1992 HAL the computer was born.

1992 Line Mode Browser v1.1 was made available by anonymous FTP.

2001 The world's oldest insole was discovered.

A famous fictional computer was born on this day in 1992. According to Stanley Kubrick's film script for *2001: A Space Odyssey,* HAL came to life at the University of Illinois in Champaign-Urbana. Ironically, on the exact same date, the World Wide Web—in the form of Line Mode Browser v1.1—was made available by anonymous FTP.

Talk radio was never the same after two births that occurred on this day. In 1951 Rush Limbaugh was born in Cape Girardeau, Missouri. And in 1954 Howard Stern was born in Jackson Heights, New York. However, outlandish opinions and outright bigotry have always had public appeal. On this day in 1971, the first episode of "All in the Family" aired on national television, introducing the world to the conservative mind of Archie Bunker.

Freedom in Africa has always been hard to win and maintain. Zanzibar Revolution Day marks this day, in 1964, when the African majority successfully revolted against the Arab leadership. A new government was formed and the country's name changed to Tanzania. It was not the first time. In 1879 the Zulu War began shortly after 17,922 British troops led by Lord Chelmsford invaded Zululand in South Africa's northeastern KwaZulu/Natal province. The 40,000 well-trained Impi (Zulu army) led by King Cetshwayo had a number of major initial victories, especially at Isandlwana and Hlobane. The six-month-long war, and the Zulu empire itself, ended at Ulundi when Zulu warriors armed with spears and clubs accepted that they could no longer match British weaponry like Martini rifles on the battlefield.

Aching feet are nothing new. The world's oldest insole was discovered on this day in 2001. Archaeologists uncovered the item while excavating a Neolithic settlement during the renovation of a major road near Zug, Switzerland. Although the shoe had decomposed during the 5,200 years it spent in the lakeland's wet soil, the thin moss insole (which measured 10 inches in length) had miraculously survived.

13th.

1920 *The New York Times* ridiculed a claim that rockets could break through the atmosphere and enter space.

1957 The Wham-O company produced its first toy flying discs.

1978 NASA selected the first women astronauts.

1993 American, British, and French warplanes wiped out radar and missile sites in southern Iraq after warning Iraqi leader Saddam Hussein to move the weapons.

1998 Linda Tripp met with Monica Lewinsky (see June 1, September 11 entries).

Friends and confidantes must always be chosen carefully. On this day in 1998, former Pentagon employee Linda Tripp met with Monica Lewinsky. Wearing a secret listening device, Tripp recorded details about Lewinsky's alleged 1995 affair with U.S. President Bill Clinton. She later turned the tapes over to the special prosecutor in the case.

The media was not convinced, until very recently, that outer space could be explored. *The New York Times* published an article on this day in 1920 ridiculing the claim that rockets could break through the atmosphere and enter space. The public's fascination with space and the potential existence of flying saucers was evident when, on this day in 1957, the Wham-O Company produced its first toy flying discs. Although mankind slipped the bonds of gravity and flew into space, and even landed on the moon during the 1960s, it took womankind a little more time. In 1978 NASA selected its first female astronauts on this same day.

14th.

1925 Yukio Mishima was born.

1978 The Sex Pistols gave their last concert (see October 8 entry).

1990 "The Simpsons" first aired as a regular TV series.

1997   Steve Fossett took off in his hot-air balloon, *Solo Spirit,* from St. Louis, Missouri, attempting to establish a new nonstop distance record (see January 20, February 21, August 7, August 16 entries).

1999   The U.S. Senate began opening arguments in its impeachment trial of President Bill Clinton.

Novelist Yukio Mishima, who was born in Tokyo, Japan, on this day in 1925, lived on the dark side of life. His first major novel, *Confessions of a Mask,* dealt with homosexuality and the ways it's concealed. The darker side of honor and chivalry was disclosed in his novel *The Sailor Who Fell from Grace with the Sea.* Mishima was enamored with Bushido—the samurai code of honor—and history of imperial Japan. In 1960 he founded the Shield Society, which was dedicated to a revival of Bushido. His 100-person private army attempted to seize Tokyo's military headquarters in 1970. The takeover failed, inspiring Mishima to commit ritual suicide like the samurai of old.

15th.

1906   Aristotle Onassis was born (see July 3, July 28, October 20 entries).

1918   Gamal Abdal Nasser was born.

1965   The Rolling Stones appeared on "The Ed Sullivan Show" (see May 12, June 3, June 14, July 30, October 25, December 5, December 6, December 18 entries).

1991   The largest hot-air balloon ever flown was launched (see January 17 entry).

2001   A chocolate spa opened in Hershey, Pennsylvania.

When Milton Hershey started making chocolate in Hershey, Pennsylvania, no one imagined the delectable treat would become such a healthy venture. On this day in 2001, the Hershey Hotel opened its $7-million spa, which features whirlpool baths of cocoa, massages, and facials made from chocolate and cocoa butter scrubs.

The movement of goods throughout the world has made many men fabulously wealthy. Perhaps the most impressive is Aristotle Socrates Onassis, who was born in Smyrna, Turkey, on this day in 1906. The son of a Greek tobacco importer, Onassis left home as a refugee when he was sixteen years old, making his way from Turkey to Greece to Buenos Aires, Argentina. Like his father, Onassis made a fortune in tobacco. He purchased his first ships when he was only twenty-six years old, quickly building one of the world's largest shipping fleets and pioneering the use of supertankers.

Transoceanic travel reached new heights on this day in 1991, when Virgin Corporation founder Richard Branson and Colt Balloons Ltd. founder Per Lindstrand launched the largest hot-air balloon ever flown, and traveled from Miyakonojo, Japan, to Yellowknife, Canada. The 220-foot-tall *Pacific Flyer* wasn't the pair's first venture. Four years earlier, they made the first transatlantic crossing in a hot-air balloon. Aboard the *Pacific Flyer,* the pair succeeded in setting a few records and breaking a few others by becoming the first men to make a transpacific crossing. Forty-six nonstop hours later, they landed, beating all previous duration and distance records in the process.

On this day in 1965, The Rolling Stones appeared on "The Ed Sullivan Show." Producers allowed the rock band to perform after they agreed to one proviso that seems quaint compared with modern censorship. The band was required to change the lyrics of their hit song "Let's Spend the Night Together" to "Let's spend some time together."

Gamal Abdul Nasser was no stranger to loss. Born on this day in 1918, in Alexandria, Egypt, Nasser had experienced poor military management firsthand as a soldier during the 1948 Palestine campaign. A corrupt government inspired him to lead the military junta that deposed King Farouk and subsequently deposed General Neguib, who had dictatorial ambitions. Elected Egypt's president in 1956, Nasser expropriated the Suez Canal and sought to unite all Arab nations into the United Arab Republic. His dreams were never fully realized. But in 1964 he did form a joint presidency council with Iraq and Yemen. After his side suffered heavy losses in the 1967 Six-Day War, Nasser tendered his resignation, but he was persuaded to remain in office.

16th.

1866   Clamp-on ice skates received a patent (see March 2 entry).

1874   Robert William Service was born.

1901   Fulgencio Batista was born.

1932 Dian Fossey was born (see December 27 entry).

1996 *The Trenton Times* reported that Pennsylvania Attorney General Ernie Preate, Jr., was living in a federal prison camp at Duluth, Minnesota.

2000 The seventh Reting Lama was enthroned (see January 3, July 6 entries).

2001 The landing craft *LST* crossed the Atlantic Ocean.

On this day in 1866, Civil War arms manufacturer Everett Barney received a patent for clamp-on ice skates, changing winter recreation forever. Even after he passed away, however, he continued to influence the lives of children. He donated hundreds of acres in Springfield, Massachusetts, for parkland. A young boy named Teddy Geisel, who played around Barney's mausoleum, was so inspired by his surroundings that he incorporated parts of it into the picture books he created when he grew up and took on the name Dr. Seuss.

The Canadian wilderness held a strong attraction for Robert William Service while he worked as a traveling reporter for the *Toronto Star.* Born in Preston, England, on this day in 1874, Service wrote ballads about rugged Canadian life, including poems like "The Shooting of Dan McGrew," "The Cremation of Sam McGee," "Songs of a Sourdough," "Rhymes of a Rolling Stone," and "The Spell of the Yukon."

When governments topple, it can spell personal trouble for the people in charge. Born in Oriente province, Cuba, on this day in 1901, Cuban dictator Fulgencio Batista was overthrown by Fidel Castro in 1959. He was forced to seek refuge in the Dominican Republic. On this same day in 1979, Iran's Mohammed Reza Shah Pahlavi was forced into exile, moving to the United States. Responsible for the modernization of Iran on both social and economic levels, Pahlavi was opposed on one side by orthodox Muslims for the imposition of too many reforms, and by liberals and leftists, on the other, for the maintenance of a so-called police state.

A two-year-old boy named Soinam Puncog was enthroned by Chinese officials in Beijing, China, on this day in 2000. As the seventh reincarnation of the Reting Lama— one of Tibet's living Buddhas—Puncog joined the physical world once again along with the Dalai Lama and the Karmapa Lama, who both live in exile in northern India. Many devout Tibetans, however, do not believe that Puncog is a true reincarnation.

The woman who opened the world's eyes to the gentle nature of mountain gorillas was born in San Francisco, California, on this day in 1932. Dian Fossey had trained as an occupational therapist before she met archaeologist Louis Leakey during a trip she made to Africa in 1963. Four years later, Fossey began to observe elusive bands of mountain gorillas in Zaire and then in Rwanda, where she started the Karisoke Research Center. Fossey was the first human to make voluntary contact with a mountain gorilla when one subject touched her hand. In 1980 she moved to Cornell University, where she wrote her book *Gorillas in the Mist*. She returned to Karisoke a few years later to continue her campaign against the poaching of gorillas and to continue her research. But in 1985 Fossey was found murdered in her cabin. The mystery has never been solved.

Lauren Whiting and a crew of twenty-eight septuagenarian war veterans completed an Atlantic crossing in a 328-foot Second World War landing craft, *LST*, which they sailed from Greece to Mobile, Alabama. The ship was slated to become a floating museum in the United States. It had been lent to the Greek government for twenty years and was taken out of service in 2000. Each crewman had to pay his way to Greece and pitch in $2,000 for expenses. Although the U.S. Coast Guard said the craft was derelict, the crew braved harsh winter conditions to accomplish their goal. Whiting said in an interview, "The most difficult part of it was the tension of trying to get her back to Mobile on time because there were lots of things planned for our reception. And of course, everybody was anxious to get home and you're relying on these two old engines."

17th.

1863 Konstantin Stanislavski was born.

1929 *Popeye the Sailor Man* first appeared in newspapers.

1934 Private ownership of gold certificates was made illegal.

1942 Muhammed Ali was born.

1944 Joe Frazier was born.

1966 A U.S. B-52 bomber collided with its refueling plane.

1991 The hot-air balloon *Pacific Flyer* made the first manned Pacific crossing (see January 15 entry).

1991 The Gulf War started (see August 2 entry).

One of the worst nuclear accidents occurred on this day in 1966. A U.S. B-52 bomber carrying four hydrogen bombs collided with its refueling plane over Palomares, Spain, killing eight people. One bomb fell into the Mediterranean Sea and two bombs exploded on the ground. To protect residents, 1,400 tons of topsoil were removed and sent to a nuclear waste site in South Carolina.

Actors seek motivation thanks to Konstantin Stanislavski, who stressed theatrical realism. Born in Moscow, Russia, on this day in 1863, Stanislavski researched the psychological makeup and background of a character. His method also demanded a precise blend of setting and gestures in order to create the perfect stage production.

Two heavyweight boxing champions were born on this day. In 1942, Cassius Marcellus Clay, Jr., was born in Louisville, Kentucky. Winner of the 1960 Olympic gold medal in boxing, Clay changed his name to Muhammed Ali in 1964 after he converted to Islam. And two years later, Joe Frazier was born in Beaufort, South Carolina, becoming the winner of the 1964 Olympic gold medal in boxing. The two pugilists met in the same ring in 1971, when Ali and Frazier's bout was hyped as the "Fight of the Century." Frazier won the competition.

On this day in 1991, the Gulf War began. American and allied missiles and planes bombed selected targets in Iraq and Kuwait. The action earned U.S. President George H. Bush the highest public approval rating since President Franklin Roosevelt declared war on Japan in 1941. Perhaps hoping to bolster his own approval ratings, U.S. President George W. Bush, on February 16, 2001, ordered airstrikes on five military sites around Baghdad.

18th.

1882   A.A. Milne was born.

1888   Sir Thomas Sopwith was born (see July 25, August 6, August 25, September 10, December 1 entries).

1896   The first college basketball game was played.

1911   Lieutenant Eugene Ely landed a plane on a platform attached to a ship.

1913   Danny Kaye was born.

1951   The polygraph was used for the first time.

1968   Eartha Kitt confronted Lady Bird Johnson about the Vietnam war (see January 26 entry).

1975   "The Jeffersons" premiered on network television.

Crime detection took a new turn on this day. In 1951 the polygraph was used for the first time in the Netherlands. Nicknamed the lie detector, the device uses four to six sensors attached to a person's body, recording any significant changes in their breathing rate, pulse, blood pressure, and perspiration that would suggest the subject is lying. However, because the results are dependent on the tester's experience, they are subjective and generally inadmissible as evidence in a court.

Slapstick and tongue-twisting songs were Danny Kaye's claim to international fame. Born in Brooklyn, New York, on this day in 1913, Kaye honed his antics singing and dancing at school and at summer camp in the Catskill Mountains. His overwhelmingly successful film and stage debuts during the late 1930s led to the filming of *The Secret Life of Walter Mitty, Hans Christian Andersen,* and *The Inspector General* during the 1940s and 1950s. Offstage, Kaye tirelessly worked as a UNICEF fund raiser and became a master cook of Chinese cuisine.

The first African-American TV show, "The Jeffersons," premiered on network television on this day in 1975. A spinoff of the hit sitcom "All in the Family," the show centered around George and Louise Jefferson's move to Manhattan's Upper East Side.

On this day, show business and politics went head to head. In 1968 Eartha Kitt told Lady Bird Johnson in a White House confrontation that American youths were in rebellion because of the Vietnam War. This incident seriously damaged Kitt's career for the next two decades.

Not everyone needed to seek their adventures in far-off lands. Born on this day in 1888, Sir Thomas Sopwith looked for his challenges in the skies, winning the 1910 Baron de Forest Prize for flying across the English Channel. Designer of the *Sopwith Camel* and founder of the Sopwith Aviation Company, Sopwith designed and built many of the planes used during the First World War. As a yachtsman, Sopwith even competed in the 1934 America's Cup. Ships and planes met for the first time on this day in 1911, when Lieutenant Eugene Ely took off and landed a Curtiss biplane on the afterdeck of the USS *Pennsylvania* in San Francisco Bay.

Born on this day in London, England, in 1882, Alan Alexander Milne seemed born to write, editing the undergraduate magazine at Cambridge University and writing light essays as a staff editor for *Punch*. But Milne's fame came from a volume of stories he wrote for his son Christopher Robin, who loved to visit the Winnipeg Infantry's mascot at the London Zoo. The bear—whose name was Winnie—had been donated by the Canadian soldiers when they left for the front during the First World War. Milne's son nicknamed the bear Winnie the Pooh.

This was a landmark day in collegiate basketball history. For the first time, five players took their places on each side of the court and the first ball was tipped off in 1896. College basketball had begun, with the University of Iowa pitted against the University of Chicago.

19th.

1935   Tippi Hedren was born.

1943   Janis Joplin was born (see June 10, July 12, July 25, August 12 entries).

1946   Dolly Parton was born.

1979   John N. Mitchell was released on parole after serving nineteen months at a federal prison in Alabama (see February 21, June 22, July 1 entries).

Born in Lafayette, Minnesota, on this day in 1935, actress Tippi Hedren is best known for her starring roles in Alfred Hitchcock's 1963 film *The Birds* and 1964 film *Marnie.* Hedren's career didn't go to the dogs as she limited the number of film projects she chose to accept; it went to the tigers and elephants. During the 1980s she established the Shambala Foundation in Antelope Valley, California, which is a retirement home for aged animal performers. Hedren did take time out, however, to appear with her daughter Melanie Griffith in the 1981 film *Roar* and the 1990 film *Pacific Heights.*

Rock and country music each gained a star today. In 1943 the raspy-voiced rock and blues singer Janis Joplin, who performed with the 1960s rock band Big Brother and the Holding Company, was born in Port Arthur, Texas. And in 1946 the country-music nightingale Dolly Parton was born in Locust Ridge, Tennessee. Parton expanded her interests into film during the 1980s, starring in the films *9 to 5* and *The Best Little Whorehouse in Texas.*

20th.

1930   Astronaut Edwin "Buzz" Aldrin was born in Montclair, New Jersey.

1964   The Beatles released their album *Meet the Beatles* (see January 1, January 24, January 30, February 7, February 9, February 12, May 9, June 6, June 12, August 29 entries).

1980   President Jimmy Carter asked the U.S. Olympic Committee to select a site other than Moscow for the Olympic Games (see October 1 entry).

1981   Iran freed fifty-two American hostages (see February 6, November 4, November 17, November 20, November 22, December 26 entries).

1982   Ozzy Osbourne bit a dead bat.

1987   Terry Waite was kidnapped (see December 2 entry).

1994   Shannon Faulkner became the first woman to attend classes at The Citadel (see August 16 entry).

1997   Steve Fossett became the first man to cross Africa by balloon (see January 14, February 21, August 7, August 16 entries).

Freedom, which Americans consider to be an inalienable right, was both stolen from and restored to a great number of people on this day. In 1981 Iran freed fifty-two American hostages who had been held captive for 444 days. British hostages were similarly released that year thanks to the negotiation efforts of special Anglican Church envoy Terry Waite. On this same day in 1987, Waite himself was kidnapped by pro-Iranian Lebanese Shiite Muslims while negotiating the release of Western hostages in Beirut, Lebanon. His own release didn't come until November 18, 1991.

Shannon Faulkner changed the face of The Citadel—South Carolina's all-male military school—on this day in 1994, when she won her case in court. It had taken a legal battle for her to become the 151-year-old institution's first female cadet. Victory was bittersweet, however. Faulkner withdrew six days after she was admitted to the school's infirmary on the first day of "Hell Week."

On this day in 1997, Steve Fossett landed his hot-air balloon, *Solo Spirit,* in Sultanpur, India, becoming the first man to cross the African continent by balloon. His journey also set both distance and duration records, clocking 10,361 miles in 6 days, 2 hours, and 44 minutes.

The face of rock music changed more than once on this day. The Beatles released their album *Meet the Beatles* on this day in 1964. For many American fans, it was their first multi-song taste of the band's music. On this same day in 1982, heavy-metal singer Ozzy Osbourne allegedly bit the head off a dead bat a fan had hurled onto the stage.

21st.

1885 Huddie "Leadbelly" Ledbetter was born.

1949 Chiang Kai-shek was defeated.

1977 U.S. President Jimmy Carter pardoned almost all Vietnam War draft evaders (see October 1 entry).

1982 B.B. King donated his entire record collection (see September 16 entry).

The University of Mississippi's Center for the Study of Southern Culture received a major donation on this day in 1982. Blues guitarist B.B. King donated his entire collection of about 7,000 rare blues records he'd played while working as a disc jockey in Memphis, Tennessee. One of the people represented in King's collection was born on this day in 1885. Huddie "Leadbelly" Ledbetter, who is credited with introducing white Americans to traditionally African-American blues music, was born in Mooringsport, Louisiana. Leadbelly's 1934 recording of his song "Goodnight Irene" occurred in unusual surroundings. This and a few other songs were taped by the Library of Congress's folklorist John Lomax while Leadbelly was imprisoned at Lousiana State Penitentiary. The song was instrumental in securing Leadbelly's pardon a few months later. Moving to New York City with Lomax in 1935, Leadbelly played his unique brand of blues to American and European audiences until his death in 1949.

Finances defeated another government on this day in 1949. When the United States terminated its aid to Chinese leader Chiang Kai-shek, his government quickly crashed. Communist forces led by Mao Zhedong took over rulership of China overnight.

22nd.

1875   D.W. Griffith was born.

1898   Sergei Eisenstein was born.

1968   "Rowan & Martin's Laugh-In" premiered on television.

1973   The U.S. Supreme Court made abortion legal.

1998   Netscape announced plans to offer its software free on the Internet.

It's rare in the modern world for a business to offer any substantial product free of charge. On this day in 1998, Netscape Communications Corporation announced its plans to make its Netscape Communicator client software source code available for free licensing on the Internet.

This date marks the birth of a nation's entertainment. Pioneer directors D.W. Griffith and Sergei Eisenstein elevated the art of filmmaking during the medium's infancy. Born in Kentucky on this day in 1875, David Wark Griffith started his film career as an actor and writer before making hundreds of film shorts in Los Angeles, California. His experiences led to the masterful production and camera techniques used in his 1915 film *The Birth of a Nation* and 1916 film *Intolerance*. Griffith also pioneered the use of documentary film footage, incorporating actual war scenes from the front in his 1918 epic *Hearts of the World*. Editing skills and tight composition made Sergei Eisenstein's films unique in their time. Born on this day in 1898 in Riga, Russia, Eisenstein was commissioned by the revolutionary government to make propaganda films during the 1920s. *Ten Days That Shook the World* and *The Battleship Potemkin* were his masterful results. Eisenstein went on to produce two historic epics, the 1938 film *Alexander Nevski* (which featured an original musical score by Sergei Prokofiev) and the 1944 film *Ivan the Terrible* (which was partially filmed in color).

A pivotal court case settled on this day in 1973 polarized the nation as few cases had ever done before. The U.S. Supreme Court handed down the decision that abortion during the first six months of pregnancy is a matter of personal choice in the case of *Roe v. Wade*.

23rd.

1870 One hundred seventy-three members of the Blackfoot nation were killed.

1899 Humphrey Bogart was born.

1907 Charles Curtis became a U.S. senator.

1910 Django Reinhardt was born.

1919 Ernie Kovacs was born.

1960 The bathysphere *Trieste* carried two men to a depth of 35,800 feet in the Pacific Ocean.

1973 U.S. President Richard Nixon announced that an accord with the North Vietnamese government had been reached.

"Greetings from your orthocon tube," comedian Ernie Kovacs would say at the beginning of his weekly comedy show. Born in Trenton, New Jersey, on this day in 1919, Kovacs performed in stock theater as a teenager, attending the New York School of Theatre and American Academy of Dramatic Art. After taking jobs as a journalist and radio announcer, Kovacs got his first break in television as the host of a cooking show and morning show on WPTZ-TV in 1950. He got his first network TV series, "It's Time for Ernie," the next year. It was almost all uphill from there. Kovacs won Emmys in 1957 and 1961 for his work. A pioneer in the use of special effects camerawork and videotaping in television comedy, Kovacs inspired many of his successors with his bizarre repertoire of on-screen characters like Percy Dovetonsils, Mr. Question Man, and the three-gorilla musical group the Nairobi Trio. One of his most famous characters, however, was the silent and innocent Eugene, whom he developed while hosting "The Tonight Show" in 1956.

Although Humphrey Bogart never actually uttered the words "Play it again, Sam" in the film *Casablanca,* it's obvious that his characterization of the cynical Rick made an indelible mark on movie audiences. Born in New York City on this day in 1899, Bogart became the face of the hero and antihero, as the romantic lone wolf in *To Have and Have Not* and *The Maltese Falcon.* His range, however, also included villainous, greedy, and psychopathic men, proving that great actors can avoid being stereotyped.

Attitudes toward Native Americans changed radically in less than four decades. On this day in 1870, U.S. Army troops massacred 173 members of the Blackfoot nation in Montana; 140 of the victims were women and children. On this same day in 1907, Charles Curtis became the first U.S. senator of Native American ancestry. Curtis lived on a Kaw reservation in Kansas for a portion of his childhood. His experiences inspired him to propose legislation in defense of reservations' self-government. In 1929 Curtis became U.S. vice president under President Herbert Hoover.

A major influence on swing-style jazz guitarists, Django Reinhardt played guitar with Duke Ellington's orchestra in 1946. Born to gypsy entertainers in Liverchies, Belgium, on this day in 1910, Reinhardt's unique playing style was derived from the loss of two fingers on his left hand in a caravan fire. He played in Paris cabarets until he joined violinist Stephane Grappelli, in 1934, to open the Quintette du Hot Club, which introduced and developed the French jazz style known as Le Jazz Hot to the world.

24th.

1962   Jackie Robinson became the first African-American player elected to the Baseball Hall of Fame (see January 31, October 15 entries).

1962   The Beatles signed their management contract with Brian Epstein (see January 1, January 20, January 30, February 7, February 9, February 12, May 9, June 6, June 12, August 29 entries).

1972   Shoichi Yokoi was discovered.

1994   The U.S. Supreme Court ruled that certain protest groups are subject to prosecution under the RICO Act.

2000   The National Security Agency's bank of supercomputers went down.

Representing almost half of the world's computer power, the National Security Agency's bank of supercomputers went down for nearly three days, starting on this day in 2000. The failure was due to human error and a computer glitch. It wasn't the first time. Three years earlier, hackers shut down the Pentagon's entire computer system at the National Military Command Center, leaving a single fax machine in operation so they could send a fax notifying officials they'd been hacked.

The U.S. Supreme Court handed down a unanimous decision on this day in 1994, holding that members of anti-abortion groups such as Operation Rescue who attempted to impede access to abortion clinics could be subject to prosecution under the RICO (Racketeer-Influenced and Corrupt Organizations) Act.

When Shoichi Yokoi arrived in Tokyo, his only comment was, "It is with much embarrassment that I return." After twenty-eight years of concealment on the island of Guam, Japanese soldier Shoichi Yokoi was discovered in the jungle on this day in 1972. It took his rescuers quite a while to convince him that the Second World War was over. Yokoi had survived for nearly three decades on a diet of nuts, berries, frogs, snails, and rats. He wove cloth from tree bark and lived in a specially constructed underground encampment. Tokyo received Yokoi as a national hero upon his return.

25th.

1927   Antonio Carlos Jobim was born.

1933   Corazon Aquino was born (see February 26, August 21 entries).

1961   John F. Kennedy held first presidential news conference over radio and television.

1971   Charles Manson, Patricia Krenwinkel, Susan Atkins, and Leslie van Houten were convicted in a Los Angeles court of the murders of actress Sharon Tate and six other people (see March 6, August 9, October 27, December 8 entries).

The world discovered the allure of Brazilian sounds thanks to a musician who was born in Rio de Janeiro, Brazil, on this day in 1927. Songwriter Antonio Carlos Jobim captured the spirit of the nation with songs like "The Girl from Ipanema" and his musical score for the 1960s film *Black Orpheus,* which present traditional samba and modern bossa nova rhythms that have become synonymous with this South American nation.

After twenty years of unquestioned power, Philippine dictator Ferdinand Marcos was overthrown by Corazon Aquino, the widow of Benino Aquino, Marcos's strongest opponent. Born in the Tarlac province of the Philippines on this day in 1933, Aquino was educated in the United States, receiving a mathematics degree. She married Benino Aquino in 1956, and her husband was imprisoned by Marcos on charges of subversion during the 1970s. He was assassinated by military guards at the Manila airport in 1983, as he was returning from three years in exile. Corazon Aquino's nonviolent campaign and strong religious backing during the 1986 presidential election helped her to win easily over Marcos despite suspected ballot tampering.

26th.

1884	Roy Chapman Andrews was born.
1928	Eartha Kitt was born (see January 18 entry).
1958	Buddy Holly and The Crickets first appeared on "The Ed Sullivan Show" (see February 3, September 7 entries).
1961	Wayne Gretzky was born.
1962	*Ranger III* was launched from Cape Canaveral, Florida.
1991	Mikhail S. Gorbachev granted search-and-seizure powers.

Rising extortion, bribery, and racketeering in Russia and the USSR forced Soviet President Mikhail S. Gorbachev to take action on this day in 1991. He granted the KGB and Soviet Interior Ministry extensive search-and-seizure powers to combat the trend.

Eartha Kitt's catlike voice and fiery personality were her sources of success and disaster. Born in North, South Carolina, on this day in 1928, Kitt debuted as a dancer after her graduation from the New York School of the Performing Arts. Director Orson Welles gave her her first break, casting her in the film *Dr. Faustus*. Her stage performance in the 1965 production *The Owl and the Pussycat* and her 1966 role as Catwoman on the TV series "Batman," however, made her name a household word. Her outspoken comments to Lady Bird Johnson during a White House incident temporarily sent her film and television career into a downward spiral. Over the past three decades, however, she has become a worldwide legend as a cabaret performer.

The first fossil dinosaur eggs were unearthed in Mongolia's Gobi Desert by explorer Roy Chapman Andrews in 1923. Born in Beloit, Wisconsin, on this day in 1884, Andrews also pioneered Alaskan exploration, studying the region before 1914. Many of his expeditions were funded by the American Museum of Natural History, where he served as director from 1935 until 1942.

Wayne "The Great One" Gretzky broke numerous records on the hockey field. Born in Bradford, Ontario, on this day in 1961, Gretzky scored more goals during a single season than any other player in the sport's history, slamming ninety-two goals during the 1981–1982 season for the Edmonton Oilers.

27th.

1918   Elmore James was born.

1926   John Logie Baird demonstrated a mechanical television.

1944   Mairead Corrigan was born.

1948   Mikhail Baryshnikov was born.

1982   U.S. President Ronald Reagan proposed a 5 percent withholding tax.

1986   José Azcona Hoyo was inaugurated.

1986   Mikhail Gorbachev demanded economic reforms.

Wealth is often accumulated through the profits gained from the interest earned on savings accounts and the dividends paid on held shares of stock. On this day in 1982, U.S. President Ronald Reagan proposed the imposition of a 5 percent withholding tax on interest and dividends to increase federal revenues.

Mikhail Baryshnikov was already a promisingly brilliant star when he entered Leningrad's Kirov Ballet. His teachers at the Riga Choreography School recognized that he had special talents at a very early age. Born in Riga, Latvia, on this day in 1948, Baryshnikov joined the ranks of other Russian dancers in 1974, defecting to the West just as Rudolf Nureyev had done ten years earlier. Baryshnikov achieved international acclaim, performing with the American Ballet Theater, the New York City Ballet, and Twyla Tharp. In 1980 he became artistic director of the American Ballet Theater.

Born in Richland, Mississippi, on this day in 1918, blues guitarist Elmore James played a self-made guitar and sang the blues when he was 10 years old. By the time he was 20, he was hanging out with other blues greats like Robert Johnson and Sonny Boy Williamson II. By the 1950s, James was known as the king of the slide guitar, playing a distinctive form of Mississippi Delta Blues on recordings for Chess Records. As rock and roll performer Little Richard once said, "There was just a few people doing real rock back when I was first starting out. Little Richard and Elmore James are the only two I know."

33

An Irish secretary and her compatriot won the Nobel Peace Prize in 1977 for their efforts to bring peace to battle-worn Northern Ireland. Born in Belfast, Northern Ireland, on this day in 1944, Mairead Corrigan began organizing peace petitions in the wake of Catholic-Protestant violence in her hometown. Interest among the city's women—of both religions—grew into the Community of Peace People. And in 1976, she founded the Northern Ireland Peace Movement with Betty Williams.

This day marked the beginning of the end of the Soviet Union's communist economic policies. On this day in 1986, Soviet Party Secretary Mikhail Gorbachev announced his plans to make radical changes in the nation's economic policy. A major shift in political power occurred on the exact same date in Honduras. The nation's first civilian president in twenty-six years was inaugurated: Liberal Party leader José Azcona Hoyo was sworn in as the nation's president.

Visionary John Logie Baird wouldn't have been surprised at the unveiling of high-definition television in 1990. Before his death in 1946, he'd drafted plans for a 1,000-line resolution television. On this day in 1926, the Scottish inventor unveiled a mechanical device he called a "televisor" in London, England. The machine used rotating discs to segment the signal into a 30-line image, which was adopted by the BBC three years later. Eventually, the broadcaster replaced his 240-line televisor with the 405-line Marconi-EMIO electronic television, which replaced the discs with cathode ray tubes.

1841   Sir Henry Morton Stanley was born.

1884   Auguste Piccard was born (see March 1, March 19, May 27, August 18 entries).

1884   Jean Piccard was born.

1902   Andrew Carnegie founded the Carnegie Institution.

1935   Iceland legalized abortion.

1974   The Israeli army lifted its siege of Suez City.

1986   The space shuttle *Challenger* exploded (see February 6, February 10, April 4, April 29, June 22, September 2, October 13 entries).

1997   Afrikaner police admitted to the killing of Steven Biko (see December 2 entry).

The truth sometimes takes a long time to be revealed. South African "black consciousness" leader Steven Biko had been arrested by Afrikaner police in 1977. During his confinement, Biko died. Government officials claimed that the death was caused by self-inflicted injuries. On this day in 1997, South Africa's Truth and Reconciliation Commission announced Afrikaner policemen's admission that Biko had been brutally beaten and was left naked and shackled to a bed in the police hospital, where he died from unattended wounds.

Twin brothers Auguste and Jean Piccard explored the world's heights and depths during their lifetimes. Born in Basel, Switzerland, on this day in 1884, the Piccard brothers studied physics and engineering, respectively, after they emigrated to the United States. Determined to explore the stratosphere, Auguste ascended 10.5 miles in a hot-air balloon in 1932. That same year, Jean and his wife ascended 10.9 miles, collecting data on cosmic rays. In 1948 Auguste descended 10,000 feet into the ocean off the west African coast in a bathysphere he'd designed. (His son, Jacques, dove a record 7 miles in the U.S. bathysphere *Trieste* off the Marianas Trench twelve years later.)

Sir Henry Morton Stanley worked as a special correspondent for the *New York Herald,* covering Lord Robert Napier's 1868 Abyssinian expedition and conflicts in Spain. He raced back to Africa in October 1869, after his editor, James Gordon Bennett, sent the message "Find Livingstone." Born in Denbigh, Wales, on this day in 1841, Stanley found the elusive missionary and explorer in Ujiji, Tanganyika, after stopping to witness the opening of the Suez Canal and traveling from Palestine to India and Zanzibar. On November 10, 1871, Stanley uttered the famous comment "Dr. Livingstone, I presume."

On this day in 1986, the American space program suffered a major tragedy, which was witnessed by millions of television viewers. The space shuttle *Challenger* exploded seventy-three seconds after blastoff from Cape Canaveral, Florida. All seven crew members lost their lives in the blast, including astronaut Judith Resnick and school teacher Christa McAuliffe.

A number of sieges and surrenders took place on the same day that France surrendered to Prussia, in 1871, ending the Franco-Prussian War. Japanese troops occupied the port town of Shanghai, China, in 1932. The Israeli army lifted its siege of Suez City in 1974, freeing encircled Egyptian troops and turning over 300,000 square miles of Egyptian territory to the United Nations.

29th.

1939   Germaine Greer was born.

1954   Oprah Winfrey was born.

1983   Chrissie Hynde and Ray Davies had their first baby.

1983   Stevie Nicks married Kim Anderson.

Some entertainers' stars rise rapidly and hover at the top. Born in Koscusko, Mississippi, on this day in 1954, Oprah Winfrey got her first broadcast job in Nashville, Tennessee. This prompted her to enter Tennessee State University to study speech and the performing arts. But she dropped out during her sophomore year to accept a news anchor position at WTVF-TV, becoming the city's first African-American newscaster. Moving to Baltimore, Maryland, in 1976, Oprah was a co-anchor until she was given her own talk show in 1978. She became the host of "A.M. Chicago" in 1984, moving to Chicago and landing a part in the 1985 film *The Color Purple*. In 1986 she hosted the nationally syndicated "Oprah Winfrey Show," set up her own production company— Harpo Productions—and bought her show from its original producers. She finally got her diploma from Tennessee State University in 1988.

Radical writer Germaine Greer blew the top off people's perceptions of marriage and sexuality during the 1970s. Born in Melbourne, Australia, on this day in 1939, Greer's 1970 book, The Female Eunuch, attacked the institution of marriage as a form of female slavery and labeled the denial of female sexuality as a male-inspired misrepresentation of fact.

The rock music world had its share of wedding bells and birth announcements on this day. In 1983 Fleetwood Mac's lead singer Stevie Nicks married Kim Anderson, who worked for Warner Records. And on the exact same date, lead singers Chrissie Hynde of the Pretenders and Ray Davies of the Kinks had their first baby.

30th.

1940   The first Social Security check was sent.

1969   The Beatles held a rooftop concert at Abbey Road Studios in London, England (see January 1, January 20, January 24, February 7, February 9, February 12, May 9, June 6, June 12, August 29 entries).

1979   The United States ordered an evacuation of Americans from Iran.

1991   The first major ground battle of the Persian Gulf War took place.

1993   Peace talks between the Serbs and Croats failed.

Retirement became a little more financially secure for one person on this day in 1940. The first Social Security check, in the amount of $22.54, was mailed to Ida May Fuller.

On this day in 1979, the federal government ordered all nonessential American officers and their dependents evacuated from Iran. In 1991 American troops engaged in the first major ground battle in Khafji, Saudi Arabia, during the Persian Gulf War. Eleven American troops died in the assault. Reports claimed that seven of those casualties were from friendly fire. And in 1993 peace talks between Bosnia-Herzegovina's Serbs and Croats failed in Geneva, Switzerland, despite American and United Nations mediation.

31st.

1786   The Treaty of Fort Finney was signed.

1876   Canadian Indians had to move onto reservations.

1919   Jackie Robinson was born (see January 24, October 15 entries).

1931   Ernie Banks was born.

1947   Nolan Ryan was born.

1958   *Explorer I* was launched.

1958   The Van Allen radiation belt was discovered.

1961   The first animal was sent into space.

1968   Nauru won its independence.

1995   U.S. President Bill Clinton approved $40 billion in loan guarantees to Mexico.

North American tribes were forced off their ancestral lands on two different occasions today. On this day in 1786, the Shawnee nation acknowledged American sovereignty over the Ohio territories east of the Miami River when tribal chiefs signed the Treaty of

Fort Finney. The tribes were subsequently forced onto reservations. On this same day in 1876, a proclamation was issued ordering all indigenous Canadians to move onto reservations or be deemed hostile. Many tribes weren't notified of the announcement, and others weren't able to meet the evacuation deadline.

The island nation of Nauru (also known as Pleasant Island) won its independence on this day in 1968. Jointly ruled by Australia, Great Britain, and New Zealand, the 10,000 people, who represent one of the world's smallest republics, had lived as a territory since the First World War.

On this day in 1995, U.S. President Bill Clinton exercised his authority to approve $40 billion in loan guarantees to Mexico. In the midst of a severe recession, the Central American nation was on the verge of default on interest payments to its government bond holders. Clinton also guaranteed the Mexican government a loan of $20 billion to boost their economic recuperation.

This was a good day to look to the stars. In 1958 America's first successful earth satellite, *Explorer I,* was launched from Cape Canaveral, Florida. The Van Allen radiation belt was discovered by NASA during the launch. In 1961 the United States sent the first animal, a chimpanzee named Ham, into space to test the safety of the *Mercury/Redstone* space capsule.

Born in Cairo, Georgia, on this day in 1919, Jackie Robinson was the first African-American baseball player to enter the professional major leagues. This Brooklyn Dodgers star was also the first African-American player inducted into the Baseball Hall of Fame. Born in Dallas, Texas, on this day in 1931, Chicago Cubs shortstop Ernie Banks was also inducted into the Baseball Hall of Fame. Born in Refugio, Texas, on this day in 1947, Nolan Ryan was rated as baseball's fastest pitcher in 1974. This New York Mets pitcher had a fast ball that clocked in at 100.8 miles per hour. The year before, Ryan set the all-time strikeout record: 383 strikeouts in a single season.

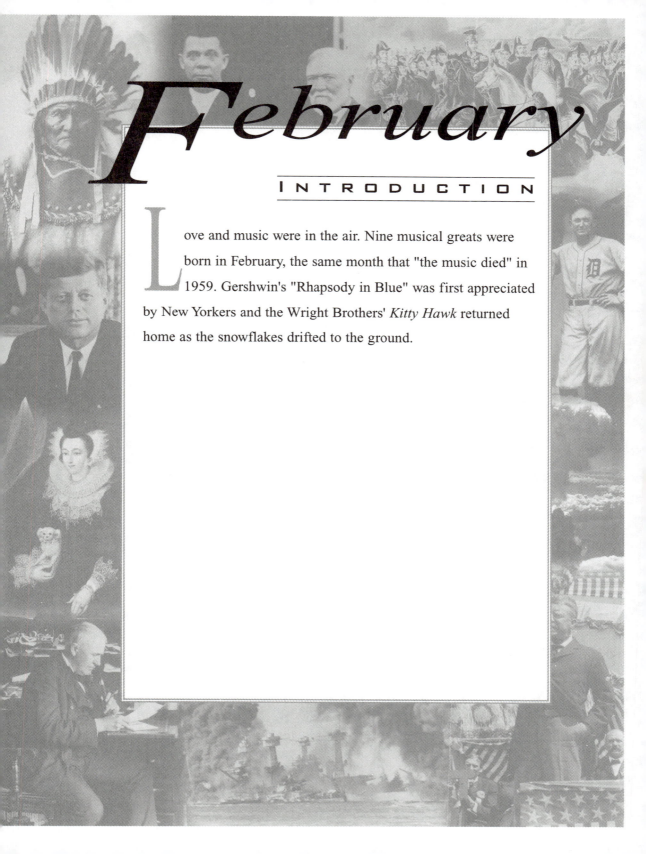

February

Love and music were in the air. Nine musical greats were born in February, the same month that "the music died" in 1959. Gershwin's "Rhapsody in Blue" was first appreciated by New Yorkers and the Wright Brothers' *Kitty Hawk* returned home as the snowflakes drifted to the ground.

1st.

1859 Victor Herbert was born.

1876 The Sioux Nation was ordered to return to their reservation.

1902 Langston Hughes was born.

1905 U.S. President Theodore Roosevelt created the U.S. Forest Service.

1931 Boris Yeltsin was born (see March 20, May 29, November 6, December 18, December 25 entries).

1948 Rick James was born.

1979 Ayatollah Ruhollah Khomeini returned to Iran.

1990 East German Premier Hans Modrow appealed for negotiations with West Germany to forge a "united fatherland."

The common use of language was a constant theme in the writings of Langston Hughes. Born in Joplin, Missouri, on this day in 1902, African-American poet and writer Langston Hughes was a leading figure in New York's Harlem Renaissance—a literary, artistic, and musical movement that brought global acclaim to African-American culture. Hughes's most famous character, Jesse B. Simple, was the subject of several racy newspaper sketches as well as several short volumes. These stories, written in the vernacular, were compiled in his 1957 book *The Best of Simple.*

Single achievements often emerge from variegated careers. Born in Dublin, Ireland, on this day in 1859, Victor Herbert was lead cellist in New York's Metropolitan Opera Company Orchestra. His range of talents, however, spanned into musical composition. He wrote the 1893 comic opera *Prince Ananias,* the serious 1914 opera *Madeleine,* and the enduring song "Ah, Sweet Mystery of Life." During the last half of the twentieth century, another performer showed his range, switching from rock and roll to punk-funk music. At fifteen years old, performer Rick James joined the U.S. Navy and went AWOL shortly after. Born in Buffalo, New York, on this day in 1948, James fled to Toronto, Ontario, where he formed the rock band Mynah Birds with Neil Young and Bruce Palmer (who later both formed the band Buffalo Springfield) as well as Goldie McJohn (who later joined the band Steppenwolf) during the early 1960s. Rick James's punk-funk career soared when he returned to the United States. He sang the top-selling song "Superfreak" during the 1970s.

Born in Sverdlovsk, Russia, on this day in 1931, Boris Yeltsin began his career in the construction business before he joined the Communist Party in 1961. Inducted into the central committee by Mikhail Gorbachev in 1985, Yeltsin became party chief that same year. Over the next two years, Yeltsin openly accused conservative party members of encouraging political corruption and sabotaging his push for *perestroika* (political and economic reform). He was downgraded in 1987 to a lowly administrative job for his efforts. Two years later he returned to public life when he was elected to the Congress of USSR People's Deputies. And in 1990, Yeltsin became the first Russian president elected by popular vote.

2nd.

1848 The first Chinese immigrants arrived in the United States (see May 6, September 2, December 17 entries).

1901 Jascha Heifetz was born.

1927 Stan Getz was born.

1942 Graham Nash was born.

1949 RCA issued the first 45 rpm record.

1961 Six hundred passengers were set free.

1976 The Centers for Disease Control determined the cause of a flu virus.

1980 A thirty-six-hour riot took place at New Mexico State Penetentiary.

1985 A popular bar was bombed in suburban Athens, Greece.

During the last half of the twentieth century, drugs and terrorism emerged in the public consciousness. On this day in 1961, 600 passengers aboard the hijacked Portuguese ocean liner *Santa Maria* were set free after being held hostage for twelve days by terrorists. In 1980 a thirty-six-hour riot instigated by New Mexico State Penitentiary inmates began. Complaining about overcrowded conditions due to the increase in drug convictions and incarcerations, the inmates caused $25 million in property damage and left thirty-three inmates dead. And on this day in 1985, a bomb set by terrorists exploded in a popular bar situated in suburban Athens, Greece, injuring seventy-eight people. Most of the clientele were U.S. military personnel and American citizens.

RCA issued the first 45 rpm record in 1949. A number of talents also appeared on the music scene on this day. Violinist Jascha Heifetz was born in Vilna, Poland, in 1901. Studying at the St. Petersburg Conservatory, Heifetz toured eastern and northern Europe when he was only twelve years old. After the Russian Revolution, Heifetz settled in the United States, where he became an international musical sensation. Jazz saxophonist Stan Getz was born in Philadelphia, Pennsylvania, on this day in 1927. Famed for his 1960s version of "The Girl from Ipanema," Getz worked with South American stars such as Astrid Gilberto and Antonio Jobim during his career. Born in Blackpool, England, on this day in 1942, rock performer Graham Nash played with the Hollies as well as Crosby, Stills, Nash, and Young, composing and performing hits such as "Bus Stop" and "Our House."

We also learned that viruses live longer than we hoped. On this day in 1976, the Centers for Disease Control (CDC) determined that four influenza cases at Fort Dix were caused by the same viral agent that initiated the 1918–1919 flu pandemic that killed 50 million people during the First World War. Because of this discovery, the federal government began a $135-million inoculation program.

3rd.

1809   Felix Mendelssohn was born.

1959   Richie Valens, Buddy Holly, and the Big Bopper died in a place crash (see January 26, May 13, September 7 entries).

1966   The Soviet spacecraft *Luna 9* landed on the moon.

1994   U.S. President Bill Clinton ended a nineteen-year-old trade embargo imposed upon Vietnam.

Born in Hamburg, Germany, on this day in 1809, Felix Mendelssohn's most famous work was his incidental music to *A Midsummer Night's Dream,* which he completed in 1843. Not all dreams, however, come true. Sometimes, the brightest stars are dimmed by fate. On this day in 1959, up-and-coming rock and roll stars Buddy Holly, J.P. "Big Bopper" Richardson, and Richie Valens died in a plane crash in Iowa on their way to a concert in North Dakota.

4th.

1902	Charles A. Lindbergh was born (see June 11 entry).
1903	The U.S. Congress passed the Elkins Act.
1906	Clyde W. Tombaugh was born.
1913	Rosa Parks was born in Tuskegee, Alabama (see December 5 entry).
1931	Isabel Péron was born (see March 24 entry).
1932	Governor of New York Franklin Delano Roosevelt opened the Winter Olympics at Lake Placid, New York (see February 8, February 11, February 13, February 14 entries).
1947	Dan Quayle was born.
1983	U.S. President Ronald Reagan condemned violence during a strike of independent truckers.
1993	General Motors was found guilty of negligence.

Illegal payoffs, strikes, and negligence were in the business news throughout the twentieth century. Urged by President Theodore Roosevelt, the U.S. Congress passed the Elkins Act on this day in 1903, making it illegal to give or receive rebates in interstate commerce transactions. It was common practice for various railroads to given certain shippers these special concessions, making fair market competition for the delivery of goods nearly impossible. Eighty years later, in 1983, U.S. President Ronald Reagan condemned the violence that accompanied a strike by independent truckers, saying he would not consider their demand for a repeal of the gasoline tax hike. And in 1993, General Motors was found guilty of negligence by a civil court in Atlanta, Georgia. The faulty fuel-tank design of a GM pickup truck was determined to be the cause of a teenager's death in a 1989 crash. The victim's parents were awarded $105.2 million.

Born in La Rioja, Argentina, on this day in 1931, Maria Estela Martinez worked as a dancer until she married Juan Péron in 1961, living with him in Spain. When Péron regained the Argentine presidency in 1973, she was appointed vice president and was lovingly referred to by the people as "Isabelita." The next year, Juan Péron died and Isabelita took his place. But her position was usurped two years later, when a military takeover forced her resignation. She was imprisoned for five years on charges of abuse of public property. When she was released, she moved to Spain.

Known for his misuse of the English language, Dan Quayle once said, "If we don't succeed, we run the risk of failure." Born in Indianapolis, Indiana, on this day in 1947, Quayle was vice president during President George H. Bush's administration. Despite his very conservative views on family values, finances, and defense, Quayle was strongly criticized by other members of the Republican party for his public persona.

Born in Streator, Illinois, on this day in 1906, Clyde W. Tombaugh became the astronomer who discovered the planet farthest from the sun in 1930. Tombaugh's sighting of the planet Pluto was later confirmed by the Lowell Observatory.

5th.

1914 William Burroughs was born.

1919 Andreas Papandreou was born.

1993 The U.S. Congress passed the Family and Medical Leave Act.

Family, business, and the government finally met eye to eye on this day. In 1993 the U.S. Congress passed the Family and Medical Leave Act, permitting employees to take up to twelve weeks of unpaid leave during any twelve-month period, following a birth or an adoption.

Born in St. Louis, Missouri, on this day in 1914, William Burroughs is known for literary work that follows a course of dark roads through the human psyche. A Harvard graduate, Burroughs bummed around the United States and Europe, becoming a drug addict while doing casual labor in New York City. His 1959 novel *Naked Lunch* and 1961 novel *The Soft Machine* outraged many critics, but established Burroughs as the voice of the 1950s Beat movement. His later works continued his search into uncharted corners of human desire.

Not every head of state rises on a continuous upward curve. Born in Athens, Greece, on this day in 1919, Andreas Papandreou was the son of Greek Prime Minister George Pappandreou, who had been placed under house arrest during the 1967 military junta. Exiled during that same period, Andreas returned to his homeland in 1974. He became Greece's first socialist prime minister in 1984, after founding the left-of-center Pan-Hellenic Socialist Movement.

6th.

1820	The first group of African-Americans emigrated to Africa (see April 19, August 2 entries).
1840	Waitangi Day was first celebrated in New Zealand.
1913	Mary Leakey was born (see August 7 entry).
1932	François Truffaut was born.
1946	Bob Marley was born.
1952	Great Britain's King George VI died and was succeeded by his daughter, Elizabeth II (see December 14 entry).
1976	The Chinese government invited former President Richard Nixon to visit Beijing.
1980	Iranian President Abolhassan Bani-Sadr denounced militants holding fifty-two Americans hostage in Tehran (see January 20 entry).
1984	The space shuttle *Challenger* launched a communications satellite, which misfired and ended up in an unusable orbit (see January 28, February 10, April 4, April 29, June 22, September 2, October 13 entries).
2000	Idaho growers gave away their potatoes.

Idaho's 1999 potato crop was so big that the total harvest was practically worthless. Since the federal government wouldn't buy the surplus, the growers donated nearly 24 million potatoes to the poor, shipping them to food banks across the nation. Their wives had come up with the idea.

Film director François Truffaut made his life into art. Born in Paris, France, on this day in 1932, Truffaut suffered from an unhappy childhood, a few years in reform school, and the stigma of being an army deserter before turning to a life in film. Writing criticisms for *Cahiers du Cinéma* in 1953, Truffaut made his cinematic début with the semi-autobiographical 1959 film *Les Quatre Cents Coups (The 400 Blows)*. Numerous projects followed, including *Shoot the Piano Player, Jules and Jim,* and *Day for Night.* A founder of the French New Wave in film, Truffaut acted in many of his films and even played a role in Steven Spielberg's *Close Encounters of the Third Kind* in 1977.

Freedom takes many forms. On this day in 1820, the first group of African-Americans made an organized emigration to Africa, leaving New York City bound for Sierra Leone. Twenty years later, British colonists and native Maori tribesmen signed a treaty, which is celebrated as Waitangi Day in New Zealand. And in 1967, the Peabody Fund—which is dedicated to the promotion of African-American education in the South—was established.

A major force in reggae music was born in Nine Miles, St. Ann, Jamaica, on this day in 1946. Robert Nesta Marley formed his own group, the Wailers, in 1964, which included Peter Tosh and Bunny Livingston. Their first hit, "Simmer Down," was the beginning of a long and successful career. Marley joined the Rastafari in 1967, growing his signature dreadlock hairdo, which became synonymous with reggae style. By 1972 the Wailers had recorded four albums, with hits like "Jamming," "I Shot the Sheriff," and "No Woman No Cry."

Archaeologists Louis and Mary Leakey revolutionized the world's perceptions of human origins, discovering that human beings dated back as far as 1.7 million years. Born in London, England, on this day in 1913, Mary was Louis's second wife. Her interest in prehistory began in childhood, when she collected stone tools and visited cave paintings in southwestern France. In 1948, it was Mary who discovered the primitive ape, *Proconsul africans,* on Lake Victoria's Rusinga Island, vaulting the Leakeys to international fame. And in 1959, Mary was being filmed when she discovered the 1.75-million-year-old hominid *Zinjanthropus.* Her most incredible discovery, however, was unearthed at Laetoli near the Olduvai Gorge. It was there that she found the 3.6-million-year-old footprints of three erect-standing hominids, proving that human beings are older than anyone had ever imagined.

7th.

1883   Eubie Blake was born.

1964   The Beatles arrived in New York City.

1965   The Beatles' George Harrison had his tonsils removed (see January 1, January 20, January 24, January 30, February 9, February 12, May 9, June 6, June 12, August 29 entries).

1969   Diane Crump became the first female jockey.

1984   Space shuttle astronauts Bruce McCandless II and Robert L. Stewart took the first untethered space walk.

1986   Haitian President Jean-Claude Duvalier fled, ending 28 years of Duvalier rule (see April 14, April 22, July 3 entries).

1990   The oil tanker *American Trader* spilled hundreds of thousands of gallons of Alaskan crude oil off the coast of Huntington Beach, California.

1995   Ramzi Yousef was arrested in Islamabad, Pakistan, two years after the World Trade Center bombing.

1999   NASA launched the *Stardust* to collect a sample of comet dust.

Born in Baltimore, Maryland, on this day in 1883, jazz pianist and composer Eubie Blake is best known for the composition "I'm Just Wild about Harry," first performed in his 1921 musical *Shuffle Along*. Blake literally lived a hundred years, recutting some of his famous songs for more contemporary player-piano rolls less than a month before he passed away. Nearly eighty years later, in 1964, The Beatles arrived in New York City for their first American concert tour. (They must have worked hard on the road. The next year, guitarist George Harrison had his tonsils removed on this day.)

Horse racing history was made in 1969, when Diane Crump became the first female jockey to compete on a major scale in the United States, running on the track at Hialeah, Florida. She was also the first female jockey to race in the Kentucky Derby, which she did in 1970.

8th.

1887   The U.S. Congress passed the Dawes Act.

1932   John Williams was born.

1960   The U.S. Congress began an investigation of music industry payola.

1972   U.S. President Richard Nixon signed the Federal Election Campaign Act.

1984   The Fourteenth Winter Olympics opened in Sarajevo, Yugoslavia (see February 4, February 11, February 13, February 14 entries).

1990   Soviet leaders agreed to surrender control.

"So much of what we do is ephemeral and quickly forgotten, even by ourselves, so it's gratifying to have something you have done linger in people's memories," composer John Williams commented. Born in Flushing, New York, on this day in 1932, Williams quickly rose to fame with his soundtrack to the film *Born Free*. He later composed the soundtracks for both the "Star Wars" and "Indiana Jones" film series and served as conductor of the Boston Pops orchestra. From the greatest heights to the lowest lows—on this same day in 1960, the U.S. Congress began an investigation of payola in the music industry, looking into under-the-counter payments made to radio station execs to guarantee that songs were frequently broadcast.

Promises and agreements are often made just so they can be broken. On this day in 1887, the U.S. Congress passed the Dawes Act, granting citizenship to Native Americans living outside the reservations. On the same day in 1971, U.S. President Richard Nixon signed the Federal Election Campaign Act, limiting media expenditures to 10 cents per voting-age person and requiring campaign contribution reports from all candidates. And in 1990 Soviet leaders agreed to surrender the Communist Party's seventy-two-year control of the government.

9th.

1906	Paul Lawrence Dunbar died.
1914	Carmen Miranda was born.
1923	Brendan Behan was born.
1944	Alice Walker was born.
1964	The Beatles made their first appearance on "The Ed Sullivan Show" (see January 1, January 20, January 24, January 30, February 7, February 12, May 9, June 6, June 12, August 29 entries).
1971	Leroy "Satchel" Paige was elected to the Baseball Hall of Fame (see July 7 entry).
1986	Halley's Comet made an appearance.
2001	India began a census.

Carmen Miranda's claims to fame were her quick delivery of Latin lyrics and her fruit-topped turbans. Born in Marco de Canavezes, Portugal, on this day in 1914, Miranda made appearances in numerous films during the 1940s, which were a favorite source of inspiration for animated film shorts. She was even caricatured by an advertising agency in a jingle and cartoon character used to sell Chiquita bananas.

On this day in 1906, poet Paul Lawrence Dunbar died. Born in Dayton, Ohio, Dunbar was the first poet to write in the African-American vernacular. His works was published in collected volumes such as *Lyrics of Lowly Life* and in four novels. Born in Eatonville, Georgia, on this day in 1944, Alice Malsenior Walker also centered her work on the African-American vernacular. Of her three best-known novels, her third, *The Color Purple,* won her the 1983 Pulitzer Prize for Fiction.

Another voice that reaches far beyond its borders is Irish. Born in Dublin, Ireland, on this day in 1923, Brendan Behan quit school when he was fourteen years old and joined the IRA. At sixteen, he was imprisoned for an attempt to blow up a Liverpool shipyard. Then he was sentenced to fourteen years for the attempted murder of two Dublin detectives. Five years in a cell in Manchester, England, were followed by deportation from England in 1952. His time behind bars afforded him the chance to read and to learn Irish from his fellow IRA inmates. The fruits of his lessons were first heard in his 1956 play, *The Quare Fellow.*

Two million census takers began to sweep India on this day in 2001, conducting a count of the nation's billion-plus population and asking questions that were outlined in a two-page document. The census takers applied a total of eighteen different languages to conduct their work. They were assigned the job of canvassing over 200 million households in 630,000 villages and 5,500 towns and cities over the course of nineteen days. "In India, with high levels of illiteracy, it takes a home visit from the census taker to gather all the details," said Census Commissioner Jayant K. Banthia. By contrast, the first U.S. Census, taken in 1790, counted a population of 4 million.

10th.

1883   Edith Clarke was born.

1890   A presidential proclamation opened eleven million acres of Sioux lands in South Dakota to homesteaders one year after they were seceded by treaty.

1957   The Southern Christian Leadership Conference was founded.

1964   The U.S. Congress passed the Civil Rights Bill.

1975 Tina Thompson was born.

1982 Twenty-eight skiers performed backflips.

1985 The space shuttle *Challenger* was moved (see January 28, February 6, April 4, April 29, June 22, September 2, October 13 entries).

1985 The USSR performed a nuclear test.

1989 Ron Brown was chosen as chairman of the Democratic Party.

1989 The United States performed a nuclear test.

1989 The World Wrestling Federation admitted that pro wrestling wasn't an actual sport.

1989 Tony Robinson became sheriff of Nottingham, England.

1990 Buster Douglas won the heavyweight boxing title.

1990 South African President F.W. de Klerk announced the release of Nelson Mandela (see March 18, July 18, December 13 entries).

1990 The world's sixth largest wrestling crowd gathered in Tokyo.

1991 Johann Koss skated to a world record.

1992 Mike Tyson was convicted of raping Desiree Washington (see June 30 entry).

1993 Jani Sievinen swam to a world record.

1995 Sun Cayun pole-vaulted to a world record.

1996 IBM's Deep Blue computer was defeated by chess champion Gary Kasparov (see May 11 entry).

1997 Comet Shoemaker-Holt 2 made its closest approach to the earth.

1997 The *Soyuz TM-25* was launched.

1998 AOL raised its rates.

The computer world stood up and jeered on this day in 1996, when IBM's Deep Blue computer was defeated by chess champion Gary Kasparov 3-1-2 in a heated, six-game chess match. (The following year, he competed against an improved version called Deeper Blue and was defeated; he scored 1 win, 2 losses, 3 draws.) Internet users were upended on this same day in 1998, when service provider America Online raised its monthly flat-rate charge for Internet access from $19.95 to $21.95.

When the Southern Christian Leadership Conference (SCLC) was founded on this day in 1957, and the U.S. Congress passed the Civil Rights Bill exactly seven years later, no one knew how far the tides of change would rise. On this same day in 1989, Jamaican-born Tony Robinson became the first non-Caucasian sheriff of Nottingham, England, and Ron Brown became the first African-American chairman of a major American political party: the Democrats. And in 1990, on this day, South African President F.W. de Klerk announced the release of civil rights advocate Nelson Mandela.

Nuclear tests occurred with great frequency during the later portion of the twentieth century. The USSR performed nuclear tests on this day in 1985, at Eastern Kazakh near Semipalitinsk. Four years later, in 1989, the United States performed tests at the Nevada test site. Neither event could have taken place if electrical engineers hadn't worked out the details. Pioneer electrical engineer Edith Clarke once said, "There is no demand for women engineers, as such, as there are for women doctors; but there's always a demand for anyone who can do a good piece of work." Born in Maryland on this day in 1883, Clarke was the first person to translate the complex equations used in electrical engineering into simpler, more usable graphics forms. And in 1947, she patented a graphical calculator for electrical design.

The same calculators were also used to make other events possible. Thanks to perfected electrical engineering techniques, it was possible for the space shuttle *Challenger* to be moved on this day in 1985 to Vandenberg Air Force Base for the mating of the *STS 51-E* mission. And in 1997 the *Soyuz TM-25* was able to launch and rendezvous with the *Mir* space station. Astronomers were also able to use high-powered electronic telescopes to view Comet Shoemaker-Holt 2 as it made its closest approach to terra firma on this day in 1997.

Aside from the twenty-eight skiers who performed backflips while holding hands in Bromont, Quebec, on this day in 1982, three world records were made on this day. In 1991 Johann Koss skated to a world record in the 10-km race, completing the event in 13:43:54. In 1993 Jani Sievinen swam to a world record for the 200-m backstroke, completing the race in 1:55:59. And in 1995 Sun Cayun pole-vaulted to a women's indoor world record, jumping 4.12 meters.

Pugilist sports such as boxing and wrestling have experienced their highs and lows. On this day in 1990, Buster Douglas knocked out Mike Tyson in ten rounds, winning the world's heavyweight boxing title. (Two years later, on the same day, Mike Tyson was convicted of raping Desiree Washington.) Wrestling took a new turn in 1989, when the World Wrestling Federation admitted that pro wrestling was an exhibition, not an actual sport, in a New Jersey courtroom in order to gain deregulation. And in 1990 the world's sixth largest wrestling crowd—63,900 spectators—gathered at Japan's Tokyo Dome to watch a sumo wrestling championship.

11th.

1928   The Second Winter Olympics opened in St. Moritz, Switzerland (see February 4, February 8, February 13, February 14 entries).

1953   The animated version of *Peter Pan* premiered (see December 27 entry).

1970   Japan became the fourth nation to put a satellite into space, joining the Soviet Union, the United States, and France.

1977   Lieutenant Colonel Mangista Haile-Mariam became Ethiopia's head of state.

2001   Space crews entered the science laboratory *Destiny*.

2001   Two former American school teachers became the first women to cross the Antarctic unaided.

The world's perception of potential crime was permanently changed on this day in 1997. Fifteen-year-old Amber Nash was suspended from school in Gobles, Michigan, for bringing a kitchen knife to class so she could cut a pan of brownies for a friend's birthday.

On this day in 2001, explorers Ann Bancroft and Liv Arnesen reached the Ross Ice Shelf, completing a 2,400-mile journey across Antarctica that began on November 13, 2000. "It's a big day for us," Arnesen said by satellite phone. This was not the first time either woman had dared such a feat. Bancroft was the first woman to ski to both the North and the South Poles. And Arnesen was the first woman to ski solo and unaided to the South Pole in 1994. They pulled their 240-pound sleds for more than nine hours down the final 12 miles of the Shackleton Glacier before making it on to the Ross Ice Shelf. The final leg of their journey required that they use parasails to ski 495 miles to meet an ice ship at McMurdo Station to take them home.

The crews of the space shuttle *Atlantis* and international space station *Alpha* entered the science laboratory *Destiny* on this day in 2001. It was the first visit after it was joined to its new home in space. The 28-foot-long laboratory was attached to the *Alpha* space station the day before during a 7.5-hour space walk by astronauts Thomas Jones and

Robert Curbeam, Jr., while astronaut Marsha Ivins used the space shuttle's robot arm to lift the laboratory from its berth on the space shuttle.

12th.

1909   The NAACP was founded, following a riot in Springfield, Illinois.

1924   George Gershwin's *Rhapsody in Blue* was first played in New York City (see September 2 entry).

1940   *The Adventures of Superman* debuted on radio.

1964   The Beatles performed in New York City's Carnegie Hall (see January 1, January 20, January 24, January 30, February 7, February 9, May 9, June 6, June 12, August 29 entries).

1992   Line mode v1.2 was announced.

1999   The U.S. Senate acquitted President Bill Clinton.

2001   The Johns Hopkins University Applied Physics Laboratory landed a space probe on the asteroid Eros.

On this day in 1992, the first revised Web language, Line mode v1.2, was announced on alt.hypertext, comp.infosystems, comp.mail.multi-media, cern.sting, comp.archives.admin, and a few Internet mailing lists.

The second presidential impeachment trial in American history ended on this day in 1999. The U.S. Senate acquitted President Bill Clinton after they voted 45-55 that he was not guilty of perjury charges and voted 50-50 with additional deliberations on charges of obstruction of justice.

The bus-sized NEAR Shoemaker space probe landed on the asteroid Eros on this day in 2001, completing history's first landing on an asteroid, which was situated 196 million miles from the earth's surface. It began signal transmissions from the asteroid's surface at 3:05 P.M. EST. The NEAR (Near Earth Asteroid Rendezvous) was the first probe to be controlled by an American agency other than NASA and the first to land on an asteroid. NASA rated the mission as a total success, hoping to learn more about the near-earth asteroid.

13th.

1903   Georges Simenon was born.

1918   Patty Berg was born.

1923   The first African-American professional basketball team, the Renaissance, was organized in New York's Harlem district.

1948   The *Kitty Hawk* was returned to the United States.

1960   France exploded its first atomic bomb, using a test site in Africa's Sahara Desert.

1974   Alexander Solzhenitsyn's Soviet citizenship was revoked and he was placed in exile.

1975   The New York Stock Exchange hit what was then a one-day record volume of 35.16 million shares (see January 4, September 20 entries).

1983   A standoff between militant tax protester Gordon Kahl and federal marshals began in Lawrence County, Arkansas (see June 3 entry).

1985   A federal panel declared that obesity was a disease that needed medical attention like smoking and high blood pressure.

1988   The Fifteenth Winter Olympics opened in Calgary, Alberta (see February 4, February 8, February 11, February 14 entries).

2001   Federal marshals seized a church in a tax dispute.

On this day in 1948, the Wright brothers' plane, *Kitty Hawk,* was returned to the United States from England, where it had been housed for twenty years. The historic aircraft was placed in the Smithsonian Museum in Washington, D.C.

Creator of the Inspector Jules Maigret mystery novels, Georges Simenon once said, "I have no imagination. I take everything from life." Born in Liége, Belgium, on this day in 1903, Simenon's reality-based inspiration produced over 500 novels during his half-century-long career. His most famous character, the pipe-smoking Inspector Maigret, was the subject of at least a hundred books, stemming from Simenon's fascination with the real-life French detective Marcel Guillaume.

For the first time in U.S. history, a church was seized as part of a tax dispute by federal marshals on this day in 2001. Five church members were inside when eighty-five federal marshals arrived at the Indianapolis Baptist Temple, supported by seventy city police officers. The dispute began when the church stopped withholding federal income and Social Security taxes from employee paychecks in 1984. Reverend Greg J. Dixon said his unregistered church was governed only by God's law and was not subject to taxation. Registered churches are exempt from certain taxes, but still must pay employee withholding taxes. Dixon refused to even apply for tax-exempt status, arguing that taxation of any church violated the First Amendment.

Born in Minneapolis, Minnesota, on this day in 1918, pro golfer Patty Berg won every major world amateur golf title by the time she was twenty years old. When she turned pro two years later, the newspapers commented that $145 per week was quite a bit of money for a girl twenty-two years old and taking her first job. Most of her male counterparts, however, were making considerably more than that at the time.

14th.

1838 Margaret Knight was born.

1896 Prince Edward became the first member of the British Royal Family to ride in a motor car.

1919 U.S. President Woodrow Wilson proposed the formation of a League of Nations.

1948 The first NASCAR modified stock car race took place.

1980 The Solar Maximum Mission Observatory was launched to study solar fires (see April 25 entry).

1980 The Thirteenth Winter Olympics opened in Lake Placid, New York (see February 4, February 8, February 11, February 13 entries).

1985 The U.S. Rabbinical Assembly of Conservative Judaism decided to admit female rabbis.

1988 Fifty-year-old Bobby Allison became NASCAR's oldest winner.

1989 Union Carbide agreed to pay $470 million in damages for the 1984 disaster in Bhopal, India (see April 8, December 30 entries).

2000 Hackers brought the Internet to its knees.

2001 Argentine paleontologists discovered a "Jurassic Park" of fossils.

In 2000 hackers brought the Internet to its knees when a virus attacked the popular web sites *Yahoo.com, buy.com, eBay.com, amazon.com, ZDnet.com, E*trade.com, Datek.com, excite.com,* and *CNN.com* during the course of three days. The computer virus triggered a loop of data that overloaded each of the systems, reducing site availability and trading by over 50 percent in each case.

Some ideas take longer to catch on than others. On this day in 1985, the U.S. Rabbinical Assembly of Conservative Judaism decided to admit female rabbis. The path had originally been opened in 1903, when New York City's Jewish Theological Seminary of America admitted its first female student, Henrietta Szold, because she promised not to seek ordination. In 1972 the first female reform rabbi, Sally Priesand, was ordained. It took another thirteen years, however, for conservatives to accept the concept and another year for it to become a reality.

You may not know it, but the patented design of the flat-bottomed paper bag has been around since 1870 thanks to Margaret Knight, who was born in Maine on this day in 1838. A prolific inventor, Knight held twenty-seven patents during her lifetime, ranging from a safety valve for the power loom, which she invented when she was twelve years old, to six shoe manufacturing devices she created later in her career. She never made a windfall profit from her inventions, yet Ms. Knight achieved a great reward: longevity. The basic machinery concept she developed for the manufacture of the flat-bottomed paper bag is still in use today.

Argentine paleontologists declared that they discovered a "Jurassic Park" of dinosaur fossils on this day in 2001, in the Patagonian province of Chubut, on an arid plateau situated 950 miles south of Buenos Aires. The finds included four unknown dinosaur species from the Jurassic period (circa 150–160 million years ago). Team member Gerardo Cladera of the Egidio Feruglio Paleontology Museum stated, "Jurassic-period fossils are very, very rare. They have only been found in China and Madagascar. . . . We know very little about the evolution of the dinosaurs, *pterosauri,* and mammals from this key period." This find left them with much to learn.

The automotive history experienced a few momentous firsts on St. Valentine's Day. The eldest son of Great Britain's Queen Victoria, Albert Edward, was known more for his frivolity than his attention to royal duty during his sixty-year apprenticeship as the Prince of Wales. His reputation, however, did include a number of firsts. He was the first prince to tour Canada and the United States, and the first British prince to be implicated in a divorce suit. On this day in 1896, Prince Edward also became the first member of the British Royal Family to ride in a motor car. Over a half-century later, the first NASCAR modified stock car race took place on a 3.2-mile course at Daytona Beach, Florida, in 1948. Most entrants drove customized pre–World War II Fords in the 150-mile race, including NASCAR's first champion, Red Byron. (The Olds 88 became the most familiar NASCAR model after the 1949 race.) Not all Daytona winners are young drivers. On the Daytona's fortieth anniversary, on this day in 1988, fifty-year-old Bobby Allison became the race's oldest winner.

15th.

1874   Sir Ernest Shackleton was born.

1957   Andrei Gromyko became Soviet foreign minister.

1965   Canada unfurled its red maple leaf flag in Ottawa.

1971   *The New York Times* began serial publication of the Pentagon Papers (see November 13 entry).

1989   The Soviet Union withdrew the last of its troops from Afghanistan after nine years of military intervention.

1995   America's "most wanted" hacker was arrested.

2000   "Who Wants to Marry a Multi-Millionaire?" premiered.

2000   The American prison population passed the 2 million mark.

On this day in 1995, the FBI arrested America's most wanted hacker in Raleigh, North Carolina. Kevin Mitnick had broken into some of the nation's most security-conscious computers, including Tsutomu Shimomura's mainframes in San Diego, California. He was sentenced to five years' imprisonment for his talents.

On this day in 2000, the Justice Policy Institute issued a statement that the American prison population had passed the 2 million mark. "Our current rate of incarceration is six to ten times that of most industrialized countries," the Institute announced. "We have more prisoners in one state, California, than do the nations of France, Germany, Great Britain, Japan, Singapore, and the Netherlands combined."

On this day in 2000, the television show "Who Wants to Marry a Multi-Millionaire?" premiered on Fox-TV before 23 million viewers. Out of the fifty initial contestants, emergency-room nurse Darva Conger won a $35,000 engagement ring, an Isuzu Trooper, a marriage to real-estate developer Rick Rockwell on camera, and a chaperoned Caribbean honeymoon cruise, which were paid for by the show's producers. Ten days later, the couple's photo appeared on the cover of *People* magazine with the title line "TV's wedding fiasco." Conger and Rockwell had broken up within twenty-four hours of saying "I do."

True heroes are a rarity in the world, but Sir Ernest Henry Shackleton certainly earned the designation when he and his crew survived the wreck of their ship without losing a single man. Born in Killee, Ireland, on this day in 1874, Shackleton was a junior officer under explorer Captain Robert Scott aboard the *Discovery* when Scott led the 1901 National Antarctic Expedition. Shackleton himself was placed in command of a 1908 expedition that came within 97 miles of the South Pole—a record for that time. During his command of a 1914 expedition, Shackleton's ship, the *Endeavour,* was crushed by ice. Pushing sledges and boats, Shackleton and his entire crew made their way to Elephant Island. Accompanied by five crew members, Shackleton then made the perilous 800-mile journey to South Georgia, where they organized a rescue party for the remaining crew on Elephant Island. Not one person died during the ordeal. In the end, Shackleton experienced a hero's death: He passed away in South Georgia during a 1920 polar expedition.

Excerpts from the Pentagon Papers first appeared in *The New York Times* on this day in 1971. The documents detailed the United States's involvement in Vietnam from the end of the Second World War through 1968. The series ran for three installments until President Richard Nixon won a restraining order to stop further publication.

16th.

1884   Robert Flaherty was born.

1948   NBC-TV aired its first nightly newscast.

1968   The 911 emergency service was inaugurated.

1990   Former U.S. President Ronald Reagan began two days of videotaped deposition for John Poindexter's Iran-Contra trial.

1998   Infertility was legally deemed a disability under the Americans with Disabilities Act.

2001   Russia launched ballistic missiles.

2001   The cause of total extinction of the dinosaurs was discovered.

2001   U.S. President George W. Bush ordered a military air strike on Baghdad, Iraq.

Phone calls were a dime back in the late 1960s. Most people, however, didn't have time to search their pockets for coins during an emergency. On this day in 1968, the problem was solved. The nation's first 911 emergency telephone service was installed in Haleyville, Alabama, allowing customers to contact local police, fire, and medical departments free of charge.

Robert Flaherty has been called the "father of the documentary film." Born in Iron Mountain, Michigan, on this day in 1884, Flaherty was raised in Canada, where he first learned about harsh life of the Inuits. This inspired his first major documentary film, *Nanook of the North,* which premiered in 1922 and astounded audiences by showing them a slice of reality few of them could ever experience in real life. The overwhelming success of this film took Flaherty to other corners of the world, from the South Sea islands and the Louisiana swamps to the Indian jungles and the Irish isle of Aran during his twenty-nine-year career.

Television networks didn't start out hiring high-priced anchorpeople to broadcast the nightly news. In fact, the first nightly news broadcast wasn't aired until this day in 1948, when NBC-TV aired "The Camel Newsreel Theatre." The program consisted of Twentieth-Century Fox Movietone newsreels, which were popular in move theaters across the nation.

Infertility was redesignated by the legal system on this day in 1998. According to an article published in the *National Law Journal,* infertility was judged to be a disability under the Americans with Disabilities Act, after Judge Suzanne B. Conlon ruled that infertility substantially limits a major life activity and is, therefore, a "physiological disorder of the reproductive system."

An asteroid or comet that was roughly the same size as the one that wiped out the dinosaurs 65 million years ago did even worse damage 250 million years ago, experts reported in the journal *Science* on this day in 2001. Space gases trapped in little carbon spheres called buckyballs that were embedded in ancient layers of sediment show that the Permian extinction event started with a cosmic collision. Trilobites died out completely—all 15,000 species of them. Ninety percent of all marine creatures and 70 percent of land vertebrates went extinct. The collision released "an amount of energy that is basically about one million times the largest earthquake recorded during the last century," Robert Poreda from the University of Rochester stated. The comet or asteroid must have been four to eight miles across. The jolt roused volcanoes, which buried huge areas in lava and sent up ash to join the dust from the explosion, plunging the world into centuries of unnatural dark and cold.

On this day in 2001, two ballistic missiles were launched—one from a land-based silo in northwest Russia and one from a nuclear-powered submarine in the Barents Sea—at a mutual target in the Kamchatka peninsula. Later that day, a Russian TU-95 bomber test-fired a strategic missile and a TU-22 bomber test-fired a pair of shorter-range tactical missiles. Colonel General Leonid Ivashov from the Russian Defense Ministry said in an interview that the rhetoric of the new American administration was "anti-Russian" and aimed at a reduction of Russia's prestige and power in the world.

U.S. President George W. Bush ordered his first military strike on this day in 2001. He sent twenty-four British and U.S. warplanes to bomb five military sites around Baghdad, Iraq, as a "self-defense measure" because they allegedly posed potential danger to British and American military patrols. Marine Lieutenant General Gregory Newbold stated, "It reached the point that it was obvious to our forces that they had to conduct the operation to safeguard those pilots and the aircraft. In fact [it was] essentially a self-defense measure."

17th.

1600 The Inquisition condemned Giordano Bruno.

1902 Marian Anderson was born (see January 7, April 9 entries).

1933 *Newsweek* was first published.

1999 The *Cable & Wireless* was launched (see March 7 entry).

No one in the history of hot-air ballooning had ever attempted to circumnavigate the world, following the jet stream north of the equator. On this day in 1999, Colin Prescot and Andy Elson took off from southern Spain in the hot-air balloon *Cable & Wireless,* marking the first attempt to complete such a daring flight.

Born in Philadelphia, Pennsylvania, on this day in 1902, Marian Anderson rose from a life in poverty to become a starring contralto singer after she gave her first recital in New York's Carnegie Hall. She toured Europe and the Soviet Union during the 1930s and became the first African-American diva to perform in New York's Metropolitan Opera in 1955. Three years later, U.S. President Dwight D. Eisenhower appointed Anderson as a delegate to the United Nations.

In the heat of religious fervor and intellectual discovery, the Roman Catholic Church frequently went head-to-head with some of the world's greatest scientific, artistic, and literary minds of the sixteenth and seventeenth centuries. Giordano Bruno was one of those thinkers, supporting Copernicus's view that the sun—not the earth—was the center of the solar system. Also publicly suggested that based on newly discovered data, there was potentially more than one solar system in the universe and, consequently, more than one inhabitable world. On this day in 1600, the Inquisition condemned Giordano Bruno for his outrageously non-Christian beliefs, branding him a heretic. For his scientific efforts, he was burned at the stake.

18th.

1922	Helen Gurley Brown was born.
1931	Toni Morrison was born.
1960	The Winter Olympics opened in Squaw Valley, California.
1977	The *Enterprise* space shuttle made its maiden flight atop a Boeing 747 over the Mojave Desert.
1980	Pierre Trudeau was returned to office for a second time as Canada's prime minister.
1995	The NAACP replaced veteran chairman William Gibson.
1999	U.S. President Bill Clinton threatened Serbian President Slobodan Milosevic with military attack.

Peace among minority groups sometimes takes extra effort. On this day in 1995, the NAACP replaced chairman William Gibson with Myrlie Evers-Williams, the widow of slain civil rights leader Medgar Evers, after members of this influential organization declared no confidence in Gibson's leadership. On this same day in 1999, U.S. President Bill Clinton warned Serbian President Slobodan Milosevic to choose peace with Kosovo's ethnic Albanians or face military attack by NATO forces.

Helen Gurley Brown and Toni Morrison made their names in the publishing world during the 1960s and 1970s. Born in Green Forest, Arkansas, on this day in 1922, Helen Gurley Brown wrote the 1962 bestseller *Sex and the Single Girl* before replacing her husband Dave Brown as editor-in-chief of *Cosmopolitan* magazine from 1965 to 1997. Toni Chloe Anthony Morrison worked as a senior editor at Random House before becoming a novelist in her own right, publishing her first book, *The Bluest Eye,* in 1970. Born Chloe Anthony Wofford in Lorain, Ohio, on this day in 1931, Morrison created works about rural African-Americans exploring the topics of incest, rape, generational conflicts, and the cultured social class. Her writings earned her the 1988 Pulitzer Prize for Literature.

19th.

1865   Sven A. Hedin was born.

1904   Alexei N. Kosygin was born.

1942   U.S. President Franklin Delano Roosevelt signed Executive Order 9066 evacuating Japanese-Americans from the West Coast (see February 24, August 4, August 10 entries).

1986   The U.S. Senate approved a treaty outlawing genocide.

1999   U.S. President Bill Clinton pardoned Henry O. Flipper (see June 15 entry).

The laws that govern ethnic relations work slowly at times. Thirty-seven years after the U.S. Congress had been asked to ratify a treaty that outlawed genocide, the governing body finally signed its approval on this day in 1986. U.S. President Bill Clinton posthumously pardoned Henry O. Flipper on this day in 1999. The first African-American West Point graduate had been dishonorably discharged in 1882 for alleged embezzlement.

Fear of the unknown frequently ignites prejudice. On this day in 1942, U.S. President Franklin Delano Roosevelt succumbed to fears about potential Japanese invasion of the United States when he signed Executive Order 9066. This simple document ordered all Japanese-Americans to be evacuated from the West Coast and moved into concentration camps situated in the Sierra Nevada and Cascade mountain ranges. A similar order was passed in Canada as well. The majority of families who complied with the order permanently lost their homes, property, and businesses. Only a small handful were financially compensated for their loss of dignity fifty years later.

Until 1908, Tibet was a virtually uncharted region of the Himalayas. Explorer Sven A. Hedin changed all that when he completed a detailed map of the area following his explorations of central Asia, Mongolia, and Tibet. Born in Stockholm, Sweden, on this day in 1865, Hedin collected over 8,000 geological specimens and artifacts from these remote areas and led the first Sino-Swedish Scientific Expeditions into China's northwestern provinces between 1927 and 1933.

Alexei Kosygin attempted some decentralization reforms while he was Soviet premier during the 1960s and 1970s, but he never had a lasting impact on domestic affairs. Born in Leningrad, Russia, on this day in 1904, Kosygin held a number of political posts before succeeding Soviet Premier Nikita Khrushchev in 1964.

20th.

1965   The *Ranger Eight* crashed on the moon after transmission of lunar surface photographs.

1980   U.S. President Jimmy Carter announced that the United States would boycott the Moscow Summer Olympics, protesting the Soviet presence in Afghanistan (see October 1 entry).

1981   The *Columbia* space shuttle fired its three engines in a 20-second test before it was given maiden launch clearance.

1999   The United States and five other nations extended the Kosovo peace agreement deadline by three days.

2001   The Sandwich family went into the sandwich business.

Orlando Montagu's father, the eleventh Earl of Sandwich, traced his line directly to the man who invented the sandwich. "There are 250 years of expectation on us," Montagu said. His restaurant, The Earl of Sandwich, catered sandwiches to London's business district, backed by Robert Earl, creator of Planet Hollywood. The business opened on this day in 2001, delivering its first sandwich to his father, John Montagu.

21st.

1925   *The New Yorker* magazine was first published.

1965   Malcolm X was assassinated.

1975   John Mitchell, H.R. Haldeman, John Ehrlichman, and Robert Mardian were sentenced to prison for their parts in the Watergate cover-up (see January 19, June 22, July 1, October 1 entries).

1995   The first solo hot-air balloon flight across the Pacific Ocean was completed (see January 14, January 20, August 7, August 16 entries).

2001   Pope John Paul II installed a record forty-four new cardinals.

On this day in 1965, Malcolm X was assassinated by three gunmen (all followers of Elijah Muhammed, founder of the Nation of Islam) as he was about to speak at a Black Muslim rally in New York City. Muslim leaders had allegedly been campaigning for Malcolm X's assassination prior to this date, although this was never officially confirmed. The three assassins were eventually arrested and convicted.

It takes more than skill and daring to fly a hot-air balloon. On this day in 1995, Chicago stockbroker Steve Fossett proved he could scale the heights when he landed his roziere—a combination gas and hot-air balloon—in Leader, Saskatchewan, Canada, completing the first solo crossing of the Pacific Ocean from Seoul, South Korea.

Forty-four new cardinals representing twenty-seven nations and five continents were installed by Pope John Paul II in St. Peter's Square at Vatican City on this day in 2001. It was a record number. Among the appointees were Fordham University theologian Avery Dulles, Archbishop Edward Egan, Archbishop Theodore McCarrick, Archbishop Lubomyr Husar, and Vietnamese Archbishop Francois Xavier Nguyen Van Thuan. For the first time, some Eastern Rite cardinals chose not to wear the biretta, opting for traditional headgear instead. Syrian patriarch Ignace Moussa I Daoud kept his black, flat-topped hat, and Archbishop Lubomyr Husar kept his traditional black hood. In naming a record number of cardinals, Pope John Paul II ignored limits set by his predecessor Paul VI on the number of cardinals younger than eighty years old who were eligible to vote for the next pontiff.

22nd.

1784 The first China trade with the United States occurred.

1924 U.S. President Calvin Coolidge aired the first White House radio broadcast.

1950 Julius "Dr. J" Erving was born.

1974 The first women's basketball game was played.

1994 Aldrich Ames and his wife were arrested on charges of Soviet and Russian counterespionage.

The way in which Americans market their wares changed when foreign trade turned a new leaf. On this day in 1784, trading between China and the United States opened up when a shipment of American-grown ginseng was delivered to Canton, China.

Born in East Meadow, New York, on this day in 1950, Julius "Dr. J" Erving played with the American Basketball Association's New York Nets, becoming an MVP who averaged 27.4 points per game. On this same day in 1974, the first women's basketball game was played at New York's Madison Square Garden. Not convinced that the female team would draw a crowd, the management scheduled a men's basketball game to follow. When the women's game ended, nearly 12,000 spectators left and the men had to play before relatively empty seats.

23rd.

1868   W.E.B. DuBois was born (see June 13 entry).

1889   Victor Fleming was born.

1940   Peter Fonda was born.

1954   The first mass polio inoculation of children occurred in Pittsburgh, Pennsylvania (see January 10, August 1, October 28 entries).

1995   The Dow Jones Industrial Average closed above the 4000 mark for the first time, at 4003.33 (see September 11 entry).

1997   Scottish scientists successfully cloned an adult sheep, producing a lamb named Dolly.

The 1939 film *The Wizard of Oz* and the 1969 film *Easy Rider* became cult classics during the late twentieth century. Born in New York City on this day in 1940, Peter Fonda not only starred as Captain America in *Easy Rider,* he also wrote and directed the film with Dennis Hopper. The son of actor Henry Fonda and brother of Jane Fonda, Peter Fonda also appeared in the films *Dirty Mary Crazy Larry* and *Ulee's Gold.* Born in Pasadena, California, on this day in 1889, Victor Fleming not only directed the musical film *The Wizard of Oz,* he also directed another cinematic blockbuster, *Gone with the Wind.* Both films were released in 1939.

Born in Great Barrington, Massachusetts, on this day in 1868, William Edward Burghardt DuBois wrote his thesis on the suppression of the African slave trade, becoming the first African-American to receive a doctorate from Harvard University. A co-founder of the National Association for the Advancement of Colored People (NAACP) in 1909, DuBois wrote numerous nonfiction and fiction works that addressed the African-American condition and slavery in general during the first half of the twentieth century. In the heat of early radical civil rights activity, DuBois moved to the west African nation of Ghana in 1959 and joined the Communist Party two years later.

Science took some major leaps to improve the human condition on this day. In 1954 medical technicians in Pittsburgh, Pennsylvania, began the first mass polio inoculation of children, using Jonas Salk's vaccine. And in 1997 Scottish scientists announced that they had successfully cloned an adult sheep, producing a lamb named Dolly.

24th.

1868   The U.S. House of Representatives impeached President Andrew Johnson.

1903   The United States acquired a naval station on the island of Cuba.

1981   Great Britain's Prince Charles's engagement to Lady Diana Spencer was officially announced (see July 1, July 29, December 9 entries).

1983   A U.S. Congress commission condemned the World War II internment of Japanese-Americans as a "grave injustice" (see February 19, August 4, August 10 entries).

1990   The duo Milli Vanilli was forced to return its Grammy Award because it was discovered the two lip-synched all of their performances and did not even sing on their own recordings.

1991   Operation Desert Storm began (see August 2 entry).

American troops were found around the world on this day. In 1903 the United States acquired a naval station in Cuba's Guantanamo Bay, part of the treaty package the United States won in the wake of the Spanish-American War. On this same day in 1991, Operation Desert Storm began in Kuwait. Within 100 hours, more than 100,000 Iraqi troops surrendered to American and allied forces. At least 100,000 additional Iraqis were killed.

25th.

1907   Mary Coyle Chase was born.

1917   Anthony Burgess was born.

1954   Gamal Abdel Nasser became premier of Egypt.

1964   Cassius Clay (Muhammed Ali) became world heavyweight champion, defeating Sonny Liston (see May 8 entry).

1986   Philippine President Ferdinand Marcos went into exile.

Unconventional views of human nature were addressed by both Mary Coyle Chase and Anthony Burgess in their work. Born in Denver, Colorado, on this day in 1907, Mary Coyle Chase wrote the Pulitzer Prize-winning play *Harvey,* which centered around a congenial, middle-aged man who befriends a six-foot-tall invisible rabbit at his local bar. Born in Manchester, England, on this day in 1917, Anthony Burgess wrote the 1962 novel *A Clockwork Orange,* which projected a wild and dark vision of life in the not-too-distant future, creating a unique vernacular in order to set the pace and voice for his tale of violent adolescence and its clash with acceptable social behavior.

On this day in 1954, Gamal Abdel Nasser took over as premier of Egypt. Although he'd been responsible for the downfall of the corrupt King Farouk and the rise of General Mohammed Neguib in 1952, Nasser sensed Neguib's dictatorial ambitions, deposing the military junta leader and taking the reins of power himself. On this day in 1986, Philippine President Ferdinand Marcos went into exile in Hawaii, ending twenty years as dictator of the island nation.

26th.

1919   The U.S. Congress passed acts to establish Grand Canyon National Park and Lafayette National Park.

1935   Robert Watson-Watt introduced the first radio-manned aircraft tracking device.

1951 The U.S. Congress passed the Twenty-second Amendment.

1985 Corazon Aquino was elected president of the Philippines, defeating Ferdinand Marcos (see January 25, August 21 entries).

1997 *The New York Times* made allegations against Democratic fundraisers.

On this day in 1951, the U.S. Congress passed the Twenty-second Amendment, which limited the presidential post to two terms. President Franklin Delano Roosevelt had served three full terms, dying while in his fourth term in office. Although he had a long and distinguished record, Congress determined that no individual should hold the presidential seat for more than eight years. During his second and final term in office, President Bill Clinton and the Democratic Party were strongly criticized in the press for their fundraising activities. On this day in 1997, *The New York Times* reported that Democratic fundraisers "explicitly sold invitations to White House coffees with President Clinton." The report further implied that overnight stays in the Lincoln bedroom of the White House were given in exchange for generous contributions to the Democratic Party.

On this day in 1935, Sir Robert Watson-Watt introduced the first radio-manned aircraft tracking device at Ditton Park, England, playing a major role in the development and use of radar in aeronautics. He was knighted for his efforts in 1942. An interest in airplanes was a family affair: Watson-Watt's wife, Katherine, was the director of the Women's Auxiliary Air Force during the Second World War.

27th.

1847 Ellen Terry was born.

1899 Charles Herbert Best was born.

1932 Elizabeth Taylor was born.

1968 The House of Commons restricted the immigration of Asians and Kenyans with British citizenship into Great Britain.

1996 U.S. President Bill Clinton banned charter flights to Cuba, after two American private planes were shot down by the Cuban Air Force.

1997 Divorce was legalized in Ireland.

Two actresses who had brilliant careers and more than enough marriages share this birthday. Born in Coventry, England on this day in 1847, Ellen Terry made her debut when she was eight years old. Married to the painter George Frederick Watts, to the architect William Godwin (with whom she had two children, Edith and Edward Gordon Craig), to Charles Kelly Wardell, and to the American actor James Carew, Terry was best known for her portrayals of Portia in *The Merchant of Venice* and Ophelia in *Hamlet* on European and American stages until 1902. She then entered theater management, commissioning her son Edward to design and produce Henrik Ibsen's *Vikings*. Born in London, England, on this day in 1932, Elizabeth Taylor made her film debut when she was ten years old. She rose to stardom with her roles in *National Velvet* and a remake of *Little Women*. As an adult, Taylor gained stature as an adult actress in the films *Cat on a Hot Tin Roof, Raintree County,* and *Suddenly Last Summer,* receiving Oscar nominations for all three roles. When she was eighteen years old, Taylor married hotel heir Nicky Hilton. Two years later, she married actor Michael Wilding. In 1957 she married film producer Michael Todd, who died in an air crash a year later. In 1959 she married singer Eddie Fisher. Five years later, she married Richard Burton; she later divorced him and the two were married again until 1976. Two years later, she married U.S. Senator John Warner. And in 1991 she married a much younger man named Larry Fortensky. That relationship lasted five years.

Born in West Pembroke, Maine, on this day in 1899, Charles Herbert Best helped to save millions of diabetics' lives when he assisted in the isolation of the hormone insulin while working as a research student to Sir Frederick Banting in Toronto, Ontario. Best himself discovered choline (which prevents liver damage often associated with diabetes) and histaminase (which aids in the assimilation of histamine) and pioneered the use of heparin, an anticoagulant drug, during his professional career.

28th.

1890   Vaslav Nijinsky was born.

1960   The residents of Geneva, Switzerland, granted women the right to vote and to hold political office (see November 3 entry).

1990   The *Atlantis* space shuttle blasted off from Cape Canaveral, Florida, secretly placing a spy satellite in orbit.

1993   Federal agents raided the Branch Davidian compound in Waco, Texas, beginning a 51-day siege (see April 19 entry).

1997   Federal regulations went into effect mandating fines of at least $250 levied on stores selling tobacco products to anyone under 18 or neglecting to card anyone under 27.

Vaslav Nijinsky was regarded as one of the twentieth century's top ballet dancers during his short but spectacular career. Born in Kiev, Russia, on this day in 1890, Nijinsky trained at St. Petersburg's Imperial Ballet School and debuted at the Maryinski Theatre. His popularity grew to international proportions in 1909, when he performed in Paris as the lead dancer in Sergei Diaghilev's Ballet Russe. His unique choreography and performances for Stravinsky's ballet *Petrushka,* Debussy's *L'Aprés-midi d'un Faune,* and Stravinsky's *Sacre du Printemps* were successfully duplicated by only two other greats of the dance world: Rudolf Nureyev and Mikhail Baryshnikov. Sadly, Nijinsky's shining star faded during the 1920s, when he was diagnosed for paranoid schizophrenia, for which he was treated until his death in 1950.

29th.

1736   Anne Lee was born.

1815   The first obscenity trial took place in the United States.

1840   John Holland was born.

1968   The first pulsar was discovered.

1995   Denver International Airport was completed.

1996   The Robert Forsyth Act of Valor Award was given to federal marshals involved at Ruby Ridge, Idaho.

1996   Thirty TV and film executives met at the White House to discuss a TV ratings system.

On this day in 1995, a major air travel hub was established in the Rocky Mountains. The 53-square-mile Denver International Airport was completed, replacing the sixty-five-year-old Stapleton Airport. Located 23 miles from downtown Denver, the $4.9-billion construction took sixteen months longer than anticipated.

Obscenity and media control are hot topics on this day. In 1815 the first obscenity trial took place in the United States. A Philadelphia court tried Jess Sharpless and found him guilty of displaying an obscene painting in his home. In 1996 about thirty television and entertainment industry executives met with President Bill Clinton at the White House to discuss the establishment of a national TV ratings system, which would aid parents in controlling their children's viewing of violent or objectionable scenes presented on television programs.

Born in Manchester, England, on this day in 1736, Anne Lee was the illiterate daughter of a blacksmith who joined the Shaking Quakers (also known as the Shakers) in 1758. Members of this religious cult saw Anne as the second coming of Christ, inspiring her to spread the word. (It didn't change her mind about marriage; she wed a blacksmith named Albert Stanley in 1762.) Arrested and imprisoned for street preaching in 1770, Anne moved her followers to the United States four years later. There she established the American Shaker settlement in Niskayuma (now Watervliet), New York.

Born in Liscannor, Ireland, on this day in 1840, John Holland emigrated to the United States in 1873, settling in Paterson, New Jersey. An inventor at heart, Holland's original design for a submarine was rejected by the U.S. Navy in 1875. Financed by the Fenian Society, in 1881 Holland did successfully launch a more practical submarine named the *Fenian Ram* on the Hudson River. Seventeen years later, he perfected his concept, demonstrating the *Holland VI* both above and below the waters of the Potomac River. This final working model convinced naval personnel from more than one nation that the submarine could become a major wartime weapon, establishing Holland as the father of the modern non-nuclear submarine.

Some stars in the sky emit regular radio waves that can be detected here on earth. These unique celestial bodies are called pulsars. On this day in 1968, the first pulsar was detected by Dr. Jocelyn Bell Burnell, who announced her find at Cambridge, England.

March

Hot-air balloons took to the skies and the American Automobile Association took to the road in March. Great leaps were also made as a planet was discovered and the Internet was predicted as the first buds of spring blossomed.

1st.

1914 Ralph Waldo Ellison was born.

1922 Yitzhak Rabin was born.

1927 Robert Bork was born (see October 23 entry).

1954 Five U.S. congressmen were wounded in the House of Representatives.

1967 U.S. Representative Adam Clayton Powell was accused of misconduct.

1974 Seven presidential aides were indicted by a federal grand jury.

1999 Bertrand Piccard and Brian Jones launched their hot-air balloon *Breitling Orbiter 3* (see January 28, March 13, March 19, May 27, August 18 entries).

Not all crimes occur within the private sector. On this day in 1954, five U.S. congressmen were wounded by Puerto Rican nationalists firing wildly from the House of Representatives gallery. U.S. Representative Adam Clayton Powell was accused of misconduct on this day in 1967. He was denied his seat in the ninetieth session of Congress. (Two years later, however, the U.S. Supreme Court ruled that the House had acted unconstitutionally in excluding Powell from the session.) And in 1974, seven of U.S. President Richard Nixon's aides were indicted by a federal grand jury on charges of covering up the Watergate scandal.

Auguste Piccard and his brother Jean made great strides in the field of aeronautics during the 1930s, achieving record heights onboard hot-air balloons. On this day in 1999, August Piccard's grandson Bertrand launched an equally ambitious feat in a similar craft. Piccard and his partner, Brian Jones, launched their hot-air balloon *Breitling Orbiter 3* from Château d'Oex, Switzerland, in an attempt to circumnavigate the world.

Many novelists achieve fame over the course of a few books. Ralph Waldo Ellison, however, born in Oklahoma City, Oklahoma, on this day in 1914, accomplished this feat with a single title. Ellison's first novel, *Invisible Man,* was a profound influence on many African-American writers when it was published in 1952. Depicting the journey of a nameless man as he travels from the South to the North in search of his identity, Ellison won the National Book Award for this singular effort.

U.S. Senator Edward Kennedy once commented that "Robert Bork's America is a land in which women would be forced into back-alley abortions, blacks would sit at segregated lunch counters, rogue police could break down citizens' doors in midnight raids, children could not be taught about evolution." The conservative right wing's choice for U.S. Supreme Court Justice, Robert Bork was rejected in the Senate. Born on this day in 1927, Bork was called upon by President Nixon to fire Watergate Special Prosecutor Archibald Cox. His appointment hearing was the longest confirmation hearing ever held for a U.S. Supreme Court Justice. He shocked even some of his supporters, modifying some of his most conservative opinions. The Senate Judiciary Committee ended up voting 9-5 against Bork's confirmation, and the Republican-based Senate voted 58-42 against his appointment. President Ronald Reagan appointed Sandra Day O'Connor to the position instead.

Born in Jerusalem, Palestine, on this day in 1922, Yitzhak Rabin decided on a military career after completing his studies in agriculture. Fighting in the 1948 War for Independence, Rabin represented the Israeli Defense Forces at the armistice on the island of Rhodes the next year. He became chief of staff in 1964 and led the winning forces in the 1967 Six-Day War. Rabin moved into politics the following year, serving as ambassador to the United States until 1973, when he rose to become Israel's prime minister from 1974 until 1977. Rabin became his nation's defense minister seven years later.

2nd.

1876   Eugenio Pacelli, who later became Pope Pius XII, was born.

1899   Mount Rainier National Park was established.

1904   Theodore Geisel was born (see January 16 entry).

1917   Puerto Rico became a territory of the United States.

1931   Mikhail Gorbachev was born.

1931   Tom Wolfe was born.

1942   John Irving was born.

1993   The Bureau of Alcohol, Tobacco, and Firearms began the surveillance of David Koresh near Waco, Texas (see April 19 entry).

Reports of child abuse and illegal arms possession at the Branch Davidian cult headquarters near Waco, Texas, prompted the U.S. Treasury Department's Bureau of

Alcohol, Tobacco, and Firearms (BATF) to begin surveillance of David Koresh and his followers on this day in 1993. The federal agents learned that their suspicions weren't completely unfounded when they discovered Koresh had stockpiled an arsenal of guns and explosives at his country compound.

Two major events in Puerto Rico's history took place on this day in 1917. The Jones Act was passed by the U.S. Congress, making the island of Puerto Rico a territory of the United States. This bill essentially granted United States citizenship to Puerto Rican nationals, allowing them to vote in federal elections and to enter the American armed forces.

The tone of adult and children's literature changed in the United States thanks to three men who were born on this particular day. Born in Springfield, Massachusetts, on this day in 1904, Theodore Geisel wrote about cats and grinches and green eggs and ham, changing youthful readers' expectations of books. *The Cat in the Hat* was only the first of Geisel stories written under the pen name Dr. Seuss. But literature transports readers to many destinations, as the title of Geisel's more adult book, *Oh, the Places You Will Go*, reminds us. Born in Richmond, Virginia, on this day in 1931, Tom Wolfe transformed our opinions of modern-day American life when he published *The Kandy Kolored, Tangerine Flake Streamline Baby* in 1966. He continued to demystify human existence with his books *The Right Stuff* and *Bonfire of the Vanities,* never allowing readers to complacently judge heroes and icons in a normal light. Born in Exeter, New Hampshire, on this day in 1942, John Irving tore away the veils of normal life in his novels *Hotel New Hampshire, The World According to Garp,* and *A Prayer for Owen Meany.*

Mikhail Gorbachev's career had numerous highlights, beginning with his education and ending with his rise to the Russian presidency. Born in Privolnoye, Russia, on this day in 1931, Gorbachev was the son of an agricultural mechanic who distinguished himself in school. He was sent to Moscow University for a law degree, where he met and married his wife Raisa. Joining the Communist Party in 1952, Gorbachev made it quickly through the ranks from regional agricultural secretary to party leader in Stavropol by 1970. Yuri Andropov appointed Gorbachev to the post of national agriculture secretary eight years later. Gorbachev had risen to general secretary of the party in 1984, introducing radical economic reforms and restructuring a corrupted government base. He further shocked the system by signing the Intermediate Nuclear Forces Abolition Treaty in 1987, ordering the withdrawal of Soviet troops from Afghanistan in 1989, and becoming Russia's president in 1990.

Born in Rome, Italy, on this day in 1876, Eugenio Pacelli was considered to be both a villain and a humanitarian during his career as Pope Pius XII. Succeeding to the papal throne in 1939, Pius XII did much to aid prisoners of war and refugees during the Second World War. He was harshly criticized, however, for his refusal to publicly speak out against the persecution of European Jews. After the war, he concentrated all of his effort on the treatment of the clergy who had been arrested and imprisoned in communist-held countries throughout Europe and Asia.

3rd.

1871 The U.S. Congress passed the Indian Appropriation Act.

1911 Jean Harlow was born.

1925 The erection of a sculpture in South Dakota's Black Hills region was authorized by federal and state governments (see July 2, July 4, August 30, September 17, October 1, October 31, December 28 entries).

1991 Rodney King was brutalized by Los Angeles police (see April 16, April 29, August 4 entries).

The life of a Hollywood movie star wasn't always glittering. Born in Kansas City, Missouri, on this day in 1911, Jean Harlow moved to Los Angeles after she eloped with a local business tycoon when she was only sixteen years old. It was the first of her three marriages on her way to the top of the dream machine. She played sharp-witted, openly sexy blonde bombshell roles while under contract with Howard Hughes's RKO Pictures before joining MGM in 1933. She had top billing at this major studio for three years in the films *Hell's Angels, Platinum Blonde, Red-Headed Woman,* and *Red Dust,* before she died unexpectedly at the age of 26.

On this day in 1871, the U.S. Congress passed the Indian Appropriation Act. Although many tribal members had already ceded their lands by signing treaties and had been moved to reservations, the government wanted to make land more accessible to settlement and negate all Native American rights to object. This bill made all tribes wards of the government and voided all previous treaties that recognized each tribe's reservation status as an autonomous nation.

4th.

1891	The U.S. Congress passed the International Copyright Act.
1902	The American Automobile Association was founded.
1909	The U.S. Congress passed the U.S. Copyright Law.
1985	The Environmental Protection Agency banned the use of leaded gasoline.

Copyright laws protect the original visual, text, and aural works created by various artists, composers, and authors. Known as intellectual property, these original works are the products of individual minds that can be licensed to book publishers, record companies, and fine art publishers in the same way patented inventions are licensed to manufacturers. On this day in 1891, the U.S. Congress passed the International Copyright Act in an effort to protect intellectual properties such as these from plagiarism. In 1909 on this same day, the U.S. Congress passed the U.S. Copyright Law, which specifically protects works created or published in the United States.

Before automobiles became the most popular form of transport in the United States, an organization was founded to aid drivers who bravely navigated the nation's roads. On this day in 1902, the American Automobile Association was founded in Chicago, Illinois. Providing emergency road services, travel advice, and other driver-related services, the organization spread nationwide in less than five decades. On this same day in 1985, the federal government influenced the American automobile industry when the Environmental Protection Agency banned the use of leaded gasoline nationwide.

5th.

1845	The U.S. Congress bought a herd of camels.
1878	Harry Emerson Fosdick was born.
1901	The Platt Amendment was passed.
1960	Elvis Presley was honorably discharged from the Army (see March 24, June 26, July 30, August 15, August 22, September 25, December 3 entries).

Not all members of the Baptist church agree with Fundamentalism. Born in Buffalo, New York, on this day in 1878, Harry Emerson Fosdick was a champion for modernism during the Fundamentalist controversy of the 1920s. The pastor of the interdenominational Riverside Church in New York City from 1926 until 1946, Fosdick was an eloquent preacher who also wrote a number of books about his particular brand of beliefs.

The harsh environment of the American deserts took their toll on the men, horses, and even mules shipped out to oversee the settlements west of the Mississippi. It was a well-known fact that camels could survive the desert heat and arid terrain. On this day in 1845, the U.S. Congress appropriated $30,000 for a shipment of camels to be sent to the western United States. Ideal though they seemed at first, the resulting U.S. Camel Corps found that camels had two weaknesses—soft feet and thin blood. Unable to endure the unforgivingly bitter winter snows and the rocky terrain, most of the camels imported didn't survive their first American winter.

The conditions by which the United States and Cuba conducted relations for three decades was established on this day in 1901. The U.S. Congress passed the Platt Amendment rider, which set the conditions for the American troop withdrawal from Cuba after the Spanish-American War. The amendment established the tone and demeanor of Cuban-U.S. diplomatic relations until 1934. This document also created the Guantanamo Naval Base, which is the oldest American military base situated in a foreign country.

6th.

1857   The U.S. Supreme Court decided that African-Americans weren't full citizens.

1897   John D. MacArthur was born.

1926   Alan Greenspan was born.

1930   Clarence Birdseye initially distributed his products.

1933   A nationwide bank holiday went into effect.

1937   Ivan Boesky was born.

1953   Georgi Maksimillianovich Malenkov became Soviet premier.

1961   The Equal Employment Opportunity Commission was established.

1970   Charles Manson released a record album (see January 25, August 9, October 27, December 8 entries).

1979   United Airlines canceled more than 400 flights a week for nearly a month.

1981   Walter Cronkite signed off as anchor of the "CBS Evening News," saying for the last time, "And that's the way it is."

1982   Muslim fundamentalists were sentenced to death.

1990   The Soviet Parliament approved a privatization bill.

Frozen foods first appeared on store shelves on this day in 1930. Clarence Birdseye initially distributed his products in ten stores located in Springfield, Massachusetts. Certain areas of business were also frozen for one reason or another on this day. In 1933 a nationwide bank holiday went into effect. Declared by U.S. President Franklin Delano Roosevelt as a way to cease the run on banks by panicked consumers, the holiday froze the cash resources of the nation's banks, allowing them time to reorganize before resuming regular business transactions. In 1979 United Airlines canceled more than 400 flights a week for the rest of the month. A jet fuel shortage—caused in part by the crisis in Iran—had frozen the airline industry, which was unable to acquire enough fuel to meet flight schedules. And in 1990 the Soviet Parliament thawed. They approved a bill that allowed private citizens to own the property and means to provide services or to create products for the first time in seventy years.

One of America's wealthiest men, one of America's most greedy men, and one of America's most financially practical men all share this birthday. Born in eastern Pennsylvania on this day in 1897, John Donald MacArthur was sole owner of the nation's largest privately held insurance company. MacArthur worked as a reporter, insurance salesman, and entrepreneur in three failed businesses before he bought the Marquette Life Insurance Company in 1928 and borrowed $2,500 to buy the Bankers Life and Casualty Company of Chicago. His investment earned him $1 million within five years, and by his death in 1978 the company was worth $5.5 billion. Born in Detroit, Michigan, on this day in 1937, Ivan F. Boesky had worked as a security analyst at L.F. Rothschild Company during the 1960s. He opened his own office, Ivan F. Boesky Corporation, in 1975. As the trend toward bond investment exponentially increased during the 1980s, so did Boesky's business. But in 1986 Boesky was charged with insider trading by the SEC and was sentenced to three years' imprisonment. Born in New York City on this day in 1926, Federal Reserve Chairman Alan Greenspan guides the U.S. economy, raising and lowering the rate of inflation by ordering the fluctuation of the prime interest rate. Appointed in 1996 by U.S. President Bill Clinton, Greenspan's practicality made him very popular with 96 percent of the *Fortune* 1000 CEOs, who agree with his less stimulating economic policies.

Crime made the headlines on this day in two different forms. To finance his defense, accused serial murderer Charles Manson released his album, *Lies,* on this day in 1970. Terrorism, however, made even bigger news around the world. In 1982 five of the twenty-four Muslim fundamentalists accused in the assassination of Egyptian President Anwar Sadat were sentenced to death.

The U.S. Supreme Court handed down the decision that African-Americans weren't considered full citizens of the United States on this day in 1857. The case of *Dred Scott v. Sandford* set back the hopes of abolitionists throughout the nation, implying that even a freed slave didn't have the same rights as any other American citizen. On this same day in 1961, U.S. President John F. Kennedy signed Executive Order 10925, establishing the Equal Employment Opportunity Commission. Dedicated to the elimination of race, creed, color, and national origin as limitations to employment and promotion, this order introduced the term "affirmative action" as a way to describe the desegregation of business in the United States.

On this day in 1953, Georgi Maksimillianovich Malenkov became the Soviet Union's premier, following the death of dictator Josef Stalin. Malenkov's political high point was quickly usurped when a power struggle ensued between him and Nikita Khrushchev, forcing Malenkov to resign by 1955. Demoted to the office of minister for electric power stations, Malenkov was accused of establishing an anti-party faction two years later. He was then sent to remote Kazakhstan to manage a hydroelectric power plant. Malenkov died in obscurity in 1968.

7th.

1932   The U.S. Congress released 40 million bushels of wheat.

1934   King Curtis was born.

1984   The U.S. Senate confirmed the first U.S. ambassador, William Wilson, to the Vatican in 117 years.

1999   Colin Prescot and Andy Elson's hot air balloon was forced down (see February 17 entry).

During the height of the Great Depression, the federal government intervened in the food business, ensuring that Americans nationwide had enough food on their tables. On this day in 1932, the U.S. Congress authorized the release of 40 million bushels of wheat to indigent families. The surplus grain from the Federal Farm Bureau was given to the American Red Cross for distribution. On July 5 of that year, another 45 million bushels were released in the same manner.

Colin Prescot and Andy Elson attempted to circumnavigate the world by following the jet stream that flows north of the equator in their hot-air balloon, *Cable & Wireless*. On this day in 1999, the pair was forced down by bad weather, ditching off Japan's coast and setting an endurance record for nonstop flight during the eighteen-day ordeal.

A musician's musician, tenor saxophonist King Curtis not only led Aretha Franklin's backup band, the Kingpins, and played on many of the Coasters' R&B hits during the 1960s, he inspired The Band's Robbie Robertson's unique style of guitar playing. Born in Fort Worth, Texas, on this day in 1934, King Curtis worked as a record producer, recording artist, and studio musician, earning a 1969 Grammy Award for best R&B instrumental for his rendition of "Games People Play." Sadly, his career was cut short when he was murdered in 1971.

8th.

1782 The Gnadenhutten massacre took place.

1859 Kenneth Grahame was born.

1971 Joe Frazier defeated Muhammad Ali in a fifteen-round decision.

On this day in 1782, the Gnadenhutten massacre took place in Delaware. One hundred sixty American volunteers from Washington County, Pennsylvania, under the command of Colonel David Williamson, attacked the neutral Moravian mission town of Gnadenhutten, killing ninety Christian Native American men, women, and children and burning the mission church. The handful of survivors fled to Canada.

A rat, a mole, a badger, and a toad became beloved children's story characters thanks to Kenneth Grahame, who was born in Edinburgh, Scotland, on this day in 1859. Author of *The Wind in the Willows,* Grahame had worked as a clerk for the Bank of England until his health forced him to stay at home and take up the pen. Although he'd written numerous essays and folktales such as the *Pagan Papers* and *The Golden Age,* it was his adventures of the four river creatures that popularized his name.

9th.

1890 Vyacheslav Molotov was born.

1933 The Emergency Banking Relief Act was passed.

1934 Yuri Gagarin was born (see April 12 entry).

1987 Chrysler Corporation purchased American Motors Corporation.

Big business and the federal government took extreme measures on this day. In 1933 the Emergency Banking Relief Act was passed, making it illegal for private citizens to own gold bullion in the United States. This step guaranteed that all gold reserves held within the nation were available to back the circulated currency during the Great Depression. On this day in 1987, Chrysler Corporation announced its purchase of the financially crippled American Motors Corporation.

The man who became the namesake of the Molotov cocktail—an incendiary device used by terrorists around the world—was born in Kukiada, Russia, on this day in 1890. Vyacheslav Molotov joined the Bolsheviks in 1905. During the 1917 Russian Revolution, he took part in the overthrow of Kerensky's provisional government and later became the youngest member of the Communist Party's Politburo. Molotov's political career was volatile. He supported a nonaggression policy toward the Nazis in 1939. Three years later, he advised Stalin at meetings with Churchill and Roosevelt. He fanned the fires of the Cold War during the late 1940s and 1950s with his public refusals to compromise the Soviet position at United Nations meetings. Nikita Khrushchev called Molotov a "saboteur of peace," eventually assigning him an ambassadorship to Outer Mongolia in 1960.

In 1961 Soviet cosmonaut Yuri Gagarin became the first man to reach the stars, orbiting the earth in the satellite *Vostok.* Born in Smolsk, Russia, on this day in 1934, Gagarin joined the Soviet Air Force when he was twenty-three years old, and was quickly assigned to the fledgling space program. Gagarin shared the Galabert Astronautical Prize in 1963 with another space pioneer, John Glenn, who had also orbited the earth, in 1962.

10th.

1894   The nation's first dog license law was signed.

1972   General Lon Nol assumed power in Cambodia.

The quality of a dog's life became a legitimate concern on this day in 1894. That's when New York Governor Roswell P. Flower signed the nation's first dog license law. Every dog had to have a collar and a registered tag that identified the animal and its owner. Besides controlling the number of stray canines within the state, the bill enabled state officials to thwart the use of dogs in "pit sports" or other abusive gambling trades.

Another monarch's rulership was officially removed on this day. Cambodian King Norodom Sihanouk had been deposed in a 1970 military coup led by General Lon Nol, who assumed complete control of the government on this day in 1972. Nol's position didn't last long, however. He was overthrown three years later by the Khmer Rouge's leader Pol Pot.

11th.

1824   The Bureau of Indian Affairs was created.

1959   *A Raisin in the Sun* opened on Broadway (see May 19 entry).

1965   Reverend James Reeb was mortally beaten.

1973   Bermuda declared a state of emergency after its governor was assassinated.

1977   Hostages were released in Washington, D.C., by Hanafi Muslims.

1978   Terrorists seized two Israeli buses.

1985   Mikhail Gorbachev became Communist Party general secretary.

1990   The Lithuanian parliament voted to break away from the Soviet Union.

1993   Janet Reno became the first female U.S. attorney general.

Terrorism took front stage on this day. In 1973 the island nation of Bermuda declared a state of emergency after its governor, Sir Richard Sharples, was assassinated. In 1977 more than 100 hostages were released in Washington, D.C., by Hanafi Muslims when ambassadors from three Islamic nations joined in peace negotiations. And in 1978 terrorists seized two Israeli buses bound for Tel Aviv, killing thirty-two Israelis and wounding seventy-six more.

Relations between the federal government and Native Americans became strained on this day in 1824, when the Bureau of Indian Affairs was created by Secretary of War John C. Calhoun. The bureau's first chief was Thomas L. McKenney. Ethnic relations became strained once again on this day in 1965, when Reverend James Reeb, a white minister from Boston, was mortally beaten by a group of white segregationists during civil rights disturbances in Selma, Alabama.

Three governments took a serious detour on this day. In 1861 American secessionists adopted the Constitution of the Confederacy at Montgomery, Alabama. This event formally split the United States into Union and Confederate factions. In 1985 Soviet officials announced Mikhail Gorbachev as successor to Konstantin Chernenko in the post of Communist Party general secretary. Gorbachev's *glasnost* and *perestroika* policies quickly brought down the old communist structure. And in 1990 the Lithuanian parliament voted to break away from the Soviet Union, restoring its independence after fifty years of forced annexation.

12th.

1795 William Lyon Mackenzie was born.

1866 Giovanni Agnelli was born.

1980 The Ford Motor Company was acquitted of three reckless-homicide charges.

2000 Pope John Paul II asked God's forgiveness for the sins of Catholics through the ages.

Back in 1899, Fiat—*Fabbrica Italiano Automobili Torino*—was founded by an ex-cavalry officer named Giovanni Agnelli. Born in Italy on this day in 1866, Agnelli put his homeland on the roadways and kept huge numbers of workers employed during the Second World War. On this same day in 1980, the Ford Motor Company was acquitted of three reckless-homicide charges. The company had been charged because a Ford Pinto was involved in an accident in which the car caught fire upon impact.

The man who caused an international incident between Canada and the United States was born in Dundee, Scotland, on this day in 1795. Emigrating to Canada in 1820, William Lyon Mackenzie was an irascible member of the provincial parliament for two years before he was expelled in 1830. He then became mayor of Toronto and declared the city's independence. In 1837 he led a group of 800 men in an attack on the city. But the Canadian army was stronger, forcing Mackenzie and his men to flee across the border, where they seized Navy Island in the Niagara River. During the sixteen days they held the island, Mackenzie claimed a provisional government. The insurgents were shipped supplies by supporters on the American steamer *Caroline* until Canadian forces burned the ship, triggering tensions across the border. Rather than surrender, Mackenzie escaped to New York City, where he was arrested and imprisoned for a year before returning to Toronto.

On this day in 2000, Pope John Paul II asked God's forgiveness for the sins of Catholics throughout the ages, which included the burning of heretics during the Inquisition, the slaughtering of Muslims during the Crusades, standing silent during the Nazi genocide of the Jews, and confessing hatred for minority groups such as the Gypsies. "We forgive and we ask forgiveness," he said during the Day of Pardon Mass at St. Peter's Basilica. Cardinal Edward Cassidy asked divine pardon for "the sins committed by not a few [Catholics] against the people of the Covenant." After a moment of silent prayer, the pope concluded, "We are deeply saddened by the behavior of those who in the course of history have caused these children of yours to suffer, and asking your forgiveness we wish to commit ourselves to genuine brotherhood."

13th.

1930 The planet Pluto was identified in a Lowell Observatory photograph, confirming Percival Lowell's 1914 calculations of its position.

1964 Kitty Genovese was stabbed to death in Queens, N.Y.

1999 *Breitling Orbiter* 3 passed the halfway mark in its nonstop circumnavigation when it crossed the Marshall Islands (see March 1, March 19 entries).

One of the most publicized instances of volunteer's dilemma occurred on this day in 1964. The term "volunteer's dilemma" refers to witnesses who won't volunteer aid until someone else does. In this case, thirty-eight people watched and listened as Kitty Genovese was stabbed to death in the courtyard of her apartment complex in Queens, New York. Although she screamed for help for an hour and a half, no one called the police until the attack had ended.

14th.

1964 A Dallas jury convicted Jack Ruby of malice aforethought.

1965 The Israeli Cabinet formally approved diplomatic relations with West Germany.

1974 The Canadian province of Quebec announced that French was the official provincial language.

1975 Presidential aide Fred LaRue was sentenced to six months' imprisonment.

1985 The United States evacuated American officials from Lebanon.

1989 The Bush administration announced an indefinite ban on imports of semiautomatic assault rifles.

1992 The Emir of Kuwait, Sheik Jaber al-Ahmed al-Sabah, returned home.

On this day in 1964, a Dallas jury convicted Jack Ruby of "murder with malice" in the mortal shooting of Lee Harvey Oswald, who had been accused of assassinating U.S. President John F. Kennedy. On this same day in 1975, presidential aide Fred LaRue was sentenced to six months' imprisonment for his role in U.S. President Richard Nixon's Watergate cover-up. And in a radical policy shift, U.S. President

George H. Bush announced an indefinite ban on imports of semiautomatic assault rifles on this day in 1989.

The Near East became a hotbed of news on this day. In 1965 the Israeli Cabinet formally approved diplomatic relations with West Germany. In 1985 the United States government evacuated American officials from Lebanon, leaving only a small diplomatic presence in war-torn Beirut. Terrorist threats against Americans and the deterioration of the Lebanese government led to the decision. And in 1992 the Emir of Kuwait, Sheik Jaber al-Ahmed al-Sabah, returned home after seven months in exile.

15th.

1892 Jesse W. Reno patented the first escalator.

1984 The acquittal of a police officer on charges of negligently killing a black youth sparked a rampage in Miami, Florida, resulting in 550 arrests.

1995 Lockheed and Martin merged.

Big business got a lift on two occasions on this day. In 1892 Jesse W. Reno patented the first escalator design. In 1995 jet plane manufacturers Lockheed and Martin merged into the Lockheed Martin Corporation, immediately requesting $16.2 million to pay for the costs of restructure.

16th.

1968 American soldiers in Vietnam killed 109 men, women, and children in the infamous My Lai massacre (see March 31 entry).

1978 Aldo Moro was kidnapped (see May 5, May 9 entries).

1985 Terry Anderson was kidnapped.

1995 Mississippi ratified the amendment to the U.S. Constitution abolishing slavery 130 years after it was passed.

Abduction made the headlines twice on this day. In 1978 Italy's former prime minister Aldo Moro was kidnapped in Rome by Red Brigade guerrillas. He later was found murdered. And in 1985. Terry Anderson, chief Middle East correspondent for the Associated Press, was abducted by three gunmen in Beirut, Lebanon. He was released in December 1991.

17th.

461 St. Patrick died.

1919 Nat "King" Cole was born (see April 10 entry).

1938 Rudolf Nureyev was born (see May 18, June 16 entries).

1973 A Cambodian Air Force officer stole a plane.

1978 The tanker *Amoco Cadiz* ran aground on the coast of Brittany, France.

1982 Four members of a Dutch television crew were shot to death.

1983 Cardinal Terence Cooke of New York City broke with tradition.

Terrorists made both hits and misses on this day. In 1973 a Cambodian Air Force officer stole a plane and bombed the presidential palace in Phnom Penh, missing President Lon Nol. He did, however, kill twenty people. In 1982 four members of a Dutch television crew were shot to death in northern El Salvador under mysterious circumstances.

"The main thing is dancing, . . . I will keep dancing to the last moment, the last drop," Rudolf Nureyev once said. Born on a train near Irkutsk, Siberia, on this day in 1938, Nureyev started dancing when he was eight years old, taking up ballet three years later. Although his father wanted him to become an engineer, Nureyev auditioned for and was accepted by both the Bolshoi Ballet School and the Kirov Ballet School in 1955; he joined the Kirov. Nureyev was immediately given solo roles after his graduation in 1958. The world first learned of Nureyev when he defected in Paris, France, while the Kirov Ballet was on tour in 1961. His work with Dame Margot Fonteyn and the London Royal Ballet was legendary, hypnotizing audiences and earning them a spot in the *Guinness World Book of Records* for garnering the longest curtain call on record in Vienna, Austria, for their performance of *Swan Lake*. In 1983 Nureyev became the director of the Paris Opera Ballet, a position he held until his death in 1993.

Born Nathaniel Coles in Montgomery, Alabama, on this day in 1919, Nat "King" Cole gained his fame as a jazz pianist and singer when he joined his brother's band, Eddie Cole's Solid Swingers, in 1936. He soon took a job conducting the musical revue *Shuffle Along* while it was on tour. In 1940 Cole recorded the hit "Sweet Lorraine" with his own trio. His stardom was assured when the song "Mona Lisa" made it to the top of the charts in 1950. Cole had his own TV series from 1956 through 1957, and he appeared in the films *Cat Ballou* and *The Nat King Cole Story* before his death at the age of 47.

History is filled with ironies. On the day Ireland's patron saint, St. Patrick, died in Saul, Ireland, in 461, another Irish patriot was turned away. Cardinal Terence Cooke of New York City broke with tradition on this day in 1983 when he refused to receive the St. Patrick's Day Parade because the marshal supported the Irish Republican Army.

18th.

1831   The U.S. Supreme Court ruled that Native American tribes could not sue for their rights in a federal court.

1922   Mohandas K. Gandhi was sentenced (see *On This Day in History:* October 2 entry).

1936   F.W. de Klerk was born (see February 10, July 18, December 13 entries; see also *On This Day in History:* February 2, May 10, July 18 entries).

1938   Mexico nationalized its petroleum industry.

1970   The first mass work stoppage at the U.S. Post Office took place.

1985   Capitol Cities Communications Inc. acquired American Broadcasting Company Inc.

Major industries took some surprising turns on this day. In 1938 Mexico nationalized its petroleum industry. In 1970 the first mass work stoppage in the U.S. Post Office's 195-year history took place. It began with a walkout by Brooklyn and Manhattan letter carriers and ended with 210,000 of the nation's 750,000 postal employees following suit. Military units were deployed to New York City's postal stations by President Richard Nixon until the strike ended two weeks later. And in 1985 Capitol Cities

Communications Inc. acquired American Broadcasting Company Inc. for more than $3.5 billion.

Human rights reached a low point on this day. In 1831 the U.S. Supreme Court handed down a decision that Native American tribes could not sue for their rights in a federal court since the tribal members themselves weren't citizens and their reservations weren't foreign nations. And in 1922, Mohandas K. Gandhi was sentenced to six years' imprisonment for civil disobedience in an Indian court. He was released two years later.

Born in Johannesburg, South Africa, on this day in 1936, Frederik Willem de Klerk came from a privileged Afrikaner family with a long history of public service; his uncle J.G. Strijdom had been prime minister from 1954 through 1958. He won the South African presidency in 1989 shortly after becoming National Party leader. Among the changes he promised his nation was the announcement that he would release ANC leader Nelson Mandela from prison. In 1994 de Klerk became one of two executive deputy presidents after Mandela himself was elected president. Three years later, de Klerk retired from active politics.

19th.

1813 David Livingstone was born.

1821 Sir Richard Burton was born.

1918 Daylight saving time was passed into law.

1929 Sergei P. Diaghilev died (see February 28 entry).

1991 The five-millionth patent was issued in the United States.

1999 Piccard and Jones broke a hot-air balloon flight duration record, flying for 17 days, 17 hours, and 41 minutes (see January 28, March 1, May 27, August 18 entries).

On this day in 1918, the U.S. Congress passed a law installing daylight saving time as an energy conservation measure. By setting the clocks ahead one hour, businesses and residences could function without turning on electrical lights, and farmers could gain an extra hour of work time during the prime growing and harvesting months. Daylight saving time officially went into effect on March 31 of that year.

The world's greatest dancers, designers, and artists were introduced by the man who died in Venice on this day in 1929. Sergei P. Diaghilev started his career as a lawyer but became an impresario in 1898, editing a fine arts magazine and arranging exhibitions throughout Europe. In 1911 he founded the Ballet Russe de Diaghilev in Monte Carlo. George Balanchine, Leonide Massine, and Vaslav Nijinsky were just a few of the choreographers and dancers who graced Diaghilev's stage. Artists and composers such as Pablo Picasso, Eric Satie, and Igor Stravinsky contributed their arts to the impresario's memorable productions.

The famous missionary and explorer who was discovered in Africa by Henry Morton Stanley was born in Low Blantyre, Scotland, on this day in 1813. Before their historic meeting in 1868, David Livingstone had found Victoria Falls in the Zambezi as well as numerous lakes. In 1866 the Royal Geographic Society had sent him to settle a dispute over the sources of the Nile River and the watershed of Central Africa. But before he could finish his task, he fell ill. Born in Torquay, England, on this same day in 1821, the explorer and translator Sir Richard Burton also searched for the source of the Nile, discovering Lake Tanganyika instead. His translations of *The Kama Sutra, The Arabian Nights,* and *The Perfumed Garden* had to be privately published to avoid prosecution for pornography during the 1880s. But these Asian classics ended up amassing him a fortune before his death.

20th.

1815 Napoleon Bonaparte became emperor of France.

1899 First woman electrocuted in U.S.

1969 John Lennon married Yoko Ono.

1970 David Bowie married Angela Barnett.

1976 Patricia Hearst was convicted.

1984 The U.S. Senate rejected spoken prayer in public schools when it failed to pass an amendment backed by U.S. President Ronald Reagan.

1993 Boris Yeltsin gave himself special powers (see February 1, May 29, November 6, December 18, December 25 entries).

1999 The *Breitling Orbiter 3* officially circumnavigated the world, nonstop, when it crossed 09° W27' (see March 1, March 21 entries).

Women were the focus of the criminal world on this day. In 1899 Martha M. Place became the first woman to be electrocuted in the United States in Sing Sing Prison. In 1976 Patricia Hearst was convicted of engaging in the armed robbery that had been staged by the militants who kidnapped her.

Wedding bells rang twice on this day in the music world. In 1969 The Beatles' John Lennon married artist Yoko Ono in Gibraltar. The next year, glam rocker David Bowie married his sweetheart, Angela Barnett, who was allegedly the subject of The Rolling Stones' hit "Angie."

Political leaders stretched the range of their powers on this day. In 1815 Napoleon Bonaparte triumphantly entered Paris, beginning his reign as France's emperor. In 1993 Russian President Boris Yeltsin announced that he'd given himself special powers, stating there would be a referendum on his presidency on April 25 of that year.

21st.

1869 Florenz Ziegfeld, Jr., was born.

1976 Rubin "Hurricane" Carter was released from jail for retrial, due to the efforts of many people including Bob Dylan who wrote a song about the case.

1994 U.S. Vice President Albert Gore addressed the International Telecommunications Union.

1999 The *Breitling Orbiter 3* landed near Mut, Egypt, 25,360 miles after it began its 19 days, 21 hours, 47 minutes of circumnavigation (see March 1, March 20 entries).

When U.S. Vice President Albert Gore addressed the International Telecommunications Union on this day in 1994, he made a statement that forecast a major wave affecting everyone's future: the Internet. He said, "The Global Information Infrastructure will help educate our children and allow us to exchange ideas within a community and among nations. It will be a means by which families and friends will transcend the barriers of time and distance. It will make possible a global information marketplace, where consumers can buy or sell products." It only took another year for the idea to blossom in the public's mind, and only five more years for it to become the international communications force we know today.

The man who glorified the American showgirl and introduced the American revue spectacular to the world was born in Chicago, Illinois, on this day in 1869. The son of the Chicago Musical College's president, Florenz Ziegfeld, Jr., decided that the French weren't the only ones who could put on a musical revue like the world-famous Follies Bergere. In 1907 Ziegfeld premiered his *Follies of 1907,* which was the first in a series of twenty-four revues staged on Broadway. Besides featuring the beautiful showgirls, Ziegfeld introduced audiences to remarkable talents like Eddie Cantor, Will Rogers, Fanny Brice, Irving Berlin, Jerome Kern, and W.C. Fields. Before his death in 1932, Ziegfeld also produced the highly successful and controversial Jerome Kern musical *Show Boat.*

22nd.

1933 U.S. President Franklin Roosevelt allowed wine and beer consumption.

1937 U.S. President Harry S Truman signed Executive Order 9835.

1961 Raymond Loewy finished the design of the Starliner Coup.

It was not business as usual on this day in twentieth-century history. In 1933, U.S. President Franklin Roosevelt signed a bill allowing Americans to consume wine and beer with a maximum 3.2 percent alcohol level, triggering the end of Prohibition. Industrial designer Raymond Loewy finished the design for a sportscar on this day in 1961. Loewy had created the Greyhound bus and the Coca-Cola bottle. And his design for the Starliner Coup was meant to save the ailing Studebaker Corporation. In 1937 President Harry S Truman signed Executive Order 9835, ordering all federal employees to sign a loyalty oath to the United States. To comply with this mandate, the FBI conducted 2 million name checks, ending the right to confidentiality for existing and potential employees.

23rd.

1857 Elisha Graves Otis installed the first passenger elevator in New York City's Haughwout and Company department store.

1857 Fannie Farmer was born.

1964 The Beatles' John Lennon published his first book, *In His Own Write* (see June 24 entry).

1966 The Anglican and Roman Catholic churches met.

1983 U.S. President Ronald Reagan proposed the Strategic Defense Initiative, popularly known as "Star Wars."

We began to measure our cooking ingredients thanks to Fannie Farmer, who was born in Boston, Massachusetts, on this day in 1857. After a stroke, she turned to cooking, eventually opening Miss Farmer's School of Cooking. In 1886 she tried to have her scientifically formulated recipes published through conventional channels. She ended up self-publishing her cookbook, which has sold more than 4 million copies since it hit the bookstore shelves.

The Anglican and Roman Catholic churches met for the very first time in four centuries on this day in 1966. The Archbishop of Canterbury, Arthur Ramsey, held an official meeting with Pope Paul VI at the Vatican.

24th.

1832 The Creek Indians signed a treaty.

1855 Andrew W. Mellon was born.

1883 The first U.S. intrastate telephone lines were connected between New York and Chicago.

1958 Elvis Presley was drafted (see March 5, June 26, July 30, August 15, August 22, September 25, December 3 entries).

1972 The Equal Opportunity Act was signed.

1973 Lou Reed was bitten by an attacker during a performance.

1976 Maria Estela "Isabel" Péron was overthrown (see February 4 entry).

1981 Vice President George H. Bush was placed in charge of the Reagan administration crisis team.

1982   The U.S. Senate unanimously voted to curb regulatory agencies' power.

1986   The federal debt hit the $2 trillion mark.

1989   The *Exxon Valdez* ruptured (see September 16 entry).

1991   Soviet military vehicles entered the capital city of Vilnius, Lithuania.

In many ways, industrialist banker Andrew W. Mellon changed the American economy for the worse during the early twentieth century. Born in Pittsburgh, Pennsylvania, on this day in 1855, Mellon joined his father's banking house after his graduation from law school, taking over the business in 1882. His wealth and financial prowess grew until 1921. That's when he became U.S. Secretary of the Treasury, serving under presidents Warren B. Harding, Calvin Coolidge, and Herbert Hoover. During his terms in office, Mellon almost eradicated taxation of wealthy Americans, plunging the nation deep into debt at the height of the Great Depression. On this same day in 1986, the federal debt passed the $2,000,000,000,000 mark.

A major conflict between man and nature occurred on this day in 1989. The oil tanker *Exxon Valdez* ran aground at the Alaskan pipeline's Valdez terminus, dumping 240,000 barrels or 11 million gallons of crude oil into Prince William Sound, poisoning thousands of marine creatures, waterfowl, and animals dependent on the sea for survival for years to come.

Opportunities were won and lost on this day. In 1832 the Creek Indians signed a treaty that handed over their lands east of the Mississippi River to the United States government. On this same day in 1972, the Equal Employment Opportunity Act was signed into law, enforcing a balance of race, color, and gender within the American workplace.

Two musical greats were bitten on this day. In 1958 Elvis Presley was bitten by the draft bug, with his induction into the U.S. Army. And in 1973 Lou Reed was bitten while performing on stage in Buffalo, New York. His attacker screamed out, "Leather!" and then bit him on the posterior.

The hands of power switched many times on this day. In 1976 an Argentine military coup toppled Maria Estela "Isabel" Perón's government, placing her under house arrest. Despite U.S. Secretary of State Alexander Haig's objections, President Ronald Reagan placed Vice President George H. Bush in charge of his administration's 1981 crisis team. The next year, the U.S. Senate unanimously voted 94-0, curbing federal regulatory agencies' power. And in 1991 a Lithuanian secessionist movement was almost quashed when Soviet military vehicles entered the capital city of Vilnius.

25th.

1908 David Lean was born.

1934 Gloria Steinem was born.

1940 Anita Bryant was born (see September 3 entry).

1942 Aretha Franklin was born (see January 3 entry).

1957 The Treaty of Rome was signed.

1958 Sugar Ray Robinson became the first five-time world champion in middleweight boxing history when he defeated Carmine Basilio in Chicago, Illinois.

1969 Pakistani President Ayub Khan resigned.

1974 Henry Kissinger and Leonid Brezhnev met (see September 21, November 10 entries).

1992 Sergei Krikalev returned home.

Few directors worked their way through the film industry ranks before directing their first productions. David Lean was one of the chosen handful. Born in Croydon, England, on this day in 1908, Lean worked as a clapperboard boy, a camera assistant, an assistant editor, and an editor before he co-directed the 1942 film *In Which We Serve* with Noël Coward. Lean's greatest claims to fame were the epic features he directed during the 1950s and 1960s: *Bridge on the River Kwai, Lawrence of Arabia,* and *Dr. Zhivago.* And his last two films, *Ryan's Daughter* and *A Passage to India,* won him critical acclaim as well.

Born in Toledo, Ohio, on this day in 1934, Gloria Steinem was a leading figure in antiwar protests, antiracism protests, and the women's movement. She co-founded the feminist publication *Ms.* magazine in 1972. She also wrote an exposé of life as a Playboy Bunny after she'd worked at the Manhattan Playboy Club in order to do her journalistic research.

An activist of another kind was born on this day in 1940. Singer Anita Bryant was Miss Oklahoma in 1958 as well as a Miss America finalist. She married a Miami Beach disc jockey and became a spokesperson for the Florida Citrus Growers Association, appearing in television commercials for orange juice during the 1970s. Her husband and her minister influenced her to become a spokesperson for two other causes as well. She became an outspoken supporter of the religious right wing and headed an antagonistic anti-homosexual campaign that sorely dampened her career.

Political power took many turns on this day. In 1957 the Treaty of Rome was signed, establishing the European Common Market, which provided a unified fiscal front for many European nations that were still struggling with post-World War II reconstruction. In 1969 Pakistani President Ayub Khan resigned after eleven years in office, turning his power over to the military. And in 1974 U.S. Secretary of State Henry Kissinger met with Soviet Premier Leonid Brezhnev in Moscow to discuss the potential for an agreement that would limit the use of strategic nuclear weapons.

Soviet cosmonaut Sergei Krikalev missed the end of communist rule in his Russian homeland. He had spent ten months on board the *Mir* space station, orbiting the earth. On this day in 1992, he returned to terra firma and to a politically reorganized Russia.

26th.

1904   Joseph Campbell was born.

1930   Sandra Day O'Connor was born.

1991   The U.S. Supreme Court handed down a 5-4 decision on the admissability of possible confessions as evidence.

The way evidence is extracted from a defendant was given a wide berth on this day in 1991. The U.S. Supreme Court handed down a 5-4 decision in the case of *Arizona v. Oreste C. Fulminante,* ruling that a confession taken from a defendant using the third degree or other forcible means can be a "harmless error" and may, therefore, be used as evidence.

Comparative folklorist Joseph Campbell once wrote, "Read myths. They teach you that you can turn inward, and you begin to get the message of the symbols." Born in New York City on this day in 1904, Campbell gained fame for his 1948 book *The Hero with a Thousand Faces,* which studied the archetype of the hero in Native American, Greek, Hindu, Buddhist, Mayan, Norse, Biblical, and Arthurian legends. His concepts were intricately woven into film director George Lucas's scripts for the "Star Wars" trilogy. Campbell's multivolume *Historical Atlas of World Mythology* was only partially completed by the time of his death in 1987.

The first woman appointed as an associate justice to the U.S. Supreme Court was born in El Paso, Texas, on this day in 1930. Sandra Day O'Connor started her legal career as an attorney and judge in Arizona. She was elected to the state senate in 1969, serving for five years. She was elected to the Arizona Superior Court in 1974 and appointed to the Arizona Court of Appeals in 1979. She was sworn in as associate justice of the U.S. Supreme Court by President Ronald Reagan on September 25, 1981.

27th.

1863   Sir Henry Royce was born.

1912   The first two two Yoshino cherry trees were planted in Washington, D.C.

1917   The Seattle Metropolitans hockey team won the Stanley Cup.

1952   Restaurants were required to display their ceiling prices.

1953   Annemarie Proell won the World Cup ski championships.

1958   Nikita Khrushchev became Soviet Premier.

1964   An earthquake rocked Alaska triggering tidal waves in Seattle.

1977   Two jumbo jets collided.

1979   OPEC raised its crude oil prices.

1980   An oil field platform capsized.

1983   Thirty Lippizaner horses were killed.

1987   The U.S. Marine Corps accused Sergeant Clayton Lonetre of espionage.

1991   British customs officials foiled an attempt by espionage agents.

1998   For the first time, Internet users judged a televised sports event.

Prices went sky high for a variety of reasons on this day. In 1863 Sir Henry Royce was born in Peterborough, England. His interest in motors led to the establishment, in 1884, of Royce Limited, a mechanical and electrical engineering firm. He built his first car in

1904, and two years later he joined Charles Stewart Rolls, forming Rolls-Royce Limited, which produced the world's most luxurious car. But Royce also designed another valuable piece of mechanics. His Merlin engine was installed in the Spitfire and Hurricane airplanes that flew for Great Britain during the Second World War. In 1952 restaurants throughout the United States were required to display their ceiling prices by the Office of Price Stabilization as a way to curb runaway consumer inflation. And in 1979 OPEC (Organization of Petroleum Exporting Countries) raised its crude oil prices by 9 percent, fueling a gas crisis worldwide.

Espionage was uncovered on this day more than once. In 1987 the U.S. Marine Corps accused Sergeant Clayton Lonetree of escorting Soviet agents through the U.S. Embassy in Moscow. This charge was later dropped, but the sergeant was still convicted of espionage. And in 1991 British customs officials foiled an attempt by espionage agents to supply Iraq with forty American-made nuclear weapon detonators.

Some of the world's worst natural and man-made disasters occurred on this day. In 1964 an earthquake rocked Alaska, centering on the city of Anchorage and triggering tidal waves as far south as Seattle and Portland. More than 100 people were killed in Alaska, and $750 million in property was destroyed. In 1977 more than 580 people died when two jumbo jets collided on a runway at Tenerife in the Canary Islands. It was recorded as the world's worst plane disaster. In 1980 a North Sea oil field platform capsized. Out of the 212 people on board, only 89 workers were saved. And in 1983 the Austrian government announced that thirty Lippizaner horses had been killed in a herpes epidemic.

Washington's famed cherry trees were first planted on this day in 1912. First Lady Helen Herron Taft and the Japanese ambassador's wife, Viscountess Chinda, planted two Yoshino cherry trees on the northern bank of the Potomac tidal basin.

Landmark sports events occurred on this day. In 1917 the Seattle Metropolitans became the first United States hockey team to win the Stanley Cup. In 1953 Austrian ski racer Annemarie Proell became the first five-time winner of the World Cup ski championships. And in 1998 Internet users got their first chance to judge a televised sports event, determining the winner of an ice skating competition among twelve world contenders.

28th.

1834 The U.S. Senate voted to censure President Andrew Jackson.

1979 A reactor at the Three Mile Island nuclear plant malfunctioned (see April 13, May 17, June 28, October 30 entries).

1982 El Salvadorans elected Christian Democratic candidate President Jose Napoleon Duarte.

1984 More than twenty tornadoes touched down in North and South Carolina.

It was a dark day in United States presidential history in 1834. The U.S. Senate voted to censure President Andrew Jackson because he removed federal deposits from the Bank of the United States without their approval.

The United States's worst nuclear disaster occurred on this day in 1979. The Unit Two reactor at the Three Mile Island nuclear plant near Harrisburg, Pennsylvania, malfunctioned, causing the reactor's core to fracture. A total core meltdown was successfully prevented. A more natural disaster also occurred on this day in 1984, when more than twenty tornadoes touched down in North and South Carolina, killing 62 people and injuring 800 others.

29th.

1936 Judith Guest was born.

1951 Julius and Ethel Rosenberg were convicted of espionage charges (see April 5, May 12, June 19 entries).

1954 Karen Ann Quinlan was born.

1995 The U.S. House of Representatives rejected a constitutional amendment.

The first unsolicited manuscript accepted by Viking Publishers in thirty years was written by the author born on this day in 1936. Judith Guest's novel *Ordinary People* also garnered Hollywood's attention when it was released as a movie in 1980. It won four Academy Awards, including one for best picture.

The U.S. Congress was divided on this day in 1995. The House of Representatives rejected a constitutional amendment that would have placed term limits on lawmakers, voting 227-204.

A landmark life began on this day in 1954. Deemed irreversibly comatose during the 1970s, Karen Ann Quinlan was kept alive for ten years. She was artificially fed and breathed with the aid of machines. Her condition brought to light the plight of those who wished to die with dignity rather than being kept only minimally functional.

30th.

1923   The *Laconia* returned to New York City.

1980   Terrorists started a stampede at the funeral of Archbishop Romero.

1981   U.S. President Ronald Reagan was shot (see August 24 entry).

Two terrorist attacks occurred on this day. In 1980 thirty El Salvadorans died at funeral services held for assassinated Archbishop Oscar Arnulfo Romero. Snipers and explosions caused a stampede of mourners. And in 1981 U.S. President Ronald Reagan, White House Press Secretary James Brady, a secret service agent, and a Washington police officer were shot and wounded outside a Washington, D.C., hotel by John Hinckley, Jr.

The first passenger ship to circumnavigate the world arrived in New York City on this day in 1923. The Cunard liner *Laconia* completed the historic voyage in 130 days.

31st.

1492   King Ferdinand of Spain extended the Spanish Inquisition (see April 16, May 3, May 9, May 13, May 20, June 13, July 31, August 23, December 5 entries).

1870   Thomas Peterson Mundy became the first African-American to vote.

1889   Muriel Hazel Wright was born.

1895   Lizzie Miles was born.

1948   U.S. Vice President Albert Gore was born.

1967   Jimi Hendrix burned his guitar on stage (see November 27 entry).

1971   U.S. Army Lieutenant William Calley was sentenced (see March 16 entry).

1980   U.S. President Jimmy Carter signed the Banking Deregulation Act (see October 1 entry).

Interest rates were freed on this day in 1980. U.S. President Jimmy Carter signed the Banking Deregulation Act, which removed the ceiling rate imposed on interest paid to small depositors. A competitive interest rate war raged through the banking industry as institutions offered higher rates for long-term deposits in the hopes of attracting new customers.

On this day in 1971, U.S. Army Lieutenant William Calley was sentenced to life imprisonment for his role in the My Lai massacre, resulting in the deaths of twenty-two Vietnamese civilians. In the end, he served only three years under house arrest.

On this day in 1492, King Ferdinand of Spain extended the Spanish Inquisition, decreeing that Granada's 150,000 Jews leave the country by July 31. The assets ceased from exiled Jews financed Christopher Columbus's second voyage to the New World.

Thomas Peterson Mundy made history on this day in 1870. He became the first African American to vote in the United States. Muriel Hazel Wright also made history when she helped organize the Choctaw Advisory Council in 1934. Born on this day in 1889, Wright fought for Native Americans' right to be financially compensated by the federal government after Oklahoma achieved statehood.

Born in New Orleans, Louisiana, on this day in 1895, Lizzie Miles developed a singing style called Gumbo French Jazz during the 1920s and 1930s. Playing in New Orleans and Los Angeles, Miles style struck a chord in many jazz fans' hearts. On this same day in 1967, rocker Jimi Hendrix burned his guitar on stage for the first time in London, England.

April

INTRODUCTION

N ovelists and musicians sprouted up like April flowers. And the same month that London's most famous castle flung open its doors to the public, people caught their first glimpse at the America's first astronauts.

1st.

1883 Lon Chaney was born.

1917 Scott Joplin died.

1920 Toshiro Mifune was born.

1938 The Wheeler-Lea Act became law (see August 1, June 27 entries).

1970 Tobacco advertising was banned on television (see August 1, June 27 entries).

1985 The Internet's first virtual community was created.

New limitations were set on the advertising world on this day in 1938, when the Wheeler-Lea Act became law. This bill empowered the Federal Trade Commission to curb false and misleading advertising in both print and broadcast forms. On this same day in 1970, a bill that banned tobacco advertising on television and included a number of other advertising restraints was signed into law by U.S. President Richard Nixon, despite massive pressure brought against it by the advertising, tobacco, and broadcasting industries.

The Internet's first virtual community was created on this day in 1985. Larry Brilliant of Networking Technologies International, Stewart Brand of the Point Foundation, and director Matthew McClure opened the Whole Earth 'Lectronic Link (WELL), charging customers $8 per month plus $2 per hour for Internet access.

The ability to create realistic characterizations highlighted the careers of Lon Chaney and Toshiro Mifune. Born in Colorado Springs, Colorado, on this day in 1883, Chaney was known as the "man of a thousand faces" because of his ability to completely change his appearance and demeanor. Starring in the silent films *The Hunchback of Notre Dame* and *The Phantom of the Opera* during the 1920s, Chaney was also the father of horror movie star Lon Chaney, Jr., who followed in his father's bone-chilling footsteps.

Famous for his portrayals of samurai, Toshiro Mifune didn't dream of becoming an actor. Born in Manchuria on this day in 1920, Mifune wanted to be on the other side of the camera. He was misdirected into an acting audition when he applied for an assistant cameraman's job at Tokyo's Toho Films. One person who witnessed his reluctant audition was director Akira Kurosawa, who cast Mifune as the leading star in sixteen out of seventeen films he made between 1948 and 1965, including *Rashomon, The Seven Samurai,* and *Red Beard.* In his autobiography, Kurosawa wrote, "It was, above all, the speed with which he expressed himself that was astounding. The ordinary Japanese actor might need ten feet of film to get across an impression; Mifune needed only three. The speed of his movements was such that he said in a single action what took ordinary actors three separate movements to express."

The African-American pianist and composer who was famous for his ragtime compositions and the opera *Treemonisha,* Scott Joplin, died in New York City on this day in 1917. Although *Treemonisha* is frequently included in major opera company repertoires nationwide, it was performed only once during Joplin's lifetime. The audience—which included potential backers—was unprepared for its avant style. Many people walked out a devastating moment that is said to have contributed to Joplin's failing health.

2nd.

1834 Fredric Auguste Bartholdi was born.

1914 Sir Alec Guinness was born.

1939 Marvin Gaye was born.

1941 Leon Russell was born.

1943 Larry Coryell was born.

1982 British soldiers surrendered to invading Argentinean troops in the Falkland Islands (see April 10, April 28, April 30 entries).

Greatness sometimes takes outside inspiration as well as outside aid. Born in Colmar, Alsace, on this day in 1834, the sculptor Fredric Auguste Bartholdi became inspired while attending a dinner at the home of Lefebvre de Laboulaye in 1865. His host suggested that he sculpt a symbol of liberty. Traveling to America in 1871, Bartholdi saw that New York Harbor was the perfect place to erect his vision: a cross between the Colossus of Rhodes and the monumental statues that lined Egypt's Nile River. Although the French government was willing to pay for Bartholdi's grand sculpture, the American government had to ask for public donations to fund the construction of the foundation and pedestal. After six years of appeals, work began on the pedestal, but it wasn't finished until publisher Joseph Pulitzer took on the job of fundraising. Bartholdi's Statue of Liberty was completed in 1886. (The statue itself was finished in 1884, although its arm was not properly attached until its restoration in 1984.)

Born in London, England, on this day in 1914, the director of London's National Theatre, Sir Alec Guinness, explained his concept of acting in his 1986 autobiography, *Blessings in Disguise:* "An actor is an interpreter of other men's words, often a soul which wishes to reveal itself to the world but dare not, a craftsman, a bag of tricks, a vanity bag, a cool observer of mankind, a child, and at his best a kind of unfrocked priest who, for an hour or two, can call on heaven and hell to mesmerize a group of innocents." Guinness starred in a number of British comedies, such as *The Lavendar Hill Mob,* as well as epic features such as *Bridge on the River Kwai* and *Lawrence of Arabia.* Although he preferred to be remembered for his live performances, it was his role as Obi Wan Kenobi in the "Star Wars" film trilogy that endeared him to millions around the world.

Some musicians are actually more revered by their peers than by the general public. Born in Washington, D.C., on this day in 1939, R&B singer and songwriter Marvin Gaye created the Motown hits "I Heard It Through the Grapevine" (which spent seven weeks at #1 in 1968), "What's Going On," "Mercy Mercy Me," and "Let's Get It On." Born in Lawton, Oklahoma, on this day in 1941, pianist and songwriter Leon Russell created the hit songs "Delta Lady" and "Evergreen." An inveterate studio musician, Russell played keyboards on the Beach Boys' "California Girls," the Byrds' "Mr. Tambourine Man," Jan and Dean's "Surf City," and even Bobby Pickett's "The Monster Mash." He also played in sessions with The Rolling Stones, Frank Sinatra, Bobby Darin, Ike and Tina Turner, and Bob Dylan. Born in Galveston, Texas, on this day in 1943, jazz guitarist Larry Coryell toured with Jimi Hendrix during the late 1960s. But he's better known in the music world for his avant-garde acoustic performances of classical works by Ravel and Stravinsky.

Territorial disputes between nations sometimes linger on for years, decades, and even centuries. On this day in 1982, a small detachment of British soldiers surrendered to invading Argentinean troops in the Falklands, marking the outset of the Falkland Islands War. Argentine dictator General Leopoldo Galtieri's military junta anticipated that a war would divert public attention from domestic troubles and restore faith in his government. Possession of the Falklands was a recurring dispute between England and Spain (and later Argentina), since each nation laid claim to the islands during the 1700s.

3rd.

1848 The first session of the Chicago Board of Trade (CBOT) was held.

1926 Virgil "Gus" Grissom was born (see April 9 entry).

1934 Jane Goodall was born.

1961 The residents of Washington, D.C., were given the right to vote.

1977 Egyptian President Anwar Sadat met with U.S. President Jimmy Carter.

1996 Theodore Kaczynski was arrested.

1998 U.S. President Bill Clinton declared National Equal Pay Day (see April 7 entry).

2000 Microsoft Corporation was officially declared a monopoly.

2000 The NASDAQ set a one-day record when it lost 349.15 points.

This was both a red- and black-letter day for the American business markets. In 1848 the first session of the Chicago Board of Trade (CBOT) was held in Chicago, Illinois. Organized by eighty-two merchants as a central grain market, the CBOT provided a much-needed counterbalance to agriculture's seasonal volatility. Since that day, the CBOT has grown into the world's largest contiguous trading facility. In 1848 a CBOT membership sold for $2. Today, memberships can sell for as much as $875,000. Software giant Microsoft Corporation was officially declared a monopoly on this day in 2000, by Judge Thomas Penfield Jackson in a Washington, D.C., courtroom. According to the judgment, Microsoft had violated American antitrust laws by keeping "an oppressive thumb" on its competitors. On the exact same day in 2000, the NAS-DAQ set a one-day record when it lost 349.15 points, with technology stocks leading the plunge, to close at 4233.68.

The letter of the law was handed down to business on this day in 1998, when U.S. President Bill Clinton declared National Equal Pay Day. In his proclamation, Clinton stated, "I call upon government officials, law enforcement agencies, business leaders, educators, and the American people to recognize the full value of the skills and contributions of women in the labor force. I urge all employers to review their wage practices and to ensure that all their employees, including women, are paid equitably for their work."

A reign of random terror was halted on this day in 1996. Unabomber suspect Theodore Kaczynski was arrested. For eighteen years, Kaczynski sent anonymous package bombs to science professors at a number of universities and to businessmen, injuring sixteen people he'd never met and killing three. He was finally brought to justice when his brother recognized his writing style in a rambling 37,000-word manifesto he'd sent to the *Washington Post,* which was published jointly by the *Post* and *The New York Times.*

To quote R. Adam Lauridsen, editor of the *Harvard Political Review,* "Politics is never easy." On this day in 1977, Egyptian President Anwar Sadat had his first meeting with U.S. President Jimmy Carter, in Washington, D.C. Their purpose was to find a way to bring about peace in the Near East. Both politicians were under fire. Sadat's popularity was at an all-time low as Egyptians rioted over increased food prices. Meanwhile, Carter's critics condemned his newly born international human rights campaign, accusing him of meddling in other countries' domestic affairs. But Sadat was right when he stated, "In the game of Middle Eastern peace, the U.S. holds 99 percent of the cards." For his peace efforts, Sadat was named *Time*'s Man of the Year for 1977. There were far fewer critics speaking out on this day in 1961, when residents of Washington, D.C., were finally given the right to vote in presidential elections by the enactment of the Twenty-third Amendment to the U.S. Constitution.

Born in London, England, on this day in 1934, Jane Goodall devoted over forty years of her life to studying wild chimpanzees in Africa, and has received over forty international awards for her work. According to her official biography, "on her second birthday, Jane Goodall's father bought her a beautiful, life-like toy chimpanzee named Jubilee in honor of a baby chimpanzee born at the London Zoo. Friends warned her parents that such a gift would cause nightmares for a child." Fortunately, her parents disregarded their warnings.

Born in Mitchell, Indiana, on this day in 1926, astronaut Virgil "Gus" Grissom went into orbit on both the *Mercury IV* and *Gemini III* missions. Chosen to be the first man to walk on the moon, Grissom was part of the crew on *Apollo I,* who died when the rocket burst into flames during a takeoff simulation on January 27, 1967. Grissom loved his profession in spite of the dangers: "If we die, we want people to accept it. We're in a risky business, and we hope that if anything happens to us it will not delay the program. The conquest of space is worth the risk of life."

4th.

1889	Lucila Godoy de Alcayaga was born.
1895	Alberta Hunter was born.
1915	Muddy Waters was born.
1922	Elmer Bernstein was born.
1922	Robert Abplanalp was born.
1924	Marguerite Donnadien was born.
1928	Maya Angelou was born.

1939 Hugh Masekela was born.

1950 Judith Resnik was born.

1979 Pakistan Prime Minister Zulfikar Ali Bhutto was hanged (see June 21, December 2 entries).

1983 The space shuttle *Challenger* made its first flight (see January 28, February 6, February 10, April 29, June 22, September 2, October 13 entries).

Three women who were born on this day introduced readers to different worlds through their writing. Born in the high Andean village of Vicuña, Chile, on this day in 1889, Lucila Godoy de Alcayaga wrote under the name Gabriela Mistral. This poet and educator won the 1945 Nobel Prize for Literature for her lyric poetry. She was also a cultural minister and diplomat, and held high administrative posts in Chile's educational system. Born in Gia Dinh, Vietnam, on this day in 1924, Marguerite Donnadien wrote under the pen name Marguerite Duras. A journalist, French resistance activist, dramatist, and novelist, she is best known for her screenplay *Hiroshima Mon Amour.* She is also known for her remarkably earnest, revealing semi-autobiographical novels *La Douleur (Pain)* and *L'Amant (The Lover),* which sold three million copies in forty languages. She began her novel *The Lover* with a bittersweet commentary on beauty: "One day, I was already old, in the entrance of a public place, a man came up to me. He introduced himself and said: 'I've known you for years. Everyone says you were beautiful when you were young, but I want to tell you I think you're more beautiful now than then. Rather than your face as a young woman, I prefer your face as it is now. Ravaged.'" Born in St. Louis, Missouri, on this day in 1928, poet Maya Angelou recited her work at U.S. President Bill Clinton's 1993 inauguration. Angelou's career has been varied and successful as a poet, educator, historian, best-selling author, actress, playwright, civil-rights activist, public speaker, producer, and director. In addition to dozens of other awards, she received both a Grammy and a Tony. "There is no agony," Angelou said, "like bearing an untold story inside of you."

The scope of music is broad as evidenced by the performers and composers associated with this particular day. Born in Memphis, Tennessee, on this day in 1895, jazz singer and composer Alberta Hunter spent a number of years performing in Chicago nightclubs, touring Europe, the Middle East, and Russia. After her mother died, in 1956, she became a nurse for two decades. She then made a spectacular comeback at eighty-two years old, attaining fame once again on the New York nightclub circuit. The parents of jazz trumpeter Hugh Masekela, who was born in Johannesburg, South Africa, on this day in 1939, boasted the city's largest collection of jazz records. This vast library—combined with the native music he heard every day—shaped Masekela's unique musical style.

Born in Rolling Fork, Mississippi, on this day in 1915, blues songwriter Muddy Waters helped to establish postwar Chicago blues through his musical style and his lifestyle. He had a tremendous influence over 1960s musicians Bob Dylan, Eric Clapton, Jimi Hendrix, and The Rolling Stones. Born in New York City on this day in 1922, film score composer Elmer Bernstein turned out works best described as chameleon-like. The symphonic *The Ten Commandments* and the jazz-driven *The Man with the Golden Arm* were his debut works. He won an Oscar for the score to the film *Thoroughly Modern Millie* and was nominated for eleven more awards.

Inventions don't have to be huge to be great. Born in the Bronx, New York, on this day in 1922, Robert Abplanalp invented the aerosol valve used in every spray can. He studied mechanical engineering at Villanova University but left before graduation to open a small machine shop. Abplanalp filed the patent for his invention in 1949 and bought out his original business partners in the Precision Valve company in 1968. Today over a billion people around the world put products made with Precision Valve components to use every day.

On this day in 1983, the space shuttle *Challenger* took off from Cape Canaveral on its first flight. The first space walk of the shuttle program was performed during this mission. Ironically, Judith Resnik was born in Akron, Ohio, on this same day in 1950. A biomedical engineer and the second American woman to travel into space, Resnik perished with the rest of the *Challenger*'s crew on January 28, 1986, when an explosion destroyed the space shuttle. Her words, however, live on. Resnik felt that nothing is impossible: "Something is only dangerous if you are not prepared for it, or if you don't have control over it or if you can't think through how to get yourself out of a problem."

5th.

1710   Marie Camargo was born.

1792   U.S. President George Washington used his veto power for the first time.

1923   The Firestone Tire Company began tire production.

1933   U.S. President Franklin D. Roosevelt ordered the surrender of private supplies of gold (see April 19, June 5, August 14, December 31 entries).

1951   Ethel and Julius Rosenberg were sentenced to death (see March 29, May 12, June 19 entries).

1980 The world's most valuable stamp was sold.

1984 Kareem Abdul-Jabbar became the NBA's highest scorer.

1995 The U.S. House of Representatives passed a tax cut bill.

1997 The U.S. Mint created a commemorative gold coin depicting Franklin Delano Roosevelt (see December 31 entry).

On this day in 1923, the Firestone Tire Company began producing low-pressure balloon tires, which replaced narrow, high-pressure pneumatic tires as the automotive standard. This innovation had a sweeping impact on transportation. Vehicles could travel faster and far more smoothly than ever before. Jacksonville, Florida, for example, witnessed bus speeds 40 percent faster than that of streetcars. New Bedford, Massachusetts, reported that their new buses ran 60 percent faster on average than streetcars.

The world's most valuable stamp—a nondescript 1856 British Guyana 1-cent magenta was sold on this day in 1980, at auction to an anonymous bidder for $935,000, including buyer's premium. The anonymous purchaser was later revealed to be chemical heir John DuPont, who was arrested for murder in 1997 and sent to a hospital for the criminally insane. The stamp was first sold to a stamp dealer for less than a dollar by a twelve-year-old Welsh boy named Vernon Vaughn, who discovered it on an envelope in his attic in 1873. The stamp began to accumulate value after the First World War, when it was publicized as the "rarest stamp in the world."

On this day in 1951, Ethel and Julius Rosenberg were sentenced to death after being convicted of conspiracy. The only evidence against them was the testimony of David Greenglass (Julius's brother-in-law), whose integrity was challenged because he blamed Julius for the failure of a joint business venture. FBI head J. Edgar Hoover warned that history would harshly view a government responsible for orphaning the couple's two young children on such poor evidence. Rumors circulated that the government would spare their lives if they confessed to their crimes and gave evidence about other Communist Party spies. However, they maintained their innocence until the end. Nobel Prize-winning author Jean-Paul Sartre called the case "a legal lynching which smears with blood a whole nation."

A dance landmark was born in Brussels, Belgium, on this day in 1710. Ballet dancer Marie Camargo refused to wear the standard dancer's costume: mask, panniers, hoop skirt, and high-heeled shoes. She shocked audiences in 1734 when she shortened her dress and wore heel-less slippers to accentuate her movements on stage, forever changing the style of dress for ballet dancers in the process. Her rival, Marie Sallé, refused to be outdone. That same year, she discarded her corset and put on Greek robes to dance in her own ballet, *Pygmalion.*

Sometimes stops and cuts mark political history more than birth or reputation. The U.S. House of Representatives passed a tax cut bill on this day in 1995, which was the final major item in the Republicans' "Contract with America." The bill passed with a vote of 246-188. U.S. President Franklin D. Roosevelt ordered the surrender of private supplies of gold to Federal Reserve banks on this day in 1933, in order to halt the hoarding of gold bullion by private individuals. Though the ban was initially to be temporary, it remained in effect until President Gerald Ford revoked it in 1974. (Ironically, on this day in 1997, the U.S. Mint issued a commemorative gold coin depicting Franklin Delano Roosevelt.) And in 1792 U.S. President George Washington used his veto power for the first time, stopping a bill that would have apportioned states' representation in Congress based on the first census, which Secretary of State Thomas Jefferson indicated contained gross errors.

Kareem Abdul-Jabbar became the highest-scoring player in NBA history on this day in 1984, topping Wilt Chamberlain, with 31,421 career points. The Lakers were playing the Utah Jazz in Las Vegas, Nevada, when the rookie Magic Johnson passed the ball to him, Abdul-Jabbar sank one of his trademark skyhook shots from the baseline. He finally ended his twenty-year career in 1989 with 38,387 regular-season points, 5,762 play-off points, and 251 All-Star Game points—all NBA records.

6th.

1866   Joseph Lincoln Steffens was born.

1892   Lowell Thomas was born.

1896   The first modern Olympics opened in Athens, Greece.

1937   Merle Haggard was born.

1985   William J. Schroeder became the first artificial-heart recipient to be discharged from a hospital.

Journalism dipped into the mud on this day. Born in San Francisco, California, on this day in 1866, journalist Joseph Lincoln Steffens wrote about corruption in city government and business for *McClure's Magazine, American Magazine,* and *Everybody's*

Magazine. Along with such other crusading writers as Upton Sinclair, Ray Stannard Baker, and Ida Tarbell, Steffens popularized "muckraking" reportage at the turn of the century. Born in Woodinton, Ohio, on this same day in 1892, journalist Lowell Thomas made his reputation by claiming to have "discovered" Lawrence of Arabia while searching for a human interest story about British military activity in the Near East to send back to American readers. At the time, some newspapers were looking for ways to encourage America's entry into the First World War.

Born in a converted boxcar in Bakersfield, California, on this day in 1937, country musician Merle Haggard started life as a manual laborer and turned to crime to survive. While serving a sentence in San Quentin Prison, he joined the prison band. It turned his life around. Paroled in 1960, Haggard found work as a musician and quickly rose to country stardom. U.S. President Richard Nixon declared Haggard to be his favorite singer. Not long after his song "I'm a Lonesome Fugitive" topped the charts, California Governor Ronald Reagan gave him a full pardon. Haggard recorded sixty-five albums, scored forty number-one hits, and earned four gold records. His song "Today I Started Loving You Again" has been recorded by over 400 artists to date.

On this day in 1985, William J. Schroeder became the first artificial-heart recipient to be discharged from a hospital, when he was released from Humana Hospital in Louisville, Kentucky. Although he moved into an apartment nearby, his Jarvik VII artificial heart remained attached to a pump the size of a washing machine.

7th.

563 B.C.	Buddha was born.
1853	Prince Leopold of England was born.
1890	Marjory Stoneman Douglas was born.
1998	U.S. President Bill Clinton declared that April 8, 1998, was "National Equal Pay Day" (see April 3 entry).

Marjory Stoneman Douglas started a movement to save the Everglades wetlands in Florida. Born in Minneapolis, Minnesota, on this day in 1890, Douglas began working to save the Everglades from development during the 1940s—long before biologists discovered how essential wetlands are to the ecosystem. Douglas's 1947 book, *The Everglades: River of Grass,* was published the same year that Everglades National Park was established. In 1970 she formed the Friends of the Everglades, which continues to fight her cause long after her death in 1998 at 108 years old.

Buddha was born on this day in 563 B.C. in the forest grove of Lumbini, in the hilly regions of what is today northeastern India and Nepal. The son of Suddhodana, who was King of the Shakya tribe, Buddha was named Prince Gautama Siddhartha at birth. The king had been forewarned by sages that his son would forsake material possessions and pursue a spiritual life. To prevent the loss of his heir, Suddhodana surrounded Siddhartha with luxury. He even married and had a son of his own before he discovered the path to enlightenment through meditation. Buddha's central tenet was the Four Noble Truths: There is suffering, there is a cause of suffering, there is an end to suffering, and there is a method to bring about this end.

Queen Victoria's seventh son, Prince Leopold, was born on this day in 1853. It was a painless delivery and a historic one, as the queen's doctor administered chloroform. Before Leopold's birth, the administration of anesthesia to a woman in labor was considered highly immoral. The Church regarded the pain of childbirth as a punishment justly inflicted by God. The queen of England is also the head of the Church of England, and Victoria quickly became an outspoken advocate of pain reduction for women giving birth.

8th.

1918 Betty Ford was born.

1946 Jim "Catfish" Hunter was born.

1974 Hank Aaron hit his 715th home run.

1985 The Indian government filed a lawsuit against Union Carbide Corporation in New York City (see February 14, December 30 entries).

The Indian government filed a lawsuit in New York City against Union Carbide Corporation on this day in 1985, following the chemical leak at Bhopal, India, that claimed more than 8,000 lives. The Indian government brought the suit in New York because it had determined that the Bhopal court didn't have jurisdiction. The suit was dismissed when Union Carbide agreed to appear in Indian court. Although no reason was stated, there is little doubt that the judgment against the company would have been considerably higher if the trial had been held in the United States.

First Lady Betty Ford shocked the world and raised awareness of breast cancer when she went public with her 1974 mastectomy. "Lying in the hospital," she recalled, "I'd come to recognize more clearly the power of the woman in the White House." Born in Chicago, Illinois, on this day in 1918, Betty Ford surprised the public again in 1978, when she admitted to drug and alcohol addiction. After completing her own treatment, she founded the Betty Ford Clinic for drug and alcohol rehabilitation, which—with its offer of "hope and a special place of healing"—has helped over 40,000 patients.

Baseball had a double-header on this day. In 1974 Atlanta Braves pitcher Hank Aaron hit his 715th home run in a game against the Los Angeles Dodgers, breaking Babe Ruth's career record. The only player in history to hit at least twenty home runs for twenty consecutive seasons, Aaron won three consecutive Gold Glove Awards and a Most Valuable Player Award. "As far as I'm concerned," Mickey Mantle once said, "Aaron is the best ballplayer of my era. He is to baseball of the last fifteen years what Joe DiMaggio was before him. He's never received the credit he's due."

Born in Hertford, North Carolina, on this day in 1946, Jim "Catfish" Hunter had a career that was truly exceptional. He never played in the minors. He spent his first year on the Oakland As' disabled list after being shot in the foot while hunting, and then went on to pitch the fourth perfect game in American League history. In 1974 he set an economic landmark for free agents in baseball, signing with the Yankees to a $3.75-million, five-year contract. Yankees owner George Steinbrenner never regretted the deal: "Catfish Hunter was the cornerstone of the Yankees' success over the last quarter century." He stacked up five straight twenty-victory seasons, earned five World Series rings, and won a Cy Young Award. Tragically, Hunter died of a disease named after another Yankees baseball legend, Lou Gehrig, on September 9, 1999, at his home in Hertford.

9th.

1898   Paul Robeson was born (see October 18 entry).

1928   Tom Lehrer was born.

1932   Carl Perkins was born.

1939   Marian Anderson performed at the Lincoln Memorial (see January 7, February 17 entries).

1959   The first seven astronauts for the U.S. space program were selected by NASA (see April 3, May 5, May 15, May 24, October 29 entries).

1992 Manuel Noriega was convicted (see January 3, September 5, December 20 entries).

1996 The power of line-item veto was granted to the U.S. president.

On this day in 1992, former Panamanian dictator Manuel Noriega was convicted by a jury in Miami, Florida, on eight out of ten counts, which included drug trafficking, racketeering, and money laundering. His extradition had cost the United States $260 million and Panama nearly $1 billion. Although Noriega had been paid by the CIA up to the time of his arrest, all of his assets were seized as drug profits. He couldn't afford counsel and was represented by court-appointed defense lawyers. (One attorney— whom he confided in at length—was a government agent who violated the sanctity of lawyer-client privilege.) Though U.S. President George H. Bush hailed the conviction as a "major victory against the drug lords," his own agencies reported that drug trafficking in Panama doubled immediately after Noriega was removed.

Born in Princeton, New Jersey, on this day in 1898, Paul Robeson was the son of an escaped North Carolina slave who had graduated from college and entered the ministry. Robeson earned a scholarship to Rutgers University. He was named twice as a football All-American. Robeson lettered in baseball, basketball, and track; became Phi Beta Kappa; and was class valedictorian. He graduated from Columbia Law School before he heeded the call of the stage. His resonant bass voice, commanding presence, and remarkable acting talent earned him international acclaim. But he was also an outspoken proponent of racial equality and socialism during the McCarthy era. Robeson made a statement in 1949 that sealed his fate: "It is unthinkable that American Negroes would go to war on behalf of those who have oppressed us for generations against a country which in one generation has raised our people to the full dignity of mankind." To silence him, the federal government revoked his passport and prevented him from performing in large American venues for more than a decade.

Born in Tiptonville, Tennessee, on this day in 1932, rockabilly musician Carl Perkins along with his brothers started life working in the fields with their parents, who were sharecroppers. A second-hand guitar given to him as a gift revealed a natural talent that changed his life. In 1954 Perkins heard Elvis Presley on the radio, and headed straight to Presley's producer Sam Phillips of Sun Records and auditioned. His first hit was inspired by two teenagers at a dance (and encouraged by Johnny Cash). "Blue Suede Shoes" skyrocketed to the top of the charts in 1956. Perkins's rockabilly style went on to influence musicians from George Harrison to Brian Setzer and the Stray Cats.

The first album by Tom Lehrer, born in New York City on this day in 1928, entitled *Songs by Tom Lehrer,* is one of the music industry's greatest success stories. Lehrer spent $15 an hour on studio time to record the entire album. He was still in college when he started selling the album around the Harvard University campus. It went on to sell 370,000 copies on his homemade label. He toured extensively and created such satirical hits as "Poisoning Pigeons in the Park" and "The Masochism Rag." Despite an enormously promising entertainment career, Lehrer felt unfulfilled and left the stage to become a math and music teacher. Lehrer became one of the most celebrated nonperforming comedians to repeatedly refuse to make an appearance.

Opera diva Marian Anderson was refused the right to perform at the Daughters of the American Revolution Constitution Hall, and in response, First Lady Eleanor Roosevelt resigned her DAR membership. Roosevelt suggested that Anderson perform at the Lincoln Memorial to protest the racial bigotry she'd experienced. And on this day in 1939, Anderson performed in front of an audience of 75,000 fans at the famous memorial in Washington, D.C.

On this day in 1996, the power of line-item veto was granted to the president by the U.S. Congress. Legislators occasionally attach unrelated items—called riders—to major legislation to force its acceptance as part of a package. The line-item veto allowed the president to reduce fund allocations in appropriations bills in the interest of national debt reduction.

On this day in 1959, the first seven astronauts for the U.S. space program were selected by NASA. Initially, 110 military test pilots were invited to inquire about the Mercury project, but the standards for acceptance were strict. Pilots needed at least 1,500 hours of flight time and a bachelor's degree, and could not be taller than 5'11" or weigh more than 180 pounds. They also faced a grueling battery of physical, psychological, and engineering tests. Finally, seven men were selected: Alan Shepard, Virgil Grissom, John Glenn, Scott Carpenter, Walter Schirra, Gordon Cooper, and Deke Slayton. Grissom was nearly disqualified due to a ragweed allergy, until he pointed out that there was no ragweed in space.

10th.

1956   Nat "King" Cole was assaulted (see March 17 entry).

1963   The USS *Thresher* went down.

1970   The New York state legislature voted to allow unrestricted abortion rights.

1982 The European Economic Community approved trade sanctions against Argentina for its actions in the Falklands (see January 1, April 2, April 28, April 30 entries).

1986 Wine drinkers were cautioned not to consume Italian wines after tainted wine was discovered.

1992 Charles Keating, Jr., was found guilty (see January 6, November 15 entries).

1996 Dan Rostenkowski accepted a plea bargain (see July 19, July 24 entries).

On this day in 1986, American wine drinkers were cautioned not to consume select imported Italian wines after twenty-two Italians died from drinking inexpensive wine that had been spiked with methanol. Although none of the tainted wines were shipped to the United States, sales of Italian wines plummeted. *Wine Spectator* magazine called the incident "wine's worst scandal in a generation."

Financier Charles Keating, Jr., was found guilty on this day in 1992 of defrauding seventeen people out of more than $900,000 through his Lincoln Savings & Loan. (His actual crime involved close to 17,000 people and $252 million.) Keating used investors' funds to support a lavish personal lifestyle, enjoying $2,500 dinners, traveling to Spain to buy tapestries for corporate offices, and building a $3-million Olympic-size pool for his grandchildren. He hired ten members of his family, paying them $34 million in salaries, bonuses, and stock profits over a five-year period.

On this day in 1963, the USS *Thresher* became the first nuclear-powered submarine to sink when it submerged 8,530 feet in the Atlantic Ocean, 22 miles east of Boston. All 129 crew members perished when it went down.

On this day in 1956, singer Nat "King" Cole was assaulted by six members of a white supremacist group, who attempted to kidnap him during a performance in Birmingham, Alabama. Cole escaped with minor injuries. However, when he refused to publicly express his outrage over the attack, many of his fans began boycotting his records.

The New York state legislature voted to allow unrestricted abortion rights during the first six months of pregnancy on this day in 1970. (This occurred three years before *Roe v. Wade* struck down other states' anti-abortion laws.) The bill was signed the next day by Republican Governor Nelson Rockefeller.

On this day in 1996, ex-congressman Dan Rostenkowski accepted a plea bargain, receiving a seventeen-month sentence and a fine of $100,000 to cover the cost of his $1,800-per-month incarceration. He'd been charged with thirteen felony counts of fraud for extensive misuse of his official House of Representatives expense account.

11th.

1865   Mary White Ovington was born.

1899   Percy Lavon Julian was born (see April 20 entry).

1900   The U.S. Navy purchased its first submarine.

1921   Iowa became the first state to impose a cigarette tax on consumers (see January 2, January 10, May 23, July 17, August 1, August 24, September 28, December 1 entries).

1980   The Equal Employment Opportunity Commission issued regulations against sexual harassment in the workplace.

The Equal Employment Opportunity Commission (EEOC) issued regulations against sexual harassment in the workplace on this day in 1980, "establishing criteria for determining when unwelcome conduct of a sexual nature constitutes sexual harassment, defining the circumstances under which an employer may be held liable, and suggesting affirmative steps an employer should take to prevent sexual harassment."

On this same day in 1921, Iowa became the first state to impose a cigarette tax on consumers, with a tax of two cents per pack. By 1991, Iowa's cigarette tax had risen to thirty-six cents.

Born in Brooklyn, New York, on this day in 1865, Mary White Ovington became involved in the campaign for civil rights in 1890 after hearing Frederick Douglass speak in a Brooklyn church. Although she was Caucasian, Ovington co-founded the National Association for the Advancement of Colored People (NAACP) after reading William English Walling's article "Race War in the North," which concluded with a plea for powerful citizens to come to their aid. Ovington served as NAACP chairperson, board member, and treasurer for thirty-eight years, until her retirement in 1947.

Born in Montgomery, Alabama, on this day in 1899, Percy Lavon Julian was the African-American chemist whose research was instrumental in the creation of drug treatments for arthritis. Julian acquired over 115 patents during his career, including one for a fire-extinguishing foam that was used on oil and gasoline fires during the Second World War. He also developed a synthetic drug used to treat glaucoma.

On this day in 1900, the U.S. Navy purchased its first submarine. The USS *Holland,* built by John Holland for $150,000, was 54 feet long and carried three torpedoes.

12th.

1961   Yuri Gagarin became the first human to orbit the earth (see March 9 entry).

1979   Kevin MacKenzie sent the very first emoticon over the Internet.

1980   The U.S. Olympic Committee's House of Delegates endorsed President Jimmy Carter's boycott of the Moscow Summer Olympics.

1981   The space shuttle *Columbia* was launched (see June 27 entry).

1994   Arizona lawyers Laurence Canter and Martha Siegel sent a mass e-mail to 6,000 Usenet groups (see June 27 entry).

Kevin MacKenzie sent the very first emoticon over the Internet in a message to the MsgGroup on this day in 1979. "Emoticon" is a condensation of "emotion" and "icon." MacKenzie's emoticon was "-)" which means "tongue-in-cheek." On this same day in 1994, Arizona lawyers Laurence Canter and Martha Siegel sent a mass e-mail to 6,000 Usenet groups, advertising their green card lottery services. This was the first spam. Canter and Seigel got far more of a response than they had anticipated. CNN-TV and *Larry King Live* discussed the event. A firestorm of furor from the Usenet groups also resulted. Netcom eventually canceled Siegel and Canter's account.

Two landmarks occurred in aerospace history on this day. In 1981 the space shuttle *Columbia* was launched, nearly six years after the last Apollo space mission. On this same day in 1961, Soviet cosmonaut Yuri Gagarin became the first human to orbit the earth. Gagarin's 108-minute orbit marked man's first venture into space and won the space race for the Soviets. Gagarin became the first of over 100 Soviet and Russian cosmonauts to go into outer space. The Russian training center, in Star City, Russia, is named after him.

13th.

1844   Edgar Allan Poe published a hoax.

1970   The *Apollo 13* crew reported that a liquid oxygen tank had burst.

1976 U.S. President Gerald R. Ford signed a bill that extended federal jurisdiction over fishing rights.

1979 Officials began the final shutdown process at the Three Mile Island nuclear power plant near Harrisburg, Pennsylvania (see March 28, June 28, October 30 entries).

On this day in 1976, U.S. President Gerald R. Ford signed a bill that extended federal jurisdiction over fishing rights to 200 miles offshore and banned the harvesting of fourteen species, including overfished cod, haddock, and yellowtail flounder. The bill also included an initiative to build up the domestic fishing fleet to take advantage of the protected fishing grounds. The bill went into effect on March 1, 1977.

Although many men dreamt of crossing the Atlantic Ocean in a hot-air balloon, no one accomplished that goal until the *Double Eagle II* landed in France, completing a crossing from Pennsylvania on August 10, 1978. Author Edgar Allan Poe, however, published a news report about such a voyage on this day in 1844. The poverty-stricken Poe had returned to New York City with his sick wife and mother-in-law, having only five dollars in his pocket. In desperation, he took on a job as a reporter for the *New York Sun*. His 5,000-word story was headlined "The Atlantic Crossed in Three Days!" According to Poe's tale, Monck Mason and Robert Holland were carried across the ocean at a speed of 60 miles per hour in their balloon *Nassau* from London to South Carolina when the propeller on their craft broke. The newspaper printed a retraction of the story two days later when no one could confirm the facts. Poe was then discharged from his journalistic duties.

14th.

1904 Sir Arthur John Gielgud was born.

1907 François "Papa Doc" Duvalier was born (see February 7, April 22, July 3 entries).

1940 Julie Christie was born.

1941 Pete Rose was born (see July 18, September 10, September 11 entries).

1994 American fighter planes shot down American helicopters.

2000 The NASDAQ, Dow-Jones Industrials, and Standard & Poor's 500 posted their biggest one-day loss in history, losing $1 trillion in value.

A grand-nephew of the actress Ellen Terry, Sir Arthur John Gielgud earned a reputation for Shakespearean roles, representing the replete classical actor to many theatergoers on both sides of the Atlantic Ocean during his seventy-five-year career. Born in London, England, on this day in 1904, Gielgud played Othello at Stratford-upon-Avon, Prospero at London's National Theatre, and Cassius in the 1952 film production *Julius Caesar*. Friend and colleague Sir Laurence Olivier once said that Gielgud had "a dignity, a majesty which suggests he was born with a crown on his head." Considered by many people to represent the epitome of Swinging Sixties London, Julie Christie gained her reputation playing free-spirited roles in the films *Darling, Far from the Madding Crowd, Dr. Zhivago,* and *The Go-Between*. Born on her father's tea plantation in Chukua, Assam, India, on this day in 1940, Christie became a staunch animal advocate during the 1980s.

Fear is the weapon of the dictator. Few twentieth-century leaders used that weapon as vigorously as François "Papa Doc" Duvalier, the Haitian dictator who was born in Port-au-Prince, Haiti, on this day in 1907. A physician and voodoo priest, Duvalier controlled the masses with threats of black magic and with a secret police force called the *Tontons Macoutes* (bogeymen).

Born in Cincinnati, Ohio, on this day in 1941, Pete Rose joined the Cincinnati Reds baseball team right out of high school and was named the National League's Rookie of the Year in 1963. Rose retired from baseball after the 1986 season as baseball's all-time career hits leader. He served as the Reds' manager from 1984 to 1988, guiding the team to four consecutive second-place finishes. In 1989, baseball commissioner Bart Giamatti banned Rose from major league basebal for gambling on the game.

On this day in 1994, two American F-15 fighter planes monitoring a UN-imposed no-fly zone in northern Iraq shot down two U.S. Black Hawk helicopters on a humanitarian mission, killing twenty-six people, including fifteen Americans and eleven foreign nationals. The fighter pilots had misidentified the Black Hawks as Iraqi helicopters. The Black Hawks were transporting American, British, French, and Turkish military officers, Kurdish representatives, and a State Department political adviser who had been observing the work of Operation Provide Comfort.

15th.

1894 Bessie Smith was born.

1930 Vigdis Finnbogadottir was born.

1979 The federal government banned the use of chlorofluorocarbons (CFCs) (see September 15 entry).

1982 Five al-Jihad terrorists were executed.

1985 The South African government declared the repeal of laws prohibiting sex and marriage between whites and nonwhites.

1995 Robert McNamara published his memoirs.

2001 Joey Ramone died (see May 19 entry).

On this day in 1982, five militant Muslim fundamentalists who were members of the al-Jihad terrorist group were executed. Claiming that they bitterly disagreed with Egyptian President Anwar Sadat's efforts toward peaceful negotiations with Israel, the men assassinated Sadat in 1981 during a military review celebrating Egypt's successful 1973 defense of the Suez and Sinai against advancing Israeli forces.

Singer Bessie Smith was known as the "Empress of the Blues" at the height of her performing and recording career during the 1920s. Born in Chattanooga, Tennessee, on this day in 1894, Smith began her career singing in vaudeville tents and small theaters throughout the South. Her outstanding stage presence shone threw when she made an appearance in the 1929 film *St. Louis Blues.*

In 1972 Vigdis Finnbogadottir became one of the first single people to adopt a child in her native Iceland. Born in Reykjavik on this day in 1930, Finnbogadottir gained one other distinction in her homeland, becoming the nation's first democratically elected female president on June 30, 1980.

16th.

1492 King Ferdinand of Spain agreed to finance Christopher Columbus's voyage to the New World (see March 31, May 3, May 9, May 13, May 20, June 13, July 31, August 23, December 5 entries).

1878   Polygamy was made illegal in the United States (see September 27, October 6 entries).

1885   Baroness Karen Blixen was born.

1926   The first Book-of-the-Month Club selection, Sylvia Townsend Warner's novel *Lolly Willowes, or the Loving Huntsman,* was chosen.

1964   Jerrie Mock became the first woman to fly solo around the world.

1990   The first African-American Internet message group began transmission.

1992   Japan's first sexual harassment suit was settled.

1993   Two former Los Angeles police officers were convicted by a federal court (see March 3, April 29, August 4 entries).

1995   Iqbal Masih died of gunshot wounds he received while riding a bicycle with a friend.

On this day in 1992, the first sexual harassment suit filed in Japan was settled in favor of the female plaintiff. The court in Fukuoka prefecture upheld her claims that her rights had been violated by male co-workers who uttered vile remarks, forcing her to quit her job.

The first African-American Internet message group, soc.culture.african.american, began transmissions on New York City's Invention Factory Bulletin Board Service on this day in 1990. The system was established to serve as a moderated newsgroup for the discussion of African-American culture and concerns as well as to provide an opportunity for fellowship on Usenet.

On this day in 1995, a thirteen-year-old Pakistani named Iqbal Masih died of gunshot wounds he received while riding a bicycle with a friend. At the age of four, Masih had been sold into servitude by his parents for $200 and spent the next six years shackled to a loom, working as a carpet weaver. He escaped when he was ten years old with the help of Ehsan Ulla Khan. Founder of the Bonded Labor Liberation Front, Khan and his group had successfully freed over 30,000 Pakistani child slaves out of the 12 million who exist—the organization's mission since it was established in 1988. Once freed, Masih spoke out about the lives of the child slaves, attracting worldwide attention as a speaker at an international labor conference held in Sweden. Masih's killers were never caught.

The Baroness Karen Blixen wrote memorable tales about romance and destiny under the pen name Isak Dinesen. Born in Denmark on this day in 1885, Dinesen's short-story collection *Seven Gothic Tales,* the story *Babette's Feast,* and the autobiographical work

Out of Africa were created after she'd married her cousin, moved with him to his African coffee plantation, divorced him, and returned to her family home in Rungstedlund.

The U.S. Supreme Court handed down the decision that made polygamy illegal in the case *Reynolds v. United States* on this day in 1878. Until that time, multiple marriages were common among practitioners of the Mormon faith and other minority religious groups.

17th.

1905 The U.S. Supreme Court deemed a New York law was unconstitutional.

1970 The *Apollo 13* crew safely splashed down in the Pacific Ocean after scuttling their mission.

1982 Canada became a commonwealth nation.

There are times when the federal and state governments don't see eye to eye. On this day in 1905, the U.S. Supreme Court handed down the decision that a New York law was unconstitutional. In the case of *Lochner v. New York,* the federal court held that a bakery owner from Utica, New York, had the right to increase workers' hours as guaranteed under the Fourteenth Amendment. Under New York state law, Mr. Lochner had been convicted of violating a state statute that limited bakery workers to a sixty-hour week.

Canada became a commonwealth nation on this day in 1982. Great Britain's Queen Elizabeth II signed the Constitution Act at Canada's capital city of Ottawa, replacing the 1867 North America Act, which had allotted the North American nation dominion status under British rule.

18th.

1882 Leopold Stokowski was born.

1897 Professor Ardito Desio was born (see August 2 entry).

1956 Grace Kelly married Monaco's Prince Rainier Louis Henri Maxence Bertrand de Grimaldi (see May 31 entry).

1978 The U.S. Senate voted 68-32 to turn over the Panama Canal to Panama on December 31, 1999 (see May 18, August 10, September 7, November 2, November 3, December 31 entries).

1989 Thousands of students demanding democracy attempted to storm Communist Party headquarters in Beijing, China.

Professor Ardito Desio was the first man to summit the world's second highest peak, K2. Born in Palmanova del Fruili, Italy, on this day in 1897, Desio was a geologist who had participated in a 1929 attempt to scale the peak. His veteran experience made him the ideal leader for the 1953 reconnaissance mission and the 1954 attempt to scale the peak with teammates Lino Lacedelli and Achille Compagnoni. Despite his age, the death of the thirty-six-year-old mountain guide Maria Puchoz during the ascent, and the complete depletion of their oxygen tanks, Desio was the first to summit. On August 2, 1953, Desio planted the Italian flag on K2, just before the onset of the monsoon season.

Born in London, England, on this day in 1882, Leopold Stokowski had the dubious distinction of making an appearance with Mickey Mouse in the 1940 animated film *Fantasia*. The conductor of the Philadelphia Symphony Orchestra, the New York Philharmonic, and the Houston Symphony Orchestra, Stokowski also founded New York's American Symphony Orchestra.

19th.

1910 Halley's Comet appeared in the skies.

1933 The United States stopped backing its currency on the gold standard (see April 5, June 5, August 14, December 31 entries).

1968 The FBI identified James Earl Ray.

1971 *Salyut 1* was launched.

1971 Sierra Leone became a republic (see February 6, August 2 entries).

1993 U.S. federal agents initiated a raid that ended in the incineration of David Koresh's enclave (see February 28, March 2, March 19 entries).

1995 The Murrah Federal Building in Oklahoma City was bombed.

The FBI identified the man wanted in the assassination of Rev. Dr. Martin Luther King, Jr., as James Earl Ray on this day in 1968. A known Missouri penitentiary fugitive and petty criminal, Ray was apprehended in London, England, and charged with the killing.

On this day in 1993, U.S. federal agents raided David Koresh's conclave, near Waco, Texas, with the ensuing incineration killing approximately eighty men, women, and children. And on this same day in 1995, the Murrah Federal Building in Oklahoma City was the target of a fertilizer bomb left in a Ryder moving truck planted by Timothy McVeigh, resulting in the deaths of 167 men, women, and children.

The nation of Sierra Leone had been populated since 1820 by freed slaves who arrived from England, the United States, and Canada. A British colony since 1807, this western African region became a republic on this day in 1971. Siaka Stevens was appointed as the new nation's executive president.

The first Russian military and civilian space station, *Salyut 1,* was launched on this day in 1971. The first vehicle of its kind, the 25-ton, solar-powered space station was launched nearly two years before its American counterpart, *Skylab.*

20th.

1853   Harriet Tubman joined the Underground Railroad.

1949   Dr. Percy Lavon Julian discovered an arthritic aid (see April 11 entry).

1972   Astronauts John Young and Charles Duke explored the moon's surface.

1980   The first Cuban refugees reached Florida.

1983   U.S. President Ronald Reagan signed a Social Security plan.

1988   Helen Thayer became the first female explorer to reach the North Pole on a solo expedition.

1999   Students Dylan Klebold and Eric Harris killed twelve fellow students and a teacher in a shooting at Columbine High School in Littleton, Colorado.

U.S. President Ronald Reagan signed a plan on this day in 1983 ensuring the Social Security System's solvency for the next seventy-five years. The plan included the delay of the 1983 cost-of-living increase for six months, a payroll deduction increase, the gradual elevation of the minimum retirement age to sixty-seven by the year 2027, the request that new federal employees join the system, and the taxation of a portion of higher-income retirees' benefits.

A series of informal, secret routes that were used by slaves in their flight for freedom, the Underground Railroad consisted of hiding places called "stations." Escapes were frequently masterminded by "conductors," who knew the location of the safest stations and routes along the way. On this day in 1853, an escaped slave named Harriet Tubman became a conductor, leading three slaves northward from Dorchester County, Maryland, to St. Catherines, Ontario. Although she was wanted throughout Maryland in violation of the Fugitive Slave Law, Tubman made nineteen trips in which she transported over 300 slaves through the dangerous 500-mile route until 1857—when she transported her own parents up to Canada. On this same day in 1971, the U.S. Supreme Court unanimously ruled that busing of students could be ordered to achieve racial desegregation in the landmark case *Swann v. Charlotte-Mecklenburg Board of Education.*

The first Cuban refugees reached Florida on this day in 1980, sailing to the United States as part of the massive Mariel boat lift. From this date until September 25, over 124,775 men, women, and children made the journey. More than 1,380 vessels were assisted to safety by the U.S. Coast Guard as they entered American waters.

On this day in 1988, fifty-year-old Helen Thayer became the first female explorer to reach the North Pole on a solo expedition. Traveling on foot and on skis while pulling a fully loaded sled attached to her belt, Thayer walked with her black husky, Charlie, whose sole job was to warn her of marauding polar bears. The 345-mile, twenty-seven-day journey was not the last time this Olympic luge racer and mountain climber made the trip. In 1990 she led the first International U.S.-Soviet Arctic Women's expedition through the same region.

The Apollo 16 space mission had landed in the moon's Descartes Highland, conducting a number of first-time experiments. It was the first time an ultraviolet camera/spectrograph was used to study the surface. And on this day in 1972, astronauts John Young and Charles Duke explored the moon's surface on a lunar rover, collecting 213 pounds of lunar rock during their seventy-one-hour stay.

21st.

1923 John Mortimer was born.

1947 James Newell Osterberg was born.

1966 An artificial heart was used to keep alive a patient awaiting a transplant in Houston, Texas.

1997 The U.S. Supreme Court ruled on government-mandated drug tests.

On this day in 1997, the U.S. Supreme Court handed down a decision that drug tests mandated by a federal, state, or local body are "searches" as defined in the Fourth Amendment in a case involving political candidates from the state of Georgia. The court also ruled that such searches require reasonable suspicion to be legal.

Although he never wrote under an assumed name, John Mortimer made his name as the author of the *Rumpole of the Bailey* series, which features a middle-aged barrister as the main character. Born in London, England, on this day in 1923, Mortimer himself was an attorney who handled a number of celebrated civil cases during the course of his legal career.

The Godfather of Punk was born in Ann Arbor, Michigan, on this day in 1947. Iggy Pop picked up his name when he first played as a drummer in a band called the Iguanas in 1964. Originally named James Newell Osterberg, he had a passion for music that inspired him to drop out of the University of Michiagn and move to Chicago to learn about urban blues from Howlin' Wolf. In 1967 Iggy returned to Detroit, forming the Psychedelic Stooges, which debuted on Halloween night. The next year they were signed to Elektra Records. Some of Iggy's early songs were issued far ahead of the punk era. "I Wanna Be Your Dog" was only moderately noticed in those early years. And his somewhat self-destructive stage performances were the stuff of legends by the time less outrageous punk performers began to top the charts during the late 1970s. Iggy's career finally took off when his friend David Bowie produced two of his albums in 1977. *The Idiot* and *Lust for Life* made it to the top of the charts.

22nd.

1952 The first live TV broadcast of an atomic explosion was shown.

1969 The first nonstop voyage around the world was completed in 312 days by Robin Know-Johnston in his sailing ketch.

1971 Haitian President François "Papa Doc" Duvalier died and was succeeded by his son, Jean-Claude (see February 7, April 14, July 3 entries).

1972   *Apollo 16* astronauts John Young and Charles Duke drove an electric car on the lunar surface.

1974   Katherine Graham became the first female member of the Associated Press board (see June 16 entry).

1976   Barbara Walters accepted an offer to co-anchor the "ABC Evening News."

1998   The Kennewick Man court case began (see July 28 entry).

2000   Eight federal agents apprehended Eliàn Gonzalez at gunpoint from his cousins' bungalow in the Little Havana area of Miami, Florida, because his cousins refused to hand the boy over to his father.

The way we view the daily news changed twice on this day. In 1952 the first live television broadcast of an atomic explosion was shown by Los Angeles station KTLA, covering an A-bomb test in the Nevada desert. On this same day in 1976, Barbara Walters accepted an offer to co-anchor the "ABC Evening News" with Harry Reasoner, becoming the first female full-time evening anchor on network television.

A landmark legal battle began on this day in 1998. The lawsuit for the ownership of Kennewick Man went before U.S. Magistrate Judge John Jelderks, involving several branches of the federal government, five Native American tribes, eight scientists, a small-town anthropologist named James Chatters, and a religious sect.

23rd.

1804   Marie Taglioni was born.

1856   Granville T. Woods was born (see November 10, November 15 entries).

1858   Max Karl Ernst Planck was born.

1891   Sergei Prokofiev was born.

Born in Stockholm, Sweden, on this day in 1804, Marie Taglioni was trained by her father to dance on point and inaugurated ballet's romantic period with her creation of the 1832 production *La Sylphide*. Taglioni introduced one more element to the ballet world: Her diaphanous costumes led to the design of the modern tutu.

Composer Sergei Prokofiev was encouraged by his teacher and lifelong friend Rimsky-Korsakov to develop a musical style that proved to be both unique and dangerous. Born in Sontsovka, Ukraine, on this day in 1891, Prokofiev's opera *The Love for Three Oranges,* ballet score *Romeo and Juliet,* the "children's piece" *Peter and the Wolf,* and the film score for Sergei Eisenstein's *Alexander Nevski* are only a few examples of his remarkable talent. But in 1948 the Soviet central committee under Josef Stalin named Prokofiev as a musical composer whose works were "marked with formalist perversions . . . alien to the Soviet people." And his last opera, *The Story of a Real Man,* was censored. It wasn't performed until his detractor, Soviet Premier Josef Stalin, and Prokofiev himself died on the exact same date: March, 5, 1953.

Two mechanical geniuses were born on this day. Although his formal education ended when he was ten years old, Granville T. Woods went on to invent the Synchronous Multiplex Railway Telegraph, which allowed trains to contact each other while in transit, thus averting numerous accidents. Born in Columbus, Ohio, on this day in 1856, Woods also invented the automatic air-brake and over forty other creations. Max Karl Ernst Planck revolutionized physics when he formulated and presented his quantum theory to the world in 1900. Born in Kiel, Germany, on this day in 1858, Planck devised a system that addressed many questions that had remained unresolved by Isaac Newton's theory. He assumed that energy changes take place in violently abrupt installments, which he called quanta.

24th.

1915   The Turkish government began a massacre of Armenians.

1916   The Easter Rebellion began.

1980   American troops attempted to rescue hostages held in Iran.

1996   The U.S. Congress passed the Anti-Terrorism and Effective Death Penalty Act.

During the 1890s a number of separatist Armenian bands started fomenting insurrection within the Turkish-Ottoman Empire in provinces such as Zeitun, Erzurum, Van, and Adana. Many of these rebels joined Russian and French troops at the outbreak of the First World War, raiding Turkish towns and cities in the hopes they could carve an independant Armenian state with their new foreign allies. In response to these vicious attacks, the Turkish Council of Ministries ordered raids on Muslim communities in and around Anatolia, Turkey, on this day in 1915. It has been recorded that 1.5 million Armenians lost their lives in the ensuing massacres. On this same day in 1916, Irish Nationalists began the Easter Rebellion in Dublin, Ireland, in the hopes of overthrowing the British rulership of the island. Their attempts, however, failed.

On this day in 1980, American troops attempted to rescue fifty-three hostages held in Iran. The mission ended in disaster when a RH-53D helicopter collided with a C-130 tanker during refueling procedures at the Desert One landing site. Eight people died in the accident. Sixteen years later, in 1996, the U.S. Congress passed and President Bill Clinton signed the Anti-Terrorism and Effective Death Penalty Act.

25th.

1908   Edward R. Murrow was born.

1959   The St. Lawrence Seaway was opened to shipping.

1967   Colorado became the first state to liberalize its abortion law.

1990   The Hubble Space Telescope was launched.

Born near Pole Cat Creek, North Carolina, on this day in 1908, Edward Roscoe Murrow had a career that spanned the worlds of journalism and politics. He traveled throughout Europe while working as assistant director of the Institute of International Education from 1932 to 1935. Murrow joined CBS as a cultural affairs journalist, but he quickly expanded his range to include the political scene. During the 1950s, Murrow explored television, producing and narrating the programs "See It Now" and "Person to Person." During that time Murrow received five Emmy Awards and contributed to the downfall of Senator Joseph McCarthy's anti-Communist "witch hunts" when he interviewed the senator on national television in 1954. Before his death in 1965, Murrow also served as head of the United States Information Agency for four years.

On this day in 1967, Colorado became the first state to liberalize its abortion law, authorizing the procedure when pregnancy resulted from rape or incest, endangered a woman's physical or mental health, or was likely to result in the birth of a child with severe mental or physical defects. The abortion had to be performed in a licensed hospital and only after unanimous approval by a panel of three physicians.

26th.

1900 Charles Richter was born.

1922 Jeanne Sauve was born.

1976 The U.S. Supreme Court affirmed the Bank Secrecy Act.

Canada's first female governor-general, Jeanne Sauve, was born in Prud'homme, Saskatchewan, on this day in 1922. A journalist and broadcaster before running for the House of Commons in 1972, Sauve was appointed the first female speaker of the House of Commons in 1980. She rose to become Canada's governor-general in 1984.

Born in Hamilton, Ohio, on this day in 1900, Charles Richter was working at the Carnegie Institute when he and Beno Gutenberg created the scale used to measure earthquake strength between 1927 and 1935. The Richter Scale measures the maximum amplitude of an earthquake's waves as observed on a seismograph and adjusts the figure for the distance from the earthquake's epicenter, applying a logarithm to derive the final result.

27th.

1927 Sheila Scott was born.

1947 Thor Heyerdahl and a small crew set out in the sail raft *KonTiki,* beginning a 4,300-mile voyage from Callao, Peru, to the Polynesian Islands (see October 6 entry).

1959 Sheena Easton was born.

1967 Expo 67 opened in Montreal, Canada (see May 1, May 12, May 27 entries).

1973 L. Patrick Gray resigned as FBI director.

1981 Ringo Starr married Barbara Bach (see July 7, August 16, September 11 entries).

Born in Worcester, England, on this day in 1927, Sheila Christine Hopkins left school when she was sixteen years old, joining the Royal Naval Section of the VAD during the Second World War. Sheila joined a repertory company after the war, using the stage name of Sheila Scott. After an unsatisfying marriage and career, Sheila took her pilot's license and then took fifth place in the first race she entered in 1959. Seven years later, Sheila flew 31,000 miles in 189 hours over the course of thirty-three days, establishing the longest solo flight record in a single-engine plane. Sheila Scott set more than 100 flying records during her career, including an equator-to-equator solo flight over the North Pole in 1971.

Born in Belshill, Scotland, on this day in 1959, pop singer Sheena Easton is best known for her hit done in collaboration with Prince. "You've Got the Look" completely changed her previously innocent image to one that was seductive. On this same day in 1981, ex-Beatle Ringo Starr must have been thinking those very words when he married actress Barbara Bach in London, England.

28th.

1919 Leslie Irving made the first jump with a parachute using a ripcord.

1967 Muhammad Ali refused induction into the U.S. Army.

1968 The musical *Hair* opened on Broadway (see October 29 entry).

1969 Charles de Gaulle resigned his post as president of France (see June 1, November 22, December 21 entries).

1977 Christopher J. Boyce was convicted of selling secrets to the Soviet Union while working for a major U.S. defense contractor.

1981 The National Academy of Sciences declared that life does not begin at conception.

1982 Great Britain announced a total blockade around the Falkland Islands (see April 2, April 10, April 30 entries).

1990 The musical *A Chorus Line* closed on Broadway.

Sometimes, the only way to test a new theory is to take a leap of faith. On this day in 1919, Leslie Irving made the first jump with a parachute using a ripcord at McCook Field, Dayton, Ohio. It was the first time the U.S. Army Air Corps tested its new parachute design. And on this day in 1981, the National Academy of Sciences declared that there was no scientific validity to the concept that life begins at conception. The comment was a direct answer to a bill proposed by U.S. Senator Jesse Helms and Congressman Henry Hyde, which defined life as starting at conception.

29th.

1845   Macon B. Allen and Robert Morris, Jr., became the first African-Americans to practice law.

1899   Edward Kennedy "Duke" Ellington was born (see September 11 entry).

1958   Michelle Pfeiffer was born.

1970   Uma Thurman was born.

1975   The United States ended its involvement in Vietnam.

1983   Harold Washington was sworn in as Chicago's first African-American mayor.

1985   Colonel Frederick Gregory became the first African-American astronaut to pilot the space shuttle *Challenger* (see January 28, February 6, February 10, April 4, June 22, September 2, October 13 entries).

1992   A California jury acquitted four Los Angeles policemen in connection with the Rodney King beating (see March 3, April 16, August 4 entries).

1992   The State Farm Insurance Company was ordered to pay.

1993   Great Britain's Queen Elizabeth II announced that Buckingham Palace would be opened to tourists (see August 7 entry).

On this day in 1992, the State Farm Insurance Company was ordered to pay $157 million to more than 814 California women who were not offered or given jobs as State Farm agents. The largest sex discrimination settlement in American history, the case began when Muriel Kraszewski sued, in 1979, because she was repeatedly turned down for positions in California. The number of female agents increased from less than 1 percent in 1979 to more than 50 percent after the suit was settled.

Two modern beauties were born on this day. Born in Santa Ana, California, in 1958, Michelle Pfeiffer starred as Catwoman in the film *Batman Returns,* as a young and vulnerable sorceress in the film *The Witches of Eastwick,* and as a spoiled young heiress in the film *Wolf.* Born in Boston, Massachusetts, in 1970, Uma Thurman starred as a drug dealer's wife in the film *Pulp Fiction* and as the goddess Venus in the film *The Adventures of Baron Munchausen.*

The balance of tolerance often swings like a pendulum. In 1845 Macon B. Allen and Robert Morris, Jr., became the first African-Americans to practice law. On this same day in 1983, Harold Washington was sworn in as Chicago's first African-American mayor. And in 1992 a California jury acquitted four Los Angeles policemen of assault and excessive force in connection with the Rodney King beating. The verdict triggered violence and looting across the United States, resulting in fifty deaths.

Born on the same day as England's Duke of Wellington, Duke Ellington was a master strategist of the non-military kind. Born in Washington, D.C., on this day in 1899, Edward Kennedy "Duke" Ellington took only formal music lessons as a child. The rest of his training came from listening to the sounds in church and in burlesque shows. His first regular group, the Washingtonians, was formed after he moved to New York City in 1924. His band grew into an orchestra, and his reputation grew as they played in a long-term contract at Harlem's Cotton Club and made regular radio appearances over the next few years. During his lifetime, Ellington wrote over 2,000 pieces. "Sophisticated Lady" was one of his most famous creations.

On this day in 1993, Great Britain's Queen Elizabeth II announced that Buckingham Palace in London, England, would be opened to tourists for the first time in history to help raise money for repairs at the fire-damaged Windsor Castle.

A year after U.S. troops invaded Cambodia in 1970, U.S. President Richard Nixon said that a residual force of U.S. troops would remain in South Vietnam indefinitely if Hanoi refused to release American prisoners of war. And on this same day in 1975, the United States ended its involvement in Vietnam with the evacuation of almost 1,500 Americans and 5,500 South Vietnamese from Saigon.

30th.

1933   Willie Nelson was born.

1982   U.S. President Ronald Reagan declared American support for Great Britain and economic sanctions against Argentina in the Falklands War (see April 2, April 10, April 28 entries).

With a career that has spanned more than five decades, country music star Willie Nelson still shows no signs of hanging up his guitar. Born in Fort Worth, Texas, on this day in 1933, Nelson was writing his own songs when he was seven years old. He landed a job as a disc jockey at a local radio station right out of high school, and in 1956 he released his first single, "Lumberjack." Five years later, Nelson moved to Nashville, Tennessee, where he was accepted into the cast of the Grand Ole Opry and signed a contract with RCA Records. It was when he moved to Austin, Texas, and released his own form of outlaw country music on the Atlantic Records label, in 1973, that his star began to rise. During the 1970s and 1980s, Nelson's musical and film career remained frenetically busy. He's recorded over one hundred albums and appeared in films such as *The Electric Horseman* and *Honeysuckle Rose.*

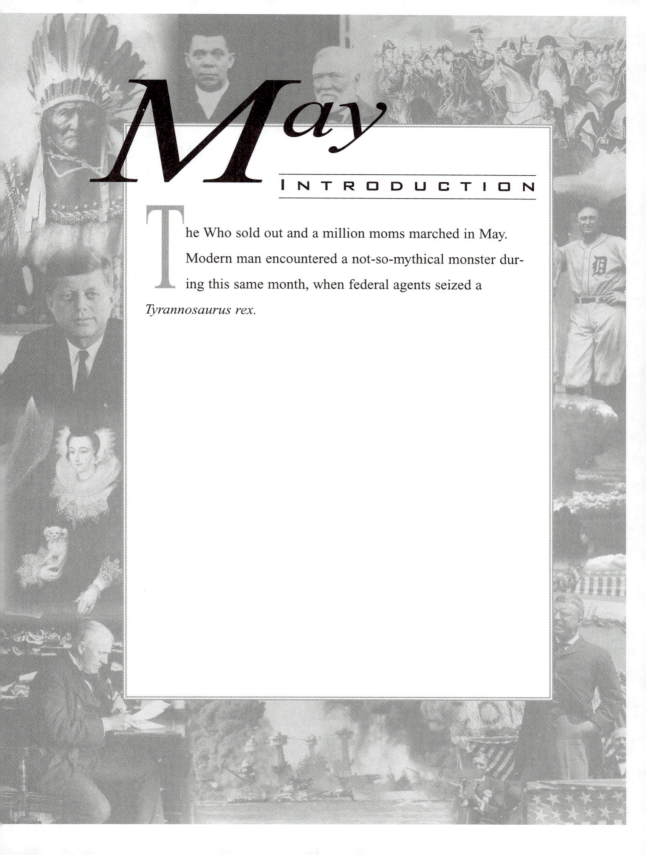

May

INTRODUCTION

The Who sold out and a million moms marched in May. Modern man encountered a not-so-mythical monster during this same month, when federal agents seized a *Tyrannosaurus rex*.

1st.

1893 The World's Columbian Exposition opened in Chicago, Illinois (see April 27, May 12, May 27 entries).

1923 Joseph Heller was born.

1924 Terry Southern was born.

1960 Francis Gary Powers's U-2 spy plane was shot down (see August 7 entry).

1961 The first American plane was hijacked to Cuba.

1966 The Beatles and The Rolling Stones played a concert.

1969 Bob Dylan and Johnny Cash taped a TV show (see May 12, May 24, June 7, July 25, July 31, August 9, August 17, September 11, December 8 entries).

1999 Conrad Anker found explorer George Mallory's body along the Northeast Ridge of Mount Everest (see June 8 entry).

Dark comedy found two new voices on this day. Born in Brooklyn, New York, in 1923, author Joseph Heller turned his Second World War experiences into the ironic novel *Catch-22*. The book's title became a catchphrase for bureaucratic absurdity when it grew from a slow seller to an international success. Born in Alvarado, Texas in 1924, screenplay writer Terry Southern once said, "The important thing in writing is the capacity to astonish." His satiric voice echoed the anti-establishment sentiments of the Sixties Generation in the films *Dr. Strangelove, Easy Rider, Barbarella, Candy,* and *The Magic Christian.*

The Cold War heated up on this day in 1960, when Soviet missiles brought down American pilot Francis Gary Powers's U-2 spy plane while he was flying over USSR territory. On this same day in 1961, the first American plane was hijacked for political purposes and forced to fly to Cuba.

1882 Baron Manfred von Richtoven was born.

1920 The National Negro Baseball League's first game was played in Indianapolis, Indiana (see January 4 entry).

1941 *Citizen Kane* premiered in New York City (see July 25 entry).

1990 The Mormon Church announced that it dropped some secret rituals that were considered offensive to women (see August 8, October 6, December 22 entries).

The skies blazed with gunfire during the First World War because of the man born on this day. Born in Schweidnitz, Germany, in 1882, Baron Manfred von Richtoven had initially joined the cavalry. But when the air force was formed, he immediately enlisted, becoming the commander of the Eleventh Chasing Squadron at the start of the war. As fighting continued, the group became known as Richtoven's Flying Circus. The commander quickly earned the name the Red Baron, winning eighty single-handed aerial battles before he was shot down behind British lines.

1494 Christopher Columbus sighted the island of Jamaica (see March 31, April 16, May 9, May 13, May 20, June 13, July 31, August 23, December 5 entries).

1849 Jacob A. Riis was born.

1923 Navy Lieutenant Oakley Kelly and Lieutenant John MacReady completed the first transcontinental air flight, landing at Coronado Beach, California.

1937 Margaret Mitchell won the Pulitzer Prize for *Gone with the Wind* (see June 10 entry).

1958 U.S. President Dwight D. Eisenhower proposed the demilitarization of Antarctica.

1971 National Public Radio made its premiere broadcast.

1977 The United States and Vietnam opened talks.

1989 Yasser Arafat urged peaceful relations.

Photojournalist Jacob A. Riis once said that the "poor were the victims rather than the makers of their fate." Born in Ribe, Denmark, on this day in 1849, Riis loudly vocalized this opinion. Unable to find work when he emigrated to New York in 1870, Riis slept in flea-ridden police station lodging houses. After three years of menial jobs, Riis found a spot at a news bureau. By 1877 he had become a *New York Tribune* police reporter. While he worked for the *New York Evening Sun* in 1888, his photos and account of urban poverty appeared in *Scribner's Magazine.* The next year, his book *How the Other Half Lives* gave an elongated depiction of slum conditions. It immediately prompted New York Police Commissioner Theodore Roosevelt to close down the lodging houses. It also encouraged city officials to establish the 1902 Tenement Law, which slightly improved municipal building codes. Riis never stopped lecturing or writing on this volatile topic until his death in 1914.

Peace was the general aim on this day. In 1977 the United States and Vietnam opened talks in Paris, France, to discuss the normalization of relations—two years after Communists had taken hold of the city of Saigon. In 1989 PLO leader Yasser Arafat ended his visit to France by stating that the PLO's mandate to destroy Israel had been superseded by a declaration to pursue peaceful relations between the two countries.

4th.

1960 The FDA approved the birth control pill.

1961 Commander Malcolm Ross and Lieutenant Commander Victor Prather launched their hot-air balloon *Strato Lab V.*

1989 Oliver North was convicted.

1994 U.S. President Bill Clinton signed the School-to-Work Opportunities Act.

2000 A prescribed burn went out of control and threatened Los Alamos National Laboratory.

This was a dark day in White House history in 1989. Former White House aide Oliver North was convicted for his involvement in the Iran-Contra affair. The court found him guilty of three charges, which included document shredding. It acquitted North, however, of nine other charges stemming from the same incident.

A prescribed burn of 1,000 acres intended to reduce the potential for future wildfires in New Mexico's Bandelier National Forest turned into a raging forest fire that damaged 50,000 acres and 400 homes when winds blew the flames out of control. The fires came dangerously close to the Los Alamos National Laboratory complex.

U.S. President Bill Clinton changed the American education system on this day in 1994. He signed the School-to-Work Opportunities Act, providing seed money to state and local governments to form partnerships among business, labor, government, education, and community organizations so that graduates could pay off student loans through special employment programs.

Ballooning rose to new heights on this day in 1961. Commander Malcolm Ross and Lieutenant Commander Victor Prather launched their hot-air balloon *Strato Lab V* from the deck of a U.S. Navy ship floating in the Gulf of Mexico. The team ascended to a record height of 113,740 feet before returning to earth.

The concept of planned parenthood in the United States was permanently changed on this day in 1960. The FDA approved a birth control pill that had been developed at the Worcester Center for Experimental Biology by Dr. John Rock.

5th.

1847 The American Medical Association was formed.

1871 The first professional baseball game was played in the United States.

1904 Cy Young pitched the American League's first perfect game (see August 6 entry).

1930 Amy Johnson began a solo flight from England to Australia.

1961   Commander Alan Shepard became the first American in outer space (see April 9 entry).

1978   The Italian terrorist group Red Brigade announced they would execute former premier Aldo Moro, whom they'd kidnapped (see March 16, May 9 entries).

1993   UN Secretary-General Boutros Boutros-Ghali recommended that a tribunal try those responsible for war crimes in Yugoslavia.

A major leap in aeronautical exploration occurred on this day in 1930. Amy Johnson began a solo flight from Croydon, England, in a de Haviland DH60 Gipsy Moth. She landed on May 24, 1930, in Port Darwin, Australia. No man or woman had ever attempted the 9,960-mile flight alone before.

Until this day in 1847, the American medical profession had no standards by which practitioners were tested and licensed to diagnose and treat patients. To protect their profession from malpractice, quacks, and snake-oil salesmen, doctors met in Philadelphia on this day to form the American Medical Association.

The skies opened to humankind on this day in 1961. Commander Alan Shepard became the first American in outer space when he made a brief suborbital flight in a single-passenger craft that was launched from Cape Canaveral, Florida.

The baseball world took the public stage more than once on this day. In 1871 the first professional baseball game was played in the United States. Two National Association teams—the Cleveland Forest Citys and the Fort Wayne Kekiongas—met at Fort Wayne, Indiana. And in 1904 Cy Young pitched the American League's first perfect game, when the Boston Red Sox beat the Philadelphia Athletics 3-0 at Philadelphia, Pennsylvania.

6th.

1856   Robert E. Peary was born.

1882   The U.S. Congress passed the Chinese Exclusion Act (see February 2, December 17 entries).

1915   Babe Ruth hit his first major league home run (see September 30 entry).

1931 Willie Mays was born.

1954 U.S. President Dwight D. Eisenhower signed the Federal-Aid Highway Act.

1974 West German Chancellor Willy Brandt resigned (see October 21 entry).

The way Americans traveled radically changed on this day in 1954. U.S. President Dwight D. Eisenhower signed the Federal-Aid Highway Act, authorizing the Interstate Highway System's construction through the use of 75 percent of federal transportation funds.

On this day in 1882, the U.S. Congress passed the Chinese Exclusion Act, hoping to stop the massive wave of Asian immigration. Railroad construction, housework, and gold rushes enticed many Chinese peasants to seek their fortune in the United States. The act banned Chinese immigration for ten years.

It took two years for Robert E. Peary to be honored with the distinction of being the first man to reach the North Pole. Born in Cresson, Pennsylvania, on this day in 1856, Peary had made eight Arctic voyages along the Greenland coast, starting in 1891. He fell three degrees short of his goal in 1906, but succeeded in April 1909. Dr. Frederick Cook claimed to have made it to the pole in 1908, but Copenhagen University determined in 1911 that he hadn't even come close, making Peary the official winner.

Some political careers fail not because of the person, but because of his or her staff members. Such was the case on this day in 1974, when West German Chancellor Willy Brandt resigned after it was disclosed that one of his staff members was an East German spy.

On the same day that Babe Ruth hit his first major league home run in 1915, another baseball great was born. In 1931 Willie Mays was born in Westfield, Alabama.

7th.

1919 Eva De Duarte (Evita) Perón was born.

1984 Agent Orange victims reach a settlement with the U.S. government.

Evita Perón was revered by many Argentinians as a champion of social welfare. Born into abject poverty in Los Toldos, Argentina, on this day in 1919, Eva De Duarte was the youngest of five children raised by their mother. As she herself commented, "I remember I was very sad for many days when I discovered that in the world there were poor people and rich people; and the strange thing is that the existence of the poor did not cause me as much pain as the knowledge that at the same time there were people who were rich." When she was 15 she ran away to Buenos Aires with a tango singer. She worked as a model and an actress before she met and married Argentine President Juan Péron in 1945. Politically astute, Evita helped her husband secure his position with the general populace, not just the estate owners, until her death in 1952.

A major wrong was acknowledged on this day in 1984. American veterans of the Vietnam War had filed a class action suit, claiming that they suffered permanent injury from exposure to the defoliant Agent Orange. The federal government announced an agreement to a $180-million out-of-court settlement with the defendants.

8th.

1932   Sonny Liston was born (see February 25 entry).

1980   The first transcontinental hot-air balloon flight was attempted (see June 27, August 12 entries).

1984   The Soviet Union withdrew from the 1984 Los Angeles Summer Olympics, citing fears over security for its athletes.

The first transcontinental hot-air balloon flight was attempted on this day in 1980. Maxie Anderson and his twenty-three-year-old son, Kristian, took off in their balloon *Kitty Hawk* from Fort Baker, California, in the hopes of making history.

One of twenty-five brothers and sisters, Charles Sonny Liston had a rough start in life, serving time in prison for armed robbery. Born in St. Francis County, Arkansas, on this day in 1932, Liston learned how to box while he was incarcerated. He'd turned professional by the time he was 21, knocking out formidable contenders until, in 1962, he became heavyweight champion of the world. Defeating Floyd Patterson in one round, Liston agreed to a rematch less than a year later. But he again managed to knock out Patterson in one round. Sonny Liston kept his title for only two years. In 1964, he was defeated by Cassius Clay (aka Muhammed Ali). Liston continued fighting until his mysterious death in 1970.

9th.

1502   Christopher Columbus set sail on his fourth voyage (see March 31, April 16, May 3, May 13, May 20, June 13, July 31, August 23, December 5 entries).

1865   Elizabeth Garver Jordan was born.

1962   The Beatles signed a recording contract with EMI's Parlophone Records (see January 1, January 20, January 24, January 30, February 7, February 9, February 12, June 6, June 12, August 29 entries).

1978   Aldo Moro was found dead in a car parked in Rome, Italy (see March 16, May 5 entries).

1979   The SALT II nuclear arms treaty was signed.

1982   U.S. President Ronald Reagan proposed a reduction of nuclear warheads.

Joseph Pulitzer hired more than one female reporter to work on his newspaper, the *New York World.* Although Nellie Bly's name is better known, Elizabeth Garver Jordan was no less notable. Born in Armstrong County, Pennsylvania, in 1865, Jordan covered the Lizzie Borden trial and specialized in interviews for Pulitzer's newspaper. She also edited *Harper's Bazaar* and served as editorial director for Harper & Brothers publishers during her long career.

Nuclear disarmament went to the discussion table more than once on this day. In 1979 the United States and the Soviet Union came to a basic agreement on the SALT II nuclear arms treaty. Sadly, the U.S. Senate never ratified the accord. And in 1982 President Ronald Reagan proposed that the United States and the Soviet Union each reduce their nuclear warheads on both land and sea by one-third.

10th.

1924   J. Edgar Hoover was named director of the FBI (see November 18 entry).

1940   Sadaharu Oh was born.

1948   President Harry S Truman ordered the U.S. Army to operate the railroads.

1957   Sid Vicious was born.

1957   Steve and Phil Mahre were born.

1960   Bono Vox was born.

1963   The Rolling Stones went into their first recording session (see January 15, May 12, June 1, June 3, June 14, July 30, October 25, December 5, December 6, December 18 entries).

1968   The Vietnam peace talks began.

1969   The Turtles and The Temptations played at the White House.

1974   The Who sold out Madison Square Garden.

1980   The U.S. federal government gave conditional approval to a loan.

1982   A British warship opened fire on an Argentine vessel.

The federal government intervened in big business on two different occasions on this day. In 1948 President Harry S Truman ordered the Army to operate the railroads, hoping to prevent a nationwide rail strike. This major arm of industry wasn't deregulated until 1952. In 1980 the federal government gave conditional approval to $1.5 billion in federal loan guarantees to aid the Chrysler Corporation.

The rock and punk music worlds witnessed some major events on this day. In 1957 the Sex Pistols' Sid Vicious was born under the name Simon Ritchie in London, England. In 1960 U2's lead singer Bono Vox was born with the name Paul Hewson in Dublin, Ireland. In 1963 The Rolling Stones worked on their first recording session, taping at London's Olympic Studios. In 1969 The Turtles and The Temptations played Tricia Nixon's White House Masque Ball. And in 1974 The Who sold out seats for all four nights at New York's Madison Square Garden in less than eight hours.

Major international sports figures were born on this day. In 1940 the Tokyo Giants' first baseman, Sadaharu Oh, was born in Tokyo, Japan. During his career, this all-time home run leader in Japanese baseball hit 868 home runs. And in 1957 Olympic gold and silver medalist skiers Steve Mahre and his twin brother Phil were born in Yakima, Washington. Both brothers won medals at the 1984 Winter Olympics in slalom events.

War and peace both began on this day. In 1968 the Vietnam peace talks began in Paris, France. And in 1982 Great Britain reported that one of its warships had opened fire on a large Argentine vessel near the Falkland Islands.

11th.

1720   Baron Karl Friedrich Hieronymus von Munchhausen was born.

1928   WGY-TV in Schenectady, New York, began scheduled broadcasts three times a week.

1978   China accused the Soviet Union of conducting border raids.

1979   China and the United States signed an agreement.

1997   IBM's Deep Blue computer defeated chess champion Gary Kasparov (see February 10 entry).

The king of tall tales was born in Bodenwerder, Germany, on this day in 1720. Baron Karl Friedrich Hieronymus von Munchhausen had served with the Russian army against the Turks, which inspired a number of exaggerated stories about his exploits. His tales, combined with sixteenth-century German jokes and the lives of other fantastic travelers such as James Bruce, inspired author Rudolf Erich Raspe to publish his book *Baron Munchhausen's Narrative of His Marvelous Travels and Campaigns in Russia,* which was released in English in 1885. During the last half of the twentieth century, the baron was the subject of three feature films.

China resolved a few territorial disputes on this day. In 1978 China accused the Soviet Union of conducting border raids across the Ussuri River. In 1979 China and the United States signed an agreement to settle claims over property confiscated during the 1940s Chinese revolution.

12th.

1918   Julius Rosenberg was born in New York City (see March 29, April 5, June 19 entries).

1925   Yogi Berra was born.

1937   George VI was crowned king, succeeding his brother Edward VIII, who had abdicated the British throne (see February 6, August 4, December 14 entries).

1942   Ian Drury was born.

1963   Bob Dylan refused to play "The Ed Sullivan Show" (see May 1, May 24, June 7, July 25, July 31, August 9, August 17, September 11, December 8 entries).

1965   West Germany and Israel established diplomatic relations.

1967   Pink Floyd played the first quadraphonic rock concert.

1967   The Rolling Stones played the *New Music Express* Reader Poll Winner's Concert (see January 15, May 10, June 3, June 14, July 30, October 25, December 5, December 6, December 18 entries).

1969   General Motors announced the end of the rear-engine Corvair.

1971   Mick Jagger married Bianca Moreno (see July 26, December 18 entries).

1982   Guards thwarted an assassin with a bayonet before he could reach Pope John Paul II while he toured the shrine at Fatima, Portugal (see May 13, May 18, June 2, July 22, October 4 entries).

1984   The New Orleans World's Fair opened (see April 27, May 1, May 27 entries).

Safety sometimes overrides profits even in big business. On this day in 1969, General Motors announced the end of production of the rear-engine Corvair. Outside sources and the media had strongly criticized the car as being unsafe; other rear-engine cars such as the Volkswagen had thrived without incident.

Molds are often made to be broken. And Ian Drury, who was born in Upminster, England, on this day in 1942, was just such a case. Although his parents were middle-class, Drury was sent to the Royal Grammar School as a boarder after he'd recovered from a bout with polio. He learned to loathe pretension while he was there. Although he studied art and had been an illustrator during the early 1970s, his heart seemed set on songwriting and singing. His break came when he formed Ian Drury and the Blockheads in 1977 and signed with Stiff Records. Two albums and two years later, the band's biggest single, "Hit Me with Your Rhythm Stick," made it to the top of the charts, selling nearly a million records. Before his death in 2000, Drury turned to television and theater work, writing the theme song for the BBC-TV series *The Diary of Adrian Mole* and tunes for the Royal Shakespeare Company's productions at Stratford-upon-Avon.

The rock music world made the news on both sides of the Atlantic Ocean on this day. In 1963 Bob Dylan refused to play "The Ed Sullivan Show" because producers wouldn't allow him to sing "Talking John Birch Society Blues." In 1967 The Rolling Stones played the *New Music Express* Reader Poll Winner's Concert in London. That exact same day, Pink Floyd played the first quadraphonic rock concert at Elizabeth Hall, England. A rock wedding also took place on this day in 1971, when Rolling Stone Mick Jagger married model Bianca Moreno.

St. Louis Cardinals general manager Branch Rickey once commented that he thought New York Yankees great Yogi Berra would "never make anything more than a Triple A ballplayer at best." Born in St. Louis, Missouri, on this day in 1925, Lawrence Peter Berra was offered $250 to play for the Cardinals in the same year Joe Garagiola had been offered $500. Yogi turned them down and accepted a $500 offer from the Yankees in 1942. After the Second World War, Berra played in fourteen World Series, hitting the first pinch-hit home run in the championship's history in 1947. He eventually put down his bat, becoming the Yankees manager in 1964. Eight years later he became manager of the New York Mets. Yogi is the only manager to guide both the Yankees (1964) and the Mets (1973) to the World Series.

13th.

1494 Christopher Columbus landed in Jamaica (see March 31, April 16, May 3, May 9, May 20, June 13, July 31, August 23, December 5 entries).

1914 Joe Louis was born (see June 15, September 24 entries).

1941 Richie Valens was born (see February 3 entry).

1950 Stevie Wonder was born.

1971 The U.S. Senate's sergeant-at-arms refused to swear in three female pages.

1981 Pope John Paul II was seriously wounded in St. Peter's Square by a Turkish gunman (see May 12, May 18, June 2, July 22, October 4 entries).

1982 Braniff became the first major airline to file for bankruptcy.

1985 A police helicopter bombed a Philadelphia row house.

The best-laid strategy can go bust, as it did on this day in 1985. A police helicopter bombed a Philadelphia row house, which ended a twenty-four-hour armed confrontation with a radical political group known as MOVE. A fire started and raged out of control, destroying sixty-one houses in the neighborhood and killing eleven people.

Some talents shine brightly even when they're very young. Such was the case of singer Richie Valens, who was born in Pacoima, California, on this day in 1941. Valens's star sparkled when he hit the top of the charts with songs like "La Bamba" and "Donna" before dying in a plane crash while on tour at the age of 17. Stevie Wonder's star has never dimmed since he rose to stardom at the age of 11, when his album *Little Stevie Wonder* topped the charts. Born in Saginaw, Michigan, on this day in 1950, Stevie Wonder also led the campaign to make Martin Luther King, Jr.'s birthday a national holiday.

The gender gap became very public in the U.S. Senate on this day in 1971. The senate's sergeant-at-arms refused to swear in three female pages who had been nominated by the senators until the Rules Committee specifically approved them. What made this a unique situation was that male pages were routinely sworn without any question of protocol.

Born in Lafayette, Alabama, on this day in 1914, Joe Louis Barrow was raised in the Black Bottom district of Detroit, Michigan, from the time he was four years old. Attracted to boxing, Louis worked at the Ford Motor Company plant during the day and took boxing lessons at night. After fifty wins as an amateur boxer and only four losses, Louis went professional, becoming heavyweight champion after he knocked out Max Baer in 1935. But the next year, German boxer Max Schmeling defeated Louis. Louis made his comeback the following year, defeating James Braddock and then knocking out Schmeling in the first round of a rematch. By the time Louis retired, in 1945, he had defended his title twenty-five times.

14th.

1992 Federal agents seized a *Tyrannosaurus rex* named Sue.

2000 The Million Mom March took place.

Instigated by Donna Dees-Thomases from suburban New Jersey, the Million Mom March took place in Washington, D.C. on this day in 2000 as a grassroots protest against handguns in the United States. An estimated 750,000 people attended in support of more sensible gun control legislation.

A dinosaur became a point of legal concern on this day in 1992. Sue is the world's largest and most complete *Tyrannosaurus rex* skeleton, standing forty feet long and weighing nearly eight tons. When the Black Hills Institute of Geological Research carefully unearthed Sue from a site near Faith, South Dakota, federal agents arrived with a warrant and seized the dinosaur on this day. Government officials claimed that Sue was found on land leased by the government to the Cheyenne River Sioux. A year later, a U.S. district court ruled that Sue had been an integral part of rancher Maurice Williams's land and, therefore, belonged to him and the Bureau of Indian Affairs, which allowed him to sell Sue to the Institute for $5,000. Sue ended up at the Chicago Field Museum, which purchased it at a Sotheby's auction in New York for $8.36 million.

15th.

1963   U.S. astronaut L. Gordon Cooper went on the final Mercury space mission, orbiting the earth twenty-two times in thirty-four hours (see April 9 entry).

1972   Alabama Governor George Wallace was shot by Arthur Bremer in Laurel, Maryland.

1973   The U.S. House of Representatives cut off funding for American bombing operations in Cambodia.

1982   British troops staged a raid on Argentine aircraft and military installations in the Falkland Islands.

1989   The first Sino-Soviet summit in thirty years began.

On this day in 1972, Alabama Governor George Wallace was shot by Arthur Bremer in Laurel, Maryland. Wallace was campaigning for the presidential nomination when the assassination attempt occurred. He was left partially paralyzed by his injuries.

For the first time in thirty years, the Russians and Chinese met on peaceful terms. The first Sino-Soviet summit began when Soviet President Mikhail Gorbachev arrived in Beijing, China, on this day in 1989. The meetings were overshadowed by pro-democracy demonstrations led by Chinese students.

War efforts were turned on and off on this day. In 1973 the U.S. House of Representatives voted to cut off funding for American bombing operations in Cambodia. And in 1982

British troops staged a raid on Argentine aircraft and military installations in the Falkland Islands.

16th.

1939   The first food stamp program began in Rochester, New York (see June 4 entry).

1955   Olga Korbut was born.

1957   Joan Benoit was born.

1982   Yugoslavia elected its first female prime minister, Milka Planinc.

1988   U.S. Surgeon General C. Everett Koop declared that nicotine is as addictive as heroin and cocaine (see January 2, January 10, April 11, July 17, August 1, September 28, December 1 entries).

Two female Olympic gold medalists were born on this day. In 1957 Joan Benoit was born in Maine. A Boston marathon winner, Benoit won the 1984 Olympic gold medal for the 26-mile marathon. It was the first time the race was an Olympic event. Born in Grodno, Byelorussia, on this day in 1955, gymnast Olga Korbut won three 1972 Olympic gold medals.

17th.

1900   Ayatollah Ruhollah Khomeini was born.

1903   James "Cool Papa" Bell was born.

1956   Sugar Ray Leonard was born.

1979   A presidential investigation panel canceled hearings into Three-Mile Island nuclear accident.

1980   A racial riot took place in Miami, Florida.

1989   The Roman Catholic Church was legalized in Poland.

1998   An artifact was found near the Queen Charlotte Islands.

The justice system doesn't always run smoothly. On this day in 1979, a presidential investigatory panel canceled hearings over the accident at the Three Mile Island nuclear power plant. The panel members claimed that they were unable to take testimony from witnesses under oath.

A Miami court handed down an unpopular decision on this day in 1980. The jury acquitted four former police officers who were accused of mortally beating an African-American suspect. Because the defendants and jury were all white, African-American ghetto residents rioted when news of the decision hit the streets, leaving fourteen people dead.

An unyielding religious and political force was born in Iran on this day in 1900. Ayatollah Ruhollah Khomeini was a devout Shiite Muslim who publicly opposed the westernization of his homeland under Shah Mohammed Reza Pahlavi's regime. He was exiled, in 1964, to Turkey, Iraq, and France for his outspokenness. When the Shah's government collapsed in 1979, Khomeini returned in triumph to Iran, where the people installed him as head of state. Khomeini instigated the Islamic Revolution, forcing the populace to return to strict Muslim values and traditions, which had been abandoned under the shah. Before his death in 1989, he received strong international criticism when he called for the death of author Salman Rushdie.

Religious freedom in Poland took a giant step on this day in 1989. The government officially granted freedom of religion to Poles, legalizing the Roman Catholic Church for the first time in decades.

A team led by archaeologist Daryl Fedje of Canada's national parks system found a 4-inch basalt cutting tool in the Juan Perez Sound a half mile off the Queen Charlotte Islands, British Columbia, on this day in 1998. Dredged up from 170-foot-deep waters, the artifact was dated as being made well before the end of the Ice Age, when the sea level was far lower than it is now.

Two sports greats share this particular birthday. Born in Starkville, Mississippi, on this day in 1903, James Thomas Bell is thought to be the fastest man to ever play professional baseball. Nicknamed "Cool Papa," Bell's style revolutionized baseball. He stole two bases on a single pitch, and he scored from first on an infield bunt. Bell was paid $90 a month when he began his career as a left-handed knuckleball pitcher with the St. Louis Stars in 1922. He played for numerous teams before the Kansas City Monarchs hired him to manage their team in 1948, where he mentored another baseball great, Ernie Banks. World welterweight champion Sugar Ray Leonard was born in Wilmington, North Carolina, on this day in 1956. He won an Olympic gold medal in 1976 and three years later gained his world title. With thirty-six wins out of thirty-nine bouts, Leonard retired in 1991 after losing to Terry Norris.

18th.

1878	Colombia granted a concession to build the Panama Canal (see April 18, August 10, September 7, November 2, November 3, December 31 entries).
1897	Frank Capra was born.
1919	Dame Margot Fonteyn was born (see March 17 entry).
1920	Karol Wojtyla was born in Wadowice, Poland (see May 12, May 13, June 2, July 22, October 4 entries).
1948	The sound barrier was broken by a female pilot.
1969	The *Apollo 10* mission was launched (see June 5 entry).
1974	India set off its first atomic explosion, becoming the world's sixth nuclear power.
1979	The Karen Silkwood estate was awarded $10.5 million (see May 19, November 13 entries).
1994	Palestinians began self-rule.

Justice doesn't always come swiftly. On this day in 1979, an Oklahoma City federal jury awarded $10.5 million to the estate of Karen Silkwood, a technician contaminated by radiation while working for the Kerr-McGee Corporation, which produced plutonium fuels. She became an activist on behalf of plant safety and died in a car crash.

Two legendary entertainers were born on this day. In 1919 Dame Margot Fonteyn was born in Reigate, England. A prima ballerina with London's Royal Ballet during her entire career, Fonteyn gained an even greater reputation when she partnered with Russia's finest ballet dancer of the 1960s, Rudolf Nureyev. Born in Palermo, Sicily, in 1897, film director Frank Capra emigrated with his family to the United States when he was six years old. Although he studied chemical engineering, he quickly moved into the film industry after graduation, working as a slapstick comedy writer until the 1930s. His 1934 film *It Happened One Night* won oscars for best picture, best director, best actor, best actress, and best screenplay. Ironically, his 1946 Christmas classic *It's a Wonderful Life* was a commercial flop, and his favorite film, *The Bitter Tea of General Yen,* never received the accolades that his earlier projects earned.

The sound barrier was broken by a woman on this day in 1948. Although it wasn't her first record flight, pilot Jacqueline Cochran flew an F-86 Sabre jet to accomplish this death-defying feat.

The tides of power changed more than once on this day. In 1878 Colombia granted a ninety-nine-year concession to a French company that intended to build the Panama Canal. In 1994 Palestinians began a regime of self-rule after twenty-seven years of Israeli military occupation.

The moon was the target of the *Apollo 10* manned satellite, which was launched on this day in 1969. Astronauts Eugene A. Cernan, Thomas P. Stafford, and John W. Young made the first lunar orbit during this historic mission.

19th.

1913   The Webb Alien Land-Holding Bill was signed.

1930   Lorraine Hansberry was born (see March 11 entry).

1941   Nora Ephron was born (see May 18, November 13 entries).

1945   Pete Townshend was born.

1952   Grace Jones was born.

1952   Joey Ramone was born.

1967   Nuclear weapons were banned in outer space.

Lorraine Hansberry's star shone brightly but briefly. Born in Chicago, Illinois, on this day in 1930, Hansberry was the first African-American female playwright to have her work produced on Broadway. *A Raisin in the Sun* played to critical and public acclaim. But sadly, Hansberry died at the age of 34.

Limitations were placed on Japanese living in the United States on this day in 1913. The California state legislature signed the Webb Alien Land-Holding Bill, which excluded Japanese from owning land in that coastal state.

Nora Ephron, was born in New York City on this day in 1941. Ephron worked as a journalist for *Esquire, The New York Times,* and *New York Magazine* before pursuing her work as an author and screenwriter. Her novel *Heartburn* was partially based on her own divorce.

Three unique musical talents were born on this day. Born in London, England, in 1945, composer and guitarist Pete Townshend wrote and performed most of The Who's chart-busting hits during the 1960s and 1970s. His "windmill" guitar-playing style and his habit of smashing instruments on stage delighted the band's thousands of fans. Townshend wrote the world's first rock opera, *Tommy,* which the band performed during the 1960s. It was made into a major motion picture in the 1970s and a Broadway musical in the 1990s. Born in Spanishtown, Jamaica, on this day in 1952, singer Grace Jones made her first mark as a model. Her exotic looks and hauntingly deep voice attracted a post-punk audience during the 1980s. Born in Forest Hills, New York, on this day in 1952, Joey Ramone and his band the Ramones stimulated punk fans during the late 1970s with hits such as "I Wanna Be Sedated" and "Rock and Roll High School." He died of lymphoma on April 15, 2001.

Outer space became a safer place on this day in 1967. The USSR ratified a treaty with the United States and Great Britain banning the shipment or use of nuclear weapons in deep space.

20th.

1506 Christopher Columbus died in poverty in Spain (see March 31, April 16, May 3, May 9, May 13, June 13, July 31, August 23, December 5 entries).

1777 The Cherokee Nation ceded all of their lands in South Carolina to the federal government when they signed the DeWitts Corner Treaty (see May 23, July 20, September 16, December 29 entries).

1915 Moshe Dayan was born (see October 21 entry).

1944 Joe Cocker was born.

1946 Cher was born.

1984 Isabel Péron returned to Argentina to lead a Péronist delegation in talks with President Raul Alfonsin.

1989 Beijing officials ordered CBS and CNN to end their live-on-scene reports of the pro-democracy protests.

1993 The ban against assisted suicides of terminally ill patients was lifted.

1993   The motor-voter bill went into effect, allowing eligible citizens to register to vote when they apply for or renew their driver's licenses.

A pair of strong musical voices were born on this day. In 1944 singer Joe Cocker was born in Sheffield, England. Known for his ability to belt out heart-pounding songs like "Delta Lady" and "Feelin' Alright" during the 1960s and 1970s, Cocker rose to fame during his Mad Dogs and Englishmen tour accompanied by Leon Russell and Delaney Bramlett. Born in El Centro, California, on this day in 1946, Cher first rose to fame when she recorded "I Got You Babe" with her husband, Sonny Bono, during the 1960s. After a successful TV variety series, numerous musical hits, and tours of the nightclub circuit, Cher became an actress, earning an Academy Award for her role in *Moonstruck.*

The ban against assisted suicides of terminally ill patients was lifted on this day in 1993. Although the state of Michigan had added the ban to an existing legislative bill, Wayne County Circuit Judge Cynthia Stephens struck down the addition, deeming it unconstitutional.

Born in Palestine on this day in 1915, Moshe Dayan was a founder of the Haganah underground militia, which fought for an independent state of Israel. Arrested and imprisoned by the British for two years, Dayan was released in 1941 to enlist in the British Army during the Second World War. He lost an eye in battle, but that didn't handicap him. When Israel won its freedom in 1948, Dayan became an officer in the Israeli army, rising to chief of staff during the 1956 Suez War. Dayan entered politics three years later and eventually was appointed defense minister. His orchestration of the Israeli victory during the Six-Day War made him a national hero until his defeat during the 1973 war. Dayan turned to peace when he became foreign minister in 1977, negotiating a reasonable treaty between Israel and Egypt.

21st.

1867   Frances Theresa Densmore was born.

1904   Fats Waller was born.

1921   Andrei Sakharov was born.

1932   Amelia Earhart flew a solo 2,026-mile flight from Newfoundland to Ireland in 14 hours, 56 minutes (see January 11, May 25, July 24, August 24 entries).

1951   Tibet conceded to takeover by the Chinese government.

1956   The United States exploded the first airborne hydrogen bomb in the Pacific Ocean.

The musical traditions of Native Americans were preserved for posterity thanks to Frances Theresa Densmore, who was born in Red Wing, Minnesota, on this day in 1867. During her long career, Densmore photographed, documented, and recorded musical performers in more than thirty tribes. She recorded nearly 2,500 songs before she died at the age of 87. Over 448 recording cylinders from her collection are still housed in the Library of Congress.

Born in New York City on this day in 1904, Thomas "Fats" Waller became a professional pianist by the time he was 15. His father—a minister—had hoped he'd follow in his footsteps. But during the 1920s, Waller played with blues singers like Bessie Smith. Then he started writing songs that have become classics, like "Ain't Misbehavin'," "Honeysuckle Rose," "Keepin' Out of Mischief Now," and "Blue Turning Gray Over You."

Physicist Andrei Sakharov was a key figure in the development of the Soviet hydrogen bomb, becoming the youngest member of the Soviet Academy of Sciences in 1953. Born in Moscow, Russia, on this day in 1921, Sakharov quickly fell into disfavor with government authorities when he publicly supported an international nuclear test-ban treaty and improved civil rights in the Soviet Union during the 1960s. His passionate campaigns earned him the 1975 Nobel Peace Prize. But five years later he was exiled by Soviet officials to the "closed city" of Gorky. In 1986 Mikhail Gorbachev personally authorized Sakharov's release. And before his death in 1989, he was elected to the Congress of the Soviet Union's People's Deputies.

22nd.

1972   Ceylon was declared a republic and renamed Sri Lanka.

1973   The Ethernet was conceived.

1992 NBC's "Tonight Show" host, Johnny Carson, retired after a nearly thirty-year run.

1995 The U.S. Supreme Court decided that states could not set term limits of federal officials.

A doctoral candidate gave birth to the Ethernet on this day in 1973. Six years before Robert Metcalfe founded the 3Com Corporation, he wrote a thirteen-page description of what would become known as the Ethernet network for his Harvard doctoral thesis. Based on his theory, Metcalfe and David Boggs later created a 2.944 Mbps connection between computers, which they named after the two nineteenth-century scientists who proved that the so-called ether didn't exist: Michelson and Morley.

A landmark decision on the fate of term limits was made on this day in 1995. The U.S. Supreme Court voted 5-4 that individual states could not limit the length of service an elected politician spent in the Senate or the House of Representatives without first amending the Constitution.

1838 General Winfield Scott ordered the forced removal of the Cherokee Nation (see May 20, July 20, September 16, December 29 entries).

1873 The Mounties were born.

1934 Robert Moog was born.

1939 A diving bell was used for the first time as a rescue vehicle.

1956 The U.S. Congress passed the Soil Bank Act.

1984 U.S. Surgeon General C. Everett Koop cited "very solid" evidence showing that a nonsmoker's exposure to secondary cigarette smoke could lead to lung cancer (see January 2, January 10, April 11, July 17, August 1, August 24, September 28, December 1 entries).

1988 The FDA approved the cervical cap for use in the U.S.

1991 The U.S. Supreme Court ruled that the federal government could prevent doctors and nurses from giving medical advice.

The federal government chose to help farmers who didn't plant crops on this day in 1956. The U.S. Congress passed the Soil Bank Act, authorizing the government to pay farmers who didn't raise corn, wheat, peanuts, cotton, tobacco, or rice for one season to stop the leeching of valuable topsoil by these nutrient-greedy crops.

A diving bell was used for the first time as a rescue vehicle on this day in 1939. When the U.S. Navy submarine *Squalus* sank off the New Hampshire coast with a crew of fifty-nine people, a diving bell was sent down with a rescue crew. Thanks to this daring scheme, thirty-three people were saved.

This was the start of a dark period in Native American history. In 1838 General Winfield Scott ordered the forced removal of the Cherokee Indians from the East to a designated "Indian Nation." Ten thousand men, women, and children were marched to the territory that's now known as Oklahoma along the Trail of Tears. Approximately one-fourth of the evacuees died along the way.

Canada's vast Northwest Territories spanned from Hudson Bay west to the Pacific coast. This untamed wilderness was the home for numerous native Métis tribes like the Assinibone and Athabascan. It also attracted many new settlers and opportunists from the East and from the United States. Naturally clashes occurred. In May 1873, however, a massacre of Métis men, women, and children by American wolf hunters prompted Canadian Prime Minister Sir John A. MacDonald to order the formation of a police force: the North West Mounted Rifles. (Political protests from the United States, however, forced a name change to the North West Mounted Police.) On this day in 1873, an army of 275 Mounties headed by Commissioner George Arthur French began their march to Fort Dufferin in Manitoba. Dedicated to the responsible treatment of the Métis as well as the enforcement of the peace, the Mounties rapidly gained an impressive reputation for fairness and efficiency during Canada's early history.

The father of synthesized music was born in New York City on this day in 1934. Originally a physicist, Robert Moog opened the R.A. Moog Company in 1954 as a part-time business that designed and manufactured electronic musical instruments. Years later it became a full-time profession when he introduced his Moog synthesizer, which electronically produced musical sounds on a keyboard. In 1978 Moog relocated to North Carolina, where he began development of more innovative music delivery systems and MIDI interfaces.

The questions of contraception and abortion highlighted this day in United States history. Although the cervical cap had been available in Germany and Hungary for over a century, it took the rest of Europe a few decades to take the concept beyond the home-made beeswax-and-linen device to a commercial contraceptive. On this day in 1988, the FDA finally approved a safe, manufactured cervical cap for use by women in the United States. On this day in 1991, the U.S. Supreme Court handed down a decision in the case of *Rust v. Sullivan* that the federal government could prevent doctors and nurses in federally funded clinics from giving medical advice about abortion to women, even if the pregnancy was a life-threatening situation.

24th.

1860 George Washington Carver was born.

1878 Lillian Moller Gilbreth was born.

1935 The first major league baseball game to be played at night took place.

1938 Tommy Chong was born (see July 13 entry).

1941 Bob Dylan was born (see May 1, May 12, June 7, July 25, July 31, August 9, August 17, September 11, December 8 entries).

1962 Astronaut M. Scott Carpenter became the second American to be launched into orbit (see April 9 entry).

1975 President Gerald Ford approved aid for the resettlement of South Vietnamese and Cambodian refugees.

1979 The United Airlines strike ended.

There weren't many female industrial engineers in the workplace when Lillian Moller Gilbreth was born in Oakland, California, on this day in 1878. But when she married Frank Bunker Gilbreth, she found her true calling. She made detailed studies of the basic elements of manual labor, like search, find, grasp, and assemble, calling them therbligs. Together the Gilbreths established the theory of scientific business management while raising twelve children. The Gilbreths' life together was immortalized by two of their children, who wrote the play and screenplay *Cheaper by the Dozen*.

Born in Edmonton, Alberta, on this day in 1938, Tommy Chong was given a guitar by his Chinese father and Scottish-Irish mother for his eleventh birthday. He formed Canada's first R&B band, The Shades, while he was in high school. Right after the group moved to Vancouver, Chong bought his own after-hours bistro called the Elegant Parlour, and The Shades recorded Chong's 1965 hit "Does Your Mama Know about Me?" for Motown Records. While on the road, Chong became fascinated by improvisational comedy. He hurried home to Vancouver and started doing stand-up at his brother's club, Shanghai Junk. "It was a topless joint and I didn't have the heart to fire the strippers," recalls Chong, "so when I turned the show into a comedy troupe known as 'City Works,' I put the girls in the skits. We had the only topless improvisational theatre in Canada." That's where he met Cheech Marin. They headed south because they were tired of the cold weather. While playing at Los Angeles's Troubadour Club, they were spotted by a record executive, who signed them to do their first gold album, *Cheech & Chong*.

Robert Allen Zimmerman was born in Duluth, Minnesota, on this day in 1941. He taught himself to play piano and guitar when he was a teen, and he played local clubs while attending the University of Minnesota. He changed his name to Bob Dylan because he thought it sounded better. Moving to New York City in 1961, Bob Dylan played clubs in Greenwich Village like Gerde's Folk City and visited his idol, Woody Guthrie, who was hospitalized with Huntington's chorea. The next year, Dylan released his first album of many original songs and was labeled a protest singer. During the 1960s, Dylan's numerous hits evolved from folk music to electric rock. His 1966 album *Blonde on Blonde* sold over 10 million copies and featured such hits as "Rainy Day Women #12 & 35" and "Just Like a Woman." During the 1970s and 1980s his music continued to evolve until he formed the Traveling Wilburys with former Beatle George Harrison, former Electric Light Orchestra leader Jeff Lynne, Tom Petty, and Roy Orbison in 1988. Dylan was toasted at the Kennedy Center for his artistic excellence in 1997.

Born in Newton County, Missouri, on this day in 1865, George Washington Carver was orphaned as an infant and raised by farmers Moses and Susan Carver. When he was twelve years old Carver went to school, supporting himself on odd jobs. By the time he was 20, he had built his own home, which he sold before moving to Iowa so he could continue his education. Although he studied art and actually had a painting exhibited at the World's Columbian Exposition in Chicago, his teachers encouraged him to study botany. Earning a master's degree, Carver took a position as head of the agricultural department at Tuskegee Institute, where he managed two farms and taught classes. He didn't feel challenged, so he moved into the chemical research department, where his creativity bloomed. He developed a rubber substitute from sweet potatoes, and he made a milk substitute, flour, ice cream flavoring, dye, instant coffee, cheese, oil, ink, and medicine from peanuts. Then he made peanut butter. Car manufacturer Henry Ford was so impressed with Carver's work that he financially supported many of the scientist's projects during his long career.

The first major league baseball game to be played at night took place in Cincinnati, Ohio, on this day in 1935. The Cincinnati Reds defeated the Philadelphia Phillies 2-1 at this landmark event.

War doesn't always end when the peace is declared. On this day in 1975, U.S. President Gerald Ford approved $400 million in aid for the resettlement of South Vietnamese and Cambodian refugees who had been displaced during the war in their respective nations.

25th.

1878 Bill "Bojangles" Robinson was born.

1878 The operetta *H.M.S. Pinafore* debuted.

1928 Amelia Earhart crossed the Atlantic Ocean in the plane *Friendship* with two passengers, starting from Boston, Massachusetts (see January 11, May 21, July 24, August 24 entries).

1929 Beverly Sills was born.

1949 Chinese communist troops entered Shanghai.

1952 Operation Desert Rock IV took place.

1961 U.S. President John F. Kennedy asked the citizens of the United States to work toward landing a man on the moon.

1994 The first international World Wide Web conference was held.

The first international World Wide Web conference was held on this day in 1994. This international subscriber computer network was the hottest topic raised at CERN—the European Organization for Nuclear Research—which is located in Geneva, Switzerland.

Tap dancer Bill "Bojangles" Robinson was famous for his stair dance, in which he used stair steps as a prop for various dance movements. Born in Richmond, Virginia, on this day in 1878, Bojangles danced in beer gardens when he was only six years old and joined the vaudeville circuit two years later. He was a highly paid dancer on the night-club circuit when he was in his twenties. Bojangles took his steps to the motion picture screen during the 1930s and 1940s, appearing in fourteen films. His co-stars included Shirley Temple and Lena Horne. For his sixty-first birthday, in 1939, Bojangles danced down New York City's Great White Way—Broadway.

The operatic world encountered two firsts on this day. In 1878, William Gilbert and Arthur Sullivan's operetta *H.M.S. Pinafore* debuted at London's Opéra Comique. And in 1929 Beverly Sills was born in Brooklyn, New York. Affectionately called "Bubbles," Sills was probably the most noted singer at the Metropolitan Opera during the twentieth century. She also served as director of the New York Opera Company after she retired from the stage. Ironically, her son never heard his mother's voice. He was born deaf.

On this day in 1961, President John F. Kennedy asked the citizens of the United States to work toward landing a man on the moon by the end of the 1960s. Despite a number of setbacks—including his assassination—the world watched a U.S. astronaut walk on the moon before the decade ended.

One of the final throes of the communist takeover of China took place on this day in 1949. Chinese communist troops entered Shanghai as nationalists abandoned their defense of this major commercial port in northern China.

Operation Desert Rock IV took place on this day in 1952. Conducting its second atomic blast to determine the effect of radiation on human subjects, the U.S. Army exposed over a thousand enlisted soldiers, who witnessed the explosion just outside the blast range. The previous experiment had involved nearly 1,600 people.

26th.

1907   Marion Michael Morrison was born.

1919   Jay Silverheels was born.

1923   James Arness was born.

1924   The U.S. Congress passed the Johnson-Reed Immigration Act.

1938   The Select Committee on Un-American Activities was formed.

1951   Dr. Sally Ride was born.

1952   West Germany, the United States, Great Britain, and France signed a peace agreement.

1972   The SALT I agreement was signed by the United States and the USSR.

1994   U.S. President Bill Clinton renewed China's most-favored-nation status despite complaints about the country's human-rights violations.

The Wild West came alive when the three actors born on this day appeared on film and television screens. Born in Winterset, Iowa, on this day in 1907, Marion Michael Morrison played numerous bit parts when he first arrived in Hollywood. He changed his name to John Wayne, hoping to improve his odds. In 1939 he landed the starring role as the Ringo Kid in the 1939 film *Stagecoach*. During the 1950s and 1960s, James Arness played Marshal Matt Dillon on the television series "Gunsmoke." Born in Minneapolis, Minnesota, on this day in 1923, Arness had played a number of characters including a monster in a B-grade film before landing his most famous role. Born on the Six Nations Reservation in Brantford, Ontario, on this day in 1919, Harold J. Smith changed his name to Jay Silverheels, seeking his fortune in Hollywood as an actor. Although he played Geronimo in the 1940s films *Broken Arrow* and *Walk the Proud Land,* it was Silverheels's role as the Native American scout Tonto in the 1950s television series "The Lone Ranger" that made his name a household word. Silverheels established a foundation in Los Angeles in 1961 to encourage Native American actors to hone their craft.

The U.S. Congress passed a very unpopular law on this day in 1924. The Johnson-Reed Immigration Act placed tight restrictions on immigration from all nations, imposing limits on how many people from each country were allowed to start a new life on American shores. The act, however, totally excluded Japanese immigration. This blatant act angered the Japanese ambassador to the United States, who warned there would be negative consequences.

The fear of communist and fascist propaganda, the actions of the Ku Klux Klan, and other subversive activities in the United States led Congress to establish a special investigative committee on this day in 1938. The Select Committee on Un-American Activities—also known as the Dies Committee—was set up to research and report on citizens thought to be involved in controversial schemes. The team was eventually renamed the House Un-American Activities Committee in 1945, and was in continuous operation until 1975.

The first American female astronaut was born in Encino, California, on this day in 1951. Dr. Sally Ride was the second woman to fly a space mission, following in the footsteps of Cosmonaut Valentina Tereshkova, who had flown in a Soviet space module during the 1960s.

Two promises for peace were signed on this day. In 1952 West Germany, the United States, Great Britain, and France signed a peace agreement. And in 1972 U.S. President Richard Nixon and Soviet leaders signed the SALT I agreement, which restricted the development of ABMs and froze for five years the numbers of ICBMs and submarine-launched ballistic missiles (SLBMs) each nation could own.

27th.

1907   Rachel Louise Carson was born.

1931   Paul Kipfer and August Piccard became the first men to reach the stratosphere in a pressurized cabin, 10 miles above Augsburg, Germany (see January 28, March 1, March 19, August 18 entries).

1933   The Century of Progress Exposition opened (see April 27, May 1, May 12 entries).

1936   The *Queen Mary* began its maiden voyage.

1937   The Golden Gate Bridge was completed.

A major proponent of the modern ecology movement, Rachel Louise Carson was born in Springdale, Pennsylvania, on this day in 1907. She learned her love of nature while growing up in the Pennsylvania countryside. After she got her master's degree in zoology in 1932, Carson was employed by the U.S. Bureau of Fisheries to write radio scripts and she wrote freelance articles on natural history for the *Baltimore Sun*. During the 1940s she served as editor-in-chief of publications for the U.S. Fish and Wildlife Service while continuing to write for magazines like *Atlantic Monthly*. The critical acclaim for her 1941 book *Under the Sea-Wind* and 1952 study *The Sea Around Us* prompted her to retire early so she could pursue a serious writing career. Distressed by the abundant use of synthetic chemical pesticides and its negative impact on both indigenous plants and animals, she wrote *Silent Spring* in 1962. The next year, she testified before the U.S. Congress, calling for federal protection of the environment and human health. Sadly, Carson died in 1964 from breast cancer.

Progress was the byword of this day on more than one occasion. In 1933 the Century of Progress Exposition opened on Chicago's lakefront. In 1936 the British luxury liner *Queen Mary* began its maiden voyage between Great Britain and the United States. And in 1937 San Francisco's Golden Gate Bridge was completed and opened to pedestrian traffic between the city and Marin County.

28th.

1830   U.S. President Andrew Jackson signed the Indian Removal Act, requiring Native Americans living in the East to be resettled west of the Mississippi.

1888   Jim Thorpe was born.

1963   The U.S. Congress passed the Equal Pay Act.

1998   U.S. President Bill Clinton signed an amendment to Executive Order 11478 prohibiting sexual discrimination in the workforce.

Equality was mandated in the workplace on this day. In 1963 the U.S. Congress passed the Equal Pay Act, which stated that men and women should receive equal pay for equal work. In 1998, U.S. President Bill Clinton signed an amendment to Executive Order 11478, prohibiting sexual discrimination in the federal civilian workforce.

One of the finest overall athletes was born in a one-room cabin near Prague, Oklahoma, on this day in 1888. Native American Jim Thorpe was voted first-team All-American halfback in his senior year in college. But football wasn't Thorpe's only game. He signed with the New York Giants baseball team after graduation. He won gold medals in decathlon and pentathlon events at the 1912 Olympics. But when a reporter revealed that he'd been playing semi-professional baseball, he was stripped of his medals. Thorpe played baseball for the Giants, Cincinnati Reds, and Boston Braves over the next sixteen years. In 1920 Thorpe served as the first president of the National Football League. But since he was not an efficient administrator, he went back to playing football between baseball seasons. During the Great Depression, Thorpe's career slid. He couldn't afford to buy a ticket to the 1932 Olympics, but was invited to sit in the presidential box. When he arrived, a crowd of over 100,000 spectators stood to cheer him. After his death in 1953, Thorpe's Olympic medals were restored after the American Athletics Union redesignated Thorpe's amateur status for the years 1909 through 1912.

29th.

1932   War veterans marched on Washington, D.C. (see July 28 entry).

1971   The Pentagon ordered drug tests of U.S. soldiers.

1979   The federal government grounded all DC-10 jets (see July 13 entry).

1990   Boris Yeltsin was elected Russian president in the third round of parliamentary ballots (see February 1, March 20, November 6, December 18, December 25 entries).

The airline industry was grounded on this day in 1979. Emergency safety inspections were ordered by the federal government after a DC-10 passenger jet crashed, four days earlier, near Chicago's O'Hare International Airport, killing 275 people.

War veterans weren't always treated honorably after they completed their service. On this day in 1932, First World War veterans marched on the nation's Capitol at the height of the Great Depression, demanding their guaranteed cash bonuses in advance of their guaranteed 1945 due date. In 1971 the Pentagon ordered mandatory drug tests for every U.S. soldier discharged from military service.

30th.

1886 Dorothy Leib Harrison Wood Eustis was born.

1922 The Lincoln Memorial was dedicated in Washington, D.C.

Born in Philadelphia, Pennsylvania, on this day in 1886, Dorothy Leib Harrison Wood Eustis became interested in breeding German shepherds after she moved to Vevey, Switzerland, in 1921. Her second husband, George M. Eustis, shared her fascination with the breed, and together they bred a strain that the Swiss Army and numerous police units found desirable. Around that same time, a school was established in Germany that trained German shepherds to become "seeing eyes" for the visually handicapped. In 1927 the Eustises learned of a school in Germany that trained dogs as guides for blind veterans. She wrote an article about the school for the *Saturday Evening Post* in 1927, which yielded interest back in the United States. Two years later, Eustis returned home and established The Seeing Eye training school for both dogs and their owners in Nashville, Tennessee. In 1932 the school was moved to Whippany, New Jersey, and then to Morristown, New Jersey, where it continues to operate with private donations to this day. Before Eustis's death in 1946, she and her staff had trained more than 1,300 dogs.

31st.

1857 Pope Pius XI was born.

1909 The National Negro Committee, which later became the NAACP, held its first conference in New York City.

1923 Prince Rainier Louis Henri Maxence Bertrand de Grimaldi III of Monaco was born (see April 18 entry).

Pope Pius XI did much to bring the Roman Catholic Church into the twentieth century. Born in Desio, Italy, on this day in 1857, Achille Ratti earned three doctorates and had been cardinal of Milan before he was enthroned as Pius XI in 1922. He gained the Vatican State's independence from the rest of Italy when he signed the Lateran Treaty with Mussolini in 1929 and smoothed long-standing strained relations with France. He ordered the standardization of the Catholic school educational system throughout the world and shocked the establishment when he appointed six Chinese bishops. Before his death in 1939, he triggered international concern when he denounced fascism in 1931, nazism in 1937, and communism in 1937, igniting a political bomb between the church and political powers during the next decade.

June

A musical prince, the last tsar, and a mysterious princess were all born in June. So was the man who wrote the book on guerrilla warfare. But the month's biggest hits were two tennis champs who slammed their way into the record books.

1st.

1958 Charles de Gaulle became premier of France (see April 28, November 22, December 21 entries).

1973 Greek Prime Minister George Papadopoulos proclaimed a republic (see August 21, August 23, November 25 entries).

1979 Zimbabwe was established.

1980 Cuban refugees rioted in Arkansas relocation center.

1981 Bangladesh said it had put down a rebellion.

1984 Alexander Gunyashev lifted a record 211 kilograms.

1990 The Cowboy Channel began television transmission.

1990 The Detroit Pistons beat the Portland Trailblazers for the first time since 1974.

1990 The United States and the Soviet Union signed an agreement to stop producing chemical weapons.

1991 Mount Pinatubo began a two-week-long eruption on the island of Luzon in the Philippines.

1992 The Pittsburgh Penguins defeated the Chicago Blackhawks.

1998 Kosovo refugees streamed into neighboring Albania.

1998 U.S. President Bill Clinton abandoned his claim of executive privilege (see January 13, September 11 entries).

A unique television event occurred ten years to the day after the Cable News Network (CNN) began its dedicated broadcast of worldwide news. On this day in 1990, the Cowboy Channel began cable television transmission of classic feature films, vintage serials, music programs, and famous television series that carried an Old West theme.

The pursuit of political power highlighted this day. A hero in both world wars, General Charles André Joseph Marie de Gaulle was France's provisional government leader after Paris was liberated in 1944. It took a series of weak, elected successors and conflicts in North Africa for him to win an election to the post. On this day in 1958, the referendum was passed that made him premier of France. On this day in 1973, Prime Minister George Papadopoulos abolished the monarchy and made himself the Greek republic's president. Six years earlier, he had led the military coup that ousted King Constantine II, exiled the royal family, and established a military dictatorship. Before the end of 1973, however, a military coup removed Papadopoulos, who was tried for high treason. On this day in 1979, Southern Rhodesia won its independence after fifty-six years of British rule, becoming the nation of Zimbabwe. Not all battles for power succeed. In 1980 Cuban refugees rioted at the Fort Chafee Refugee Relocation Center in Arkansas, injuring at least fifteen law enforcement officers. And in 1981 a rebellion by army officers was put down in Chittagong, Bangladesh. Political power does affect common people, as it did in 1998, when thousands of refugees fled Serbia's Kosovo province to escape persecution by crossing into nearby Albania.

Three record events occurred on this day in the sports world. In 1984 Soviet weight lifter Alexander Gunyashev pressed a record 211 kilograms. The Detroit Pistons basketball team beat the Portland Trailblazers in Portland, Oregon, in 1990—an event that had not occurred since 1974. And in 1992, on this same day, the National Hockey League's Pittsburgh Penguins beat the Chicago Blackhawks, winning the Stanley Cup for the second year in a row.

2nd.

1904   Johnny Weissmuller was born.

1946   Italy abolished its monarchy, becoming a republic.

1979   Pope John Paul II arrived in his native Poland, becoming the first pontiff to visit a communist country (see May 12, May 13, May 18, July 22, October 4 entries).

1980   The Sex Pistols' Glen Matlock was ejected from the punk band because he liked The Beatles (see October 8 entry).

Most people equate the name Johnny Weissmuller with the actor who played the title role in nineteen Tarzan films from 1932 through 1948. But few people realize that he was an Olympic medalist swimmer long before he appeared on the silver screen. Born in Windber, Pennsylvania, on this day in 1904, Weissmuller broke all records when he swam 100 meters in less than a minute and 440 yards in less than five minutes. His agility and speed won him five gold medals in the Olympics, making him the undisputed champion from 1921 through 1928.

3rd.

1865	Great Britain's King George V was born.
1868	Tsar Nicholas II was born (see June 6, June 18 entries).
1897	Memphis Minnie was born.
1942	Curtis Mayfield was born.
1948	Korczak Ziolkowski began the Crazy Horse Monument.
1964	The Rolling Stones made their U.S. television debut, appearing on "The Dean Martin Show" (see January 15, May 10, May 12, June 1, June 14, July 30, October 25, December 5, December 6, December 18 entries).
1965	The first human being walked in space.
1972	Sally Priesand became the United States's first female rabbi (see February 14 entry).
1976	Lieutenant Beverly Kelley became the U.S. Coast Guard Officer Candidate School's first female graduate.
1983	Militant tax protester Gordon Kahl died in a gun battle with federal authorities in Arkansas (see February 13 entry).
1998	The Crazy Horse Monument was dedicated.
2000	Great Britain's Queen Elizabeth II publicly recognized Camilla Parker Bowles.

A major monument was started and dedicated on this day. In 1948 sculptor Korczak Ziolkowski began carving the face of Lakota chief Crazy Horse in the side of a mountain near the town of Crazy Horse, South Dakota, in the Black Hills near Mount Rushmore. Using his own money to fund the project, he died before seeing its completion, but his family continued to work on his dream. On this same day, fifty years later, the nine-story-tall Crazy Horse Monument was dedicated. Like its neighbors at Mount Rushmore, however, Crazy Horse's full figure has not been completed.

Two exceptional music talents are celebrated this day. Born in Algiers, Louisiana, on this day in 1897, delta blues singer Memphis Minnie made her way up north to Beale Street in Memphis, Tennessee, where Johnny Shines commented that "any men fool with her she'd go right after them right away. She didn't take no foolishness off them. Guitar, pocket-knife, pistol, anything she get her hand on she'd use it." The first Blues Unlimited Reader's Poll—taken in 1973, which was the same year as her death—cited Minnie as being rungs ahead of her contemporaries Bessie Smith and Ma Rainey. Born in Chicago, Illinois, on this day in 1942, soul singer Curtis Mayfield worked with The Impressions during the 1950s and 1960s before he released his solo funk album in 1970. His soundtrack for the 1972 film *Superfly* elevated his career, winning Mayfield four Grammys. More albums and production projects followed until Mayfield was injured in a 1990 accident that left him quadriplegic.

Not all rulers have an easy reign. Some experience the tides of change firsthand. Born at Marlborough House, England, on this day in 1865, Great Britain's King George V watched his empire crumble. He sat on the throne while the British South African colonies formed an independent union in 1910, and while Ireland rebelled and became a free state in 1922. The political pressure surrounding his family's German last name, Saxe-Coburg, during the First World War led to an official name change to Windsor. And he presided while the 1935 Government of India Act was signed, leading to the colony's eventual independence. Russia's last tsar was also born on this day in 1868. Nicholas II ascended the throne in 1894. Although he managed to redirect diplomatic relations with both France and Great Britain, he experienced major defeat in the 1904 Russo-Japanese War. On the verge of revolution, his powers were diminished by the Duma's establishment in 1906. The First World War's strains didn't improve matters, leading to the eventual 1917 Russian Revolution. Nicholas was forced to abdicate his throne and was executed along with his wife, Alexandra, and their children in 1918.

Another monarch had to deal with modern times on this day in 2000. Great Britain's Queen Elizabeth II recognized her son Prince Charles's long-time mistress Camilla Parker Bowles. While both women attended a weekend barbecue at the prince's Highgrove estate, they exchanged pleasantries for the first time, even though Charles and Camilla's affair had gone on for more than three decades.

The second female rabbi in recorded Judaic history was ordained on this day in 1972. A graduate of Hebrew Union College, Sally Priesand took her first position as assistant rabbi at Stephen Wise Free Synagogue in New York City, becoming the United States's first female rabbi. She stayed for seven years, until she realized she was not going to succeed the senior rabbi who was about to retire. In 1981 she became the rabbi of the Monmouth Reform Temple in Tinton Falls, New Jersey.

A human being walked in space for the first time on this day in 1965. U.S. astronaut Edward White took a step outside the *Gemini 4* spacecraft and floated for twenty-one minutes while tethered to the capsule exterior.

4th.

1784   The first female aeronaut flew over France.

1964   The 1939 food stamp program was reactivated on a national scale by the U.S. Department of Agriculture (see May 16 entry).

1972   U.S. Representative Shirley Chisholm announced she was a presidential candidate (see November 5 entry).

1985   The U.S. Supreme Court disallowed silent prayer in schools.

1989   Tanks rolled into Beijing's Tiananmen Square and Chinese soldiers fired on the thousands of unarmed pro-democracy demonstrators.

A French opera singer reached the highest notes yet on this day in 1784. The diva Marie Elisabeth Thible earned the distinction of being the world's first female aeronaut when she flew in a hot-air balloon high over Lyon, France, while Sweden's King Gustav watched her ascent from the ground.

In politics, winning isn't everything. Sometimes, making your stand sets the winds of change in motion. On this day in 1972, U.S. Representative Shirley Chisholm did just that when she announced she was a presidential candidate. At her press conference, she commented that "as a black person and as a female person, I do not have a chance of actually gaining that office in this election year. I make that statement seriously, knowing that my candidacy itself can change the face and future of American politics—that it will be important to the needs and hopes of every one of you—even though in the conventional sense, I will not win."

The federal government took a neutral stand on religion on this day in 1985. The U.S. Supreme Court handed down a decision striking down an Alabama law that permitted daily "silent meditation or prayer" in public schools. The court stated in its final comments that the "government must pursue a course of complete neutrality toward religion."

5th.

1887   Ruth Fulton Benedict was born.

1933   The United States went off the gold standard (see April 5, April 19, August 14, December 31 entries).

1966   Eugene Cernan took a record space walk (see May 18 entry).

1980   The United Nations Security Council voted to condemn Israel.

1983   The musical *Cats* and the play *Torch Song Trilogy* won Tony awards.

A major landmark in the conquest of outer space took place on this day in 1966. Astronaut Eugene Cernan stepped out of the *Gemini 9* spacecraft and took a two-hour, ten-minute tethered walk in space.

An essential failure based on prejudice was publicly censured on this day in 1980. The United Nations Security Council voted to condemn Israel for its failure to protect Arabs living in the West Bank. The action came three days after three West Bank mayors were wounded in bomb attacks executed by Jewish extremists. The United States abstained from participation in the voting procedure.

Under normal circumstances, people tend to adopt the ideal personality that's dictated by the culture in which they live. This groundbreaking assessment of culture's influence on populations was strongly supported in the 1930s and 1940s by anthropologists Franz Boas and Ruth Fulton Benedict, who was born in New York City on this day in 1887. While working at Columbia University, she wrote her theories about the uniqueness of cultures. She also served as president of the American Anthropological Association. It was her 1946 book *The Chrysanthemum and the Sword: Patterns of Japanese Culture* that became the foundation for American postwar policy toward Japan. Benedict was not made a full professor at Columbia, however, until a few months before her death in 1948.

6th.

1872	Tsarina Alexandra Fyodorovna was born (see June 3, June 18 entries).
1924	George Leigh Mallory and Andrew Irvine set out from Camp IV on Mount Everest (see May 1, June 8 entries).
1956	Bjorn Borg was born (see June 15 entry).
1962	The Beatles began their first session with EMI producer George Martin at London's Abbey Road Studio (see January 1, January 3, January 20, January 24, January 30, February 7, February 9, February 12, May 9, June 12, August 29 entries).
1966	Stokely Carmichael launched the Black Power movement.
1969	The U.S. Department of Justice admitted that it tapped Rev. Dr. Martin Luther King's phone lines.
1978	Californians voted in favor of Proposition 13.

Fear and misunderstanding frequently breed anger and unfounded suspicions, as evidenced on this day in history. In 1966 the leader of the Student Nonviolent Coordinating Committee (SNCC), Stokely Carmichael, coined the term "Black Power" during a speech that called for African-Americans to "unite, to recognize their heritage, and to build a sense of community," segregating themselves from the American culture and value system. And in 1969 attorneys revealed that the Rev. Dr. Martin Luther King's phone lines had been tapped by the U.S. Department of Justice. The statement made during a hearing in a federal courtroom in Houston, Texas, further substantiated that the U.S. attorney general had authorized the taps even though President Lyndon Johnson had ordered the action be taken only for reasons of national security.

A political earthquake started in California on this day in 1978. California voters overwhelmingly approved Howard Jarvis's Proposition 13, which cut the state's property taxes by 30 percent. No small measure, this action triggered a nationwide tax revolt on federal, state, and local levels. Its ramifications are still being felt today in the form of reduced governmental support for educational programs and mandated tax increases to recoup funds lost during nearly two decades.

One of the world's youngest tennis champions, Bjorn Borg led the pack before his twenty-first birthday. Born in Sodertalge, Sweden, on this day in 1956, Borg left school when he was fourteen years old to concentrate on his game. It paid off. Two years later he was the Wimbledon junior champion. Between 1974 and 1981, Borg won six French

Open titles, five consecutive Wimbledon singles titles, and two Italian championships. Shortly after he was defeated by John McEnroe at Wimbledon in 1981, Borg retired at 25 a rich man.

7th.

1940   Tom Jones was born.

1948   Czechoslovak President Eduard Benes resigned.

1955   The television quiz show "The $64,000 Question" debuted.

1958   Prince was born.

1965   The rights to privacy and contraception were assured by the U.S. Supreme Court.

1969   The Bob Dylan and Johnny Cash television special aired on ABC-TV (see May 1, May 12, May 24, July 25, July 31, August 9, August 17, September 11, December 8 entries).

1983   The United States ordered six Nicaraguan consulates to close.

A pair of strong, distinctive voices arose on this day. Known for his form-fitting suits and resonant voice, Welsh pop singer Tom Jones was born in Pontypridd, South Wales, on this day in 1940. His career hit a high note with 1960s chart toppers like "What's New Pussycat?" and "It's Not Unusual." In 1958 Prince Nelson was born in Minneapolis, Minnesota. Famed for his erotic pop lyrics, exotic outfits, and elaborate stage productions, Prince crossed from the R&B charts to the top of the rock list with hits like "Little Red Corvette" and "Purple Rain." Many of his songs have also been hits for singers like Chaka Khan, the Bangles, and Sheena Easton.

Access to contraceptive devices and the right to privacy for married couples were assured by the federal government on this day in 1965. The U.S. Supreme Court handed down a decision in the case of *Griswold v. State of Connecticut* that an 1879 law banning contraceptives was unconstitutional, violating six constitutional amendments.

An eye for eye was the order of the day in 1983. It was on this day that the United States ordered the Nicaraguan government to close six of its consulates. The action was taken after Nicaragua expelled three U.S. diplomats whom it accused of plotting to poison a Sandinista official.

8th.

1892   Homer A. Plessy refused to move to a segregated railroad coach.

1924   George Mallory and Andrew Irvine vanished along Mount Everest's northeast ridge near a 90-foot wall at the 28,300-foot level (see May 1, June 6 entries).

1953   The U.S. Supreme Court ruled that restaurants in the District of Columbia could not refuse to serve African-Americans.

1996   U.S. President Bill Clinton invoked the Antiquities Act.

The freedom to function in society has been contested in the U.S. Supreme Court on more than one occasion. On this day in 1892, Homer A. Plessy refused to move to a segregated railroad coach while it was stationed in New Orleans, Louisiana. His arrest and subsequent trials eventually led to the Supreme Court's hearing of the case *Plessy v. Ferguson*. On this same day in 1953, the U.S. Supreme Court handed down a decision that restaurants in the District of Columbia could not refuse to serve African-American patrons.

Obscure or unused laws are sometimes invoked decades after they're passed. On this day in 1996, U.S. President Bill Clinton invoked the 1906 Antiquities Act for the first time since it was passed to establish the 1.9-million-acre Grand Staircase-Escalante National Monument in Utah. Controversy in Congress immediately ensued because of the size of the parcel. On January 11, 2000, the president established three additional monuments: the 1.014-million-acre Grand Canyon-Parashant National Monument in Arizona, the 71,100-acre Agua Fria National Monument in Arizona, and the California Coastal National Monument. He also expanded the Pinnacles National Monument by 7,900 acres. And on April 15, 2000, he created the 327,769-acre Giant National Monument in California.

9th.

1943   The U.S. Congress passed the Current Tax Payment Act.

1972   Bruce Springsteen signed a deal with CBS Records.

Withholding tax from paychecks and wage packets became a reality on this day in 1943. The U.S. Congress passed the Current Tax Payment Act, which mandated that employers retain income taxes from employees and make payments on their behalf to the federal government. Inaugurated at the height of the Second World War, the bill ensured the timely and prompt payment of taxes by all American wage earners and was meant as an emergency provision to provide needed government funds.

10th.

1847   The *Chicago Tribune* newspaper was first published.

1898   Hattie McDaniel was born (see May 3 entry).

1910   Howlin' Wolf was born.

1966   Janis Joplin sang with Big Brother and the Holding Company for the first time (see January 19, July 12, July 25, August 12 entries).

1966   The Beatles issued their single "Rain."

The first African-American actress to win an Oscar was born in Wichita, Kansas, on this day in 1898. Hattie McDaniel had played numerous roles on stage and screen before she landed the part of Mammy in the 1939 film *Gone with the Wind.* Her characterization garnered the respect of the Academy of Motion Picture Arts and Sciences. McDaniel also gained popularity in the title role of Beulah on her nationally broadcast radio series.

Two major musical firsts occurred on the same day that blues great Howlin' Wolf was born in West Point, Mississippi, in 1910. On this same day in 1966, blues-style singer Janis Joplin played for the first time with the San Francisco rock band Big Brother and the Holding Company. On the exact same day, The Beatles released their first recording, "Rain," to employ reverse tape tracks as part of the background music.

11th.

1806   John A. Roebling was born.

1910   The Printers' Association of America sought to ban billboards that portrayed women's skirts (see April 1, April 12, June 27 entries).

1927   Charles Lindbergh was presented with the first Distinguished Flying Cross to be awarded (see February 4 entry).

1995   The U.S. Supreme Court ruled that preferential treatment of minorities was unconstitutional, effectively making affirmative action unconstitutional.

Invention is a gradual process from inspiration to actualization. Civil engineer John A. Roebling proved this when his fascination with hemp rope led to the design of the Brooklyn Bridge. Born in Muehlhausen, Prussia, on this day in 1806, Roebling worked with his brother farming in Pennsylvania after arriving in the United States in 1831. It didn't take long for him to progress to a job as a canal engineer, where he became inspired through his observations of the effect of hemp rope on inclines to develop a machine that could make wire rope—the first to be manufactured in the United States. He started thinking about suspension bridges employing his wire rope. Roebling completed his first bridge in 1846. He built another near Niagara Falls in 1851. And then he designed his masterpiece—the Brooklyn Bridge—which was finished by his son. Roebling had contracted tetanus from a foot injury while supervising construction of the famous bridge. He died fourteen years before the bridge was completed.

Women's ankle-length skirts were considered too delicate a subject for public display at the beginning of the twentieth century. On this day in 1910, the Printers' Association of America decided to foil the exploitation of such intimate apparel. They called such advertising immoral and campaigned for the banning of women's skirts on billboards.

Affirmative action was ruled as unconstitutional on this day in 1995. The U.S. Supreme Court handed down a 5-4 decision in the case of *Adarand v. United States* that federal programs that give preferential treatment to minority applicants are presumably unconstitutional in nature. On July 19 of that same year, President Bill Clinton stated that affirmative action has been "good for America," but the University of California's Board of Regents voted the next day to end the preferential treatment of minority applicants.

12th.

1924   U.S. President George H. Bush was born in Milton, Massachusetts.

1929   Anne Frank was born (see June 15 entry).

1947 Babe Didrikson Zaharias became the first American-born winner of the British Women's Amateur Golf Tournament (see June 26 entry).

1965 The Beatles were awarded the Member of British Empire designation by Queen Elizabeth II (see January 1, January 20, January 24, January 30, February 7, February 9, February 12, May 9, June 6, August 29 entries).

1967 The U.S. Supreme Court decided that anti-interracial marriage laws were unconstitutional.

1972 The U.S. Supreme Court upheld the right of private clubs to exclude African-Americans from their membership.

1973 The first female pilot was hired to fly a passenger airline.

1991 CERN held a computer seminar on the World Wide Web.

1995 The U.S. Supreme Court decided that contracts awarded on the basis of race were unconstitutional.

1996 A panel of federal judges in Philadelphia blocked a law intended to ban indecency on the Internet.

The first female pilot was hired to fly a passenger airplane on this day in 1973. Emily Howell was employed by the regional carrier Frontier Airlines to fly regularly scheduled passenger flights.

The Internet and the World Wide Web were on the minds of people on this particular day in history. In 1991 CERN—the European Organization for Nuclear Research—held a computer seminar on the World Wide Web. And in 1996 a panel of federal judges presiding in Philadelphia, Pennsylvania, blocked a law banning the posting of indecent materials over the Internet and the World Wide Web.

It's a fine line between discrimination and the methods used to prevent it. On this day in 1967, the U.S. Supreme Court handed down a decision in the case of *Loving v. Virginia* that the Constitution was violated by state legislation that outlawed interracial marriage. But in 1972 the Supreme Court upheld the right of private clubs to exclude African-Americans from their membership rolls. And in 1995 the Supreme Court handed down a decision that contracts awarded on the basis of race as defined by affirmative action were unconstitutional in the case of *Adarand Constructors, Inc. v. Pena.*

13th.

1502 Christopher Columbus discovered the island of Martinique (see March 31, April 16, May 3, May 9, May 13, May 20, July 31, August 23, December 5 entries).

1894 W.E.B. DuBois became the first African-American to receive a Harvard University doctorate (see February 23, November 1 entries).

1903 Harold "Red" Grange was born.

1978 Israel completed its withdrawal from Lebanon.

1994 The U.S. Supreme Court curtailed the powers of cities to curb the display of signs on private property.

1996 The antigovernment group the Freemen ended their eighty-one-day standoff at their Montana ranch, surrendering to the FBI.

1996 The U.S. Supreme Court placed greater limits on congressional districts.

Limitations were imposed by the U.S. Supreme Court on this day. In 1994 the Supreme Court handed down a decision to limit the power municipal governments have to curb the display of signs on private property whether they are of a political or commercial nature. And in 1996 the Supreme Court handed down a decision to impose greater limits on the establishment of congressional districts.

It was a winning day in sports. Football great Harold "Red" Grange was born in Forksville, Pennsylvania, on this day in 1903. He earned the nickname the Galloping Ghost while he played for the University of Illinois, gaining 4,280 yards in three years of play. One commentator said that he was "the greatest broken-field runner in the history of the game." But that was before he signed with the Chicago Bears in 1925, causing quite a stir within the league because he was still a student at the time. Grange became the first football player to earn the unheard-of sum of $100,000 per season during his career.

The process of withdrawal was difficult and slow, but on this day in 1978, Israel removed the last of its invasion forces from southern Lebanon under the supervision of United Nations peace keepers. But rather than handing over the six-mile-wide strip at the border to the UN, Israeli commanders entrusted the land to the Christian militia.

14th.

1906 Margaret Bourke-White was born.

1928 Ché Guevara was born (see October 9, October 11 entries).

1933 Jerzy Kosinski was born.

1969 Steffi Graf was born.

1969 The Rolling Stones announced they'd formed their own record label, Sticky Fingers (see January 15, May 10, May 12, June 3, July 30, October 25, December 5, December 6, December 18 entries).

1993 U.S. President Bill Clinton chose Judge Ruth Bader Ginsburg to serve on the Supreme Court.

Through the eyes of Margaret Bourke-White, the world saw the faces of the rural poor in the southern United States; the 1941 siege of Moscow; civil unrest in India, Pakistan, and South Africa; the opening of the Nazi concentration camps; and the faces of great men such as Gandhi. Born in New York City on this day in 1906, Bourke-White became a staff photographer for *Fortune* magazine in 1929, but changed jobs in 1936 when *Life* magazine was launched. As an associate editor and staff photographer for the famed publication, Bourke-White was the first female photographer assigned to cover the U.S. forces during the Second World War and was the official United Nations correspondent during the Korean War. Ill health prevented her from circling the globe after 1952, but she continued to produce photo essays for the publication until she retired in 1969.

Author Jerzy Kosinski wrote about survival. The subjects of his novels sometimes skewed reality to make a situation work for them despite the odds. Born in Lodz, Poland, on this day in 1933, Kosinski studied and taught political science before he emigrated to the United States in 1957, turning his sights toward writing. His 1965 novel *The Painted Bird* was heralded as a classic of Holocaust literature, and his 1971 novel *Being There* took an ironic look at modern American life. It was made into a film that starred Peter Sellers.

A symbol of guerrilla warfare and revolution to an entire generation of 1960s youth, Ernesto Ché Guevara played a pivotal role in revolutionary politics throughout Central and South America. Born in Buenos Aires, Argentina, on this day in 1928, Guevara graduated with a degree in medicine two years before he joined Fidel Castro's revolutionary campaign in Mexico. The next year, he joined Castro's guerrillas in Cuba, winning a victory over a corrupt dictatorship on that island nation. After the takeover, he held a few political posts before returning to South America in 1965. It was while he was forming revolutionary forces that he was captured and shot by government troops. His 1961 book *Guerrilla Warfare* was considered to be the best handbook on the staging of a revolution, becoming a bestseller on U.S. college campuses for over a decade.

One of the world's top female tennis players was born in Bruehl, Germany, on this day in 1969. Steffi Graf won the Olympic demonstration event and took sixteenth place at Wimbledon in 1984. Four years later, she won an Olympic gold medal and the Grand Slam—the French, Australian, and U.S. Opens plus Wimbledon—in singles events. The next year, she won Wimbledon but was defeated by Arancha Sanchez at the French Open.

15th.

1877   Henry O. Flipper became West Point's first African-American graduate (see February 19 entry).

1938   Johnny Vander Meer pitched his second no-hitter baseball game in a row.

1951   Joe Louis reclaimed his heavyweight champion title (see May 13, September 24 entries).

1952   *Anne Frank: Diary of a Young Girl* was published in the United States (see June 12 entry).

1975   Bjorn Borg won the French Open (see June 6 entry).

1983   The U.S. Supreme Court limited the powers of states and cities to place curbs on legal abortions.

Access to legal abortions was secured on this day in 1983. The U.S. Supreme Court handed down a decision that limited the powers of states and cities to place curbs on legal abortions, allowing women who wanted the service access to appropriate local treatment.

Titles abounded in sports on this day. In 1938 Cincinnati Reds pitcher Johnny Vander Meer threw his second no-hitter baseball game in a row. This made the left-hander the only major league player to pitch successive no-hit, no-run games. In 1951 boxer Joe Louis reclaimed his heavyweight champion title in a comeback bout with Lee Savoid. And in 1975 Bjorn Borg won the French Open tennis championship.

16th.

1892   Jennie Grossinger was born.

1902   Barbara McClintock was born.

1903   Pepsi Cola registered its patent.

1903   The Ford Motor Company was incorporated.

1917   Katherine Graham was born (see April 22 entry).

1961   Rudolf Nureyev defected (see March 17 entry).

1963   Soviet cosmonaut Valentina Tereshkova became the first woman to travel into space (see June 17, June 19 entries).

Two major American brands were born on this day in 1903. The Pepsi Cola Company registered its patent for the recipe of its popular soft drink. The owners waited one year after they opened for business to protect their successful formula. And on the exact same day, the Ford Motor Company was incorporated by founder Henry Ford.

A respite from New York City life, Grossinger's was one of the world's most famous resorts. Over the years it expanded from a small farm hostel into a thirty-five-building hotel because of Jennie Grossinger, who was born in Austria on this day in 1892. Jennie's parents borrowed $450 to buy the small farm in the Catskill Mountains after they emigrated to the United States. To make ends meet, they took in summer boarders. Jennie was the chambermaid and bookkeeper. Her mother was the cook. Her father took care of maintenance. Word spread about their hospitality and excellent cuisine, making it a major destination for New Yorkers wishing to escape the city heat. By the time Jennie handed the business over to her children during the 1960s, she had built the enterprise into a 1,200-acre luxury resort that welcomed 150,000 guests each year.

It takes nerves of steel to run a newspaper like the award-winning *Washington Post*. And Katherine Graham proved that she could take the heat with the best of them. Born on this day in 1917, she started out as a reporter at *The San Francisco News* until she found a job at the *Washington Post* in 1938. She became the newspaper's president in 1969. Within a few years, her publication gained international acclaim when she okayed the investigation of the Watergate scandal by Bob Woodward and Carl Bernstein. She also approved the publication of the Pentagon Papers before a restraining order was obtained by U.S. President Richard Nixon to stop their release.

We know that some genes can control other genes. We also know that genes can move on a chromosome. Barbara McClintock discovered these facts while doing research on the genetics of maize at the Carnegie Institution labs. Born on this day in 1902, McClintock's groundbreaking studies went largely unnoticed when she first published them in 1951. It took three decades for the world to learn how valuable her work truly was: She received the 1983 Nobel Prize for Physiology or Medicine.

17th.

1900   The Boxer Rebellion began (see July 14, September 7 entries).

1944   The Republic of Iceland was established, ending its union with Denmark.

1963   Soviet cosmonaut Valentina Tereshkova became the first female astronaut to orbit the earth (see June 16, June 19 entries).

1982   Argentine President Leopoldo Galtieri resigned after his nation's defeat in the Falklands.

1991   The U.S. Supreme Court ruled that poor prison conditions don't violate the Eighth Amendment.

1999   The Cape Hatteras Lighthouse (North Carolina) was moved.

The concept of cruel and unusual punishment was decided on this day in 1991. The U.S. Supreme Court handed down a decision that poor prison conditions—overcrowded cells, poor sanitation, and exposure to violence—don't violate the Eighth Amendment's prohibition of cruel and unusual punishment.

Relations between people can end graciously or violently. On this day in 1900, the Boxer Rebellion began, pitting China against Austria-Hungary, France, Germany, Great Britain, Italy, Japan, Russia, and the United States. The Boxers were a secret society dedicated to driving the "foreign devils" out of China. Their followers believed that their nation had been economically and physically ravaged not only by natural disasters, but by sanctions placed on them by Western nations and the seizure of Chinese cities by the Japanese, Germans, Russians, British, and French. In 1944 Icelanders politically broke ties with the Danes. The Republic of Iceland was established, ending its union with Denmark.

It's not often that a lighthouse needs to be moved to prevent its destruction. But on this day in 1999, workmen moved the Cape Hatteras Lighthouse 10 feet from its original position on a beam and roller system. Built in 1870, the 208-foot lighthouse was threatened by beach erosion. By August of the same year, the crew managed to move the lighthouse 1,500 feet to its new, protected position on the slim island.

18th.

1901   Princess Anastasia Romanov was born (see June 3, June 6 entries).

1901   Jeanette MacDonald was born.

1952   Carol Kane was born.

1952   Isabella Rossellini was born.

1979   U.S. President Jimmy Carter and Soviet Chairman Leonid Brezhnev signed the SALT II agreement, limiting the production and placement of long-range missiles and bombers (see October 1 entry).

1981   The Lockheed F-117 stealth fighter made its first flight.

Three women with distinctive film careers share a birthday. Born on this day in 1901, Jeanette Macdonald earned top dollar for her singing ability, especially when she paired up with Nelson Eddy in a number of musical films. Their most famous duet, however, appeared in the film *Indian Love Song,* in which she and Eddy (dressed as a Canadian Mountie) croon beside a crystal-clear lake. Born in Rome, Italy, on this day in 1952, actress Isabella Rossellini made immediate headlines. The daughter of actress Ingrid Bergman and filmmaker Robert Rossellini, Isabella's birth horrified the American film industry because her parents were not married. Her sultry voice and looks have graced films such as *Blue Velvet, Death Becomes You,* and *Immortal Beloved.* Also born in 1952, actress Carol Kane has a voice that cannot be mistaken. Besides playing opposite Andy Kaufmann in the television series "Taxi," Kane has taken broad character roles in films like *Hester Street, Addams Family Values,* and *The Princess Bride.*

19th.

1897 Moe Howard was born.

1934 The U.S. Congress passed the Equal Time Act.

1947 Salman Rushdie was born.

1953 Julius and Ethel Rosenberg were executed at Sing Sing prison (see March 29, April 5, May 12 entries).

1963 Soviet cosmonaut Valentina Tereshkova returned to earth (see June 16, June 17 entries).

1973 Soviet Chairman Leonid Brezhnev asked for trade concessions (see October 15 entry).

The Three Stooges had the honor of holding the longest single motion picture contract ever signed by a comedy team. They spent twenty-four years making two-reel comedies for Columbia Pictures. The business head of this remarkably successful trio was Moe Howard. Born in Bensonhurst, New York, on this day in 1897, Moe always wanted to be in show business, spending every moment he could playing in little theater productions and watching plays and musicals. His brothers Shemp and Curly were no better. Neither was his cousin Larry. Despite his outrageous antics on screen, Moe was a serious, introverted man who was devoted to his family, rarely associating with Hollywood film people during his long career.

Author Salman Rushdie worked as an actor and as an advertising copywriter before he devoted himself completely to writing. Born in Bombay, India, on this day in 1947, Rushdie emigrated to Great Britain in 1965, to read at Cambridge University. Although his first novel, *Grimus,* sold poorly in 1975 when it was published, his 1981 novel *Midnight's Children* made him an international success. However, it was his 1988 novel *Satanic Verses* that caused the great stir. The book was banned in India, and the next year Iran's Ayatollah Khomeini issued a death threat, declaring that the author had blasphemed again the name of Islam. He was forced into hiding under police protection for nearly a decade.

Politicians want to be heard, and on this day in 1934, the U.S. Congress passed the Equal Time Act, which ensured that every one would have his or her moment. This law mandated that radio stations throughout the United States had to provide equal time to every potential political candidate. And in 1973 Soviet Communist Party Chairman

Leonid Brezhnev asked to be heard by congressional leaders, contending that the Cold War was over and asking for trade concessions on behalf of the USSR.

20th.

1898   The U.S. Navy seized Guam during the Spanish-American War.

1909   Errol Flynn was born.

1924   Audie Murphy was born.

1936   The U.S. Congress passed the Robinson-Patman Anti-Price Discrimination Act.

1977   Menachem Begin became Israel's prime minister (see August 15, September 15 entries).

1982   The British reoccupied the South Sandwich Islands.

1997   The nation's biggest tobacco companies announced that they agreed to submit to strict federal control (see July 17, August 10 entries).

The federal government placed a few restrictions on big business on this particular day in history. In 1936 the U.S. Congress passed the Robinson-Patman Anti-Price Discrimination Act. This law made it illegal for large corporations to drive prices down so low that smaller companies are driven out of business. And in 1997 the nation's biggest tobacco companies made a formal announcement that they agreed the day before to submit to strict federal control over the manufacture and marketing of cigarettes. They also agreed to pay $368.5 billion over the next twenty-five years to compensate states and individuals for tobacco-related health costs.

Film heroes sometimes appear more real than they truly are. Such was the case with actor Errol Flynn, who was born in Hobart, Tasmania, on this day in 1909. The son of a marine biologist, Flynn was an adventurer, working as a tobacco plantation manager, a journalist, and prospector before taking the role of Fletcher Christian in the 1933 film *In the Wake of the Bounty*. Some dramatic training in England led to a major break in Flynn's career. His title role in the 1935 film *Captain Blood* made him a swashbuckling box office hero for the next five years. His drinking and womanizing throughout Hollywood during the 1940s diminished his public appeal. On the other side of the coin, actor Audie Murphy was a Second World War hero who had earned thirty-three awards and decorations, including the Medal of Honor, while he was in service. Born in Texas on this day in 1924, Murphy was invited to come to Hollywood by actor James Cagney after the war. It took a couple of years for him to get a break, starring in the 1949 *Bad Boy,* which led to a twenty-six-film contract with Universal Studios. In 1955 he starred in the autobiographical film *To Hell and Back,* which was the studio's highest-grossing film until the 1975 film *Jaws* was released.

Islands were a focal point in history on this day. In 1898 the U.S. Navy seized the largest island in the Marianas—Guam—during the Spanish-American War. And in 1982 British forces reoccupied the South Sandwich Islands and established the 150-mile Falkland Islands Protection Zone (FIPZ).

21st.

1846   The saxophone was patented by Antoine-Joseph Sax (see January 17, November 6 entries).

1953   Benazir Bhutto was born (see April 4, December 2 entries).

1963   Cardinal Giovanni Battista Montini was elected pope, taking the name Paul VI (see June 30, July 29, September 26, October 28, November 27, December 9 entries).

1974   Former presidential aide Charles Colson was sentenced to one to three years' imprisonment for obstruction of justice in the Daniel Ellsberg case (see February 15, July 12, November 13 entries).

1989   The U.S. Supreme Court decided that flag burning as a form of political protest is constitutional.

In 1990 Pakistan Prime Minister Benazir Bhutto became the first governmental head to give birth to a child while in office. It was her second. Her first was born just before her election. Born in Pakistan on this day in 1953, but educated in England, Bhutto was president of the student union when she studied at Oxford University. Returning to Pakistan in 1977, she was placed under house arrest for seven years during a military coup. Her father, Prime Minister Zulfikar Ali Bhutto, had been accused of vote rigging, corruption, and conspiracy by his opponent General Zia al-Haq. Despite international protest, he was convicted and executed in 1978. Bhutto and her mother were released in 1984, at which time they moved to England. Benazir Bhutto became joint leader in exile of the Pakistan People's Party. She returned to Pakistan in 1986 to campaign for open elections as well as reforms. She married Asif Ali Zardari the next year. With the death of General al-Haq and the call for a general election, Bhutto herself became prime minister in 1988, three months after giving birth to her first child.

The patriotic wishes of a president were quashed on this day in 1989. The U.S. Supreme Court voted in a 5-4 decision that burning the American flag as a form of political protest was constitutional. President George H. Bush had attempted to have an amendment added to the U.S. Constitution that would ban desecration of the national flag, but the justices determined that individuals are protected under the First Amendment to physically display their opinions in this manner.

The son of a Belgian woodwind and brass instrument maker, Antoine-Joseph Sax developed a new instrument while refining a bass clarinet design. A cross between a woodwind and a brass horn, his saxophone was first displayed in 1841. The next year, Sax moved to Paris and opened his own instrument-making business. On this day in 1846, Sax received a fifteen-year patent for his design from the French government.

22nd.

1933　Dianne Feinstein was born (see December 4 entry).

1948　Todd Rundgren was born.

1977　Former U.S. Attorney General John Mitchell was incarcerated at the federal minimum-security prison at Maxwell Air Force Base, Alabama, for his part in the Watergate scandal (see January 19, February 21, July 1 entries).

1983　The space shuttle *Challenger*'s crew deployed and retrieved a satellite, using the shuttle's mechanical arm (see January 28, February 6, February 10, April 4, April 29, September 2, October 13 entries).

U.S. Senator Dianne Feinstein's political career has been a series of firsts. She was the first woman to serve as president of San Francisco's Board of Supervisors when she was elected in 1969. But that was only the beginning. Born in San Francisco, California, on this day in 1933, Feinstein became the city's mayor in 1978, after Mayor George Moscone and board member Harvey Milk were assassinated. Serving as mayor for nine years, she reduced the city's crime rate by 27 percent and balanced the budget each year she was in office. She was one of the first women considered for vice presidential candidate in 1984 and the first woman nominated as the Democratic candidate for California's governorship in 1990. When she was elected to the U.S. Senate in 1992, she became the first woman to represent her home state in that capacity.

Eclectic and eccentric talents mark Todd Rundgren's musical career. Born in Philadelphia, Pennsylvania, on this day in 1948, Rundgren played in a local bar band before he formed the Nazz in 1967. After three albums the group broke up, in 1970, and Rundgren worked as a studio engineer for a while. Getting together with Hunt Sales and Tony Sales, he recorded a Top 20 hit, "We Got to Get You a Woman." He quickly followed that success with the hits "Hello It's Me," "I Saw the Light," and "It Wouldn't Have Made Any Difference." He departed from pop rock, writing a few soul ballads, and then shifted into radically progressive rock with the band Utopia during the late 1970s. He also produced a number of successful albums for the New York Dolls, Grand Funk Railroad, Hall & Oates, and Meatloaf.

23rd.

1784 The first teenage balloonist flew in the United States.

1894 Alfred Kinsey was born.

1927 Bob Fosse was born.

1940 Wilma Rudolph was born.

1961 U.S. President John Kennedy assigned Vice President Lyndon Johnson the task of unifying the United States satellite programs.

1988 The U.S. Senate Committee on Energy and Natural Resources was cautioned about global warming.

Choreographer and film director Bob Fosse put the sizzle in Broadway musical steps. Born to a vaudeville entertainer in Chicago, Illinois, on this day in 1927, Fosse made his stage debut when he was thirteen years old. He made his Broadway dance debut in 1950, but it was the "Steam Heat" number he designed for the musical *Pajama Game* that launched his career. The dance numbers seen in the musicals *Damn Yankees, Sweet Charity, Pippin,* and *Dancin* tip their hats to Fosse's hip-swinging, gyrating style. His film direction and choreography for the 1972 film *Cabaret* and the 1979 film *All That Jazz* confirmed his reputation as a visual genius.

A teenager made aeronautic history on this day in 1784. Thirteen-year-old Edward Warren flew a thirty-five-foot-diameter silk hot-air balloon over Baltimore, Maryland, becoming the first teenage balloonist in the United States.

Nothing stopped Wilma Rudolph from reaching her goal. Born in Clarksville, Tennessee, on this day in 1940, Wilma was the twentieth of twenty-two children. She was stricken with polio as a child, but she managed to overcome her frailties, becoming a member of the Tennessee Belles athletic team when she was a teenager. She went to the 1956 Olympics, winning a bronze medal in the sprint relay event. At the 1960 Olympics, Wilma took gold medals for the 100-meter, 200-meter, and sprint relay events. For the next four years, she set and broke her own track records before retiring from the sport at the age of 24.

It took a trained zoologist to establish the scientific study of human sexual behavior. Born in Hoboken, New Jersey, on this day in 1894, Alfred Kinsey studied and taught zoology during the 1920s and 1930s. He turned his attentions to the human animal in 1942, when he established the Institute for Sex Research. The results of his work at this landmark facility were published in his 1948 book *Sexual Behavior in the Human Male*—which is popularly known as the Kinsey Report—and his 1953 sequel *Sexual Behavior in the Human Female*.

Global warming was a matter of great concern on this day in 1988. NASA scientist James E. Hansen testified before the U.S. Senate Committee on Energy and Natural Resources that global warming had become a threat to humankind. Blamed as the cause of extreme weather shifts, depletion of the ozone layer, and an increase in the incidence of skin cancer throughout the world, the concept of global warming is still being debated in the political and scientific arenas worldwide.

24th.

1895   Jack Dempsey was born (see September 22 entry).

1932   Siam's absolute monarchy was replaced with a constitutional monarchy.

1940   Hope Cooke was born.

1965   The Beatles' John Lennon published his second book, *A Spaniard in the Works* (see March 23 entry).

1968   The exchange of a one-dollar U.S. silver certificate for one troy ounce of silver bullion was discontinued.

1981 Former Israeli Defense Minister Moshe Dayan said that Israel had the capacity to produce an atomic bomb (see May 20, October 21 entries).

1985 Canada increased airport security following two disasters on flights originating in Canada.

1993 Eight Muslim fundamentalists were arrested in New York City.

1996 After repeated threats via e-mail and snail mail, Network Solutions dropped 9,272 domain names from its DNS tables for failure to pay their domain name fees.

1996 U.S. Supreme Court justices upheld civil forfeiture.

Terrorism and potential double jeopardy made the news on a few occasions on this day. In 1985 the Canadian government increased airport security following two disasters on flights that originated in Canada: An Air India jumbo jet had crashed into the Atlantic ocean, and an unloading CP Air flight exploded after it landed in Japan. In 1993 eight Muslim fundamentalists were arrested in New York City, suspected of plotting to bomb United Nations headquarters, a federal building, and the Holland and Lincoln tunnels. And in 1996 the U.S. Supreme Court handed down a decision that prosecution and civil forfeiture paired together did not constitute double jeopardy.

A lavish Asian monarchy made the headlines on this day in 1932. A military coup put an end to the absolute monarchy of Siam's King Prajadhipok of the Chakri dynasty. As a result, a constitutional monarchy was established that was administered by military leaders. And the future wife of an Asian monarch was born in New York City on this day in 1940. Hope Cooke was made the ward of former U.S. Ambassador to Iran Selden Chapin after her parents had divorced, her mother died, and her grandparents passed away. A graduate of Oriental studies at Sarah Lawrence College, Cooke met her future husband while vacationing at a resort in Darjeeling, India. In 1963 Cooke became the first Westerner to marry into the Sikkimese royal family, becoming Queen of Sikkim when she married Chogyal Palden Thondup Namgyal at the age of 22.

Before heavyweight boxer Jack Dempsey earned his world title, he'd worked in the copper mines until 1914. Born in Manassa, Colorado, on this day in 1895, Dempsey entered the ring as Kid Blackie, winning his first match at the age of 19. He won the world heavyweight title five years later, defeating Jess Willard. And he managed to retain his belt until he was knocked out by Gene Tunney in 1926, losing by only a few points after having knocked down the contender in a long count. Dempsey retired in 1940 and became a successful New York City restaurateur until his death in 1983.

25th.

1910 The U.S. Congress passed the Mann Act.

1962 The U.S. Supreme Court declared that prayer in public schools is unconstitutional.

1987 Former U.S. Treasury Secretary Robert Anderson was sentenced to one month of imprisonment and five years of probation for tax evasion.

1996 A tanker truck exploded at the Al-Khobar Towers in Saudi Arabia, killing 19 U.S. military personnel and injuring hundreds of others where they were in residence.

The white slave trade and prostitution were outlawed in the United States on this day in 1910. The U.S. Congress passed the Mann Act, which prohibited the transportation of women across state or international lines for immoral purposes. The business of white slavery and prostitution had grown in major American cities to such a point that New Orleans was officially off limits to naval personnel because of its numerous brothels, and Chicago boasted over 600 brothels within its municipal limits.

Prayer in public schools was declared unconstitutional on this day in 1962. The U.S. Supreme Court handed down a decision in the case of *Engel v. Vitale* that the reading of a prayer in public schools violated the Constitution's First and Fourteenth Amendments.

26th.

1909 Colonel Tom Parker was born (see March 5, March 24, July 30, August 15, August 22, September 25, December 3 entries).

1911 Babe Didrikson Zaharias was born (see June 12 entry).

1961 Greg LeMond was born (see July 24, July 27 entries).

1983 U.S. Secretary of State George Schultz criticized the Soviet Union.

1986 Irish voters decided against the end of a constitutional ban on divorce by more than a 3-2 ratio.

_1989_ The U.S. Supreme Court ruled that the death penalty can be imposed on murderers who are age 16 and older regardless of their mental state (see July 2, December 7, December 18 entries).

_1993_ U.S. military forces fired long-range missiles into the heart of Baghdad, Iraq.

_1997_ The Communications Decency Act was declared unconstitutional.

Levels of decency across communications lines in the United States were in question on this day in 1997. The U.S. Supreme Court handed down a decision in the case of _Reno v. ACLU_ that the Communications Decency Act, which was part of the 1996 Telecommunications Reform Act, was unconstitutional.

Colonel Tom Parker was a natural promoter. Born Andreas van Kujik in Breda, the Netherlands, on this day in 1909, Parker ran away from home and headed to the United States when he was 16. As an illegal alien, he joined the U.S. Army and took the name of a commanding officer who'd showed an interest in him: Colonel Tom Parker. After he got out of the service, he became an advance man for the carnival show. In 1940 he became director of the Tampa Humane Society and was elected the city's dog catcher. The society turned a profit for the first time under his leadership and promotion. He opened the nation's first pet cemetery after that, which also turned a profit. He then turned to music promotion, signing country singer Eddy Arnold, who fired Parker in 1953. But two years later, Parker signed Elvis Presley just after he'd finished recording for Sam Phillips at Sun Records. He continued to work as Presley's manager until the superstar's death in 1977, earning a 50-percent cut of all earnings. Parker continued to manage the estate until he was found guilty of malfeasance.

Two major American athletes celebrate their birthday on this day. Born in Texas on this day in 1911, Babe Didrikson Zaharias never knew her limits. She won two track-and-field gold medals at the 1932 Olympics, setting world records in the javelin throw and 80-meter hurdles. And she won 114 golf tournaments as well as 83 amateur golf tournaments. It's not surprising that she was named sportswoman of the year in 1931, 1945, 1946, 1947, 1950, and 1954. Born in Lakewood, California, on this day in 1961, cyclist Greg LeMond won gold, silver, and bronze medals in the 1978 junior world championship time trial. He went on to win senior world titles in 1979 and 1983. As a professional cyclist, LeMond was the first American to win the 1986, 1989, and 1990 Tour de France. (A serious hunting accident had kept him from the competition in 1987 and 1988.) LeMond retired in 1994 after being diagnosed with a rare muscular disease.

The use of missiles made the headlines on this day. In 1983 U.S. Secretary of State George Schultz criticized the Soviet Union for rejecting an American interim solution to the storage and use of medium-range missiles in Europe. And in 1993 U.S. military forces fired long-range missiles into the heart of Baghdad, Iraq. The attack was justified as a reprisal for the attempted assassination of U.S. President George H. Bush during his visit to Kuwait two months earlier.

27th.

1888   Antoinette Perry was born.

1934   The U.S. Congress passed the National Housing Act.

1961   U.S. President John F. Kennedy signed an executive order allowing public gifts for the purpose of paying down the National Debt.

1976   Seven Arab guerrillas hijacked a jet in Athens, Greece.

1977   The U.S. Supreme Court ruled that lawyers cannot be prevented from advertising fees charged for routine legal services (see April 1, April 12 entries).

1978   The first Polish astronaut was launched.

1979   The U.S. Supreme Court ruled that employers and unions could establish affirmative action programs that include the use of quotas.

1982   The space shuttle *Columbia* was launched (see April 12 entry).

1983   Balloonists Maxie Anderson and Don Ida were killed when their hot-air balloon crashed in a German forest during a race (see May 8, August 12 entries).

1984   The motion picture industry incorporated the PG-13 category into its voluntary system of film ratings (see April 1, April 12 entries).

1985   New York's first hotel strike ended.

1985   The United States demanded the release of seven American hostages held in Lebanon.

Industrial relations were a major focal point on this day in business history. In 1934 the U.S. Congress passed the National Housing Act, which created the Federal Housing Administration. By empowering the federal government to back home finance, the real estate industry got it first major stimulus as millions of Americans applied for reasonably priced mortgages. In 1977 the U.S. Supreme Court handed down a decision that attorneys can't constitutionally be prevented from advertising the fees they charge for routine legal services. In 1979 the U.S. Supreme Court handed down a decision that employers and unions could establish affirmative action programs that include the use of quotas. And in 1985 the month-long New York hotel strike ended. The first event of its kind, which involved 16,000 employees and fifty-three major hotels, the strike ended with a wage hike agreement.

International terrorism escalated between the late 1970s and mid-1980s. On this day in 1976, seven Arab guerrillas hijacked an Air France jetliner shortly after takeoff from Athens, Greece, carrying 258 passengers and 12 crew members. And in 1985 the United States demanded that seven other American hostages held in Lebanon be included in any arrangement to free thirty-nine hostages from a hijacked TWA passenger jet.

Antoinette Perry was the queen of the American stage during her career. Born in Denver, Colorado, on this day in 1888, she started out as an actress but found her niche as a director. She has nearly thirty plays to her credit. And in 1947, she established the American Theatre Wing. In honor of her dedication, the Antoinette Perry Awards were created to honor the best in American theater. They are affectionately known today as the Tony Awards.

Aerospace made the headlines on this day. In 1978 the first Polish astronaut was launched into space, joining the Russian commander of a new type of Soviet spacecraft. And in 1982 the U.S. space shuttle *Columbia* blasted off from Cape Canaveral, Florida, carrying two astronauts and the shuttle program's first military cargo.

28th.

1926 Mel Brooks was born.

1946 Gilda Radner was born.

1980 Officials at the Three-Mile Island nuclear plant began venting radioactive gas (see March 28, April 13, October 30 entries).

1983 The U.S. Supreme Court ruled that life imprisonment with no possibility of parole is unconstitutional.

1984 Israeli officials freed 291 Syrian soldiers captured in Lebanon in exchange for three Syrian-held Israeli soldiers and three diplomats.

1992 The strongest earthquake in the United States in forty years occurred.

1993 The National Commission on AIDS ended its four-year project.

Insult was followed by further injury on this day in 1980. Out of necessity, officials at the Three-Mile Island nuclear plant in Pennsylvania ordered the venting of radioactive gas from the damaged reactor's containment tower. Unfortunately, the two-week-long procedure forced the immediate evacuation of hundreds of nearby families.

The strongest earthquake recorded in the United States in forty years took place on this day in 1992. The initial shake was followed by an equally severe tremor, both of which had their epicenter in Southern California. During the disaster a young boy died in Yucca Valley and more than 400 people were injured.

A master and mistress of comedy celebrate their birthday on this particular day. Mel Kaminsky got his start in show business playing stand-up comedy at Catskills Mountain resorts like Grossinger's. Born in Brooklyn, New York, on this day in 1926, Mel changed his name to Mel Brooks, teaming up with Carl Reiner and creating characters like the 2,000-Year-Old Man. Brooks's international fame came when he wrote and directed the 1960s film *The Producers* and the 1970s film *Blazing Saddles,* which both starred a later collaborator, Gene Wilder, who wrote and acted in Brooks's film *Young Frankenstein.* Born in Detroit, Michigan, on this day in 1946, comedienne Gilda Radner was playing in the Toronto production of the musical *Godspell* when she auditioned for the first cast of the Toronto branch of Second City. She spent eighteen months with the improv group before moving on to the "National Lampoon Radio Hour" and the first cast of NBC-TV's "Saturday Night Live," where she played from 1975 through 1980. Married to Gene Wilder during the 1980s, Radner appeared with her husband in a few films before she died in 1989.

Not all projects have pleasant conclusions. On this day in 1993, the National Commission on AIDS ended its four-year study. Sadly, all they had to report was that national leaders had done very little to combat the disease.

29th.

1920 Ray Harryhausen was born.

1972 The U.S. Supreme Court ruled that the death penalty was unconstitutional.

1976 Palestinian hijackers threatened to blow up a plane.

1992 The U.S. Supreme Court ruled that women have a constitutional right to abortion.

The tactics of terrorism can be drastic, as was proven on this day in 1976. An Air France jetliner had been hijacked by Palestinian terrorists, who ordered that the plane land in Uganda. They then demanded that Israel and four other nations release fifty-three Arab prisoners or they would blow up the plane, its crew, and its passengers.

Born in Los Angeles, California, on this day in 1920, Ray Harryhausen fell in love with the movies from the very start. His aunt got free passes to Grauman's Chinese Theater because she was Grauman's mother's nurse. She took Ray to see the 1925 film *The Lost World* and the 1933 film *King Kong,* which both featured stop-motion animation techniques created by Willis O'Brien. A few years later, Ray bought a 16mm camera and fashioned his own clay dinosaurs, filming stop-motion shorts. He noticed a girl at school reading the original *King Kong* screenplay, who turned out to be Willis O'Brien's niece. He got to meet his hero before he enlisted during the Second World War. When he finished the service, O'Brien asked him to work with him on the 1949 film *Mighty Joe Young.* It was the beginning of a long career. Harryhausen created amazing sodium process effects in the 1960 film *The Three Worlds of Gulliver,* and he perfected his signature Dynamation technique in the 1963 film *Jason and the Argonauts* and the 1974 film *The Seventh Voyage of Sinbad.* His last project, the 1981 film *Clash of the Titans,* combined the best of his skills and knowledge, the production of epic effects before the inception of computer-generated imagery.

The rights of women to a safe and legal abortion were slightly diminished on this day in 1992. The U.S. Supreme Court handed down a decision in the case of *Planned Parenthood of Southeastern Pennsylvania v. Casey* that reconfirmed a woman's constitutional right to abortion. However, the divided court stipulated that individual states should be allowed to express a "compelling interest" in preserving life and allowed additional restrictions not previously required.

30*th.*

1864 U.S. President Abraham Lincoln signed the Yosemite Land Grant.

1917 Lena Horne was born.

1927   Phoebe Fairgrave Omlie became the first woman in the United States to receive a pilot's license.

1963   Pope Paul VI was crowned (see June 21, July 29, September 26, October 28, November 27, December 9 entries).

1966   Mike Tyson was born (see February 10 entry).

1971   Three Soviet cosmonauts, who had been in space for more than three weeks, were found dead when their *Soyuz 11* spacecraft landed.

1980   Vigdis Finnbogadottir became the first democratically elected female head of state.

1982   The Equal Rights Amendment failed ratification.

1985   All thirty-nine remaining American hostages seized during the hijacking of a TWA jet were freed in Beirut, Lebanon.

One of the jazz world's most elegant singers was born in Brooklyn, New York, on this day in 1917. The daughter of an actress and a hotel operator, Lena Horne once called herself a "sepia Hedy Lamarr." She made her debut at Harlem's Cotton Club when she was sixteen years old. She had good teachers in those days: Duke Ellington, Cab Calloway, Billie Holiday, and composer Harold Arlen. She was playing the nightclub circuit when MGM music supervisor Roger Edens noticed her. In 1943 she starred in *Cabin in the Sky* and *Stormy Weather.* From that point on she was an overnight sensation, appearing in musical films and recording hit after hit. After her marriage to conductor Lennie Hayton in 1947, Horne's career continued uphill until she was blacklisted during the McCarthy era of the 1950s for her friendship with actor Paul Robeson and for her work in the civil rights movement. But she continued to record and play the clubs while her husband managed her career. In 1979 she received an honorary doctorate from Harvard University.

The status of women gained and lost on this day in history. In 1980 Vigdis Finnbogadottir became the first democratically elected female head of state. She was elected president of Iceland, defeating three male opponents. In 1982 the Equal Rights Amendment failed ratification. The extended deadline to get the support of two-thirds of the American states expired. With three states shy of the thirty-eight states required, Illinois failed to endorse the hard-fought amendment.

One of boxing's hardest punchers and players was born in Brooklyn, New York, on this day in 1966. Mike Tyson went to reform school when he was twelve years old, but was released into the custody of a boxing trainer. Quickly, Tyson became a seasoned amateur and was selected as an alternate for the 1984 Olympic team. He turned pro the next year and the following year became history's youngest heavyweight champion. That's when his troubles began. A stormy marriage and divorce with actress Robin Givens, numerous charges of assault, and one rape conviction colored the career of a champion who's won more than forty knockouts and lost only three bouts in the ring.

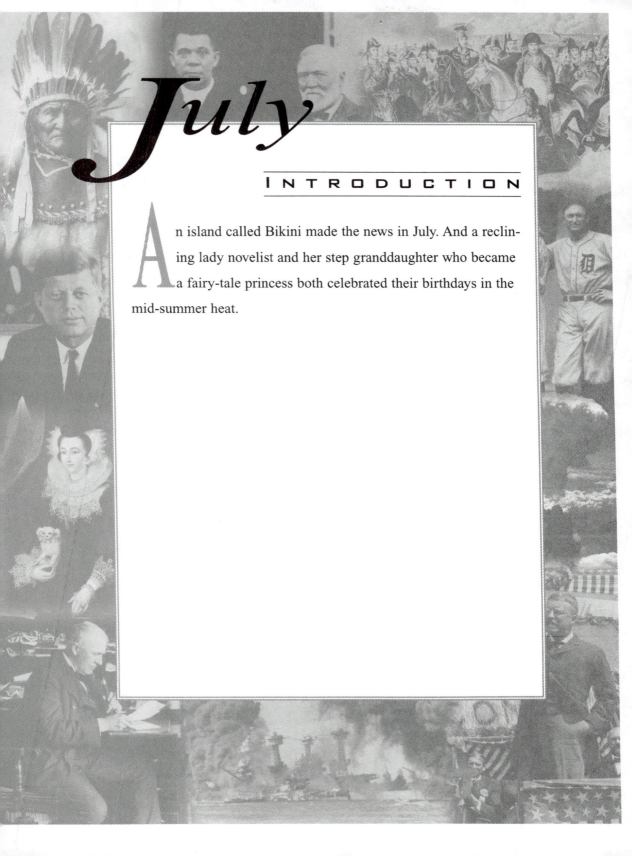

July

An island called Bikini made the news in July. And a reclining lady novelist and her step granddaughter who became a fairy-tale princess both celebrated their birthdays in the mid-summer heat.

1st.

1915   Willie Dixon was born.

1946   The first postwar atomic bomb test was conducted at Bikini Atoll in the Marshall Islands by the United States.

1961   Carl Lewis was born (see August 8 entry).

1961   Lady Diana Spencer was born (see February 24, July 9, July 29, December 9 entries).

1972   U.S. Attorney General John Mitchell resigned to reenter private law practice (see January 19, February 21, June 22 entries).

1972   The Bureau of Alcohol, Tobacco, and Firearms (BATF) was created.

1980   U.S. President Jimmy Carter signed the Motor Carrier Act (see October 1 entry).

1981   The United Auto Workers rejoined the AFL-CIO.

1984   Liechtenstein became the last European nation to grant women the right to vote (see November 3 entry).

1992   The U.S. Congress passed the National Plumbing Products Efficiency Act.

Controlled substances and goods became subject to a new federal monitoring system when the Internal Revenue Service's Alcohol, Tobacco, and Firearms Division (ATFD) was given full bureau status within the Treasury Department. On this day in 1972, the Bureau of Alcohol, Tobacco, and Firearms (BATF) was created.

Some changes were made to the way business in the United States works on this day. In 1980 U.S. President Jimmy Carter signed the Motor Carrier Act, which curbed federal control over interstate trucking. And in 1992 the U.S. Congress passed the National Plumbing Products Efficiency Act, which limited the amount of water used for flushing to 1.6 gallons per toilet. But one thing returned to business as usual. In 1981 the United Auto Workers rejoined the AFL-CIO after a thirteen-year separation that began over a policy dispute.

A blues great who crossed over from urban blues to rock and roll was born in Vicksburg, Mississippi, on this day in 1915. Songwriter Willie Dixon created numerous hits that he recorded during the 1950s and 1960s, including "Seventh Son," "Spoonful," "Wang Dang Doodle," and "I Just Wanna Make Love to You." These same songs were also covered by other chart-topping blues musicians like Albert King, Howlin' Wolf, and Muddy Waters, as well as British rock greats like The Rolling Stones, Cream, and The Yardbirds.

Lady Diana Frances Spencer was born at Park House in Sandringham, England, on Queen Elizabeth II's estate on this day in 1961. Although she led less than a charmed childhood, her adult life was like one of her step-grandmother Barbara Cartland's romance novels. Diana became a fairytale princess when she married Prince Charles during the 1980s, becoming Princess Diana. A well-loved member of the British royal family, she took her public duties seriously, contributing to numerous groups that supported the welfare of children and families worldwide. She broke with tradition when she divorced the prince in 1996.

Born in Birmingham, Alabama, on this day in 1961, Frederick Carleton Lewis is one of track and field's greatest athletes. Winning gold medals in the 100-meter, 200-meter, long jump, and 400-meter relay events at the 1984 Olympics, Carl Lewis matched Jesse Owens's historic accomplishments at the 1936 Berlin Olympics. In 1991 Lewis achieved records in the 100-meter, 400-meter relay, and long jump at the World Championships in Tokyo, Japan. It was an inherited talent. Lewis's mother won sixth place in the 80-meter hurdles at the 1951 Pan-American Games. His sister won eighteen national championships in the hurdles and long jump. And his brother was a professional soccer player.

2nd.

1921 The first million-dollar prize fight was held.

1939 Mount Rushmore's Theodore Roosevelt figure was dedicated (see March 3, July 4, August 30, September 17, October 1, October 31, December 28 entries).

1960 Dr. Barbara Moore arrived in Los Angeles, California, after walking the 3,027-mile route from New York City in eighty-six days.

1976 The U.S. Supreme Court ruled that capital punishment wasn't cruel or unusual punishment (see June 26, December 7, December 18 entries).

1979 The Susan B. Anthony $1 coin was placed into circulation.

1989 Japanese Prime Minister Toshiki Kaifu appointed two women to his cabinet for the first time in Japanese history.

The U.S. Supreme Court handed down a grave decision on this day in 1976. The justices determined that capital punishment does not constitute "cruel and unusual punishment." This meant that the death penalty wasn't considered to be too harsh a sentence in some criminal cases.

An unprecedented pair of political appointments were made on this day in 1989. Japanese Prime Minister Toshiki Kaifu named two female cabinet members. What prompted his move was the fact that his predecessor had been forced out of office after an illicit affair he'd had with a geisha was exposed.

Pugilism became an expensive sport on this day in 1921. The first million-dollar heavyweight prize fight took place in Jersey City, New Jersey. Jack Dempsey won the prize when he knocked out Georges Carpentier in the fourth round.

3rd.

1893   Mississippi John Hurt was born.

1909   Stavros Spyros Niarchos was born (see January 15, July 28, October 20 entries).

1951   Jean-Claude Duvalier was born (see February 7, April 14, April 22 entries).

1981   Tennis player Chris Evert won her third successive Wimbledon singles title, defeating Czechoslovakia's Hana Mandlikova.

1988   The USS *Vincennes* fired a missile at an Irani passenger jet.

Greek shipping magnate Aristotle Onassis's major business competitor was his brother-in-law Stavros Spyros Niarchos. Born in Athens, Greece, on this day in 1909, Niarchos pioneered the construction of the supertanker and controlled the world's largest independent fleet of marine transport vessels.

Born in Teoc, Mississippi, on this day in 1893, Mississippi John Hurt was one of ten children who all taught themselves to play music. When he was asked by his landlord, years later, how he came up with his songs, Hurt replied, "Well, sir, I just make it sound like I think it should." Rather than continuing to sharecrop like his father, Hurt worked day labor and picked up extra money playing at church suppers and dances. Hurt's life changed when fiddler Willie Narmour was signed by Columbia Records during the

1920s. Narmour had been asked to recommend other local talent, and Hurt's name came to mind. In 1928 Hurt recorded "Frankie" and "Nobody's Dirty Business" in Memphis, Tennessee. He recorded additional work in New York City, such as "Avalon Blues," and then returned home to sharecrop. In 1963 two blues archivists named Tom Hoskins and Mike Stewart heard Hurt's recording of "Avalon Blues." With the aid of an 1878 atlas and a local gas station attendant, they found the 71-year-old Hurt, whom they recorded on the spot. Hurt became an overnight success, playing East Coast nightclubs and folk festivals before his death in 1966.

Born in Port-au-Prince, Haiti, on this day in 1951, Jean-Claude Duvalier inherited his father's position and a portion of his nickname. The son of Haitian dictator François "Papa Doc" Duvalier, Jean-Claude became the nation's president-for-life after his father's death in 1971. Ruling through a private army, Duvalier is known as "Baby Doc" throughout his island nation.

On this day in 1988, the USS *Vincennes* fired a missile at an Irani passenger jet, killing 290 passengers and crew. The vessel had responded to an alleged attack by an Irani F-14 fighter plane.

4th.

1900   Louis Armstrong was born.

1916   Tokyo Rose was born.

1930   Mount Rushmore's George Washington figure was dedicated (see March 3, July 4, August 30, September 17, October 1, October 31, December 28 entries).

1946   The Philippines gained independence from United States rule.

Jazz great Louis Armstrong learned to play the cornet in less than opportune circumstances. Born in New Orleans, Louisiana, on this day in 1900, Armstrong had been sent to a reform school for delinquency. He learned to play the cornet while he lived there until 1914. He got a job playing at the local bars when he was released, getting encouragement from top names like King Oliver and Kid Ory. During the 1920s, he went from recording with Ory's band and the Creole Jazz Band in Chicago to putting down tracks with his own Hot Five and Hot Seven studio groups. He changed over to trumpet, appeared in over fifty films, and toured the world as a star soloist from the 1930s until his death in 1971.

The Philippine Islands were given their independence from United States rule on this day in 1946. The island nation had been given commonwealth status in 1936, but the outbreak of the Second World War delayed the final process of total autonomy.

Born in the United States on this day in 1916, Iva Ikoku Toguri became one of the Second World War's most infamous figures. A UCLA graduate, Toguri had gone back to Japan to visit her mother in 1941. But when the attack on Pearl Harbor took place that December, Toguri found herself trapped in Japan—unwanted by both sides. She found a job as a typist at Radio Tokyo and was later chosen to read scripts on the *Zero Hour.* Organized and presented by Allied POWs under the supervision of Japanese military intelligence and directed by Australian Army Major Charles Cousens, the show transmitted popular music and reports about the war. (The former Sydney radio celebrity had picked Toguri because she had no broadcast experience and didn't have an attractive voice.) When the war was over, Toguri returned home to the United States, speaking openly to reporters about her overseas job. Her innocence led to her arrest and conviction as a traitor. Tapes of her "Tokyo Rose" broadcasts and the testimony of two former Japanese-American supervisors who lied under oath led to her imprisonment for ten years and a $10,000 fine. During the 1970s a *Chicago Tribune* journalist reinvestigated her story, which led to her pardon by U.S. President Gerald R. Ford in 1977.

5th.

1911 Georges Jean Raymond Pompidou was born.

1982 The Penn Square Bank of Oklahoma was declared insolvent, touching off a bank crisis that affected most of the United States.

1993 Peter Steiner's cartoon "On the Internet, nobody knows you're a dog" appeared in *The New Yorker* magazine.

Born in Montboudif, France, on this day in 1911, Georges Jean Raymond Pompidou was a gregarious and accessible symbol of the France that emerged during the 1970s. A member of Charles de Gaulle's staff since 1944, Pompidou had been promoted to numerous posts until de Gaulle himself showed signs of jealousy during the 1960s. Pompidou had turned out to be a more successful instrument for international and domestic diplomacy than anyone had realized. After de Gaulle retired in 1969, Pompidou was elected France's president, offering a more liberal and globally minded future for his nation.

6th.

1935   Tenzin Gyatso was born (see January 3 entry).

1957   Althea Gibson became the first African-American to win a Wimbledon singles title (see July 10, August 25 entries).

The Buddha of Compassion was born in Takster, Tibet, on this day in 1935. Tenzin Gyatso's birth was auspiciously visited by a pair of crows who watched over the house. Monks sent from the monastery at Lhasa to test the toddler selected two-year-old Tenzin as the fourteenth Dalai Lama, the Compassionate Buddha. He was enthroned in 1940, but a regent managed his political affairs until 1950. The Chinese invasion of Tibet forced the Dalai Lama to flee to Chumbi, on the southern Tibet border. He continued to live there after negotiating an eight-year autonomy agreement with the People's Republic of China. But in 1959 a Tibetan national uprising failed and the Dalai Lama fled to Dharamsala, India, where he established his alternative government seat. He was awarded the 1989 Nobel Peace Prize for his nonviolent pursuit of Tibetan independence. And in 2000, the seventeenth Karmapa Lama joined him in exile.

7th.

1906   Leroy Robert "Satchel" Paige was born (see February 9 entry).

1915   Billie Holiday was born.

1940   Ringo Starr was born (see April 27, August 16, September 11 entries).

1992   Muslim holy men incited riots against women in Zinder, Niger.

Muslim holy men incited riots in Zinder, Niger, on this day in 1992. Mobs of men went on a rampage against hundreds of women, burning buildings and attacking women in the streets. The holy men blamed a severe drought on the immoral and indecent behavior of the nation's women.

Billie Holiday—who was known as Lady Day—led a tragic life but had a successful career, contributing one of the best jazz voices of the twentieth century. Billie Holiday was born in Baltimore, Maryland, on this day 1915. She had been jailed for prostitution as a teenager, but by the mid-1930s she was singing in New York City. Her voice led to work with Benny Goodman, Lester Young, Count Basie, and Artie Shaw. She even appeared with Louis Armstrong in the 1940s film *New Orleans*. Sadly, by the end of the 1940s, her voice had deteriorated as a result of severe drug addiction. Her life was portrayed in the 1970s film *Lady Sings the Blues*.

Born in Mobile, Alabama, on this day in 1906, Leroy Robert "Satchel" Paige was the starring pitcher in the National Negro Baseball League even though he was a late bloomer. He was forty-two years old before he entered the league, and he pitched fifty-five no-hitters.

8th.

1805 Bill Richmond won a world boxing championship.

1838 Count Ferdinand von Zeppelin was born in Constance, Germany (see May 6 entry).

1951 Evonne Goolagong was born.

1959 The first American soldiers were killed in Vietnam.

1969 U.S. troops began their withdrawal from Vietnam.

1985 Seventeen-year-old Boris Becker became Wimbledon's youngest winner and the first German winner of the men's singles title.

1993 Randy Weaver and a co-defendant were acquitted or slaying a federal marshal in Ruby Ridge, Idaho (see August 17, August 22, September 6 entries).

On this day in 1993, a jury in Boise, Idaho, acquitted white separatist Randy Weaver and a co-defendant. They had been charged with slaying a federal marshal in a shootout at a remote mountain cabin in Ruby Ridge, Idaho.

Two unique sportspeople have something to celebrate on this day. The first Australian Aborigine tennis player, Evonne Goolagong, was born on this day in 1951. During her professional career, she won the Wimbledon singles title in both 1971 and 1980. And on this day in 1805, Bill Richmond became the first African-American pugilist to win a world boxing championship. He knocked out Jack Holinwin after twenty-six rounds in a bout at Cricklewood Green, England.

The Vietnam War took two different routes on this day in military history. In 1959 Major Dale R. Buis and Major-Sergeant Chester M. Ovnand were the first American soldiers to be killed in Vietnam. Ten years later, in 1969, U.S. troops began their withdrawal from Vietnam.

9th.

1893   Dr. Daniel Hale Williams performed the first successful open heart surgery operation at Chicago's Provident Hospital.

1901   Barbara Cartland was born (see July 1 entry).

1973   The Drug Enforcement Administration (DEA) was established.

The author of over 400 romance novels, biographies, and health books, Barbara Cartland was born in Edgbaston, England, on this day in 1901. She published her first book, *Jigsaw,* when she was twenty-three years old. In 1983 she gained a place in the *Guinness World Book of Records* by writing twenty-six books in one year. Selling more than 450 million copies during her lifetime, Cartland dictated most of her work while reclining on a sofa.

10th.

1927   David Dinkins was born.

1938   Howard Hughes and a crew of four people completed a flight around the world.

1943   Arthur Ashe was born (see July 6, August 25 entries).

1952   The Republican Party adopted the Equal Rights Amendment plank.

1962   Telstar was launched (see July 18 entry).

1981   Race riots erupted in England.

1990   Mikhail S. Gorbachev won reelection as Soviet Communist Party leader.

1992   Manuel Noriega was sentenced.

Former Panamanian leader Manuel Noriega was sentenced on this day in 1992. A federal judge in Miami, Florida, ordered forty years' imprisonment for Noriega, who had been convicted of drug and racketeering charges.

Racially motivated violence erupted in over eighty cities and towns including Liverpool, London, and Manchester in England on this day in 1981. In London alone, 350 people were arrested in the Brixton district's Loughborough estate and north London's Broadwater Farm.

A landmark effort was made by the Republicans on this day in 1952. The political party adopted the Equal Rights Amendment plank as part of their party platform.

Former New York City Mayor David Dinkins once said, "You can be anything you want to be. You can be a street sweeper, if you want. Just be the best blasted street sweeper you can be. . . . And, you know you can be mayor." Born in Trenton, New Jersey, on this day in 1927, Dinkins moved to New York as a child with his parents. In 1965 he joined the New York State Assembly and in 1972 was president of elections for the city. In 1989 Dinkins defeated Rudolph Giuliani, becoming the city's first African-American mayor. After he lost his reelection bid to Giuliani, he began a teaching career at Columbia University.

On this day in 1962, the Telstar communications satellite was launched into orbit from Cape Canaveral, Florida. Its sole mission was to relay television and telephone signals between the United States and Europe.

Arthur Ashe was the first tennis player to earn $100,000 in one year. Born in Richmond, Virginia, on this day in 1943, Ashe accomplished numerous firsts during his career. In 1968 Ashe became the first male African-American to win the U.S. Open and Wimbledon. (Althea Gibson had been the first African-American woman to accomplish the same feat.) He won the Davis Cup in 1968 through 1970 as a player, as well as in 1981 and 1982 as captain. After he had heart surgery in 1983, he spent time creating a tennis program for inner-city kids. In 1992 he announced that he had contracted AIDS from a blood transfusion he had received during heart surgery. In 1997 the new home for the U.S. Open was named the Arthur Ashe Stadium.

11th.

1897	Blind Lemon Jefferson was born.
1897	Scientist Salomon August André and two companions headed for the North Pole (see April 6, August 3, August 29 entries).
1984	The U.S. Transportation Department announced that air bags or automatic seat belts were mandatory.
1987	The five-billionth person was born.
1989	The Chrysler Corporation agreed to double the number of minority representatives and women in management.
1995	U.S. President Bill Clinton extended full diplomatic recognition to Vietnam.

Transportation and cars were a focal point in the news on this day. In 1984 the U.S. Transportation Department announced that air bags or automatic seat belts were mandatory on all American-made cars by 1989 unless states representing two-thirds of the population made use of seat belts compulsory. In 1989 the Chrysler Corporation agreed to double the number of minority representatives and women in managerial administrative positions after it had been pressed by the NAACP. That meant that 20 percent of management had to fulfill those minority quotas.

A tragic expedition began on this day in 1897. Scientist Salomon August André and two companions left Spitsbergen, Norway, for the North Pole. Shortly after their journey began, they disappeared. Seal hunters found the expedition's diaries, logs, and exposed film in 1930.

Blind Lemon Jefferson was one of the blues' first commercially successful recording artists. Born in Couchman, Texas, on this day in 1897, Jefferson recorded his nearly one hundred titles between 1926 and 1929. Because of his success, other male blues artists were able to secure contracts at a time when only female singers like Bessie Smith and Ma Rainey were being courted by record labels. Lightnin' Hopkins, B.B. King, and T-Bone Walker were just a few of his disciples. It took time for him to achieve that fame. At one time, he played in the streets of Dallas for tin-cup donations to support his wife and child. Some of the most famous songs he wrote and recorded were "See See Rider," "Boll Weevil Blues," and "Match Box Blues."

The world's population got exponentially larger on this day in 1987. The five-billionth person joined the human race: Yugoslavian-born Matej Gaspar.

12th.

1895   R. Buckminster Fuller was born.

1937   Bill Cosby was born.

1970   Janis Joplin premiered her Full Tilt Boogie Band (see January 19, June 10, July 25, August 12 entries).

1974   White House aide John Ehrlichman and three other defendants were convicted of conspiracy to violate Daniel Ellsberg's civil rights (see February 15, June 21, November 13 entries).

1986   The U.S. Senate voted to permanently televise coverage of its proceedings.

Born in Philadelphia, Pennsylvania, on this day in 1937, Bill Cosby earned a track and field scholarship to Temple University. But he abandoned this pursuit when he started playing in local nightclubs. His 1965 appearance on "The Tonight Show" led to a deal as co-star of the television series "I Spy" that same year. Over the course of four years, Cosby won three consecutive Emmys. He never stopped working from that point on, acting and producing "The Bill Cosby Show," "The Cosby Show," the cartoon series "Fat Albert and the Cosby Kids," as well as appearing in numerous motion pictures. He also recorded over twenty comedy albums and won eight Grammy awards. Cosby is considered to be one of show business's wealthiest men.

The way people perceive the structure of things changed when Richard Buckminster Fuller introduced his trouble-free Dymaxion house design in 1927. Born in Milton, Massachusetts, on this day in 1895, Fuller experimented with economical and efficient design systems. His three-wheel, V-8 engine Dymaxion car was a hit at the Century of Progress Exposition during the 1930s. But it was after 1945 that Fuller's creativity flourished, with his development of polyhedral space-frame enclosures and geodesic domes. His most famous domes were the U.S. Pavilion at the 1967 Montreal Exposition and the dome at Disney's EPCOT Center in Florida.

Chinese philosopher Confucius was born on September 28, 551 B.C.

Napoleon Bonaparte became Emperor of France on March 20, 1815.

On August 8, 1844, Brigham Young was chosen to head the Mormon Church, following the murder of founder Joseph Smith.

American inventor Thomas Edison finished the model for his first phonograph on August 11, 1877.

One of the greatest all-around athletes who ever lived, Jim Thorpe was born on May 28, 1888 in a one-room cabin near Prague, Oklahoma.

On December 22, 1894, Captain Alfred Dreyfus, the only Jewish officer on the French General Staff, was sentenced to life imprisonment for selling military secrets to the Germans.

The Boxer Rebellion, aimed at driving the "foreign devils" out of China, began on June 17, 1900.

Aviator Charles Lindbergh was born on February 4, 1902.

$\mathcal{S}$andra Day O'Connor, the first woman to serve on the United States Supreme Court, was born on March 26, 1930.

$\mathcal{O}$n January 24, 1962, Brooklyn Dodger great Jackie Robinson became the first African-American elected to the Baseball Hall of Fame.

*M*alcolm X was assassinated on February 21, 1965 as he was about to speak at a Black Muslim rally in New York City. The three gunmen were all followers of Elijah Muhammed, founder of the Nation of Islam.

*A*stronaut Edward White became the first human being to walk in space on June 3, 1965.

The worst nuclear disaster in United States history occurred on March 28, 1979, when a reactor malfunctioned at the Three Mile Island nuclear power plant in Middletown, Pennsylvania.

J. Edgar Hoover was named director of the FBI on May 10, 1924

On February 20, 1980, President Jimmy Carter announced that the United States would boycott the Moscow Summer Olympics.

The space shuttle Challenger exploded shortly after blastoff on January 28, 1986, killing all seven crew members.

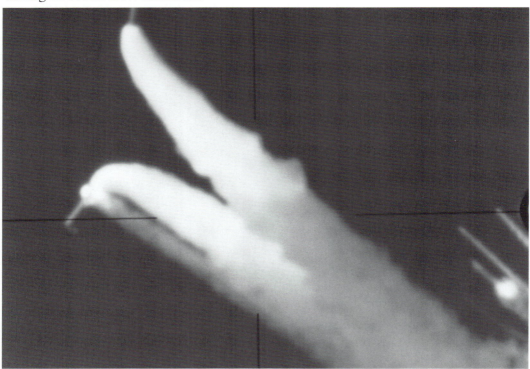

13th.

1939   Frank Sinatra made his recording debut.

1942   Harrison Ford was born.

1946   Cheech Marin was born (see May 24 entry).

1979   The Federal Aviation Administration allowed DC-10s back into service (see May 29 entry).

1985   The Live Aid concerts took place.

Just like he sang in his hit song "Born in East L.A.," Cheech Marin really was born in East Los Angeles, California, on this day in 1946. Although his real name is Richard Marin, his nickname comes from the Chicano word for deep-fried pork skins: *cheecharone*. During high school Cheech played hooky to cruise with the "lowriders" and still graduated with straight A's. He studied for an English degree while working as a dishwasher and janitor. In 1968 he went to Calgary, Alberta, to study pottery with a famous teacher who lived there. The next year, Cheech met a nightclub owner in Vancouver, British Columbia, named Tommy Chong. The rest is comedy history. Cheech and Chong won a Grammy and gold records, and made half a dozen films together before they split up in 1984.

Harrison Ford was a nerdy little kid who was always getting picked on while he was growing up in Des Plaines, Illinois. Born in Chicago on this day in 1942, Ford tried his hand at acting while he was in college, just to raise his grade point average. It didn't help. So he left for Los Angeles with his new wife and a summer-stock theater job on his resumé. A few bit parts led to nothing big in television, so he worked as a carpenter. He made friends with director George Lucas, who changed his life, offering him a role in the film *American Graffiti*. Ford initially turned it down because he was making better money as a carpenter. Lucas upped the pay a little and Ford accepted the job. From there he went on to play Han Solo in the "Star Wars" trilogy, Indiana Jones in another trilogy, and the starring role in Ridley Scott's *Blade Runner*. He married Melissa Mathison shortly after *Star Wars* premiered. Ford is still one of the highest-paid actors in Hollywood.

Two forms of music encountered landmark events on this day. In 1939 Frank Sinatra made his recording debut, singing "Melancholy Mood" and "From the Bottom of My Heart" with the Harry James Band. In 1985 Live Aid concerts were concurrently held in Philadelphia and London to raise money for African famine relief. Forty bands played for a total of sixteen hours before an audience of 1.6 billion people, viewing in 156 countries.

14th.

1865 British illustrator Edward Whymper became the first man to climb Switzerland's Matterhorn.

1868 Gertrude Margaret Lowthian Bell was born.

1900 An international military expedition took control of the Chinese port of Tientsin during the Boxer Rebellion (see June 17, September 7 entries).

1914 Robert Goddard was granted a liquid-fuel rocket patent.

2000 A solar eruption took place.

A massive solar eruption took place on this day in 2000. The National Oceanic and Atmospheric Administration reported, "The storm is expected to reach strong to severe levels, which can adversely affect satellite operations and power grids." The large, complex sunspot group produced one of the largest solar flares seen in over a decade, ejecting billions of tons of plasma and charged particles into space and causing a geomagnetic storm on earth. As the earth's magnetic field deflected the particles, they produced the Aurora Borealis as well as some radio blackouts.

Born in Washington Hall, England, on this day in 1868, Gertrude Margaret Lowthian Bell learned to speak Persian and Arabic while traveling through the Near East. A trained archaeologist, she had worked on a number of excavations in the area before the First World War. When the British Army set up headquarters in Cairo, Egypt, she was appointed to the Arab Bureau, just like her friend and colleague T.E. Lawrence (who later became known as Lawrence of Arabia). Her job was to assess regional conditions based on her comprehensive knowledge of Arab history and culture. After the war, she was sent to Baghdad, where she became oriental secretary to the British High Commission. Bell was part of the forum that chose Faisal I as king of the newly formed nation of Iraq. She bequeathed the money to fund Iraq's British Institute of Archaeology upon her death.

15th.

1830   The Sac and Fox Indians ceded all their lands east of the Mississippi to the United States.

1834   The Spanish Inquisition ended by decree after 356 years.

1949   The U.S. Congress passed the Federal Housing Act.

1979   U.S. President Jimmy Carter proclaimed a national energy supply shortage.

1991   U.S. troops left northern Iraq, ending the Persian Gulf war.

The days of ice-cold air conditioning and desert-hot heating were over after this day in 1979. U.S. President Jimmy Carter proclaimed a national energy supply shortage and established strict temperature restrictions in nonresidential buildings. The temperature was to be maintained at 72 degrees Fahrenheit.

The era of housing projects began on this day in 1949. The U.S. Congress passed a Federal Housing Act, which funded the removal of tenement buildings in slum areas and the erection of low-rent public housing projects like Chicago's Cabrini Green and New York's Queenbridge.

16th.

1872   Roald Amundsen was born.

1948   Ruben Blades was born.

Abandoning his medical studies to pursue adventure, Roald Amundsen conquered both the Arctic and the Antarctic during his lifetime. Born in Borge, Norway, on this day in 1872, Amundsen set sail for Antarctica as first mate on the first vessel to winter near the South Pole, the *Belgica,* in 1897. He began a four-year voyage to cross the Northwest Passage in both directions in 1902, and found the magnetic North Pole. But when he discovered that Robert Peary had actually crossed the pole in 1910, he set his sights southward. The next year, he achieved his goal one month before Captain Robert Scott. Amundsen didn't stop there. In 1926 he circled the North Pole in a plane with Umberto Nobile. Ironically, in 1928 Amundsen disappeared with his plane while searching for Nobile, who had been reported missing near the pole on a second flight.

"I do not believe in the notion that one is condemned to do something because he looks in a certain way or speaks a certain language," Ruben Blades once said. Born in Panama City, Panama, on this day in 1948, Blades's career has encompassed singing, law, and politics. In 1968 he went to New York City on $20, thanks to his brother's job with an airline company. He managed to get a singing job at a Pete Rodriguez band recording session. Then he went home to finish his law degree. Just before his graduation in 1973, however, his family was forced to flee to Miami, Florida. (His father—a State Corps detective—was inadvertently accused by Colonel Manuel Noriega of an assassination attempt on General Omar Torrijos Herrera.) Blades moved back to New York in 1976, singing for a number of bands. Six years later he went out on his own, winning numerous Grammy awards. During the 1980s and 1990s, Blades pursued an acting career, starring in films like *The Milagro Beanfield War* and *The Two Jakes,* as well as TV shows like "The X-Files." In 1994 Blades ran for the Panamanian presidency. But as he said, "At no moment did I think I was going to become president . . . but if I would have been, it would not have been through a desire for power. What we attempted was to bring to the fore the existence of an important sector of the Panamanian population that disagrees and cannot identify with the policies applied to them. My political campaign fully achieved that purpose."

17th.

1968   The animated Beatles' film *Yellow Submarine* premiered at London's Pavilion.

1989   The Boeing B-2 stealth bomber made its first successful test flight.

1997   Human error disrupted the Internet.

1998   A federal judge threw out an EPA report (see January 2, January 10, April 11, June 20, August 1, August 10, September 28, December 1 entries).

In a landmark case against cigarettes and smoking, Federal Judge William Osteen threw out the Environmental Protection Agency's 1993 report as evidence on this day in 1998. The report documented the agency's findings that secondhand tobacco smoke causes lung cancer.

Human error seriously affected the computer world on this day in 1997. A programmer at Network Solutions erroneously caused the DNS tables for domain names that ended in *.net* and *.com* to become corrupted, leaving most domain names unreachable by Internet surfers while empty databases were downloaded to visitors' monitors.

18th.

1918 Nelson Mandela was born (see February 10, March 18, December 13 entries.

1927 Ty Cobb made his four-thousandth hit (see December 18 entry).

1929 Screamin' Jay Hawkins was born.

1937 Hunter S. Thompson was born.

1940 Igor Ivan Sikorsky flew the first VS-300 helicopter at Stratford, Connecticut.

1950 Richard Branson was born.

1962 Telstar relayed the first satellite-broadcast TV program in both North America and Europe (see July 10 entry).

1990 Pete Rose was sentenced to five months in prison for tax evasion (see April 14, September 10, September 11 entries).

Born in England on this day in 1950, Richard Branson has led a life full of hard work and risk. School wasn't much fun. Branson was both myopic and dyslexic, so he didn't get much encouragement. But when he developed a newspaper called *Student at the Age of Sixteen,* which presented politics, rock music, and celebrity interviews, educators took note. When his headmaster saw the first issue, he remarked, "Congratulations, Branson. I predict you will either go to prison or become a millionaire." In 1970

Branson formed a mail-order company that sold discounted records. Branson & Company grew rapidly. The management opened a store, which they called Virgin because they were all business virgins. Within two years, Branson founded Virgin Records, which recorded Mike Oldfield's first album, *Tubular Bells.* It sold over 5 million copies. In 1984 Virgin Airlines was born, becoming the second largest British international airline. Branson also takes personal risks. His boat *Virgin Challenger II* broke the record for crossing the Atlantic Ocean; in 1987 Branson flew the first and largest hot-air balloon to cross the Atlantic Ocean, the *Virgin Atlantic Flyer;* he crossed the Pacific Ocean; and he made an attempt to circumnavigate the world.

Gonzo journalist Hunter S. Thompson once said, "I wouldn't recommend sex, drugs or insanity for everyone, but they've always worked for me." Born in Louisville, Kentucky, on this day in 1937, Thompson published his first novel, *The Rum Diary,* in 1959. It's been all up- and downhill from there. Thompson has been a regular contributor to numerous national and international magazines, including *Rolling Stone.* He has also written such fiction and nonfiction cult classics as *Hell's Angels, Fear and Loathing in Las Vegas, Fear and Loathing on the Campaign Trail '72,* and *Better Than Sex.*

The man who inspired "ghoul rockers" like Alice Cooper was born on this day in 1929 in Cleveland, Ohio. Jalacy J. Hawkins joined Tiny Grimes & His Rocking Highlanders in 1951, playing piano and saxophone as well as singing. Known as Screamin' Jay Hawkins, he played with Fats Domino for a while, but was kicked out when he started sporting leopard skins and a turban on stage. It made no matter. He recorded and released a chart-topping hit of his own in 1956: "I Put a Spell on You." His road shows were extravaganzas for their time. Hawkins would be carried out on stage in a coffin. Dressed in a suit and cape, he performed while brandishing a smoking skull he named Henry.

Sentenced to life imprisonment in 1964, Nelson Rolihlahla Mandela became a symbol of resistance until he was released in 1990. Born in Transkei, South Africa, on this day in 1918, Mandela was a successful lawyer in Johannesburg before he joined the African National Congress (ANC) in 1944, becoming a defiant organizer against apartheid and eventually the ANC's president. Even after South African President F.W. de Klerk banned the ANC in 1960, Mandela continued his campaign and was arrested. Despite his four-hour defense speech, he was convicted. After his release from prison at the age of 71, Mandela was elected as South Africa's first non-white president, replacing de Klerk, who had stepped down when apartheid was finally lifted.

19th.

1993 U.S. President Bill Clinton fired FBI Director William Sessions for incompetence and lying.

1994 U.S. Representative Dan Rostenkowski was indicted for fraud and misuse of government funds (see April 10, July 24 entries).

1996 A blind cow made a remarkable river journey.

A blind cow started a remarkable journey on this day in 1996. Rosie fell into the raging Fraser River while grazing at the Rosebank Ranch near Lytton, British Columbia. Only two years old, she had gone blind after chewing on an old battery she found in the forest. Cows aren't known for their swimming ability, and the river itself has been known to claim the lives of bridge jumpers and river rafters. Two days later, she was seen bobbing up and down in the rapids by a cable-ferry operator. And three days after that, she was spotted on the river bank, standing half on the rocks just south of Hell's Gate: a gorge that shoots 900 million liters of water through the chasm every minute. All she got from her experience was a cold.

20th.

1777 The Cherokee Nation ceded all their lands east of the Blue Ridge Mountains (see May 20, May 23, September 16, December 29 entries).

1881 Chief Sitting Bull surrendered.

1976 The *US Viking* spacecraft landed on Mars's surface.

1979 FEMA was created.

1984 Miss America 1984, Vanessa Williams, was asked to return her crown because *Penthouse* magazine had published nude photographs of her.

1984 Running expert Jim Fixx died of a heart attack while jogging at the age of 52.

Native Americans surrendered both land and lives to the federal government on this day. In 1777 the Cherokee Nation ceded all their lands east of North Carolina's Blue Ridge Mountains when they signed the Treaty of Long Island. And in 1881 the Sioux Nation's Chief Sitting Bull surrendered to federal troops.

The Federal Emergency Management Agency (FEMA) was created by an executive order on this day in 1979. Established to handle disaster mitigation, preparedness, response, and recovery throughout the nation, FEMA also interfaces with the Department of Defense to plan and fund necessary civil defense during a natural disaster such as a flood, earthquake, tornado, or hurricane.

21st.

1911 Marshall McLuhan was born.

1938 Janet Reno was born.

1948 The first 33-1/3 rpm long-playing record was introduced by Columbia Records at the Waldorf-Astoria Hotel in New York City.

1952 Robin Williams was born.

1984 The Polish government proclaimed amnesty for 652 political prisoners.

Born in Chicago, Illinois, on this day in 1952, Robin Williams studied political science at Claremont McKenna College before transferring to the Juilliard School in New York City, where he studied theater. He got his big break when he auditioned for the role of the alien Mork, who first appeared on the TV series "Happy Days." When he was asked to sit down at the audition, he sat on his head on the chair. He got the part since he was "the only alien who auditioned." In 1979 Williams starred in the spin-off series "Mork & Mindy," in which he rarely stuck to the script. He won the 1979 Golden Globe for Best TV Actor in a Comedy. During the 1980s Williams got into film, starring in *Popeye, The World According to Garp, Moscow on the Hudson, Good Morning Vietnam, The Dead Poets Society,* and *The Fisher King,* to name a handful of his projects. He has been nominated for Academy Awards four times, finally winning a supporting actor Oscar for the 1997 film *Good Will Hunting.*

Before anyone really thought how far the electronic information revolution could go, Marshall McLuhan hypothesized on its effect. Born in Edmonton, Alberta, on this day in 1911, Herbert Marshall McLuhan became internationally famous for his studies on the effect mass media has on group thought and social behavior. His most famous work, *The Medium Is the Message: An Inventory of Effects,* was a cult classic during the 1960s and 1970s. He published dozens of other articles and books describing the strength of television and other visually oriented media on future thought before his death in 1980.

Janet Reno's father worked as a *Miami Herald* police reporter after he emigrated to the United States. Her mother was a *Miami News* investigative reporter. So it's not surprising that Janet herself delved deeper into righting wrongs when she grew up. Born in Miami, Florida, on this day in 1938, Reno majored in chemistry at Cornell University, receiving her degree in three years before she enrolled in Harvard Law School. By 1971, she was staff director of the Judiciary Committee of the Florida House of Representatives, revising the court system. Two years later, she worked at the State's Attorney's Office. Five years later, she was appointed State Attorney General for Dade County. She became the first female U.S. attorney general in 1993.

22nd.

1892 Emperor Haile Selassie I was born.

1940 George Clinton was born.

1969 General Francisco Franco named Prince Juan Carlos as his successor as Spain's head of state (see October 30, December 4 entries).

1981 Mehmet Ali Agca was convicted and sentenced to life in prison for shooting Pope John Paul II (see May 12, May 13, May 18, June 2, October 4 entries).

1988 The U.S. Congress passed the Stewart B. McKinney Homeless Assistance Act.

The man who pioneered funkadelic music during the 1970s with his band Parliament-Funkadelic was born in Kannapolis, North Carolina, on this day in 1940. Known for his outrageous costumes and live shows, George Clinton used to work as a barber in Plainfield, New Jersey, while singing in a doo-wop group as a teenager. He began to develop funkadelic after he moved to Detroit, Michigan, in 1967. Over the course of thirty years, Clinton has written and released over thirty albums. His success and influence on modern music earned him and Parliament-Funkadelic an induction into the Rock and Roll Hall of Fame in 1997.

A modicum of help for the homeless was given by the federal government on this day in 1988. The U.S. Congress passed the Stewart B. McKinney Homeless Assistance Act, which donated federal surplus personal property to tax-exempt providers who assist homeless individuals.

Emperor Haile Selassie I was said to be a direct descendant of Israel's King Solomon and the Queen of Sheba. Born on this day in 1892 with the name Ras Tafari Makonnen, Selassie forced the abdication of Lij Yasu in 1916, placing his cousin Zauditu on the throne as empress. Twelve years later, Selassie crowned himself king, and—after Zauditu mysteriously died—in 1930 he became emperor. When other African nations were still ruled by western powers, Ethiopia and its emperor stood for African independence, even when his country was invaded by Italian troops in 1935. Selassie became JAH, the everlasting god of the Jamaican Rastafarian cult, which grew up around his legend. Despite the abolition of slavery and the establishment of a National Assembly, Selassie didn't manage to modernize Ethiopian culture, combat corruption, or ease the starvation of his people. He was deposed by the Marxist dictator Menghistu Haile Mariam in 1974 and placed under house arrest, dying under mysterious circumstances a year later.

23rd.

1851   The Sioux Nation ceded their lands in Iowa and a portion of their holdings in Minnesota when they signed a treaty (see May 20, May 23, July 20, December 29 entries).

1991   The U.S. Senate voted to curb trade with China.

1994   The first female Japanese astronaut returned to earth.

Trade means a great deal to nations in this day and age. On this day in 1991, the U.S. Senate voted to curb trade with the People's Republic of China in order to force the release of a select number of political prisoners.

The first Japanese female astronaut returned from space on this day in 1994. A heart surgeon named Chiaki Mukai had spent fifteen days on board a U.S. spacecraft, conducting experiments.

24th.

1897   Amelia Earhart was born in Atchison, Kansas (see January 11, May 21, May 25, August 24 entries).

1946   The United States conducted the first underwater test of an atomic bomb off Bikini Atoll in the Pacific Ocean.

1969   The *Apollo 11* astronauts splashed down.

1974   The U.S. Supreme Court ruled that President Richard Nixon had to hand over the subpoenaed White House documents for the Watergate trials.

1975   An *Apollo* spacecraft successfully splashed down.

1993   Russia announced that it was taking billions in pre-1993 rubles out of circulation, invalidating the currency.

1993   U.S. Representative Dan Rostenkowski denied allegations he had received embezzled funds (see April 10, July 19 entries).

The Apollo space missions made the news on two different occasions on this day. In 1969 the *Apollo 11* astronauts made a safe splashdown in the Pacific Ocean after accomplishing the first manned lunar landing. And in 1975 another *Apollo* spacecraft splashed down safely in the Pacific Ocean, ending an orbital rendezvous with a Soviet *Soyuz* spacecraft.

25th.

1909   French pilot Louis Blérlot became the first aviator to cross the English Channel (see January 7, January 18, August 6, August 25, September 10, December 1 entries).

1936   *Macbeth* closed at the Park Theater in Bridgeport, Connecticut (see May 2 entry).

1956 The Italian oceanliner *Andrea Doria* collided with the Swedish ship *Stockholm* in heavy fog off the New England coast, killing fifty-one people.

1965 Bob Dylan was booed off the stage at the Newport Folk Festival (see May 1, May 12, May 24, June 7, July 31, August 9, August 17, September 11, December 8 entries).

1968 Janis Joplin with Big Brother and the Holding Company released their album *Cheap Thrills* (see January 19, June 10, July 12, August 12 entries).

1976 The space probe *Viking's* robot arm, which had balked earlier, began picking up soil samples off Mars's surface.

1999 American cyclist and cancer survivor Lance Armstrong won the Tour de France (see June 26, July 27 entries).

Affordable entertainment eased much of the stress caused by the Great Depression. And on this day in 1936, a federally funded project did just that. The audience at the Park Theater in Bridgeport, Connecticut, applauded the closing-night performance of *Macbeth*. The Shakespearean play had been produced by John Houseman and directed by Orson Welles in cooperation with the Federal Theatre Project, which was a branch of the Works Progress Administration (WPA).

New musical ideas were cheered and jeered on this day. When Bob Dylan introduced an electric guitar to his repertoire at the Newport Folk Festival on this day in 1965, he was booed off stage by his loyal acoustic fans. In 1968, however, a new audience of fans cheered Janis Joplin as well as Big Brother and the Holding Company for the release of their album *Cheap Thrills*.

1847 Liberia gained its independence (see August 15 entry).

1894 Aldous Huxley was born.

1943 Mick Jagger was born (see May 12, December 18 entries).

1979   The punk band The Clash debuted their album in America, two years after its release in Great Britain.

1984   American bank regulators announced they had created a $4.5-billion bailout package for Chicago's Continental Illinois National Bank & Trust Company.

1990   U.S. President George H. Bush signed the Americans with Disabilities Act.

Africa's first sovereign, democratic nation to be ruled by non-whites became a republic on this day in 1847, when Joseph Jenkins Roberts declared Liberia's independence. The country had existed under colony status, controlled by the American Colonization Society.

Born in Godalming, England, on this day in 1894, author Aldous Huxley studied English at Oxford University because an eye disease prevented him from taking up his favorite subject, biology. His novels explored the future and mysticism in almost prophetic tones. His 1932 novel, *Brave New World,* described the lives of people who had been scientifically bred and conditioned to achieve social harmony. The degeneration of humankind in a post-atomic world was the subject of his 1948 novel, *Ape and Essence.* And the achievement of superficial nirvana through the use of mescalin was the topic of his 1954 book, *The Doors of Perception,* which became a cult classic during the 1960s.

Rock music giant Mick Jagger once said, "It is all right letting yourself go, as long as you can get yourself back." Born in Dartford, England, on this day in 1943, Michael Philip Jagger fell in love with American blues music as a kid. He met Keith Richards on a train platform while they were in grammar school, and the two became immediate friends. While Jagger studied at the London School of Economics, he and Richards formed a band, which they named after a Muddy Waters song: The Rolling Stones. Jagger's lanky bad-boy looks and powerful voice attracted a strong following in London, which carried over to the United States after the band appeared on "The Ed Sullivan Show" to promote the single from their second album, "Satisfaction." After four decades of recording and performing, Jagger is still considered one of rock music's greatest icons.

Physically and mentally challenged individuals were assured a new level of civil rights on this day in 1990. U.S. President George H. Bush signed the Americans with Disabilities Act, which banned discrimination against the disabled, including workers diagnosed with the AIDS virus.

27th.

1965 U.S. Public Law 89-92 went into effect, requiring caution labels on cigarette packages and establishing the National Clearinghouse for Smoking and Health (see January 2, January 10, April 11, July 17, August 1, August 24, December 1 entries).

1971 George Harrison announced his Concerts for Bangladesh (see July 31 entry).

1986 Greg Le Mond became the first American to win the 2,500-mile Tour de France bicycle race (see June 26 entry).

1996 A pipe bomb exploded at the Atlanta Centennial Olympic Park.

Terrorism attacked the Olympics once again on this day in 1996. But this time, it occurred in the United States. A pipe bomb exploded at the Atlanta Centennial Olympic Park during an outdoor concert that was intended to entertain visitors to the Olympic Games. One concertgoer, Alice Hawthorne, was killed and 111 more people were injured when the bomb went off under a bench in the park. A security guard, Richard Jewell, was initially arrested by the FBI as a suspect, but was later cleared and released.

28th.

1929 Jacqueline Lee Bouvier Kennedy Onassis was born (see January 15, July 3, October 20 entries).

1932 The Bonus Army gathered in Washington, D.C. (see May 29 entry).

1934 The *Explorer I* crew bailed out.

1984 The Summer Olympic Games opened in Los Angeles, California, minus fifteen nations, including the Soviet Union.

1996 Kennewick Man was discovered (see April 22 entry).

A near tragedy occurred after an altitude record was reached on this day in 1934. Major William E. Kepner, Captain Albert W. Stevens, and Captain Orvil A. Anderson were forced to bail out of their hot-air balloon, *Explorer I,* after it had reached the 60,613-foot level. The balloon had ripped after they began their descent.

Jacqueline Lee Bouvier Kennedy Onassis was one of the twentieth century's most famed First Ladies. Born in Southampton, New York, on this day in 1929, Onassis worked at the *Washington Times-Herald* as a human-interest photographer after her 1951 college graduation. Two years later, she married U.S. Senator John F. Kennedy. Onassis won the world's heart when she became First Lady in 1960. Her elegant fashion sense was contagious. The world wept with her and admired her composure following Kennedy's assassination. Five years later, the world watched as she married Greek shipping magnate Aristotle Onassis and began a shopping spree that never seemed to end. After his death in 1975, she returned home to New York, where she worked as an editor at Doubleday Publishing and protectively raised her two children, John F. Kennedy, Jr., and Caroline Kennedy.

The Great Depression led to many incidents of civil unrest in which the government sent National Guardsmen and Army troops to keep the peace. In June 1932, a group of 25,000 First World War veterans and their families—known as the Bonus Army—arrived in Washington, D.C. They set up a tent city just outside city limits. They came to demand immediate payment of the cash bonus they had been promised for their war service, which the government agreed they would receive in 1945. Many jobless veterans whose savings had been wiped out in the 1929 stock market crash were destitute. A bill that proposed the immediate payment of those bonuses had died in the U.S. Senate. On this day in 1932, General Douglas MacArthur was ordered by U.S. President Herbert Hoover to evict the 10,000 remaining veterans. Wearing gas masks, sabres, and rifles with fixed bayonets, squadrons under the command of Major George S. Patton herded marchers on Pennsylvania Avenue and torched the remaining makeshift huts and tents. In the skirmish, two veterans were mortally shot by panicked policemen.

A 9,300-year-old man was discovered on this day in 1996. The oldest, best-preserved human to be found in North America—Kennewick Man—was uncovered by two college students who were watching a hydroplane race along the banks of the Columbia River in eastern Washington. The students pulled the skull from the river bank and the county coroner, Floyd Johnson, toted it in a bucket to local amateur archaeologist James Chatters's house. A few days later, Johnson and Chatters went back to the site and, miraculously, found almost all of Kennewick Man's bones, which the current had scattered downstream.

29th.

1829 Native Americans from the Chippewa, Ottawa, and Potawatomi nations ceded their land in the Michigan Territory when they signed a treaty.

1953 Ken Burns was born.

1958 U.S. President Dwight D. Eisenhower signed the NASA and Space Act, creating the National Aeronautics and Space Administration (NASA).

1965 The Beatles' second film, *Help!,* premiered.

1968 Pope Paul VI reaffirmed the Roman Catholic Church's opposition to artificial birth control methods (see June 21, June 30, September 26, October 28, November 27, December 9 entries).

1977 Oil began to flow through the 800-mile Alaska pipeline.

1981 Great Britain's Prince Charles married Lady Diana Spencer (see February 24, July 1, December 9 entries).

1985 U.S. President Ronald Reagan invited Soviet observers to witness a nuclear test.

Documentary filmmaker Ken Burns has revitalized history. Born in Brooklyn, New York, on this day in 1953, Burns studied film and design at Hampshire College before he became a cinematographer for the BBC and Italian television. In 1975 he established Florentine Films in a small New Hampshire village, which has produced award-winning PBS-TV mini-series specials on the Civil War, the Brooklyn Bridge, the Shakers, jazz music, the Statue of Liberty, and baseball. His unique production style incorporates vintage photographs, drawings, and film clips coupled with narrated quotes from memoirs, personal letters, diaries, and newspaper items of the period as well as expert commentaries.

Diplomatic relations between the United States and the Soviet Union took an interesting turn on this day in 1985. U.S. President Ronald Reagan invited Soviet observers to witness an underground nuclear test in the Nevada desert. In return for this open-handed gesture, Soviet Premier Mikhail Gorbachev proposed a five-month moratorium on all nuclear weapons testing.

30th.

1932   The Tenth Summer Olympics opened in Los Angeles, California.

1936   Buddy Guy was born.

1954   Elvis Presley made his first public appearance (see March 5, March 24, June 26, August 15, August 22, September 25, December 3 entries).

1970   The Rolling Stones fired their manager, Allen Klein (see January 15, May 10, May 12, June 3, June 14, October 25, December 5, December 6, December 18 entries).

Long before Jake and Elwood became known as the Blues Brothers during the 1980s, urban blues greats Junior Wells and Buddy Guy were billed as the Blues Brothers, playing in their mutually unique styles in Chicago blues clubs during the 1960s. Born in Lettsworth, Louisiana, on this day in 1936, electric guitarist Buddy Guy once said, "I must have been put here for a reason. Ain't nobody ever taught me nothing. There wasn't nobody to teach me nothing. So my talent got to be God-gifted, 99.5 percent. The rest of the stuff I watched, looked, and learned." Rock music greats Jimi Hendrix and Eric Clapton both called Guy the world's greatest blues guitarist. When Guy first moved to Chicago in 1957, he won a "Battle of the Blues" contest, beating Otis Rush and Magic Sam. Two years later, he was a session musician in high demand, backing Muddy Waters, Willie Dixon, Koko Taylor, Sonny Boy Williamson, and Little Walter on recordings for Chess Records. He hit the top of the R&B charts with his own album, *Stone Crazy,* in 1962. Guy has since played around the world and, in 1989, he opened his own club, Legends, in Chicago, where he's known to cook up a pot of gumbo for customers when he comes to play.

31st.

1498   Christopher Columbus discovered the island of Trinidad (see March 31, April 16, May 3, May 9, May 13, May 20, June 13, August 23, December 5 entries).

1912   Milton Friedman was born.

1964   The *Ranger 7* spacecraft sent back the first close-up pictures of the moon.

1971   The Concerts for Bangladesh took place (see May 1, May 12, May 24, June 7, July 25, July 27, August 9, August 17, September 11, December 8 entries).

1981   General Omar Torrijos Herrera died.

1995   *Newsweek's* cover announced the rise of the high-paid, high-tech workers they called "the Overclass."

The champion of monetarism was born in New York City on this day in 1912. Economist Milton Friedman worked at the National Bureau of Economic Research for eight years, before becoming a professor at the University of Chicago in 1946. His controversial theory of monetarism states that a nation's economy can be controlled through its money supply. Friedman was awarded the 1976 Nobel Prize for Economics and was policy adviser to U.S. President Ronald Reagan during his terms in office.

One of the 1970s greatest rock music extravaganzas was a benefit concert dedicated to raise money for refugee families in war-torn Bangladesh. Organized by ex-Beatle George Harrison and classical sitarist Ravi Shankar, the Concerts for Bangladesh began on this day in 1971 at New York City's Madison Square Garden. Rock royalty took the stage to a packed house, featuring Harrison, Shankar, The Rolling Stones' Mick Jagger and Keith Richards, ex-Beatle Ringo Starr, Bob Dylan, Eric Clapton, Billy Preston, and Mad Dogs & Englishmen's Joe Cocker and Leon Russell. The house band for the concert was Badfinger.

The Panamanian dictatorship headed by Chief of Government General Omar Torrijos Herrera ended on this day in 1981, when the general was killed in a plane crash. He was succeeded by Colonel Manuel Noriega.

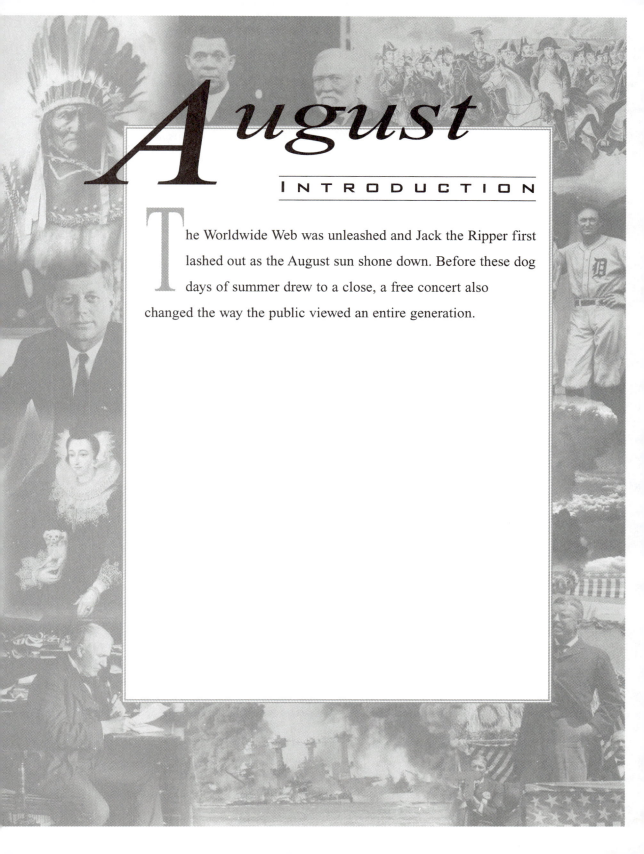

August

INTRODUCTION

The Worldwide Web was unleashed and Jack the Ripper first lashed out as the August sun shone down. Before these dog days of summer drew to a close, a free concert also changed the way the public viewed an entire generation.

1st.

1779   Francis Scott Key was born.

1818   Maria Mitchell was born (see October 1 entry).

1931   Ramblin' Jack Elliot was born.

1942   Jerry Garcia was born (see August 9 entry).

1956   Dr. Jonas P. Salk's first vaccine was made available. (see January 10, February 23, October 28 entries).

1965   Great Britain banned cigarette advertising from commercial television (see January 2, January 10, April 1, April 11, July 17, August 24, September 28, December 1 entries).

1966   Charles Whitman fired a gun from atop a tower at the University of Texas.

1966   U.S. President Lyndon B. Johnson called for enactment of gun control legislation.

1981   MTV began broadcasting on cable television.

2000   Air France Flight 4590 crashed on takeoff.

The battle for gun control began on this day in 1966, after Charles Whitman mortally wounded fourteen people and injured thirty others with a rifle while positioned atop a tower at the University of Texas before being slain by police. Later that day, U.S. President Lyndon B. Johnson called for enactment of gun control legislation.

The first major airline disaster involving one of the twelve existing Concorde supersonic jets occurred on this day in 2000. Air France Flight 4590 crashed on takeoff from Charles de Gaulle Airport in Paris, killing 109 passengers and crew as well as five hotel guests when the jet smashed into a small hotel in Gonesse.

Music speaks to the hearts of many Americans. On this day, one of the creators of the nation's anthem was born. In 1779 Francis Scott Key, who was an attorney and the lyricist of "The Star Spangled Banner," was born in Maryland. A protegé of famed folksinger Woody Guthrie, cowboy balladist Ramblin' Jack Elliot was born in Brooklyn, New York, on this day in 1931. No one expected that Jack, raised in a Jewish household, would find his roots in the West. He'd met his first cowboy when he was a child, running away from home at age 15 to the West, where he could experience the romance of American cowboy life firsthand. A voice of 1960s American youth was also born on this day in 1942. Jerry Garcia, lead guitarist for the Grateful Dead, was born in San Francisco, California. On this same day in 1981, MTV began broadcasting on cable television, permanently changing the way Americans heard and saw their favorite musicians and singers.

Not all comets are discovered by university-taught scientists. On this day in 1818, Maria Mitchell was born in Nantucket, Massachusetts. A librarian by trade, she viewed the skies with a home telescope, discovering Mitchell's Comet just above the North Star in 1847. A self-taught astronomer, Mitchell became the first elected female member of the American Academy of Arts and Sciences. Her work eventually led her to become a professor of astronomy at Vassar College.

2nd.

1920 Marcus Garvey presented his "Back to Africa" program (see February 6, April 19, August 17 entries).

1939 The Hatch Act, barring federal employees from political campaigns, was passed.

1946 The Battle of Athens (Tennessee) took place.

1953 Ardito Desio summited K-2 (see April 18 entry).

1958 Johnny Cash signed a record deal with CBS Records (see December 3 entry).

1974 Former White House counsel John Dean was sentenced to a maximum four years in prison for his role in the Watergate scandal.

1977 The Department of Energy was established.

1990 Iraqi troops invaded Kuwait (see January 17, February 24 entries).

1995 Executive Order 12968, establishing a uniform federal personnel security program, was signed.

A new movement began on this day in 1920. Marcus Garvey presented his "Back to Africa" program during a speech in New York City, inspiring African-Americans to move to Liberia as a way to return to their origins rather than suffer prejudice in the United States.

Sometimes the government itself needs to impose self-restraints. In 1995 Executive Order 12968 was signed by U.S. President Bill Clinton, establishing a uniform federal personnel security program for employees to have initial or continued access to classified information. In 1939 the Hatch Act was passed by the U.S. Congress. The law barred federal employees from taking an active role in political campaigns. In 1946 the Battle of Athens took place. Some 3,000 ex-GIs in Athens, Tennessee, took up arms against the local police force in retaliation to what they perceived as an abuse of power.

3rd.

1795	The U.S. government established the Ohio Territory.
1872	Haakon VII of Norway was born.
1923	U.S. Vice President Calvin Coolidge was sworn in as president.
1951	The U.S. Military Academy dismissed ninety cadets.
1958	The first undersea crossing of the North Pole was made (see April 6, April 20, May 9, May 12, July 11, August 29 entries).
1973	The U.S. Justice Department ordered a new investigation of Kent State University (see January 4 entry).
1983	The U.S. Justice Department sued General Motors Corporation.
1988	The Soviet Union released Mathias Rust, who had landed a light plane in Moscow's Red Square (see September 4 entry).
1993	Ruth Bader Ginsburg was appointed to the U.S. Supreme Court.

Government intervention was a highlight in the business world on this day. In 1981 U.S. air traffic controllers went on strike after negotiations with the federal government broke down. In 1983 the U.S. Justice Department sued General Motors Corporation, charging the company with willful neglect. Allegedly, the manufacturer knew that its X-model cars had defective brakes.

Two cases of criminal activity on campus came to light on this day. In 1951 the U.S. Military Academy dismissed ninety cadets for cheating on their final exams. In 1973 the U.S. Justice Department ordered a new investigation into the deaths of four Kent State University students during a campus demonstration.

In 1795 the U.S. government signed treaties with Native American tribes establishing the Ohio Territory. It wasn't the first or last time land was negotiated to be taken by treaty. But as Chief Seattle said in 1887, "But how can you buy or sell the sky? The land? The idea is strange to us. If we do not own the freshness of the air and the sparkle of the water, how can you buy them?"

Appointment to a high position occurs in many ways. In 1872 Haakon VII was born in Charlottenlund, Norway. Unlike many monarchs, he was elected king when Norway voted, in 1905, for its independence from Swedish rule. In 1923 U.S. Vice President Calvin Coolidge was sworn in as the nation's thirtieth president, succeeding Warren Harding, who had died the day before. And in 1993 the U.S. Senate voted 96-3 to confirm the appointment of Ruth Bader Ginsburg to the U.S. Supreme Court.

4th.

1900   The Queen Mother was born (see December 14 entry).

1921   Maurice Richard was born.

1962   Roger Clemens was born.

1964   The bodies of murdered civil rights workers were found in Mississippi.

1966   Several U.S. radio stations banned the broadcast of The Beatles' songs.

1976   Police clashed with black students in Soweto South Africa.

1988   The U.S. Congress voted to pay Japanese-Americans (see February 19, February 24, August 10 entries).

1993   A federal judge sentenced two Los Angeles police officers (see March 3, April 16, April 29 entries).

Many times, relations between people from different ethnic backgrounds need time to heal. In 1988 the U.S. Congress voted to pay $20,000 to each living Japanese-American who had been interred in a concentration camp in the western United States during the Second World War. There are times, however, when differences cannot be easily mended. In 1976, on this day, simmering tensions exploded in South Africa as police clashed with black students in Soweto Township. And in 1993 a federal judge sentenced Los Angeles police officers Stacey Koon and Laurence Powell to two-and-a-half years' imprisonment for violating Rodney King's civil rights. Not all events begin or end well. On this day in 1964, the bodies of murdered civil rights workers Michael A. Schwerner, Andrew Goodman, and James E. Chaney were found by federal agents in an earthen dam in Mississippi.

Comments are not always taken lightly, even from musicians. In 1966 several U.S. radio stations banned the broadcast of The Beatles' songs because John Lennon sarcastically commented during a conversation that the band was more popular than Jesus Christ.

The lives of few people have crossed so many important events in history as that of the Queen Mother Elizabeth. Born as Lady Elizabeth Bowes-Lyon in St. Paul's Walden Bury, England, on this day in 1900, she married the Duke of York in 1923 and had two daughters, Elizabeth and Margaret. She became Great Britain's Queen-Consort in 1936, when her husband was enthroned as King George VI, after his brother Edward abdicated to marry Wallis Warfield Simpson. She made her first royal visits to Paris, Canada, and the United States before the Second World War broke out. And rather than flee to the countryside during the London Blitz, she stood by her husband as Buckingham Palace was attacked by aerial bombs. Even after her husband died in 1952 and her daughter Elizabeth II was enthroned, she continued to perform her public duties. Her hundredth birthday celebration in 2000 was filled with great fanfare for Great Britain's most beloved royal.

Two major sports figures were born on this day. In 1921 Canadian hockey player Maurice Richard was born in Montreal, Quebec. Richard played on eight Stanley Cup Championship teams and became the first player to score 50 points in a single season during his eighteen-year career. In 1962 five-time Cy Young Award-winning baseball pitcher Roger Clemens was born in Dayton, Ohio.

5th.

1858   Julia Archibald Holmes reached the summit of Pikes Peak.

1930   Neil Armstrong was born.

1963   The United States, Great Britain, and the Soviet Union formally signed a treaty outlawing nuclear tests in the atmosphere, in space, and at sea.

1974 U.S. President Richard Nixon admitted that he ordered a halt to the investigation of the Watergate break-in six days after it occurred (see September 15, September 19, October 1, October 23, November 21 entries).

1981 Under orders from U.S. President Ronald Reagan, the Federal Aviation Administration began to dismiss air traffic controllers who had gone on strike.

1985 U.S. President Ronald Reagan revealed that a sore removed from his nose the previous week was an easily curable form of skin cancer.

Julia Archibald Holmes made exploration history on this day in 1858. She became the first woman in recorded history to summit Pikes Peak in Colorado.

Born in Wapakoneta, Ohio, on this day in 1930, astronaut Neil Armstrong became the first man to set foot on the moon on July 20, 1969. He had commanded the *Gemini 8* space mission in 1966, but he made his mark in history on board the *Apollo 11* space mission in 1969.

6th.

1890 Baseball player Cy Young pitched his first professional game (see May 5 entry).

1922 Sir Freddie Laker was born.

1926 Gertrude Ederle became the first female swimmer to cross the English Channel, finishing two hours faster than her male predecessors (see January 7, January 18, July 25, August 25, September 10, December 1 entries).

1965 The Voting Rights Bill was signed by U.S. President Lyndon B. Johnson.

1991 The World Wide Web was unleashed (see December 14, December 16 entries).

2000 A rare coin was sold.

Transatlantic air travel took a unique turn when Sir Freddie Laker pioneered low-cost air fares for flights between Great Britain and the United States. Born in Kent, England, on this day in 1922, Laker started his aviation career working for Short Brothers. During the Second World War, he was attached to the Air Transport Auxiliary, where he got his greatest experience as a pilot. In 1960 he was hired as a manager at British United Airways, where he stayed until he opened Laker Airlines Ltd. in 1966.

A newspaperman from Mountain Home, Arkansas, Frank Wallis found an unusual coin in a roll of new golden Sacagawea dollar coins he had purchased at a bank. Known by coin collectors as a double-denomination mule error, the coin was minted with both quarter and dollar faces. The front bore the portrait of George Washington, which normally appears on a quarter. And the back was minted just like a regular Sacagawea dollar. Only four such misprinted coins are known to have been sent into circulation. Wallis's was the first to be reported and was sold to coin dealer Dwight Manley for $29,900 at the American Numismatic Association's annual fair. Two of the other three that have been discovered were auctioned previously, one selling for $31,000 and the other selling at an on-line auction for $41,395. The error is believed to be the first of its kind in the 208-year history of the U.S. Mint.

The World Wide Web was officially unleashed on this day in 1991. The line-mode browser (www) was released on alt.hypertext. A few weeks later, the browser was posted on comp.sys.next, comp.text.sgml, and comp.mail.multi-media.

7th.

1876   Mata Hari was born (see October 15 entry).

1888   Jack the Ripper killed his first victim.

1894   The United States formally recognized the Republic of Hawaii.

1903   Louis Leakey was born (see February 6 entry).

1904   Ralph J. Bunche was born.

1912   Delegates at the Progressive Party's first national convention nominated Theodore Roosevelt for U.S. president.

1934   The U.S. Court of Appeals struck down the federal government's attempt to ban James Joyce's novel *Ulysses.*

1957   Colonel Rudolf Abel was indicted as a Soviet spy (see May 1 entry).

1959   The U.S. satellite *Explorer 6* transmitted the first view of earth from outer space.

1972   The Federal Council on Environmental Quality released its annual report.

1974   French stuntman Philippe Petit walked a tightrope strung between the World Trade Center's twin towers in New York City.

1985   British radio and television journalists staged a twenty-four-hour strike, protesting the BBC's cancellation of a documentary on Northern Ireland.

1993   Queen Elizabeth II of England opened the doors to Buckingham Palace (see April 29 entry).

1998   Steve Fossett took off in his hot-air balloon *Solo Spirit 3* from Mendoza, Argentina, attempting to circumnavigate the world (see January 14, January 20, February 21, August 16 entries).

A federal grand jury in New York City indicted Colonel Rudolf Abel as a Soviet spy on this day in 1957. He was eventually sentenced to thirty years' imprisonment. But he didn't fulfill his entire term: Abel was exchanged for U-2 pilot Francis Gary Powers in 1962.

One of the world's most famous unsolved mysteries began on this day in 1888. The body of the first of seven women murdered by Jack the Ripper was discovered in London's East End. A prostitute named Martha Tabram was found slashed in her room in the Whitechapel district. From that night until November 10, all seven slasher murders took place within a square-mile area edged by Whitechapel, Spitalfields, Aldgate, and the City of London proper. Jack's name originated from a letter written by someone who claimed to be the killer. But while the crime spree raged, he was sometimes referred to as the Whitechapel Murderer and Leather Apron. Although some criminologists believe the killer was a member of the Royal Family, most people think it was simply the work of a woman-hating psychopath.

The grandson of a slave, political scientist Ralph J. Bunche became a distinguished international diplomat attached to the United Nations during the 1950s and 1960s. Born in Detroit, Michigan, on this day in 1904, Bunche advised the federal government on questions of strategy in Africa during the Second World War. He was then consulted as an expert on trusteeship territories, drafting the sections of the UN charter that related to their interests. He won the 1950 Nobel Peace Prize after arranging a cease-fire as UN mediator in Palestine. And as UN undersecretary, he played an important role in relations during the Suez, Congo, and 1965 Indo-Pakistani crises.

"Don't drink the water, but you can breathe the air" was the conclusion made on this day in 1972. The Federal Council on Environmental Quality released its annual report, stating that the air in the United States was cleaner, while the water was more polluted than before.

The man who helped us realize that humankind is millions of years old was born in Kabete, Kenya, on this day in 1903. Paleontologist Louis Leakey returned to Africa after graduating from Cambridge University, acting as curator of Nairobi's Coryndon Memorial Museum. Along with his wife and partner, Mary, he discovered the earliest human remains in Africa's Olduvai Gorge. When they discovered the two-million-year-old remains of *Homo habilis,* he postulated that two human-like species, *Homo habilis* and *Australopithecus robustus,* actually coexisted. Only *Homo habilis* survived, becoming the precursor of *Homo sapiens* or human beings.

One of the world's most famous spies was born in Leeuwarden, the Netherlands, on this day in 1876. Marguerite Gertrude Zelle had grown up to become an oriental dancer in France by 1905. Known as Mata Hari, her exotic looks naturally attracted the interest of many men who held high-level military and governmental posts in France and Germany. Legend has it that she had her clandestine affairs on board the Oriental Express as it coursed through Europe, gathering information from her lovers about war tactics at the height of the First World War. The French government arrested her in 1917 and convicted her of espionage on Germany's behalf. She was executed before a firing squad in Paris that same year.

8th.

1844 Brigham Young became leader of the Mormons (see May 2, October 6 entries).

1863 Florence Augusta Merriam Bailey was born (see May 2, October 6 entries).

1945 U.S. President Harry S Truman signed the United Nations charter.

1973 U.S. Vice President Spiro Agnew denounced reports that he had taken kickbacks from contractors as "damned lies."

1984 Carl Lewis won his third gold medal out of the four he received in track and field events at the 1984 Summer Olympic Games (see July 1 entry).

2000 The Confederate submarine *H.L. Hunley* was raised.

The Mormons were the subject of two historic events on this day in religious history. In 1844 Brigham Young was chosen to head the Mormon church, following Joseph Smith's murder. And in 1863 Florence Augusta Merriam Bailey was born. Although she was primarily an ornithologist whose studies won major scientific awards, she made another major contribution. In 1894, after observing the lives of women living within the Mormon community, she published an exposé entitled *My Summer in a Mormon Village.* Her book portrayed the suffering of women who lived in this polygamous society but still maintained their faith.

The Confederate submarine *H.L. Hunley* was raised from the Atlantic Ocean on this day in 2000. The submarine went down for no apparent reason with nine crew members, in 1864, after sinking the Union blockade vessel *Housatonic* off Sullivans Island, South Carolina. The salvaged submarine was placed on a barge and taken to Charleston, where it was housed in a conservation facility at the old Charleston Navy Base. Made from locomotive boilers, the *Hunley* was a hand-cranked vessel with a sad history. The first crew drowned in 1863 when the sub was flooded by the wake of a passing ship near its mooring on James Island. A few weeks later, a second crew that included its designer, H.L. Hunley, died during a testing accident.

1814   The Creeks signed the Treaty of Fort Jackson.

1866   Matthew Henson, the first African-American to reach the North Pole, was born.

1888   The Dawes Act went into effect.

1927   Marvin Minsky was born.

1962   Robert Zimmerman legally changed his name to Bob Dylan (see May 1, May 12, May 24, June 7, July 25, July 31, August 17, September 11, December 8 entries).

1963   Whitney Houston was born.

1969   Actress Sharon Tate was murdered by the Manson Family (see January 25, March 6, October 27, December 8 entries).

1989   U.S. President George H. Bush signed the Financial Institutions Rescue, Recovery, and Enforcement Act.

2000   Millie Jeffrey was awarded the Presidential Medal of Freedom.

2000   The fifth anniversary of Jerry Garcia's death was observed (see August 1 entry).

The savings and loan industry got a much-needed shot in the arm on this day in 1989. U.S. President George H. Bush signed the Financial Institutions Rescue, Recovery, and Enforcement Act, which provided $166 billion over the course of ten years to close or merge insolvent savings and loan institutions throughout the United States.

A pioneer in the study of artificial intelligence, Marvin Minsky built the first wired neural network learning machine called SNARC (Stochastic Neural-Analog Reinforcement Computer) in 1951. Born in New York City on this day in 1927, Minsky began his academic career studying psychology. But he quickly realized that he disagreed with professors like B.F. Skinner, who relied on environment and behavior to explain human mind functions. He, on the other hand, believed the human brain works like thousands of microcomputers that each have a special function. In 1959 he and John McCarthy co-founded the MIT Artificial Intelligence Laboratory, which Minsky headed from 1964 through 1973.

A large Native American tribe was convinced to move west of the Mississippi River on this day in 1814. Major General Andrew Jackson ended his campaign against the Creeks when both sides signed the Treaty of Fort Jackson. The Creek tribal leaders agreed to cede all their land to the United States and were eventually moved west of their homeland. On this same day in 1888, the Dawes Act became effective. This bill allowed white men to marry Native American women, protecting the property rights of both parties within the marriage.

Back in the 1920s, the Ku Klux Klan had a strong following in the Midwest. In Cherokee, Iowa, their targets weren't African-Americans, but Roman Catholics and Jews. As a child, Millie Jeffrey got hit with stones by other children because she was Catholic. "No Catholic could get elected to public office, and I thought it was very wrong and that's when I became interested in justice and politics," she remembered. Jeffrey dedicated her life to civil rights after she left her hometown, joining Reverend Dr. Martin Luther King, Jr., and James Meredith on marches in Alabama and Mississippi during the 1960s. Jeffrey was also the director of the first women's United Auto Workers department, and she was the president of the Michigan Women's Foundation. On this day in 2000, Jeffrey was awarded the Presidential Medal of Freedom by U.S. President Bill Clinton for her special contributions to the way Americans live.

Born in Newark, New Jersey, on this day in 1963, singer Whitney Houston once said, "I ain't no diva. I know what I don't want. I know how to say no. I know how to hire and fire. I've learned my craft and I've learned it well." Houston's mother was a successful R&B backup singer, and her aunt Dionne Warwick topped the charts more than once. Houston herself became the first female artist to have an album enter the Billboard charts in the number-one position. And she became the first female artist to do this twice when she issued her next album.

The power of music was noted on this day in 2000. On the fifth anniversary of Grateful Dead guitarist Jerry Garcia's death, the band's publicist, Dennis McNally, noted, "The Grateful Dead is an enormous cottage industry. . . . In our last full year, 1994, we sold about $65 million worth of tickets." Since 1995, sales of Grateful Dead-related products were estimated at tens of millions of dollars. But unlike many rock bands, the group and its leader encouraged fans to tape concerts for free and charged one-fifth the price of the standard $200 concert ticket. Even though the band stopped working when Garcia died, the Dead's loyal fans (known as Deadheads) continue to gather for reunions to this day.

1943   Ronnie Spector was born.

1974   The Election Reform Act was passed, limiting individual contributions to candidates for federal offices to $1,000.

1977   The United States and Panama agreed to transfer the Panama Canal to Panamanian control by the year 2000 (see April 18, May 18, September 7, November 2, November 3, December 31 entries).

1988   U.S. President Ronald Reagan signed legislation to compensate Japanese-Americans interred during the Second World War (see February 19, February 24, August 4 entries; see also *On This Day in History:* June 23 entry)

1995   U.S. President Bill Clinton ordered the Food and Drug Administration to curb sales of tobacco to children (see June 20, July 17 entries).

2000   It was announced that a bald eagle chick had hatched in Washington, D.C.

Japanese-Americans who had been interred in West Coast concentration camps during the Second World War received nominal compensation on this day in 1988. U.S. President Reagan signed the legislation, giving $20,000 and an apology to each of the 120,000 Japanese-Americans who had survived imprisonment, humiliation, and the loss of personal property because of national hysteria.

Ronnie Spector is the only American vocalist to be backed by The Beatles, on her 1970 single "Try Some, Buy Some." Born as Veronica Yvette Bennett in New York City's Spanish Harlem on this day in 1943, Ronnie Spector performed as one of disc jockey Murray Kauffman's dancing girls for his staged rock and roll revues, along with her sister Estella and her cousin Nedra, while recording demos for Colpix Records. The trio were working as go-go dancers at the famed Peppermint Lounge when they were spotted by record producer Phil Spector. It was Estelle who followed up the contact. They broke their demo contract and signed with Phil Spector, who vaulted them to fame with hits like "Be My Baby," "Walkin' in the Rain," and "I Can Hear Music." Ronnie and the Ronnettes went down in the record books as the most famous girl group in rock history.

For the first time in fifty years, the nation's symbol nested in the nation's capital. On this day in 2000, the National Park Service announced that a bald eaglet had hatched in a nest and was flying on its own on park service land in Washington, D.C. Residents had spotted a pair of bald eagles building a nest in January. The female was seen sitting on the nest in March. And the next month a chick was spotted. Loss of habitat and peril from pesticides had placed bald eagles on the endangered species list. After the pesticide DDT was banned in 1972, their numbers had been increasing in some portions of the United States.

11th.

1807   David Rice Atchison was born.

1863   Carrie Jacobs-Bond was born.

1873   J. Rosamond Johnson was born (see December 12 entry).

1877   Thomas Edison is said to have finished the model for the first phonograph.

1943   A group of WASPs were assigned flight duty.

1950   Steve Wozniak was born.

A computer pioneer was born in San Jose, California, on this day in 1950. Steve Wozniak was the electronics engineer who built and introduced the Apple computer, the extremely user-friendly alternative to IBM's personal computer, in 1976. Together with Steve Jobs, Wozniak saw his Apple Corporation grow into a billion-dollar concern. But nine years later, he left the firm to pursue his interest in home video.

Female songwriters highlighted two events on this day. A co-composer of the African-American anthem "Lift Every Voice and Sing" was born in Jacksonville, Florida, on this day in 1873. J. Rosamond Johnson co-wrote the song with James Weldon, and it became an overwhelming success. Born on this same day in 1863, Carrie Jacobs-Bond was widowed and penniless when she began to sell her songs to support herself and her son. As her work grew in popularity, she realized she could make more money running her own publishing company. Taking out a loan, she established Carrie Jacobs-Bond and Son Publishing Company. Her most famous song, "I Love You Truly," sold more than 5 million copies during her life.

A U.S. president who held office for only one day was born in Frogtown, Kentucky, on this day in 1807. David Rice Atchison was a U.S. senator from Missouri and president pro tempore of the Senate in 1849. When U.S. President James K. Polk ended his term on a Sunday that year and President-elect Zachary Taylor refused to take the oath of office on a Sunday, Atchison took office for the entire day of March 4, 1849, between the United States's eleventh and twelfth presidents.

A fleet of tiny PQ-8 planes had to be flown from the factory to March Field on this day in 1943. But because the cockpits were filled with radio equipment, male pilots couldn't fit in the planes. A group of Women's Airforce Service Pilots (WASPs) assigned to fly the new models, sitting on their parachutes with their legs stuck straight out in front of them while in flight.

12th.

1831 Madame Helena Petrovna Blavatsky was born.

1868 The U.S. Army forced Navajo Nation chiefs to sign a treaty establishing a 3.5-million-acre reservation within their old territory.

1970 Rock singer Janis Joplin gave her final concert, performing at Harvard University (see January 19, June 10, July 12, July 25 entries).

1978 Maxie Anderson, Ben Bruzzo, and Larry Newman left Presque Island, Maine, aboard their hot-air balloon *The Double Eagle,* heading for France (see May 8, June 27 entries).

Americans were introduced to the world of Eastern religion and psychic phenomena thanks to Madame Helena Petrovna Blavatsky, who was born in Ekaterinoslave, Russia, on this day in 1831. The principal founder of the Theosophy movement, Blavatsky traveled throughout India and Tibet before joining forces with Henry Steel Olcott in New York City to establish a center for esoteric study. Although she made many claims about her psychic powers, she did not pass rigorous investigation by the Society for Psychical Research.

13th.

1812 Alfred Krupp was born (see September 6, October 17 entries).

1927 Fidel Castro was born (see September 5, October 5, October 11, November 30, December 2 entries).

The man who forged the German armaments industry was born in Essen, Germany, on this day in 1812: Alfred Krupp. The son of forge owner Friedrich Krupp, Alfred exhibited the first flawless ingot of cast steel at the British Association for the Advancement of Science's Great Exhibition, which was held in London, England, in 1851. Manufactured in the world's first Bessemer steel plant, it weighed 8000 pounds. Four years earlier, Krupp had begun production of the world's first steel gun. To feed the growing demand for his steel and arms, Krupp acquired numerous mines and built docks to ship his products throughout the world.

The fight against corruption and oppression in Cuba was led by a singular inspirational figure who was born on his father's sugar plantation in Cuba on this day in 1927. Fidel Castro had studied law and had a busy practice in Havana, defending the rights of the poor against corrupt government officials under the Batista regime. In 1953 he joined his brother Raul in an unsuccessful uprising attempt. He was sentenced to fifteen years' imprisonment for his involvement, but got out on amnesty in a year. Fleeing to the United States and then to Mexico, Castro organized support and began guerrilla warfare activities in Cuba in 1956. Overthrowing Batista in December 1958, Castro established a "Marxist-Leninist regime," which he still heads to this day.

14th.

1928   Lina Wertmuller was born.

1945   Wim Wenders was born.

1947   Danielle Steel was born.

1974   Congress authorized the personal ownership of gold by U.S. citizens for the first time since the 1930s (see April 5, April 19, June 5, December 31 entries).

Controversial avant-garde films have turned many heads at the Cannes Film Festival, influencing more mainstream features years and decades after they first appeared on the screen. Two directors who are known for their radical cinematic approaches share this birthday. Born in Rome, Italy, on this day in 1928, Lina Wertmuller rose to prominence with her visual attacks on the male-oriented Italian culture with her 1972 film *The Seduction of Mimi.* She quickly followed up her success, in 1975, with the films *Swept Away* and *Seven Beauties,* both of which starred actor Giancarlo Giannini. Born in Düsseldorf, Germany, on this day in 1945, Wim Wenders focused his cinematic sights on the isolation and alienation felt by individuals in search of enlightenment. Among his most famous works are the 1984 film *Paris, Texas* and the 1987 film *Wings of Desire.*

One of the world's most prolific romance novelists was born in New York City on this day in 1947. Danielle Steel worked as an advertising copywriter before she began hitting the top of best-seller lists with regular frequency. When her first novel, *Going Home,* gained popularity in 1973, she devoted her time totally to writing books. It was her 1979 novel, *The Promise,* that made her a best-selling author despite critics' constant dislike for her work. Ten years later, Steel had sold 85 million copies of her novels in forty-two countries.

15th.

1824 Freed African-American slaves established the country of Liberia along Africa's west coast (see July 26 entry).

1876 The U.S. Congress passed a law removing Native Americans from the Black Hills of South Dakota after gold was discovered.

1912 Dame Wendy Hiller was born.

1912 Julia Child was born.

1913 Menachem Begin was born (see June 20, September 15 entries).

1923 Shimon Peres was born.

1955 Elvis Presley signed with Colonel Tom Parker (see March 5, March 24, June 26, July 30, August 22, September 25, December 3 entries).

1969 The Woodstock Music and Arts Fair opened on Max Yasgur's New York farm.

2000 Two hundred North and South Koreans were reunited.

Two great dames were born on the same day in 1912. Born in Bramhall, England, Dame Wendy Hiller made her name during the 1930s for her stage portrayal of Eliza Doolittle in George Bernard Shaw's *Pygmalion*. She played such a convincing role that the playwright himself requested her to recreate Eliza for the 1938 film version. Although she devoted most of her time to the stage, Hiller starred in the 1940 film *Major Barbara* and the 1945 film *I Know Where I'm Going*. But it was her role in the 1958 film *Separate Tables* that won her an Academy Award. Chef and television host Julia Child was born in Pasadena, California, on the exact same day. While her husband Paul Child was working at the American Embassy in Paris, France, Julia attended the Cordon Bleu cooking school. The culmination of her education was published in 1961: She wrote *Mastering the Art of French Cooking* with two French co-authors, Simone Beck and Louisette Bertholle. It was the first of nine cookbooks that she has published over four decades. She then produced the first of her popular television series, *The French Chef,* on PBS-TV.

Two former Israeli prime ministers share the same birthday. Born in Brest-Litovsk, Poland, in 1913, Menachem Begin was elected prime minister in 1977 and formed a coalition government. In 1978 he and Egyptian President Anwar Sadat were jointly awarded the Nobel Peace Prize. Born in Poland in 1923, Shimon Peres served as defense minister before he was elected prime minister in 1984.

On June 24, 1950, thousands of Korean families were separated on either side of the Demilitarized Zone on the Korean peninsula. On this day in 2000, two hundred North and South Koreans were reunited with their families for four days in the capital cities of Seoul and Pyongyang. The reunion was the result of summit talks that had taken place two months earlier. The South Korean delegation was selected based on age (most people were in their 70s, 80s, or 90s) out of a pool of 76,000 applicants.

16th.

1960   A parachute was tested from a hot-air balloon.

1962   The Beatles' drummer Pete Best was fired and replaced by Ringo Starr (see April 27, July 7, September 11 entries).

1995   Shannon Faulkner entered The Citadel (January 20 entry).

1998   Steve Fossett survived a crash of his hot-air balloon (see January 14, January 20, February 21, August 7 entries).

Two hot-air balloonists made death-defying descents on this particular day in history. In 1960 Captain Joe W. Kittinger rose to 102,800 feet in a hot-air balloon before jumping from the open gondola in a parachute. He reached speeds of more than 600 mph before pulling the rip cord to test a new type of parachute during his spectacular descent. On this same day in 1998, Steve Fossett survived the crash of his hot-air balloon, *Solo Spirit 3,* when it ruptured during a thunderstorm. The craft was 500 miles from Australia's east coast and Fossett had flown 14,236 miles when the tragedy occurred. Falling 29,000 feet, Fossett was rescued the next day in a life raft thanks to the emergency beacon he carried on board.

One of the military's last male bastions was invaded on this day in 1995. Shannon Faulkner entered The Citadel military academy, after a court order allowed her to become the school's only female cadet. She dropped out in less than a week—along with thirty male cadets—when temperatures in the classrooms and dormitories reached 116° Fahrenheit.

17th.

1862	Facing starvation, the Sioux Nation began an uprising in Minnesota.
1887	Marcus Garvey was born in Jamaica (see August 2 entry).
1897	W.B. Purvis patented the electric railway switch (see January 7 entry).
1963	Folksinger Joan Baez introduced Bob Dylan to an audience of 14,000 at Forest Hills, New York (see May 1, May 12, May 24, June 7, July 25, July 31, August 9, September 11, December 8 entries).
1978	The hot-air ballon *Double Eagle* completed the first transatlantic flight, landing in France (see January 14 entry).
1992	The siege at Ruby Ridge, Idaho, began (see August 22, September 6 entries).

A tragic confrontation began at a mountain cabin near Ruby Ridge, Idaho, on this day in 1992. Federal marshals began a siege in an attempt to bring Randy Weaver to justice. He had been charged with possession of a sawed-off shotgun.

18th.

1891	The Oklahoma Territory was opened.
1894	The U.S. Bureau of Immigration was established.
1932	Auguste Piccard made his second hot-air balloon flight from Zurich, Switzerland (see January 28, March 1, March 19, May 27 entries).
1950	The American Broadcasting Company began airing Saturday morning television shows for children.

At the turn of the nineteenth century, the world was on the move as evidenced by events that took place on this day in 1891. Once designated as Cherokee Nation reservation land, 900,000 acres of the Oklahoma Territory were opened to white settlement by presidential order. In an attempt to limit the overwhelming immigration to the United States by people from around the world, the U.S. Congress established the Bureau of Immigration—forerunner of the Immigration and Naturalization Service—on this day in 1894.

Physicist and engineer August Piccard had already reached the skies during his lifetime: He'd ascended to the stratosphere in a hot-air balloon. On this day in 1932, he rose to the heights once again. But this time he flew up in a hot-air balloon to study cosmic rays at high altitude.

19th.

1902 Ogden Nash was born.

1964 The Beatles began their second U.S. tour (see January 1, January 20, January 24, January 30, February 7, February 9, February 12, May 9, June 6, June 12 entries).

1978 The Who released their album *Who Are You?*

1994 U.S. President Bill Clinton halted an open-door policy toward Cuban refugees.

The door closed on this day in 1994. After three decades of openly welcoming Cuban refugees to its shores, the United States closed the door on free entry. President Bill Clinton ordered the Coast Guard to intercept refugees at sea and ship them to the U.S. Navy base at Guantanamo Bay, Cuba.

Poet Ogden Nash loved to twist the English language into an amusing pretzel. Born in Rye, New York, on this day in 1902, Nash showed no fear of tripping himself up in a turn of a phrase, whether it appeared in *The New Yorker* magazine or in a collected volume of verse. He wrote his poems for people everywhere who go just about anywhere. As he wrote in *Oh to Be Odd,* "Oh to Be Odd! Hypochondriacs / Spend the winter at the bottom of Florida and the summer on top of the Adirondriacs. / You go to Paris and live on champagne wine and cognac / If you're dipsomognac."

Rock and roll landmarks occurred with great regularity during the 1960s and 1970s, and this day was no exception. In 1964, The Beatles' second American tour began when they played a concert at the Cow Palace in San Francisco, California. After they appeared on the television program "The Ed Sullivan Show" during their first tour, their army of fans had grown to staggering millions. No regular concert hall could handle the numbers of teens who wanted to see the "Fab Four," so they were booked into huge convention centers in every major city. On this same day in 1978, the last Who album to feature Keith Moon as drummer was released. Sadly, Moon died before he could celebrate with his band mates the overwhelming success of *Who Are You?* which sold over a million copies.

20th.

1818   Emily Brontë was born.

1890   H.P. Lovecraft was born.

1916   The National Park Service was established.

1926   Jacqueline Susann was born.

1955   Bill Haley made it to the top of the charts.

1980   John Lennon and Yoko Ono began recording together.

Some writers achieve fame while others succeed in garnering cult status. Science fiction author H.P. Lovecraft found his audience among a fanatical group of French and American readers. Born in Providence, Rhode Island, on this day in 1890, Lovecraft actually made his living as a ghostwriter and revisionist. But his consuming passions were set to print during the 1920s and 1930s in the magazine *Weird Tales*. He contributed about sixty short stories that wove a tale around fish-like beings called the "Old Ones" who roamed the earth before humankind existed. Much of his work, however, was published after his death, in 1937, such as the 1965 collection *Dagon and Other Macabre Tales*.

The lives and loves of women have changed over the centuries, as evidenced by the works of two female authors who share this birthday. Born in Halifax, England, on this day in 1818, Emily Brontë wrote about social stigma and its effect on the eternal love of a well-to-do young girl and a farm boy who grew to become a wealthy land owner in her novel *Wuthering Heights*. Born in Philadelphia, Pennsylvania, on this day in 1926, Jacqueline Susann wrote about the world of show business and its influence on the ambitious women who strive to make it to the top, losing love and sometimes life in the process. A former actress, Susann experienced a runaway best-seller in her first novel, *Valley of the Dolls*.

Two musical landmarks occurred on this particular day. One of the earliest rock and roll hits made it to the number-one slot. In 1955 Bill Haley and the Comets' song "Rock Around the Clock" hit the top of the Billboard charts. Another rock and roll hit was born on this same day in 1980. John Lennon and Yoko Ono began recording their chart-topping album *Double Fantasy*.

The number of national parks and monuments set aside for the preservation of wilderness had exponentially grown since the first park—Yellowstone National Park—was designated in 1872. Concern for the care and management of forty fragile environments was manifested on this day in 1916, when the U.S. Congress established the National Park Service to "conserve the scenery and the natural and historic objects and the wild life therein and to provide for the enjoyment of the same in such manner and by such means as will leave them unimpaired for the enjoyment of future generations." A division of the Department of the Interior, this agency now oversees and maintains more than 365 separate federal properties from coast to coast.

1878   The American Bar Association was established.

1901   The first transcontinental automobile trip was completed (see September 1 entry).

1904   Count Basie was born.

1952   Joe Strummer was born.

1958   The Small Business Investment Act was signed.

1973   The new civilian government freed political prisoners under the amnesty granted by Greek President George Papadapoulos (see June 1, August 23, November 25 entries).

1975   A ban against Cuban exports was lifted.

1982   Palestine Liberation Organization guerillas retreated from Beirut, Lebanon, as Israeli troops invaded the area.

1983   Benigno Aquino was mortally wounded at the Manila airport while returning from self-imposed exile in the United States (see January 25, February 26 entries).

1986 A toxic gas cloud escaped from a volcanic crater.

1999 A giant panda was born in captivity.

The way business is conducted in the United States has undergone more than a few evolutionary changes. On this day in 1958, U.S. President Dwight D. Eisenhower gave small businesses financial encouragement when he signed the Small Business Investment Act, which allowed firms to get low-cost government loans to improve or expand their current ventures. And in 1975 American companies—both large and small—gained access to the wealth of sugar and tobacco exports from Cuba. A twelve-year-old ban was lifted, allowing American companies access to these valuable goods through their foreign subsidiaries.

Many professions have organized self-monitoring bodies to test and license members as well as establish codes of ethical conduct. On this day in 1878, one such group was created by lawyers, judges, and law professors in Saratoga, New York. The American Bar Association was founded to maintain a high quality of practice within the legal profession.

Sometimes nature takes its own tragic course, proving that human beings cannot always control their environment. On this day in 1986, a gas cloud escaped from a volcanic crater in the Cameroons, spreading toxins in the atmosphere that could not be controlled. The eruption killed more than 17,000 people in its wake.

The public's conception of automobile travel was transformed when, in 1901, the first transcontinental automobile trip was completed by Tom Fetch and Marcus Karup. Their Packard Model F arrived in New York City after a sixty-one-day journey from San Francisco. The event proved that automobiles were not limited to local transport.

Two forms of music have a reason to celebrate this particular day. In 1904 jazz pianist and bandleader William "Count" Basie was born in Red Bank, New Jersey. Although he'd played drums in a band as a child, his mother convinced him to take up piano. While he was still in his teens, Basie made money as an accompanist at a silent film house. When he moved to New York City, encouragement from Fats Waller led to Basie's work as a touring backup musician for a number of blues singers during the 1920s. His own big band gained international fame over the next fifty years. A prominent figure in punk rock was born in Ankara, Turkey, on this day in 1952. The Clash's lead singer, Joe Strummer, was the son of a diplomat, but his political leanings directed him toward less middle-class attitudes. Unlike the nihilistic Sex Pistols, Strummer's band extolled a world filled with possibilities.

Giant pandas require a delicate balance of elements to survive in the wild. The fragile line between survival and extinction becomes even finer in captivity. On this day in 1999, a rare event took place in the animal world: A giant panda was born at the San Diego Zoo. Its mother was one of three giant pandas living in capitivity in the United States. The first successful captive birth in the Western Hemisphere since 1990, the newborn gave scientists fresh hope for this fading species. Fewer than 1,000 giant pandas live in the wild in China, and there are only 110 living in captivity in the entire world.

22nd.

1911   The Louvre Museum announced that Leonardo da Vinci's *Mona Lisa* had been stolen.

1922   Michael Collins was killed.

1969   Elvis Presley made his comeback, performing at the International Hotel in Las Vegas, Nevada (see March 5, March 24, June 26, July 30, August 15, September 25, December 3 entries).

1973   U.S. Secretary of State William Rogers resigned (see March 25, September 21, November 10 entries).

1984   U.S. President Ronald Reagan was nominated for a second term in office.

1992   Federal agents killed Randy Weaver's wife during the standoff at Ruby Ridge, Idaho (see August 17, September 6 entries).

Political leaders come and go, but a few linger for a little more time. On this day in 1922, one of the Irish Republican Army's founders—Michael Collins—was killed in an ambush near Bandon, Ireland. The previous year, he had negotiated a treaty between the Sinn Fein and Great Britain, ending a bloody rebellion. In 1973 U.S. President Richard Nixon announced that Secretary of State William Rogers had tendered his resignation. The president announced the appointment of National Security Adviser Henry Kissinger as his replacement. And in 1984 U.S. President Ronald Reagan and Vice President George H. Bush were nominated for a second term in office at the Republican National Convention in Dallas, Texas.

23rd.

1500 Christopher Columbus was accused of mistreating West Indian natives and was sent back to Spain in chains (see March 31, April 16, May 3, May 9, May 13, May 20, June 13, July 31, December 5 entries).

1946 Keith Moon was born (see September 7 entry).

1947 Margaret Truman sang at the Hollywood Bowl.

1970 Lou Reed played with the Velvet Underground for the last time.

1975 Former Greek President George Papadapoulos and two officers involved in the 1967 military coup were sentenced to death by a special court (see June 1, August 21, November 25 entries).

1994 Cuban refugees were rescued by the U.S. Coast Guard.

Waves of refugees have fled Cuba for political or economic reasons since Fidel Castro overthrew the corrupt Batista government during the late 1950s. One of the largest exoduses occurred in 1980, when over 125,000 emigrants made it to the Florida shores. But the largest single-day total since that time took place on this day in 1994. More than 3,000 Cuban refugees were rescued at sea by the U.S. Coast Guard as they entered Florida waters.

Two events on opposite ends of the musical spectrum occurred on this particular day. In Los Angeles, California, an audience of 15,000 people gathered to hear U.S. President Harry S Truman's daughter, Margaret, sing at the Hollywood Bowl in 1947. It was her first public performance. A man who couldn't stop entertaining people on or off the stage was born on this same day in 1946, in Wembley, England. The Who's drummer, Keith Moon, had dropped out of school and picked up the drums when he was 14. Three years later, he joined Pete Townshend, John Entwhistle, and Roger Daltrey to form the punk rock band The Who. For the next fourteen years, rumors about Moon's gregarious, almost self-destructive lifestyle became the stuff of legends, from his accidentally driving over his personal chauffeur and trashing hotel rooms to binge-drinking himself nearly to death. Only a few days after The Who released their album *Who Are You?* in 1978, Moon died of an accidental overdose of medication that had been prescribed to help him curb his addiction to alcohol. On this same day in 1970 another punk rock icon made the news. Lou Reed decided to pursue a solo career, playing his last show with the band made famous by pop artist Andy Warhol—the Velvet Underground.

24th.

1932   Amelia Earhart became the first female pilot to fly nonstop across the United States (see January 11, May 21, May 25, July 24 entries).

1956   The first nonstop transcontinental helicopter flight was completed.

1968   France became the world's fifth thermonuclear power, exploding a hydrogen bomb in the South Pacific.

1973   The United States and Thailand announced an agreement for a phased withdrawal of American troops.

1981   John W. Hinckley, Jr., was indicted for assassination attempt on U.S. President Ronald Reagan (see March 30 entry).

1982   Mark David Chapman was sentenced for murder of John Lennon (see December 8 entry).

1996   U.S. President Bill Clinton set new limits on sales of cigarettes to minors (see January 2, January 10, April 11, July 17, August 1, December 1 entries).

An assassin and a would-be assassin made the headlines on this day. In 1981 John W. Hinckley, Jr., was indicted for his attempt to assassinate U.S. President Ronald Reagan. The next year, Mark David Chapman was sentenced to twenty years to life imprisonment for the assassination of songwriter and former Beatle John Lennon.

A pair of momentous flights were completed on this day in aeronautic history. In 1932 Amelia Earhart became the first female pilot to fly nonstop coast to coast—from Los Angeles, California, to Newark, New Jersey. Her trip took 19 hours, 5 minutes. In 1956 the first nonstop transcontinental helicopter flight was completed by a pilot working for Piasecki Aviation. The 2,610-mile journey took 31 hours and 40 minutes.

25th.

1875   Captain Matthew Webb became the first man to cross the English Channel without a life jacket, swimming the breaststroke (see January 7, January 18, July 25, August 6, September 10, December 1 entries).

1927 Tennis player Althea Gibson was born in Silver City, South Carolina (see July 6, July 10 entries).

1930 Sean Connery was born.

1958 Tim Burton was born (see August 27 entry).

1972 The People's Republic of China cast its first veto on the Security Council (see October 25 entry).

1981 The *US Voyager 2* spacecraft sent back a report.

1992 Reverend Sun Myung Moon married about 20,000 couples (see January 6 entry).

1997 The state of Florida reached an $11.3-billion out-of-court settlement with the tobacco industry, recovering Medicaid expenditures spent on smokers' health costs (see January 2, January 10, April 11, July 17, August 1, August 24, November 6, December 1 entries).

A stickler for visual detail, film director Tim Burton's work frequently exhibits gothic overtones. Born in Burbank, California, on this day in 1958, Burton went to work at the Disney Studios after he graduated in animation from the California Institute of the Arts. He got his first job as a director, however, when Paul Reubens (aka Pee Wee Herman) asked him to direct the 1985 film *Pee Wee's Big Adventure.* Burton's darker side emerged when he next directed *Beetlejuice.* During the 1990s, his distinctive style was also seen in films like *Batman, Edward Scissorhands, The Addams Family,* and *Sleepy Hollow.*

Born in Edinburgh, Scotland, on this day in 1930, actor Sean Connery introduced the role of British superspy James Bond to the silver screen in the 1962 film *Dr. No.* Connery's childhood didn't exactly prepare him to play the part of an elegant, well-educated espionage agent. The son of a truck driver, he worked a morning milk route before heading off to school. After a number of false starts and odd jobs, Connery eventually was drawn to television and film during the late 1950s. He recreated the James Bond role five more times before he moved on to other projects after 1971. *The Man Who Would Be King, The Untouchables, Indiana Jones and the Last Crusade, The Name of the Rose,* and *The Hunt for Red October* are just a few of the films he's starred in during the past thirty years.

The People's Republic of China hadn't been a member of the United Nations for more than a year before it exercised its rights. On this day in 1972, Chinese delegates cast their first veto in the United Nations Security Council, blocking Bangladesh's bid for UN membership.

An unusual report was sent to the planet earth on this day in 1981. The *US Voyager 2* spacecraft had come within 63,000 miles of the planet Saturn. At this relatively close distance, it began transmission of photos back to earth as well as other information about this far-off celestial body.

Reverend Sun Myung Moon married about 20,000 couples from 131 nations in the world's largest mass marriage, which was held in Seoul, Korea, on this day in 1992. An additional 10,000 couples were wedded by simultaneous satellite transmissions shown in Brazil, the Philippines, Zaire, Kenya, and Nigeria.

26th.

1900 A man was bitten by a mosquito in the name of science.

1904 Christopher Isherwood was born.

1992 The Animal Enterprise Protection Act was passed.

1994 The Anti-Crime Act was signed.

A new law was passed by the U.S. Congress on this day in 1992 to prevent terrorist attacks by animal rights groups, which had become more vigilant in their protests during the late 1980s. The Animal Enterprise Protection Act gave courts latitude to sentence animal rights terrorists in the hopes of discouraging the unlawful disruption of commerce involving animals. The bill was also designed to protect individual owners of animals and scientists from those who are radically opposed to the use of nonhuman animals in business and industry.

In the hopes of curbing increased crime rates throughout the nation, U.S. President Bill Clinton signed the Anti-Crime Act on this day in 1994. This piece of legislation promised that 100,000 police would be placed on U.S. streets with the help of federal funds.

Many writers have achieved their place in the record books by creating one memorable piece of work. Born in Disley, England, on this day in 1904, Christopher Isherwood earned his time in the limelight for more than one project. In 1939, he wrote a book that served as the basis for the Broadway hit, *I Am a Camera,* and then for the musical *Cabaret. Goodbye to Berlin* wasn't the only work he wrote about pre-Nazi life in Berlin, but it was his most popular. In 1944 Isherwood took a bizarre detour, translating the

Hindu epic poem *The Bhagavad-Gita* along with Swami Prabhavananda. He then moved to Hollywood, where he worked as a screenplay writer for MGM studios.

A man allowed a mosquito to feed on him for a good cause on this day in 1900. U.S. Army physician James Carroll allowed himself to be bitten as part of his research into the transport of the yellow fever virus. Carroll was an assistant to Walter Reed, who headed the U.S. Army Yellow Fever Commission. Stationed in Havana, Cuba, since the Spanish-American War, the team, which also included Aristides Agramonte and Jesse Lazear, proved that the *Aedes aegypti* mosquito carried the yellow fever virus, eradicating the notion that the disease was spread by direct contact with infected human beings or objects.

27th.

1928 Chief Mangosuthu Buthelezi was born.

1929 Yasser Arafat was born.

1952 Paul Reubens was born (see August 25 entry).

1998 The Washington State Supreme Court ruled that the police must advise citizens that they have the right to refuse a warrantless search of their homes.

It's Pee Wee Herman's birthday! Born as Paul Reubens in Peekskill, New York, on this day in 1952, Reubens introduced his character Pee Wee Herman while working with an improvisational comedy troupe. The success of this childlike character led to Reubens writing the script for *Pee Wee's Big Adventure* in 1985. The next year, Reubens signed a deal with CBS-TV to create the children's show *Pee-Wee's Playhouse*. Reubens also appeared in two other Tim Burton films, *Batman Returns* and *The Nightmare Before Christmas*.

Two passionate political leaders were born on this day in twentieth-century history. In 1928 Chief Mangosuthu Buthelezi was born in Mahlabatini, South Africa. The founder and president of the Zulu Inkatha Party, Buthelezi dedicated his life to the achievement of a nonracist democratic political system in his country. Born in Jerusalem in 1929, Palestinian Liberation Organization leader Yasser Arafat dedicated his life to the creation of a Palestinian state that would exist separately from the state of Israel. This Nobel Peace Prize winner became the head of the newly formed nation after repositioning his stance from rebel leader to international diplomat.

28th.

1828 Count Leo Tolstoy was born.

1928 An all-party conference in Lucknow, India, voted for dominion status within the British empire.

1971 A Brookfield Zoo elephant named Ziggy was allowed outdoors.

1976 Massachusetts Institute of Technology scientists announced that they had created an artificial gene.

1983 Israeli Prime Minister Menachem Begin announced his resignation (see September 15 entry).

The man who inspired Mohandas K. Gandhi to adopt the doctrine of nonresistance was born on his parents' estate in Russia's Tula province on this day 1828. Most people know of Count Leo Tolstoi's novels *War and Peace* and *Anna Karenina*. But few people know that this father of thirteen children had inspired an entire sect who turned to nonresistance after reading the pamphlets and short stories he wrote during the 1870s and 1880s. Gandhi even carried on a correspondence with the somewhat eccentric author until his death in 1910.

Animals kept in captivity have been known to exhibit aggressive behaviors during mating season or when they feel threatened by outside stimuli. Back in the 1940s, an elephant at the Brookfield Zoo in Illinois had seriously attacked his trainer. At the time, little was understood about the fragile nature of the elephant psyche, so Ziggy was kept in solitary confinement to be studied. Fortunately, zoo officials did not deem it necessary to kill the beast. On this day in 1971, Ziggy was allowed outdoors for the first time in 30 years.

29th.

1758 The New Jersey Legislature established the first Indian reservation.

1947 The United Nations authorized the establishment of the state of Israel.

1957 U.S. Senator Strom Thurmond ended a twenty-four-hour filibuster against a civil rights bill.

1958 George Harrison joined the Quarrymen, which included John Lennon and Paul McCartney (see September 20 entry).

1966 The Beatles gave their final live concert at Candlestick Park in San Francisco, California (see January 1, January 20, January 24, January 30, February 7, February 9, February 12, May 9, June 6, June 12 entries).

1979 The Sheridan Broadcasting Corporation made a purchase.

1982 British explorers Ranulph Fiennes and Charles Burton completed the first aerial circumnavigation of the globe by way of the North and South poles.

2000 Adam Nash was born.

Reservation land was set aside for the nation's Native American tribes throughout the 1700s and 1800s in the United States. The first such reservation was established in New Jersey on this day in 1758. The colonial legislature set aside 1,600 acres of land, which was designated as tribal territory, separating settlers from these original residents.

The world's first entirely African-American owned and operated radio network came into existence on this day in 1979. The Sheridan Broadcasting Corporation of Pittsburgh, Pennsylvania, purchased the Mutual Black Network of Arlington, Virginia, moving its operations into Sheridan's main headquarters.

A test-tube baby named Adam Nash was born in Denver, Colorado, on this day in 2000. He was conceived in order to save his six-year-old sister's life. In a painless procedure, doctors collected cells from his umbilical cord and transplanted them into his sister Molly, who suffered from Fanconi anemia—a hereditary bone marrow deficiency—a month later. Lisa and Jack Nash used genetic tests to screen the embryos before implanting one in Lisa's womb, ensuring that Adam would have the exact type of cells needed.

30th.

1936 The Thomas Jefferson figure on Mount Rushmore was dedicated (see March 3, July 2, July 4, September 17, October 1, October 31, December 28 entries).

1943 Jean-Claude Killy was born.

1986 Nicholas Daniloff was arrested (see September 29 entry).

1993 Israel's Knesset approved the framework for Palestinian autonomy in the occupied territories.

The press is not immune to arrest. On this day in 1986, *U.S. News and World Report* correspondent Nicholas Daniloff was arrested by KGB police in Moscow, Russia. He was charged with espionage after receiving secret documents from a Soviet acquaintance.

An Olympic gold medal skier was born in Val d'Isere, France, on this day in 1943. Jean-Claude Killy won three gold medals in the 1968 Olympics in the slalom, giant slalom, and downhill events. Rather than entering another olympiad, Killy turned professional immediately after his landmark win, endorsing ski products and manufacturing ski equipment.

31st.

1870 Maria Montessori was born.

1881 The first U.S. tennis championships were played in Newport, Rhode Island.

1964 U.S. President Lyndon B. Johnson signed the federal Food Stamp Act.

1996 Three scientists found Martian fossils.

The creator of the Montessori educational system was born in Rome, Italy, on this day in 1870. Maria Montessori was the first female medical graduate from the University of Rome when she received her degree in 1894. She developed her educational system for three- to six-year-old children after she'd worked with feeble-minded youngsters at a school she had opened in 1899. The Montessori system encourages independence and responsibility in a specially equipped environment, and was originally taught in a school she opened in Rome's slum district in 1907.

Martian fossils were found on this day in 1996. NASA announced that three Houston-based scientists hd found the potato-sized Martian meteorite ALH84001 in Antarctica, containing what appeared to be fossils of Martian life.

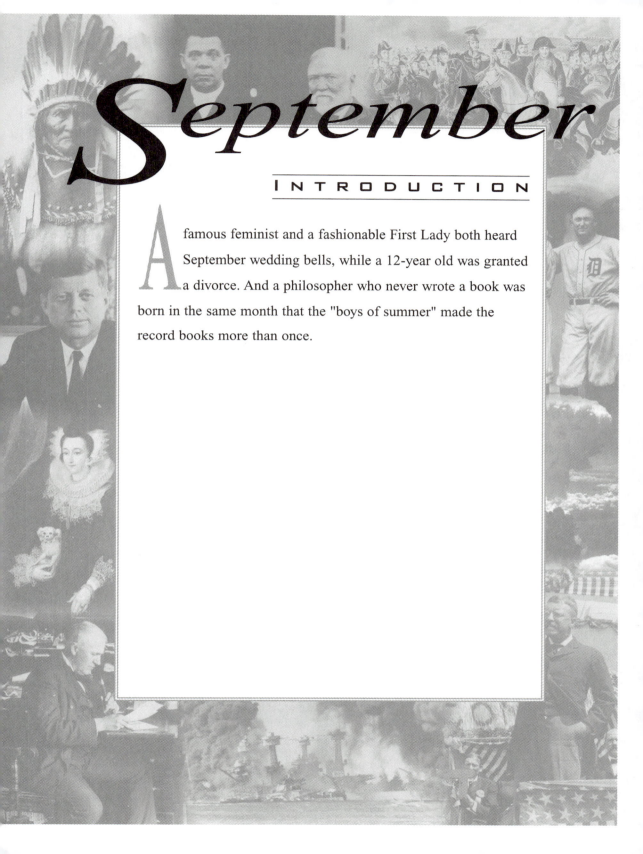

September

A famous feminist and a fashionable First Lady both heard September wedding bells, while a 12-year old was granted a divorce. And a philosopher who never wrote a book was born in the same month that the "boys of summer" made the record books more than once.

1st.

1910 Nan Aspinwall became the first woman to ride across the United States on horseback, making it from San Francisco to New York City (see August 21 entry).

1958 A U.S. spy plane was shot down for violating Soviet airspace.

1969 Colonel Moammar Ghadafi overthrew the Libyan government in a bloodless coup.

1983 A Korean passenger plane was shot down for violating Soviet airspace.

A U.S. spy plane was shot down on this day in 1958. George P. Petrochilos and sixteen other crewmen were downed by Soviet MIGs as the plane skimmed the Soviet border. On this same day in 1983, a Soviet jet fighter shot down a Korean Air Lines 747 passenger jet over the Sea of Japan. The plane had violated Soviet airspace, which cost 269 passengers and crew their lives.

2nd.

1885 White coal miners violently attacked their Chinese co-workers in Rock Springs, Wyoming (see February 2, May 6, December 17 entries).

1935 George Gershwin signed his name to the completed orchestral score of his opera *Porgy and Bess* (see February 12 entry).

1945 Ho Chi Minh's troops seized power in Hanoi and proclaimed an independent Vietnam.

1948 Christa McAuliffe was born (see January 28, February 6, February 10, April 4, April 29, June 22, October 13 entries).

1962 The Soviet Union agreed to send arms to Cuba (see October 22 entry).

1985 A joint U.S.-French expedition announced it had located the *Titanic's* remains about 560 miles off the coast of Newfoundland (see October 21 entry).

2000 North Korean spies and guerrillas were returned home.

Another step toward reconciliation between North and South Korea took place on this day in 2000. Hundreds of thousands of people welcomed home sixty-three North Koreans, who had been convicted of espionage and guerrilla warfare activities during the Korean War, when they arrived in Panmunjom, North Korea. The aging ex-convicts—who ranged in age from 66 to 90—had been captured in South Korea, tried, and imprisoned because they refused to renounce their allegiance to communist ideals. Although some of the returnees had been freed long ago, they weren't allowed to go back to North Korea until this day.

A special astronaut was born in New Hampshire on this day in 1948. Christa McAuliffe was a school teacher who was part of a six-person crew that included Dr. Judith Resnick on board the space shuttle *Challenger,* in 1986. Tragically, McAuliffe and the entire crew died when the space shuttle exploded on liftoff.

3rd.

1954 The Espionage and Sabotage Act was signed.

1964 The National Wilderness Preservation System was established.

1996 The United States launched twenty-seven cruise missiles at "selected air defense targets" in Iraq in retaliation for the Iraqi invasion of Kurdish areas.

2000 Gloria Steinem got married.

Punishment for the crime of espionage became more severe in the United States on this day in 1954. U.S. President Dwight D. Eisenhower signed the Espionage and Sabotage Act, establishing the death penalty for anyone convicted of commiting sabotage and spying within the nation during alleged peace time.

U.S. President Lyndon B. Johnson turned some federal land into permanent wilderness on this day in 1964 when he signed a bill establishing the National Wilderness Preservation System. It had taken eight years and sixty-six drafts to create this project in the U.S. Congress. A lot of land was at stake. Fifty-four wilderness areas within national forests found in thirteen states—constituting 9.1 million acres—were set aside to be protected in their natural condition. No roads, artificial structures, or permanent improvements were allowed to be built or maintained within these pristine areas, saving a portion of the true wilderness for generations to come.

An icon of feminism got married for the first time on this day in 2000. The founder of *Ms.* magazine and feminist pioneer, Gloria Steinem, married South African businessman and anti-apartheid activist David Bale in a ceremony held at the Oklahoma home of former Cherokee Nation chief Wilma Mankiller. Often quoted as saying that "a woman needs a man like a fish needs a bicycle," the sixty-six-year-old Steinem had agreed to be Bale's fourth wife while both attended a spiritual retreat.

4th.

1886 Apaches led by Geronimo surrendered to General Nelson Miles at Skeleton Canyon, Arizona.

1937 Dawn Fraser was born.

1957 Arkansas Governor Orval Faubus called out the National Guard to prevent desegregation.

1957 The Ford Motor Company introduced the Edsel.

1972 Mark Spitz won his seventh Olympic gold medal.

1987 Mathias Rust was convicted by a Soviet court on charges of illegal border entry (see August 3 entry).

1993 The Al Fatah faction of the Palestinian Liberation Organization endorsed a peace accord with Israel.

1997 The Supreme Court refused to block a California law prohibiting affirmative action.

2000 *Beetle Bailey* turned fifty years old.

Some stunts are not well rewarded, as was evidenced on this day in 1987. A Soviet court convicted West German pilot Mathias Rust on charges of illegal border entry without a visa and potential espionage, all stemming from his landing in Moscow's Red Square on May 28, 1987. For his frivolity, Rust was sentenced to four years in a labor camp. He served less than one year and was released on August 3, 1988.

Two opposing events occurred on this day. In 1957, Arkansas Governor Orval Faubus called out the National Guard in an attempt to prevent nine African-American students from entering Central High School in Little Rock. Forty years later, the U.S. Supreme Court refused to block a California state law that prohibited preferential treatment to certain races in government employment and school admissions.

Private Beetle Bailey turned fifty on this day in 2000. Still avoiding work, this comic strip character was the invention of Mort Walker, who fashioned him after a real-life high school chum. (Walker once had to flip his friend's mattress to wake him up for school.) A half century is a long time to keep coming up with fresh ideas for a comic strip, and *Beetle Bailey* is King Features Syndicate's third-largest-selling product, after *Blondie* and *Hagar the Horrible.* It appears daily in 1,800 newspapers in fifty countries. But as the strip's seventy-seven-year-old creator remarked, "I write myself into a corner until I have to come up with a punch line."

A major athlete was born in Australia on this day in 1937. Dawn Fraser became the first three-time winner of the same event in three separate Olympics. She won gold medals in the freestyle swimming event at the 1956, 1960, and 1964 Olympics and set twenty-seven individual swimming records before she was suspended for pulling a prank at the 1964 Olympics. On this same day in 1972, Mark Spitz won a record seventh Olympic gold medal in men's swimming events at the Munich Olympics.

5th.

1698 The first tax on beards was imposed by Russia's Tsar Peter the Great.

1978 A Near East summit began at Camp David.

1981 Poland's Solidarity labor movement convened.

1991 The trial of former Panamanian leader Manuel Noriega began in the United States (see January 3, December 20 entries).

2000 Fidel Castro shook hands with U.S. President Bill Clinton (see August 13, October 5, October 11, November 30, December 2 entries).

2000 Tuvalu joined the United Nations.

Three very remarkable meetings took place in the international arena on this day. In 1981 Poland's Solidarity labor movement commenced its first national convention while approxiamtely 100,000 communist troops practiced maneuvers just outside the nation's border. In 1978 U.S. President Jimmy Carter, Egyptian President Anwar Sadat, and Israeli Prime Minister Menachem Begin began a Near East summit meeting at Camp David. And in 2000 Cuban President Fidel Castro shook hands with a current U.S. president for the first time since he overthrew the Batista government in 1959.

While attending a United Nations summit conference, Castro shook hands with President Bill Clinton. During his regime, he had seen eight other presidents serve terms in the White House before this landmark event occurred.

One of the world's most peaceful countries became an official United Nations member on this day in 2000. Formerly known as the Ellice Islands, Tuvalu is inhabited by 9,000 people who live on 10 square miles of coral atolls situated over 600 miles north of Fiji. Although the economy of the United Nations' 189th member has been largely focused on fish, coconuts, and a national investment trust, the country has enjoyed a newfound wealth from the Internet. Their domain name suffix—*tv*—seems to be highly valued by television stations around the world. Broadcasters agreed to pay Tuvalu $50 million over a period of ten years to use the suffix. This doubled their gross national product and enabled them to afford UN membership.

6th.

1899 The United States proposed an open-door policy to give foreign powers equal trade rights in China.

1974 George Harrison formed his own label: Dark Horse Records (see August 29, September 20 entries).

1983 The Soviet Union admitted shooting down Korean Air Lines Flight 007.

1996 The Ruby Ridge hearings began in the U.S. Senate, chaired by Senator Arlen Specter (see July 22, August 17, August 22, entries).

2000 MP3.com was ordered to pay a penalty for copyright violation.

2000 For the the first time since 1851, the British Association for the Advancement of Science conference opened in the city of London (see August 13 entry).

A major Internet lawsuit was decided in the courts on this day in 2000. The nine-month-old MP3.com listening service had been sued by Universal Music Group. As U.S. District Judge Jed S. Rakoff commented, the Internet company supposed that "because their technology is somewhat novel, they are somehow immune from the ordinary applications of laws of the United States, including copyright law." The MP3.com company had copied between 5,000 and 10,000 of Universal Music Group's CDs, for which

Judge Rakoff penalized the fledgling Internet company $25,000 per CD in reparations to be paid to the music publishing giant.

The truth eventually comes to the surface even in international incidents. On this day in 1983, the Soviet Union admitted shooting down Korean Air Lines Flight 007 when it passed into Soviet airspace over Sakhalin Island five days earlier. All 269 people on board the Korean Air Lines Boeing 747 were killed.

A major science show opened on this day in 2000. For the first time since the Great Exhibition of 1851, the city of London, England, hosted the British Association for the Advancement of Science annual conference. The twenty-four-day event, which presents new findings in scientific research, debates, workshops, concerts, and experiments that involve the conference's visitors, showcased the work of 400 scientists and artists who apply scientific technology in their work. The Imperial College of London's rector Lord Oxborough commented, "The message of this festival is that at no time in civilization has civilization been more dependent on science than it is today."

7th.

1901	The Boxer Rebellion ended with the Peace of Peking (see June 17, July 14 entries).
1921	The first Miss America bathing beauty contest took place in Atlantic City, New Jersey.
1936	Buddy Holly was born in Lubbock, Texas (see January 26, February 3, May 17 entries).
1954	SEATO was formed.
1975	Martina Navratilova defected (see September 9, October 18 entries).
1977	U.S. President Jimmy Carter and Panamanian Chief of Government Omar Herrara signed the Panama Canal Treaty and Neutrality Treaty (see April 18, May 18, August 10, November 2, November 3, December 31 entries).
1978	Keith Moon died in an apartment in London, England (see August 23 entry).
2000	A prized bull was cloned.
2000	The National Debt Clock was turned off.

A separation began on this day in 1977. U.S. President Jimmy Carter and Panamanian Chief of Government Omar Herrara signed the Panama Canal Treaty and Neutrality Treaty. These combined treaties gradually returned control of the Panama Canal to the nation of Panama. A union was also begun on this day in 1954, when a number of Southeast Asian nations formed an alliance similar to NATO (the North Atlantic Treaty Organization). The Southeast Asian Treaty Organization (SEATO) united Australia, Great Britain, France, Pakistan, the Philippines, Thailand, New Zealand, and the United States under a pledge to fight against the communist takeover of any nation within their sphere of influence and mutual defense against "massive military aggression" by any outside source.

A prized Canadian Holstein bull was cloned by scientists at the Artificial Insemination Center and the University of Montreal veterinary department on this day in 2000. Starbuck had sired nearly 200,000 calves throughout the world during his twenty-year lifespan. Before his death in 1998, researchers had taken tissue and cells from this near-perfect animal. On this day, Starbuck 2 was born, using a cloned embryo that had been implanted in a cow the previous year. The calf weighed 120 pounds.

The National Debt Clock that loomed above New York's Times Square for eleven years was turned off on this day in 2000. Funded and installed by Manhattan real estate developer Seymour Durst in 1989, the clock presented a second-by-second accounting of the nation's ballooning debt. The computerized mechanism crashed at one point during the mid-1990s when the rate of increase grew so rapidly, even the computer couldn't keep up with the calculation. The week before the clock was shut off, the numbers displayed were slowly edging downward; and in its last few seconds, the sign read: "Our national debt: $5,676,989,904,887. Your family share: $73,733."

8th.

1935 U.S. Senator Huey Long was mortally wounded by Dr. Carl Weiss in Baton Rouge, Louisiana.

1951 The Japanese Peace Treaty was signed.

1965 Bert Campaneris played nine positions.

1974 U.S. President Gerald Ford granted former President Richard Nixon an unconditional pardon for any crimes he might have committed while in office.

1989 The Department of Veterans Affairs was created.

An unusual first took place on the baseball field on this day in 1965. Bert Campaneris of the Kansas City A's became the first major league player to play in all nine field positions during the same baseball game.

Although Japan had surrendered in 1945, ending the Second World War, it took another six years before the matter was settled on paper. On this day in 1951, the Japanese Peace Treaty was signed in San Francisco, California, by the United States, Japan, and forty-seven other nations.

9th.

1900 James Hilton was born.

1941 Otis Redding was born.

1948 The Democratic People's Republic of Korea was formed in North Korea, claiming authority over both North and South Korea.

1989 Tennis star Steffi Graf defeated Martina Navratilova in the women's singles event at the U.S. Open in New York City (see September 7, October 18 entries).

1993 The Palestinian Liberation Organization and Israel agreed to recognize each other.

1998 Independent Counsel Kenneth Starr said he had grounds for impeachment of U.S. President Bill Clinton (see September 11 entry).

2000 The hole in the ozone layer stretched over an entire city (see September 15, October 11 entries).

A man who opened the world's eyes to the beauty of Shangri-La was born in Leigh, England, on this day in 1900. James Hilton had heard numerous tales about explorers' encounters with the tranquil Hunza and other tribes high in the Himalaya Mountains who reputedly live well past one hundred years. Fascinated by their accounts, he wrote the 1933 book *Lost Horizon,* which captured millions of readers' imaginations. But Hilton also opened people's eyes to the cloistered world of the academician in his equally successful 1934 novel *Goodbye Mr. Chips.*

It took millions of dollars and thousands of worker hours, but on this day in 1998, Independent Counsel Kenneth Starr told congressional House leaders that he had found substantial and credible information "that may constitute grounds for impeachment" of U.S. President Bill Clinton. To substantiate his claim, Starr delivered 36 boxes to the House of Represenatives containing two copies of his lengthy report as well as supporting evidence.

For the first time in the world's history, the hole in the earth's ozone layer stretched over a populated city: Punta Arenas, Chile. The hole—which originated in Antarctica—was caused in greater part by the use of CFCs in aerosols, solvents, and foam-blowing agents prior to their outlawing when the 1989 Montreal Protocol was signed. A threat to human beings, animals, and small plant life, the hole allows too much ultraviolet light to enter the atmosphere, damaging plants and causing skin cancer in humans and animals. Although ozone levels had begun to recover in recent years, a warm weather pattern triggered the expansion of the hole to just under 11 million square miles—the largest it had been in its twenty-year recorded history.

10th.

1928   Yma Sumac was born.

1934   Roger Maris was born.

1940   Buck Buchanan was born.

1946   James Hines was born.

1947   Larry Nelson was born.

1948   Bob Lanier was born.

1951   Florence Chadwick became the first American woman to swim the English Channel from both coasts (see January 7, January 18, July 25, August 6, August 25, December 1 entries).

1955   Bert Parks began a twenty-five-year career hosting the Miss America Pageant.

1955   "Gunsmoke" premiered.

1961   Mickey Mantle hit the 400th home run of his major league career.

1969   The New York Mets beat the Montreal Expos in both ends of a doubleheader.

1972   Muhammad Ali defeated Ken Norton.

1974   Lou Brock broke Maury Wills's 1962 record.

1980   Bill Gullickson fanned eighteen batters.

1982   Pete Rose broke Hank Aaron's record (see April 14, July 18, September 11 entries).

1986   Sprinter Evelyn Ashford was defeated for the first time.

Television personality Bert Parks began a twenty-five-year career as host of the Miss America Pageant on NBC-TV on this day in 1955. A viewing tradition for millions of people, Parks sang the words "There she is, Miss America" to each newly crowned beauty queen until he retired. Another long-standing television career began on this exact same day in 1955. James Arness brought Marshal Matt Dillon to life when the series "Gunsmoke" premiered on CBS-TV. It was the beginning of a twenty-year, record-breaking run.

One of the world's most exotic voices was born in Peru on this day in 1928. Yma Sumac's five-octave range first came to the public's attention when she got a job singing on a Peruvian radio show in her early teens. Bandleader and composer Moises Vivianco heard her remarkable vocal range and decided to promote her career throughout Latin America. The couple married in 1947 and moved to New York City, where she sang with her husband's band Conjunto Folklorica Peruano for three years. Capitol Records signed her to a multi-record deal in 1950. Sumac's exotic looks also appealed to the camera. She appeared in two films during the 1950s, *Secret of the Incas* and *Omar Khayyam*. Although she stayed out of the public eye during the 1960s, Sumac recorded the album *Miracles* in 1971, which critics believe was her best.

The sports world had much to cheer about on this particular day in history. In 1934 New York Yankees baseball outfielder Roger Maris was born in Houston, Texas. Maris broke Babe Ruth's single-season home run record. In 1940 football hall-of-famer Buck Buchanan was born in Birmingham, Alabama. Buchanan was a member of winning teams in both Superbowl I and Superbowl IV. In 1946 track and field great James Hines was born. Before joining the Miami Dolphins football team, Hines won a gold medal in track at the 1968 Olympics. In 1947 golf champion Larry Nelson was born in Fort Payne, Alabama. During the 1980s, Nelson won the U.S. Open Golf Tournament in 1983 and won the PGA Tournament on two separate occasions. In 1948 Detroit Pistons basketball great Bob Lanier was born. Lanier was NBA All-Star on eight different occasions during his career. In 1951 Florence Chadwick of San Diego, California, became the first American woman to swim the English Channel from both coasts. In 1961

Mickey Mantle hit his 400th home run. In 1969 the New York Mets beat the Montreal Expos in both games of a doubleheader. It was the first time the baseball team moved into first place in the National League East Division. In 1972 Muhammad Ali defeated Ken Norton in a rematch, regaining his heavyweight boxing title. In 1974 St. Louis Cardinals batter Lou Brock broke Maury Wills's 1982 major league record for stolen bases in a single season, taking his 105th steal. In 1980 Montreal Expos rookie pitcher Bill Gullickson sent eighteen White Sox batters to the bench, setting a major league record for a rookie pitcher in a single game. In 1982 Pete Rose played in his 3,077th baseball game, breaking Hank Aaron's National League record. In 1986 sprinter Evelyn Ashford was defeated for the first time in eight years, losing to Valerie Brisco-Hooks in the 200-meter event.

11th.

1910   The first electric bus line opened.

1917   Ferdinand Marcos was born (see September 23 entry).

1946   The first mobile phone conservation took place.

1959   Duke Ellington won the Springarn Medal (see April 29 entry).

1961   Bob Dylan made his first New York City appearance at Gerde's Folk City. (see May 1, May 12, May 24, June 7, July 25, July 31, August 9, August 17, December 8 entries).

1962   Ringo Starr joined John, Paul, and George for his first recording session (see April 27, July 7, August 16 entries).

1967   US Surveyor 5 made the first chemical analysis of lunar material.

1973   Chilean President Salvador Allende was deposed.

1974   The St. Louis Cardinals baseball team defeated the New York Mets.

1984   Secretary of State George Schultz announced a change in policy in Vietnamese immigration to the United States.

1985   Pete Rose broke a major-league hitting record (see April 14, July 18, September 10 entries).

1986 Dow Jones Industrial Average encountered its biggest one-day decline in history, plummeting 86.61 points to 1792.89 points as 237.57 million shares were traded (see February 23 entry).

1998 The Starr Report was released (see January 13, June 1, September 9 entries).

2001 Terrorists attacked New York City and Washington, D.C. (see On This Day in History: February 26 entry).

Local commutes got easier on this particular day. In 1910, the first electric bus line to enjoy commercial success began operations in Hollywood, California. Wireless phone service for commuters was actually born on this day in 1946, when the first long-distance mobile telephone conversation took place between two moving vehicles.

Ten years after the close of the Vietnam War, the true byproducts of that war came to light on this day in 1984. U.S. Secretary of State George Schultz announced that the United States was willing to admit 8000 Eurasian children who had been fathered by American GIs with Vietnamese mothers. Schultz also said that the nation would accept 10,000 Vietnamese political prisoners into the United States.

 As commuters headed to their offices throughout New York City and Washington D.C. on this day in 2001, tragedy struck. In an attempt to spark a war between Muslim and western nations, a group of terrorists launched simultaneous attacks on American shores. Terrorists crashed two hijacked Boeing 767 jetliners filled with passengers into the World Trade Center's twin 110-story towers—which they considered to be icons of capitalism and the nation itself. The first jet tore into the north tower at 8:48 AM; the second jet hit the south tower at 9:03 AM. Less than two hours later, both buildings collapsed as the intense heat of the ensuing fires melted the towers' steel frame, killing and injuring thousands of civilians as well as rescue workers who had rushed to the scene. Hijackers on board another Boeing 767 jet crashed into the Pentagon in Washington D.C. at 9:30 AM, demolishing a segment of the nation's defense headquarters. A fourth passenger jet crashed near Shankside, Pennsylvania, at 10:15 AM, after passengers thwarted the hijackers' attempt to hit an unknown target. Before the day's end, two smaller office towers at the World Trade Center also collapsed. And the United States, as a people, experienced the grief and agony of terrorism on a scale that had previously been unthinkable.

Two dictators share a common day in history. Philippine dictator Ferdinand Marcos was born on this day in 1917. Even while Marcos was still studying law at the University of the Philippines, he found himself in trouble. He was accused, in 1939, of the murder of his father's political rival. He defended himself and was acquitted of the charge. During his 20-year reign as dictator—which began in 1966—Marcos imposed martial law throughout his nation. He was accused of both fraud and corruption after he was deposed by in a general election by Corazon Aquino. On this same day in 1973, Chilean President Salvador Allende was deposed in a military coup by General Augusto Pinochet. Although the new government reported that Allende committed suicide rather than surrender. The dictator had been mortally wounded in a shoot out at the presidential palace in Santiago.

The world of baseball experienced two landmarks on this day. In 1974, the St. Louis Cardinals baseball team defeated the New York Mets 4-3. This wouldn't seen so unusual, except that it took 7 hours, 4 minutes to play the record twenty-five innings to accomplish the feat. Spectators went home at 3:10 AM from the second longest game in professional baseball history. In 1985, player Pete Rose broke a major-league record: he hit his 4192nd run, breaking Ty Cobb's career record.

12th.

1897	Irene Joliot-Curie was born.
1922	The word "obey" was deleted from the bride's vow in the Episcopal marriage ceremony.
1953	U.S. Senator John F. Kennedy married Jacqueline Bouvier (see July 28, October 20 entries).
1966	"The Monkees" premiered on NBC-TV.
2000	The space shuttle *Atlantis* arrived at the *Zvezda* service module.

It's not often that the phrase "like mother like daughter" can be applied to the scientific world. But on this day in 1897, Irene Joliot-Curie became an exception to that rule when she was born in Paris, France, to physicist Marie Curie and her husband, chemist Pierre Curie. Irene followed in her mother's steps. She assisted her mother at the Radium Institute and married another of Madame Curie's assistants, Jean Joliot. She took over her mother's research work at the institute in 1932. The year after her mother died of cancer from radiation exposure, Irene and Jean received the 1935 Nobel Prize in Chemistry for their work in the artificial production of radioactive elements—just as Irene's parents had done in 1903. Sadly, Irene died of cancer in 1956, after lifelong exposure to radiation.

A major moving project took place in outer space on this day in 2000. The space shuttle *Atlantis*'s crew entered the Russian service module *Zvezda*. *Atlantis* commander Terrence Wilcutt and cosmonaut Yuri Malenchenko opened the hatch and checked the interior of this permanent orbiting space station. Five astronauts and two cosmonauts unloaded 1,300 pounds of supplies from the unmanned Russian supply ship *Progress,* which was docked on one end of the *Zvezda;* and another 4,800 pounds of supplies— including an oxygen generator, color TV monitor, exercise machine, and toilet—were taken off *Atlantis.*

13th.

1845   The Knickerbocker Club was founded.

1916   Roald Dahl was born.

1938   Judith Martin was born.

1989   Francis "Fay" Vincent became baseball commissioner.

Manners played a pivotal role in the careers of two writers who were born on this particular day. Born in Washington, D.C., on this day in 1938, columnist Judith Martin covered the White House and diplomatic social scene during her twenty-five-year career at the *Washington Post.* She's best known, however, for the columns and books she's written about social etiquette under the pen name Miss Manners. Known for the rude nature of his youthful characters, Roald Dahl became internationally recognized and criticized for his children's books. In truth, his 1964 novel *Charlie and the Chocolate Factory* was simply a re-creation of some of his own children's playmates and the evil fate he wished upon some of the more unruly ones. An earlier work, *James and the Giant Peach,* was equally successful in later years. Born in Llandaff, Wales, on this day in 1916, Dahl also wrote adult tales, like his 1946 collection of wartime short stories, entitled *Over to You.* He also wrote the screenplay for the James Bond thriller *You Only Live Twice,* which was based on Ian Fleming's novel.

Two firsts occurred in the world of professional baseball on this day. In 1845 the Knickerbocker Club was founded in New York City. This professional playing organization was the first of its kind, writing the rules of conduct and play for the United States's favorite sport. And in 1989 Francis "Fay" Vincent was named major league baseball's eighth commissioner, succeeding the late A. Bartlett Giamatti.

14th.

1898 Margaret Fogarty Rudkin was born.

1950 United Nations peacekeeping forces landed on the Korean peninsula.

1959 The Soviet space probe *Lunik 2* became the first vehicle to make a lunar landing.

1984 Joe W. Kittinger launched his hot-air balloon, *Rosie O'Grady,* from Caribou, Maine, attempting to make the first solo transatlantic crossing.

1995 An annual fee was imposed on domain name registrations.

Some success stories occur later in life. This was certainly the case for Margaret Fogarty Rudkin, who was born in New York City on this day in 1898. Margaret, her husband, and their three sons had moved to Pepperidge Farm in Fairfield, Connecticut, where she quickly adapted to country life, growing fruits and vegetables and raising livestock. When she discovered that one of her sons had an allergy to commercial breads, she began baking her own loaves from her mother's favorite recipe. Her son's doctor and her neighbors convinced her that her healthy bread was also delicious. So she started selling her Pepperidge Farm breads by mail order out of her kitchen. Grocers began clamoring for her bread, too. Soon the bakery moved out of the house and into its own building in Norwalk, Connecticut. The business continued to grow throughout the late 1940s and 1950s, adding cookies to the list of products. She sold the business to the Campbell Soup Company in 1968.

The National Science Foundation (NSF) and its licensee Network Solutions, Inc. (NSI) came to a profitable agreement on this day in 1995. Both the NSF and NSI announced that domain name registration on the Internet was no longer a free service. This meant that all new domain name registrants had to pay $100 for a two-year registration of their proprietary names with the suffixes *.com, .net, .org,* and the like. Owners who had registered prior to this day would be charged $50 per year on the first anniversary of their initial registration. Educational institutions using the suffix *.edu,* however, were absolved from this charge: The NSF took responsibility for paying their registration fees.

15th.

1830   The Choctaw Indians ceded their lands east of the Mississippi River.

1961   The atomic nightmare was revealed in *Life* magazine photo-essay.

1972   A federal grand jury indicted seven men, including two former White House aides, in connection with the Watergate break-in (see August 5, September 19, October 1, October 23, November 21 entries).

1983   Israeli Prime Minister Menachem Begin resigned (see June 20, August 15, August 28 entries).

1995   José Prieto was sentenced (see April 15, September 9, October 11 entries).

A criminal offense against the environment was punished on this day in 1995. José Prieto was sentenced to twenty-six months in federal prison for smuggling CFC-12—a refrigerant gas known as dichlorodifluoromethane—into the United States. The illegal importation of this ozone-depleting gas had become a crime after the United States signed the 1989 Montreal Protocol.

The terror of the atomic nightmare came home to roost in photographs and words on this day in 1961. *Life* magazine published a photo-essay entitled "A New Urgency, Big Things to Do—and What You Must Learn," which described the potential devastation that could occur in the United States if a nuclear bomb were dropped. Many people who read this perturbing article began building fallout shelters, stockpiling supplies, and practicing evacuation procedures both at home and in offices to prepare for what seemed the inevitable event of a nuclear war.

16th.

1893 The Cherokee Strip was open to settlement (see May 20, May 23, July 20, December 29 entries).

1925 Blues performer B.B. King was born in Itta Bena, Mississippi (see January 21 entry).

1974 U.S. President Gerald Ford offered conditional amnesty to Vietnam War draft evaders and deserters who agreed to serve two years in public service jobs.

1976 The Episcopal Church approved the ordination of female priests and bishops.

1978 The Grateful Dead played a concert beside Egypt's Great Pyramid (see August 1 entry).

1985 The United States became a debtor nation for the first time in 71 years, with a balance-of-payments deficit of nearly $32 billion.

1994 Exxon Corporation was ordered to pay fishermen harmed by oil spill (see March 24 entry).

It took five years for Alaskans to win their just rewards. But on this day in 1994, a federal jury in Anchorage ordered Exxon Corporation to pay $5 billion in punitive damages to Alaskan residents, tribal members, and business owners who had been harmed by the spill left in the wake of the *Exxon Valdez* oil tanker rupture in 1989.

On this day in 1893, a six-million-acre tract of land in the Oklahoma Territory's Cherokee Strip was opened to white settlers, even though it had originally been designated as Native American reservation land. Set aside for the Cherokee Nation, who had been moved there from the East Coast, the federal government decided to recant on its treaty and reclaim the land for the onslaught of newcomers. At the sound of a gun, 100,000 potential residents rushed in by stagecoach, covered wagon, horseback, and on foot to claim a plot of this land under the homesteader rules.

17th.

1901 Sir Francis Chichester was born.

1923 Hank Williams was born.

1937 The Abraham Lincoln figure on Mount Rushmore was dedicated (see March 3, July 2, July 4, August 30, October 1, October 31, December 28 entries).

A brave yachtsman was born in Barnstable, England, on this day in 1901. Francis Chichester moved to New Zealand when he was eighteen years old, seeking and finding his fortune as a land agent. That's when his life really took off. He returned to England to learn how to fly in 1929. And to prove his abilities, he flew to Australia in a Gipsy Moth plane. Chichester battled lung cancer in 1957. But he won the first transatlantic yacht race, in 1960, sailing his *Gipsy Moth III* from Plymouth, England, to New York City in forty days. Six years later, Chichester took on his biggest challenge: He sailed his *Gipsy Moth IV* from Plymouth, England, to Sydney, Australia, in 107 days; he then returned to Plymouth via Cape Horn in 119 days. Lord Francis Chichester became the first person to circumnavigate the world in a sailing craft.

A country classic was born in Mount Olive, Alabama, on this day in 1923. Although Hank Williams was a superstar for only four years, he was the brightest star in the musical sky in his time. Blues singer Rufus Payne taught him how to play guitar and sing before Hank and his mother moved to Montgomery, Alabama, when he was 14. Hank quickly formed a band and got a regular gig on WSFA radio in 1941. Two years later, he met and married Audrey Mae Sheppard, who became his personal manager. With Audrey's encouragement, the couple went to Nashville and met Fred Rose of Acuff-Rose Publishing in 1946. The meeting was a success: Hank recorded two demos, which led to an MGM Records contract the next year. It was seemingly all uphill from that point: Hank joined the Lousiana Hayride, made numerous radio appearances, went on tour, and made more records. Some of his hits—"Your Cheatin' Heart," "Jambalaya," and "Kaw-Liga"—even crossed over into the pop charts. Sadly, his success took a downward spin when he started drinking too much, divorced his wife, and became addicted to morphine after suffering a back injury. He died on his way to a concert in 1953, after a doctor had given him vitamin B-12 and morphine injections without knowing that he was drinking whiskey.

1819   Jean Foucault was born.

1961   United Nations Secretary General Dag Hammarskjöld was killed in an airplace crash in northern Rhodesia (see *On This Day in History:* April 7, July 29 entries).

1984   Joe W. Kittinger landed his hot-air balloon, *Rosie O'Grady,* in Savona, Italy, breaking his ankle when he set down.

1996   Residents of Okinawa, Japan, voted to have 28,000 U.S. troops removed from the island after numerous criminal incidents against Japanese citizens occurred.

The man who proved that the earth rotates was born in Paris, France, on this day in 1819. Physicist Jean Foucault proved the earth's rotation in 1851, by placing objects in a circular pattern around a freely suspended pendulum. The swinging object knocked down every object in the circle during the course of the experiment. But Foucault's pendulum wasn't his only discovery. The next year, he developed the gyroscope, and in 1857 he developed Foucault's prism, which was a vast improvement over earlier spectrum separators.

1888   The world's first beauty contest took place.

1957   The United States conducted its first underground nuclear test in the Nevada desert.

1974   Former U.S. President Richard Nixon was subpoenaed to appear at the Watergate trial by special prosecutor Leon Jaworski (see August 5, September 15, October 1, October 23, November 21 entries).

1978   Egypt's cabinet ministers unanimously approved President Anwar Sadat's Camp David agreement to sign a peace treaty with Israel.

1992   The Salem witches were readmitted to the First Church of Salem.

1994 U.S. armed forces invaded Haiti to restore Haitian President Jean-Bertrand Aristide to the presidency.

Justice takes time, and some times are longer than others. On this day in 1992, Rebecca Nurse and Giles Corey were readmitted to the First Church of Salem, in Salem, Massachusetts. The two had been, excommunicated, and executed as witches during the Salem witch hunts of the late 1600s. Justice had taken 300 years to right itself.

The world's first beauty contest took place on this day in 1888. It didn't happen in Atlantic City, New Jersey, but at the Spa Belgium in Belgium. The Concours de Beauté's first reigning beauty queen was Bertha Souret, a Creole from the archipelago of Guadeloupe in the Caribbean.

20th.

1853 Phra Paramindr Maha Chulalongkorn was born.

1873 Financial panic forced the New York Stock Exchange to close; it remained shut for ten days (see January 4, February 13 entries).

1934 Sophia Loren was born.

1963 U.S. President John F. Kennedy went before the United Nations, proposing a joint U.S.-Soviet expedition to the moon.

1966 George Harrison made his first pilgrimage to India (see August 29, September 6 entries).

A woman who became one of the world's great beauties was born in Rome, Italy, on this day in 1934. Sophia Loren was a model before she was placed under contract with film producer Carlo Ponti in 1950. Under his tutelage, she went from walk-ons to starring roles in major motion pictures. She later married Ponti. In 1961 she won an Oscar for her work in *Two Women.* She also co-starred with Marcello Mastroianni in numerous films, including *Marriage Italian Style* and *Yesterday, Today, and Tomorrow.*

The monarch whose father inspired the book *Anna and the King of Siam* as well as the musical and film *The King and I* was born in Siam on this day in 1852. Before he put in his prescribed time in a Buddhist monastery before succeeding his father to the throne when he was 20, Phra Paramindr Maha Chulalongkorn had been educated by British tutors (including Anna Leonowens) and taught Western ways. When he became king, he traveled through India and Indonesia. Then he returned home. He abolished slavery; built roads, schools, hospitals, and railways; standardized the Siamese currency; installed electricity in Bangkok; and hired a Western governess for his many children. Chulalongkorn even visited England and met with Queen Victoria before his death in 1910.

21st.

1902   Sir Allen Lane was born.

1947   Stephen King was born.

1973   Henry Kissinger was confirmed as secretary of state by the U.S. Senate (see March 25, August 22, November 10 entries).

1981   Sandra Day O'Connor was confirmed as Supreme Court justice by the U.S. Senate.

1982   After contract talks failed, National Football League players began their first regular-season strike.

Two great pioneers of the publishing industry have this day in common. Born in Bristol, England, on this day in 1902, Sir Allen Lane apprenticed at the Bodley Head publishing house under its founder, his cousin John Lane. In 1935 Allen Lane had made it to managing director but resigned in order to open his own imprint—Penguin Books. Dedicated to the reprinting of novels with paperback covers, Lane created a publishing revolution by selling classic works for sixpence apiece. Born in Portland, Maine, on this day in 1947, horror novelist Stephen King published a local newspaper with his brother when he was twelve years old. Four years later, he self-published a short story collection entitled *People, Places, and Things, vol. I.* The next year, he self-published *Star Invaders.* His first commercially published story, "I Was a Teenage Grave Robber," appeared in *Comics Review* in 1965. After a rejection by Random House, King stopped thinking about writing and pumped gas while he finished his degree from the University of Maine. King married Tabitha Spruce in 1971 and took a high school teaching job for $6,400 a year. He started work on the novel *Carrie,* which he tossed out. Tabitha pulled it out of the garbage, read it, and encouraged him to finish it. Doubleday bought the book in 1973, giving him enough money to quit his teaching job. Over 300 million copies of his numerous novels—*Pet Sematary, Cujo, The Dead Zone,* and others—have been sold in over thirty-five countries since that day. King shocked the world in 2000, when he sold the first installment of a novel directly to readers over the Internet without a publisher's intervention.

22nd.

1927 Gene Tunney successfully defended his heavyweight title against ex-champion Jack Dempsey in a ten-round decision at Soldiers Field in Chicago, Illinois (see June 24 entry).

1961 U.S. President John F. Kennedy signed the Juvenile Delinquency and Youth Offenses Control Act.

1970 U.S. President Richard Nixon requested the assignment of FBI agents to college campuses.

1975 U.S. President Gerald Ford escaped an assassination attempt by former Manson Family member Sara Jane Moore in San Francisco, California (see December 12 entry).

1980 The Solidarity union was formed under leadership of Lech Walesa in Poland.

Adolescence and youth was a major concern in the political arena on this day. In 1961 U.S. President John F. Kennedy signed the Juvenile Delinquency and Youth Offenses Control Act. Many local law enforcement agencies required extra funds to handle teenage crime in the streets and on school property. In 1970 U.S. President Richard Nixon requested that 1,000 new FBI agents be recruited and installed on college campuses throughout the United States. Radical political activities had made both educators and federal officials concerned that the nation's colleges and universities had become hotbeds for anarchistic activities.

23rd.

1949   U.S. President Harry S Truman announced that the Soviet Union had detonated its first nuclear device.

1950   The McCarran Internal Security Act became law.

1952   U.S. vice-presidential candidate Richard Nixon disputed charges of wrongdoing in his campaign finance plans.

1957   Martial law began in the Philippines (see September 11 entry).

1973   Former Argentine president Juan Perón was reinstalled after an eighteen-year exile (see October 17 entry).

1993   The South African Parliament voted to allow blacks to take a role in government.

1997   Iranian President Mohammad Khatami was elected to office.

Despite the protestations and veto by U.S. President Harry S Truman, a controversial bill was temporarily put into effect in the United States on this day in 1950. The McCarran Internal Security Act called for the registration of all "communist-front" and "communist-action groups," declaring an alleged national emergency. The bill also called for the construction of internment camps, similar to those erected for Japanese-Americans during the Second World War. Within the next two years, six of these camps were built for the imprisonment of "communist subversives." The camps were maintained until the 1960s on a standby basis.

24th.

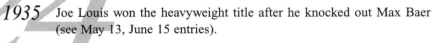

1935   Joe Louis won the heavyweight title after he knocked out Max Baer (see May 13, June 15 entries).

1936   Jim Henson was born.

A puppet master was born in Greenville, Mississippi, on this day in 1936. Jim Henson studied commercial art before he landed a job at a local television station in

Washington, D.C. He got his own show, "Sam and Friends," which ran from 1955 until 1961—enough time for him to finish college. Puppet creations like Kermit the Frog began appearing in commercials and national television shows such as the "Jimmy Dean Show" during the early 1960s. His real break came when he developed "Sesame Street" in 1969, which continues to appear on PBS-TV. Kermit, Miss Piggy, and other characters also crossed over to "The Muppets Show," which was viewed by over 235 million people in over 100 countries. The Muppets also appeared in numerous feature films. Henson also developed characters for the 1982 film *The Dark Crystal* and the 1986 film *Labyrinth* before his death in 1990.

25th.

1931   Barbara Walters was born.

1954   Elvis Presley made his only appearance at the Grand Ole Opry (see March 5, March 24, June 26, July 30, August 15, August 22, December 3 entries).

1965   "The Beatles" animated television series premiered on ABC-TV.

1992   A twelve-year-old boy got a divorce.

Born in Boston, Massachusetts, on this day in 1931, Barbara Walters wanted to become a teacher after she got her master's degree in education. But she was already writing news releases in New York City for WNBT-TV. Before she knew it, she was the youngest producer at WNBC-TV in New York and was then hired as a writer for NBC's "Today Show." Thirteen years later, Walters was a co-host for the long-running morning program. It didn't take long before Walters became the first female anchor for the "ABC Evening News." Because of her talent for securing exclusive interviews with celebrities and controversial personalities, she also hosted the "Barbara Walters Special." Since the 1990s, Walters has become anchor of "20/20" as well as the producer and co-host of the morning show "The View."

A landmark divorce case was finalized on this day in 1992. A judge in Orlando, Florida, ruled in favor of Gregory Kingsley's divorce proceedings. The twelve-year-old boy sought a divorce from his biological parents in order to pursue a more reasonable life.

26th.

1849   Ivan Pavlov was born.

1897   Pope Paul VI was born (see June 21, June 30, July 29, October 28, November 27, December 9 entries).

1914   The U.S. Congress established the Federal Trade Commission.

1957   *West Side Story* opened on Broadway.

1983   *Australia II* won the America's Cup, ending a 132-year United States winning streak.

1990   The Soviet Union ended its ban on religion.

After seventy years of repression, the Soviet Union lifted its ban on religion on this day in 1990. During the early days of the communist regime, the government had halted all public religious ceremonies and gatherings. Officials also forbade the study of any religion in homes or private schools. Today, Russians are free to practice Christianity, Judaism, Islam, and numerous other religious beliefs.

The man who discovered the reflex response was born near Ryazan, Russia, on this day in 1849. Ivan Pavlov was the son of a village priest. After completing his medical studies in St. Petersburg, Breslau, and Leipzig, he worked at the Institute of Experimental Medicine, becoming a professor and then director between 1890 and 1913. He was awarded the Nobel Prize for Physiology or Medicine in 1904, for his studies of conditioned reflex.

27th.

1894   U.S. President Grover Cleveland proclaimed amnesty for anyone convicted of polygamy (see April 16, October 6 entries).

1912   W.C. Handy published the first blues song, "Memphis Blues" (see November 16 entry).

1938   The *Queen Elizabeth* ocean liner was launched.

1939   Kathy Whitworth was born.

1964   The Warren Commission concluded that Lee Harvey Oswald had acted alone in U.S. President John F. Kennedy's assassination (see *On This Day in History:* November 24 entry).

1973   The Soviet Union launched its first manned spacecraft in two years.

1991   U.S. President George H. Bush announced unilateral reductions in nuclear arms.

Professional golf's all-time female tournament leader, Kathy Whitworth, was born in Monahans, Texas, on this day in 1939. She took up golf when she was 15 and was mentored by Harvey Penwick. After winning the New Mexico State Amateur Tournament in both 1957 and 1958, she turned professional. It took Whitworth four years to win a tournament. But after her victory at the 1962 Kelly Girl Open, she slid into easy wins at eighty-eight other tournaments, including three LPGA titles in the United States. During the 1960s, Whitworth was the first female golfer to earn more than $1 million in prize money and was named Player of the Year seven times. She continues to play senior tournaments and captain golf teams in international competition to this day.

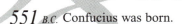

551 B.C.   Confucius was born.

1904   New York City police arrested a woman for smoking a cigarette in public (see January 2, January 10, April 11, May 23, July 17, August 1, August 24, December 1 entries).

1924   Two U.S. Army planes landed in Seattle, Washington, completing the first around-the-world flight in 175 days.

1976   Muhammad Ali retained his heavyweight title, defeating Ken Norton in a close fifteen-round decision in New York City (see September 10 entry; see *On This Day in History:* January 15 entry).

1977   Bing Crosby and David Bowie recorded the song "Peace on Earth," but Crosby died before it was released.

The punishment for smoking in New York City was tough if you were a woman on this day in 1904. Police arrested a woman for smoking a cigarette in public and invoked the Sullivan ordinance. This law made smoking in public by women punishable by ten days' imprisonment plus payment of a $5 to $25 fine.

The most famous Chinese philosopher and teacher taught his disciples that benevolence, reciprocity, respect, and personal effort were the keys to a successful existence. Born in Shantung province, China, on this day in 551 B.C., Confucius didn't win immediate acceptance of his concepts. After leaving a promising government career, he became an itinerant scholar for twelve years. Although he traveled from court to court, he never found a mentor to care for him and his disciples. He returned to his home, where he continued to teach until his death in 479 B.C. Confucius never wrote down any of his thoughts. His disciples, however, gathered his sayings and recorded his actions in collected volumes, which became the basis for alleged Confucianism in later centuries.

1817 Ohio tribal members were given a reservation.

1953 Carson Pirie Scott & Company in Chicago, Illinois, became the first department store to sell insurance.

1962 U.S. President John F. Kennedy activated the Mississippi National Guard (see September 30 entry).

1965 The Federal Aid to the Arts Act was signed.

1978 Pope John Paul I was found dead by his personal secretary after serving for only thirty-four days.

1980 The U.S. Senate reported that the Justice Department had shown no favoritism in its investigation of Libyan ties with President Jimmy Carter's brother, Billy (see October 1 entry).

1982 More than 1,200 U.S. Marines were ordered to land in Lebanon.

1983 The War Powers Act was invoked.

1986 The Soviet Union released journalist Nicholas Daniloff (see August 30 entry).

1988 The space shuttle *Discovery* was launched, reinstituting NASA's manned space program.

1993 The Bosnian Parliament decided to reject an international peace plan.

Fine art, theater, music, and other forms of artistic expression created in the United States received a federal boost on this day in 1965, when President Lyndon Johnson signed the Federal Aid to the Arts Act. This bill established the National Foundation on the Arts and the Humanities, which eventually became the National Endowment for the Arts.

Ohio tribal members were given a few small concessions in exchange for their signatures on the Fort Meigs Treaty, which ceded 4 million acres of the Ohio Valley to the United States government on this day in 1817. For their peaceable agreement, the Ohio Indians received 144 square miles—called the Grand Reserve—situated on the Upper Sandusky. They also received one square mile of cranberry bog on Broken Sword Creek, which the government called Cranberry Reserve. They were also given a sawmill, a blacksmith, and a $4,000 annuity. In 1820 they were given a grist mill for their generosity.

The Mississippi National Guard was activated on this day in 1962. U.S. President John F. Kennedy ordered these troops to enforce federal court orders allowing James Meredith to enroll at the University of Mississippi. State officials had defied the order to grant this African-American student the right to enter a state university.

Thoughts about war were on many people's minds on this particular day throughout late-twentieth-century history. In 1982 U.S. President Ronald Reagan ordered more than 1,200 U.S. Marines to participate in an international peacekeeping force in Lebanon. In 1983 the U.S. Congress invoked the War Powers Act, authorizing President Reagan to retain troops in Lebanon for another eighteen months. And in 1993 the Bosnian Parliament decided to reject an international peace plan unless Bosnian Serbs returned land they had taken by force.

30th.

1787	The *Columbia* left Boston, Massachusetts, on the first circumnavigation by an American vessel.
1809	The Treaty of Fort Wayne was signed.
1927	Babe Ruth hit his sixtieth home run of the season (see May 6 entry).
1962	A confrontation ensued over James Meredith's enrollment at the University of Mississippi (see September 29 entry).
1970	The United States and the Soviet Union signed agreements designed to prevent accidental nuclear war.
1976	The state of California enacted the nation's first euthanasia (right to die) legislation in the case of Karen Ann Quinlan (see March 29 entry).

The Treaty of Fort Wayne was signed by Governor Harrison and chiefs from the Delaware, Miami, and Potawatomi tribes on this day in 1809. The agreement ceded more than 3 million acres in Indiana and Illinois to the federal government. Only two tribal leaders refused to sign—Tecumseh and Tensquatawa.

Although U.S. President John F. Kennedy had ordered Mississippi National Guard to enforce a federal court order on the previous day, a riot ensued on the University of Mississippi campus on this day in 1962. Over 2,000 Ku Klux Klan members and student demonstrators had tried to keep African-American student James Meredith from enrollment. Thirteen out of the 200 National Guardsmen sent to enforce the order and the peace were shot by sniper fire. And 29 of 200 federal marshalls were critically injured in the fifteen-hour riot.

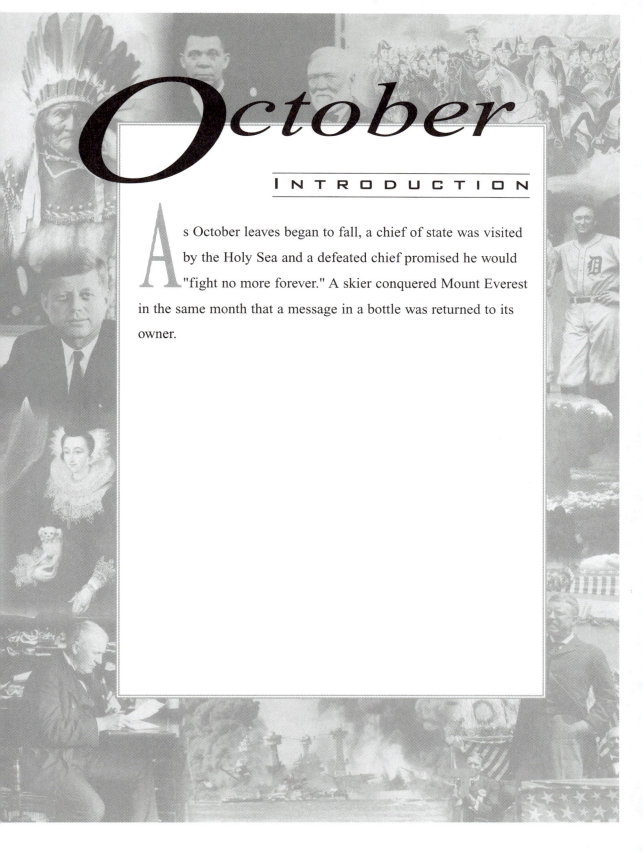

October

As October leaves began to fall, a chief of state was visited by the Holy Sea and a defeated chief promised he would "fight no more forever." A skier conquered Mount Everest in the same month that a message in a bottle was returned to its owner.

1st.

1847 Maria Mitchell found a comet (see August 1 entry).

1903 The first World Series of Baseball opened (see October 4, October 5 entries).

1924 U.S. President Jimmy (James Earl) Carter, Jr., was born in Plains, Georgia (see January 4, January 7, January 20, January 21, February 20, March 31, June 18, July 1, September 1 entries).

1924 U.S. Supreme Court Justice William Rehnquist was born in Milwaukee, Wisconsin.

1925 Mount Rushmore was dedicated as a national monument (see March 3, July 2, July 4, August 30, September 17, October 4, October 31, December 28 entries).

1974 The Watergate trial began (see February 21, August 5, September 15, September 19, October 23, November 21 entries).

1993 A new student loan program began, allowing students to borrow directly from the federal government.

Until this landmark day in 1847, most comets had been discovered by male astronomers. On this day, however, the first female astronomer set her sights on one of these icy celestial bodies. A Massachusetts school teacher and amateur astronomer named Maria Mitchell found a comet flying just above the North Star. After it was confirmed, she became the first female member elected to the American Academy of Arts and Sciences. She even received a gold medal from King Frederick of Denmark in recognition of her sharp vision. But besides numerous other honors and awards, Mitchell was given the most lofty recognition: A crater on the moon was named after her.

2nd.

1904 Graham Greene was born.

1919 James McGill Buchanan was born.

1950   Charles Schulz's comic strip, *Peanuts,* was first published.

1986   The United States imposed sanctions on South Africa.

A prolific novelist was born in Berkhamsted, England, on this day in 1904. Graham Greene wrote a number of short stories, verses, and a few novels before he saw his first success with his 1932 novel *Stamboul Train.* After a few more hits, he embarked on a series of "Catholic novels," which he wrote shortly after his conversion to that religion. The 1938 thriller *Brighton Rock* was the first of four works with this thematic approach. Greene's most popular books, however, came later: *The Third Man, The End of the Affair, Our Man in Havana,* and *The Comedians* were all made into feature films during his lifetime.

Economics walks hand in hand with politics. A controversial economist was born in Murfreesboro, Tennessee, on this day in 1919. James McGill Buchanan was awarded the 1986 Nobel Prize for Economics after he presented his creative theories of public choice, which are based on the concept that politicians are motivated by self-interest. And in 1986, on this same day, the United States applied economic sanctions to South Africa to entice that nation to end its apartheid policies. The government even banned South Africa Airlines from landing within the United States.

3rd.

1929   The Kingdom of Yugoslavia was formed.

1935   Italy defied a League of Nations covenant, invading Ethiopia.

1957   The world's first man-made satellite was launched.

1962   Astronaut Wally Schirra made six orbits around the earth (see April 9 entry).

1974   Frank Robinson was named Cleveland Indians manager, becoming major league baseball's first African-American manager.

1989   The Canadian government cut its passenger rail service.

1990   East and West Germany were officially reunited.

1994   The number of people living below the poverty line increased.

Economic blues affected both the United States and Canada on this particular day. In 1989 the Canadian government cut passenger rail service from 405 scheduled runs per week down to 191. This was one of many cost-cutting measures designed to reduce the nation's increasing national deficit. Canadian VIA rail service was costing the government $400 per passenger to operate outside of the fares paid by users. In 1994 *Time* magazine reported that the U.S. Census Bureau had found that "the number of Americans living under the poverty line last year—defined as an income of $14,763 for a family of four—climbed to more than 39 million, or 15 percent of the nation's population."

Major milestones were made in aerospace on this day. In 1957 the world's first man-made satellite was launched from Tyuratam, Soviet Union. The race for space had begun. And in 1962 astronaut Wally Schirra blasted off Cape Canaveral, Florida, in the *Sigma 7* space capsule. During his nine-hour flight, Schirra made six orbits around the earth.

4th.

1877 Chief Joseph surrendered.

1927 Work began on the Mount Rushmore monument (see March 3, July 2, July 4, August 30, September 17, October 31, December 28 entries).

1959 The Chicago White Sox and the Los Angeles Dodgers met in the first World Series played west of the Mississipppi River (see October 1 entry).

1969 China announced two nuclear test explosions (see October 5 entry).

1981 Pope John Paul II celebrated mass in St. Peter's Square in his first appearance in the Vatican since an attempt was made on his life (see May 12, May 13, May 18, June 2, July 22 entries).

1984 The government sent workers home.

1989 Televangelist Jim Bakker was convicted of fraud.

2000 The last Morris Mini rolled off the production line.

The last unit of Great Britain's favorite car—the Morris Mini—rolled off the production line at MG Rover's Longbridge factory in Birmingham, England, on this day in 2000. An icon of England's Swinging Sixties, the Mini had been designed to be gas efficient and economical to maintain. In the wake of the 1956 Suez Crisis, the car's design was a response to the needs of Europeans whose gas supplies had been drastically rationed.

Drawn on a paper napkin by designer Alec Issigonis in 1957, the Mini was meant to transport a family of four, two small suitcases, and a lady's handbag—nothing more. As body engineer John Sheperd commented as the last car rolled away, "I don't think even [Issigonis] realized at that time what we had on our hands. He thought it would have a 10-year life span." Inexpensively priced, the Mini was driven by royalty, the working class, rock and roll stars, and movie idols alike, from Peter Sellers, Ringo Starr, and Brigitte Bardot to Great Britain's Princess Margaret and Jordan's King Hussein.

It was on this day in 1877 that the Nez Perce leader Chief Joseph said, "From where the sun now stands I will fight no more forever." After successfully evading 2,000 U.S. Army troops sent to capture Joseph and 700 tribal members and escort them to a 6,000-acre reservation in Idaho, the chief surrendered only a few miles from the Canadian border and freedom. He had led the army on a 1,400-mile wild goose chase from Oregon via Yellowstone National Park into Montana over the course of three months. With his people exhausted from hunger, cold, and travel, Joseph stopped in Montana's Bear Paw Mountains. The disagreement had begun when the government reclaimed the six-million-acre Nez Perce reservation, because gold had been discovered there. In punishment, Joseph and his band were sent to the non-Nez Perce Colville Reservation in eastern Washington to live out their days. Joseph is said to have died of a broken heart in 1904.

The federal government closed up shop on this day in 1984. The White House told hundreds of thousands of federal workers to go home around midday to save money. The U.S. Congress had failed to approve a $50-billion spending plan that morning. The money was needed to keep most of the government's agencies and offices solvent for the year.

Televangelism went on a downward spiral on this day in 1989. Former televangelist Jim Bakker—who hosted the "PTL Club" on national television—was convicted on twenty-four counts of fraud and conspiracy. Evidence had proven that he had bilked his television congregation out of $158 million in contributions. He'd embezzled nearly $4 million of that sum to build himself a few mansions and an air-conditioned doghouse, as well as to purchase fleets of Mercedes and Rolls-Royces for himself and his family. For his overly zealous behavior, Bakker was sentenced to forty-five years' imprisonment plus payment of a $500,000 fine.

The first World Series to be played west of the Mississippi River commenced on this day in 1959. The Chicago White Sox and the Los Angeles Dodgers met in the Los Angeles Coliseum before a record crowd of 92,394 spectators. The Dodgers won this first game 3-1. Eventually, they won the title in four games to two.

Most nuclear tests performed by major nations were executed underground or underwater after the 1950s. But on this day in 1969, China announced it had completed two nuclear tests, including the explosion of a hydrogen bomb in the atmosphere.

5th.

1921 The first radio broadcast of the World Series was transmitted by WJZ in Newark, New Jersey (see October 1 entry).

1931 The first transpacific nonstop flight was completed.

1936 Vaclav Havel was born.

1953 Earl Warren was sworn in as U.S. Supreme Court Chief Justice.

1970 Anwar Sadat was elected to succeed Egyptian President Gamal Abdul Nasser.

1975 U.S. Senator Frank Church announced that the CIA had made several attempts on Fidel Castro's life (see August 13, September 5, October 11, November 30, December 2 entries).

1976 Scientists announced that radioactive fallout from a Chinese nuclear test was detected in the eastern United States (see October 4 entry).

2000 The three surviving members of The Beatles published their own history of the band, after 400 unofficial versions had already hit the bookshelves.

2000 Sotheby's auction house entered a guilty plea to charges of conspiring to fix fees.

2000 Yugoslavian President Slobodan Milosevic was overthrown (see October 7 entry).

The famed Sotheby's auction house pleaded guilty to conspiracy on this day in 2000. Sotheby's and its rival Christie's—which together controlled 95 percent of the world's auction market—had been in collusion, fixing their fees since 1993. Their actions had stifled competition in the $4-billion collectibles industry. As a result of the three-year federal investigation, the auction house giant agreed to pay a $45-million fine for its violation of antitrust laws, and it agreed to pay buyers and sellers $256 million in reparations in the matching civil suit.

The first transpacific nonstop air flight was completed on this day in 1931. Clyde Panghorn and Hugh Herndon, Jr., had taken off from Japan, flying for 41 hours before they landed in Washington state.

A playwright who became a president was born in Prague, Czechoslovakia, on this day in 1936. Vaclav Havel had worked as a stagehand before becoming a resident playwright at Prague's Theatre on the Balustrade in 1960. Although his works were critically acclaimed, the communist-controlled government deemed some of them to be subversive. He was arrested numerous times after premiere performances and was even jailed for four and a half years for his writings. In fact, Havel was imprisoned for three months in February 1989 and was released six months before the government was overthrown and he was elected the nation's first democratic president by direct popular vote.

After thirteen years of "iron-fisted" socialist rule, Yugoslavian President Slobodan Milosevic was overthrown in a relatively peaceful takeover by followers of opposition leader Vojislav Kostunica on this day in 2000. When thousands of demonstrators stormed the parliament and executive buildings in Belgrade, most police and army troops stood aside or joined the demonstrators. Milosevic himself had already fled the city before the takeover erupted. And the nation's official news agency, Tajung, proclaimed Kostunica as the newly "elected president of Yugoslavia."

6th.

1890   A Mormon church conference held in Salt Lake City, Utah, renounced the practice of polygamy (see April 16, May 2, August 8, September 27 entries).

1914   Thor Heyerdahl was born (see April 27 entry).

1958   The American nuclear submarine *Seawolf* surfaced.

2000   An unborn calf, the clone of a prize-winning Holstein, was sold for $82,000.

A prize-winning Holstein named Mandy earned a great reputation for producing more than twice the national average: She normally provides 3,300 gallons of milk per year. Because of her abilities, the company Infigen had cloned Mandy, hoping to sell her genetic duplicate for about $50,000. Although the calf hadn't even been born yet, Mandy's clone sold for $82,000 at auction on this day in 2000 at the World Dairy Expo in Madison, Wisconsin. Purchased by the Landox Syndicate from Minneapolis, Minnesota, the new owners were willing to wait for the calf to be born and grow to six months old before it was shipped.

An explorer who dared to disprove historical claims was born in Norway on this day in 1914. Thor Heyerdahl set out to prove that ancient civilizations crossed the great oceans and influenced each other long before European navigators set their sails toward the New World. To prove that the Polynesian culture had potential contact with the Peruvian Incas or other South American natives, in 1947 he and five colleagues drifted on a balsa wood raft—the *Kon-Tiki*—for 101 days from Callo, Peru, to Tuamoto Island: a distance of 4,300 miles. To prove that Mediterranean people had encountered the Americas long before Christopher Columbus, in 1970 he sailed his reed boat—*Tigris*—from the Moroccan coast of Africa to the Barbados in 57 days. When he wasn't sailing, Heyerdahl conducted important archaeological digs in the Galapagos Islands and Easter Island during the 1950s.

A world record was established by the American nuclear submarine *Seawolf* on this day in 1958, after it surfaced off the New England coast. The craft and its crew had managed to stay submerged for two months without surfacing for air change or supplies.

7th.

1963 U.S. President John F. Kennedy signed an international nuclear test ban treaty.

1973 Egypt and Syria attacked Israel, starting the Yom Kippur War.

1979 Pope John Paul II visited the White House.

1985 Four Palestinian terrorists commandeered a cruise ship.

2000 Former law professor Vojislav Kostunica was sworn in as Yugoslavia's president (see October 5 entry).

2000 A mountain climber skiied down Mount Everest.

A happy holiday cruise turned into a political tragedy on this day in 1985. The Italian cruise ship *Achille Lauro* and its 511 passengers were commandeered by four Palestinian terrorists off the Egyptian coast. The terrorists threatened to blow up the cruise ship unless Israel freed Palestinian prisoners. In the heat of the moment, American passenger Leon Klinghoffer was killed, before the terrorists surrendered to authorities on the second day of the hijacking.

It takes nerves of steel to make the ascent on the Himalayas' Mount Everest. Not everyone makes it to the top, and some adventurers don't survive the trip back down. But on this day in 2000, a successful climber didn't just make the descent in slow steps; he skied from the mountain's 29,035-foot summit down to base camp at the 17,000-foot level in a single run. David Karnicar—a thirty-eight-year-old Slovenian ski instructor—had taken four days to summit the world's tallest peak. Placing a camera on his helmet and donning his skis at the 29,028-foot level, Karnicar took five hours to descend. He stopped three times: to adjust equipment, to meet other expedition members, and to take a good look before heading under the Icefall, a group of precariously balanced ice blocks that could break and fall at any time. It wasn't the first time he'd succeeded in such the feat. The previous year, Karnicar had skied down the Himalayas' 26,700-foot Annapurna with his brother Andre.

Pope John Paul II has experienced many firsts since he ascended the pontifical throne. On this day in 1979, he made history both at the Vatican and in the United States. Entering the White House, the pope met with U.S. President Jimmy Carter, becoming the first pontiff to set foot on the presidential grounds.

A still-unratified treaty was signed on this day in 1963. U.S. President John F. Kennedy signed an international nuclear test ban treaty, which was agreed upon among the United States, Britain, and the Soviet Union. Shockingly, the U.S. Senate has still not ratified this agreement after nearly four decades, despite overwhelming support by U.S. citizens.

8th.

1890 Eddie Rickenbacker was born.

1906 Hairdresser Karl Ludwig introduced the first permanent wave at his hair salon in London, England.

1970 Soviet author Alexander Solzhenitsyn was awarded the Nobel Prize for Literature.

1976 The punk band the Sex Pistols signed a record deal with EMI in London, England (see January 14, June 2, December 10 entries).

1998 The U.S. House of Representatives voted to proceed with an impeachment inquiry into President Bill Clinton's conduct.

Most business figures are not known for their wartime heroics or their sports abilities, but Eddie Rickenbacker was. Born in Columbus, Ohio, on this day in 1890, Eddie drove race cars when he was 16, entering the first Indianapolis 500 in 1911. Eddie held the world speed record of 134 mph before he enlisted in the army during the First World War. Within a year, Captain Eddie Rickenbacker was in the 94th Aero Pursuit Squadron, which fought Baron Manfred von Richthofen's "flying circus." Eddie personally downed twenty-two airplanes and four observation balloons, becoming the "ace of aces." When he returned home, he bought a controlling interest in the Indianapolis Speedway. In 1935 he became general manager and vice president of Eastern Airlines. Three years later, he was president. During the Second World War, Eddie was appointed special representative for Secretary of War Henry L. Stimson. On his second mission over the Pacific, in 1942, his B-17 crashed 600 miles north of Samoa. Eddie and seven crewmen drifted on rubber rafts, living on fish and rainwater for twenty-three days. Two weeks after his rescue, he was back on inspection duty throughout the Pacific. After the war, Eddie continued his job as Eastern Airlines' president, becoming its chairman in 1954.

9th.

1930 The first transcontinental flight completed by a female pilot took place.

1934 Yugoslavian King Alexander was assassinated during a visit to Marseilles, France.

1967 Ché Guevara was executed in Bolivia (see June 14, October 11 entries).

1975 Andrei Sakharov became the first Russian to win the Nobel Peace Prize (see December 19 entry).

1976 A four-person, all-female team set the record for chicken plucking, finishing twelve birds in 32.9 seconds.

1976 Chinese Prime Minister Hua Guofeng succeeded Mao Zhedong as Communist Party chairman.

1981 Israeli Prime Minister Menachem Begin met Egyptian President Hosni Mubarak.

1995 U.S. President Bill Clinton approved a challenge grant.

U.S. President Bill Clinton issued a financial challenge on this day in 1995. The president approved a $510,241 challenge grant, which was issued to the San Diego Unified School District for the implementation of the Triton Project. The district had proposed using a combination of technologies in order to improve student performance in mathematics and science courses.

The first female pilot completed a transcontinental flight across the United States on this day in 1930. Laura Ingalls completed her flight from Roosevelt Field in New York to Glendale, California, making only nine stops along the way.

Political news and business are sometimes conveyed unconventionally. On this day in 1976, wall posters spread throughout Beijing, China, announcing that Prime Minister Hua Guofeng was chosen to succeed Mao Zhedong as Communist Party chairman. And in 1981 Israeli Prime Minister Menachem Begin met with Egyptian President Hosni Mubarak for forty minutes, pledging a continuation of peace discussions. Begin had come to attend assassinated president Anwar Sadat's funeral in Cairo, Egypt.

10th.

1911 Dr. Sun Yat-Sen's revolutionary troops overthrew China's Manchu dynasty.

1914 Ivory Joe Hunter was born.

1935 *Porgy and Bess* opened on Broadway (see September 2 entry).

1964 The first Olympics Games to be held in Asia opened in Tokyo, Japan.

1973 U.S. Vice President Spiro Agnew resigned after being accused on bribery and tax evasion charges.

1975 Israel and Egypt signed the Sinai accord.

2000 A message in a bottle was returned to its owner after forty-four years at sea.

"Prolific" is too mild a word to describe songwriter Ivory Joe Hunter, who had a catalogue of 2,500 songs to his name before he died. Hunter was born in Kirbyville, Texas, on this day in 1914; his father was a guitarist and his mother was a gospel singer. It was no surprise that, in 1933, he made his first recording for the Library of Congress when a federal song collector heard about his music. Unlike many performers of his day, Hunter started his own label—Ivory—in the 1940s and sold to African-American and white audiences alike. His hits on other labels, like "Pretty Baby Blues," "Landlord Blues," "Since I Met You Baby," and "Guess Who," made it to the top of the R&B charts. In 1974 the man who was once described as the "big Texan with the owl eyes and Cheshire-cat smile" was given a benefit at the Grand Ole Opry—which featured music greats such as George Jones, Tammy Wynette, and Isaac Hayes—to help pay for his mounting medical bills. That same year, Hunter died from cancer.

When Hans Schwarz sailed from Austria to attend the 1956 Olympics in Melbourne, Australia, he was caught by a muse. Writing a note in both German and English, he placed his message in a bottle, sealed it, and tossed it into the Indian Ocean. On this day in 2000, the bottle and its contents were returned to Schwarz, who had moved to Wellington, New Zealand, five years after he'd made his 1956 visit. Shortly after the close of the 2000 Olympics in Sydney, Australia, the bottle washed up on a shore on the New Zealand coast, not far from Schwarz's home. The finder called Schwarz and on this day handed the bottle to its originator.

A simple but significant peace was made on this day in 1975. Israel signed the Sinai accord with Egypt, pledging to withdraw its troops from 2,000 square miles of Egyptian territory.

11th.

1958   The *Pioneer 1* lunar probe was launched by NASA.

1967   Bolivian government officials reported that Ché Guevara was buried in a secret grave (see June 14, October 9 entries).

1975   "Saturday Night Live" premiered on NBC-TV with George Carlin as its first host.

1976   The Toxic Substances Control Act was signed (see September 9, September 15 entries).

1979   Fidel Castro visited New York City for the first time in nineteen years to address the United Nations assembly (see August 13, September 5, October 5, November 30, December 2 entries).

1984   Kathy Sullivan became the first American female astronaut to walk in space.

1995   Paul Crutzen, Mario Molina, and F. Sherwood Rowland won the Nobel Prize in Chemistry.

2000 U.S. President Bill Clinton promoted explorer William Clark.

2000 The 100th space shuttle mission was launched from Cape Canaveral, Florida.

Two centuries after he completed his historic expedition with Meriwether Lewis, William Clark was promoted from lieutenant to captain in the U.S. Army by President Bill Clinton. "Unfortunately, issues of budget and bureaucracy intervened—some things never change—and Clark never received his commission," Clinton commented at the ceremony. On this day in 2000, Clinton presented the plaque to a pair of Clark's great-great-great-grandsons. Both the Native American guide Sacagawea and Clark's African-American servant York were awarded the honorary title of sergeant at the same ceremony.

Concern for the health and well-being of an entire planet drove certain events that occurred on this day. In 1976 U.S. President Gerald R. Ford signed the Toxic Substances Control Act, which mandated a three-year phase-out of the production and sale of PCBs, which had been linked to human illnesses and the near extinction of many indigenous plants and animals. On this same day in 1995, Paul Crutzen, Mario Molina, and F. Sherwood Rowland received the Nobel Prize in Chemistry for their research and discoveries on the nature and cause of the ozone layer hole that had opened up over Antarctica. This scientific team pointed the finger at the massive use of CFC-based aerosols throughout the world, which threatened the only protective layer the population has against ultraviolet rays, which have been directly linked to skin cancer in humans and animals.

12th.

1928 The first artificial respirator—the iron lung—was used at a Boston hospital.

1984 A terrorist bombed a bathroom in Brighton, England.

On this day in 1984, British Prime Minister Margaret Thatcher narrowly escaped injury while she attended a meeting in the coastal resort of Brighton Beach, England. A terrorist had placed a bomb in the bathroom of her hotel suite. Fortunately, the device went off when Mrs. Thatcher wasn't even near the hotel.

13th.

1903 The Boston Pilgrims (now the Red Sox) won the first World Series, defeating the Pittsburgh Pirates.

1939 An airplane instructor's license was issued to a woman for the first time.

1962 *Who's Afraid of Virginia Woolf?* premiered on Broadway.

1984 The space shuttle *Challenger* made a perfect landing at Cape Canaveral, Florida (see January 28, February 6, February 10, April 4, April 29, June 22, September 2 entries).

2000 The space shuttle *Discovery* docked at the international space station *Alpha*.

Because of military-based air training programs that had been introduced during the First World War, many men had received their pilot's licenses and earned enough flight hours to also get instructor's licenses during the 1920s. Female aviators did not have that advantage. On this day in 1939, Evelyn Pinckert Kilgore had logged her 2,000 flight hours and was granted the first airplane instructor's license given to a female pilot by the Civil Aeronautics Administration.

Trouble with navigational equipment forced the space shuttle *Discovery* to rendezvous with the international space station *Alpha* on this day in 2000 without the help of radar. Instead, commander Brian Duffy used the shuttle's star-tracking system to detect beams cast by handheld lasers operated by the rest of the crew. The team's mission was to collect air samples in the still-uninhabited space station and to drop off four gyroscopes and two antennas, which were to be installed by the next shuttle crew.

14th.

1832 Chickasaw chiefs ceded tribal lands east of the Mississippi River to the United States government.

1906 The Chicago White Sox beat the Chicago Cubs in the World Series.

1912 Theodore Roosevelt was shot in the chest.

1916 James Barnes won the first Professional Golfers' Association tournament, which was held at Mount Vernon, New York.

1968 The first live telecast from a manned U.S. spacecraft was transmitted from the *Apollo 7* capsule.

2000 The Grand Ole Opry turned seventy-five years old.

The world's longest continuously running show celebrated its seventy-fifth birthday on this day in 2000. Country fiddler Uncle Jimmy Thompson took his first audience request on a live radio show that was broadcast on WSM-AM in Nashville, Tennessee, in 1925. As its popularity grew, the show earned the name the Grand Ole Opry. As the Country Music Association's head, Ed Benson, commented, "There's no question that without the commanding influence of the Grand Ole Opry, Nashville would have never become 'Music City USA.'" Certainly no one outside of Nashville would ever have heard of performers like Skeeter Davis, Porter Waggoner, Dolly Parton, Hank Williams, Patsy Cline, Loretta Lynn, Elvis Presley, Ernest Tubb, or the thousands of other country greats who have graced the stage with its distinctive red barn backdrop.

Not every presidential candidate has been fortunate enough to have an assassination attempt fail. On this day in 1912, a New York City saloon keeper shot Theodore Roosevelt in the chest while the former president was campaigning in Milwaukee, Wisconsin. Running for a second chance at the presidency under the Bull Moose ticket, the undaunted Roosevelt went ahead and made his scheduled speech before he sought medical attention for his wound.

15th.

1917 Mata Hari was executed (see August 7 entry).

1951 "I Love Lucy" premiered on CBS-TV.

1964 Soviet officials announced that Nikita Khrushchev was replaced by Alexei Kosygin as premier and Leonid Brezhnev as party general secretary (see June 19 entry).

1966 The Endangered Species Preservation Act went into effect.

1971 Simon Kuznets received the Nobel Prize in Economics.

1972 Jackie Robinson threw out the first pitch to open the second game of the World Series (see January 24, January 31 entries).

1973 UNIX was introduced.

1984 Astronomers displayed the first photographic evidence of a separate solar system situated 293 trillion miles from earth at a conference held in Pasadena, California.

A unique concept was given the highest commendation on this day in 1971. Simon Kuznets received the Nobel Prize in Economics for his contribution to the way the world measures its wealth and economic health. Kuznets developed the concept that a country's gross national product is the perfect measuring stick for that nation's economic health.

The computer language that drives the Internet was first presented on this day in 1973. Developers Ken Thompson and Dennis Ritchie presented their first paper on the UNIX programming langauge at the Symposium on Operating Systems Principles.

An important step toward the preservation of the environment for the benefit of future generations went into effect on this day in 1966. The Endangered Species Preservation Act initially protected the lives and habitats of seventy-eight species in the United States. These animals had been researched and identified as critical cases by the U.S. Fish and Wildlife Service. By April 1999, species such as the bald eagle and the black-footed ferret had come back in suffcient numbers to be taken off the critical list, but in that same year 925 species remained on the endangered list.

A major league anniversary was celebrated on the baseball field on this day in 1972. Baseball great Jackie Robinson threw out the ceremonial first pitch to open the second game of the World Series. It was the twenty-fifth anniversary of the day he became the first African-American to play in baseball's major leagues.

16th.

1793 Queen Marie Antoinette of France was guillotined.

1916 Margaret Sanger opened the first birth control clinic in New York City.

1951   Prime Minister Ali Khan of Pakistan was assassinated.

1962   U.S. President John F. Kennedy was shown reconnaissance photographs that revealed the presence of missile bases in Cuba, triggering the Cuban missile crisis (see October 22, October 25 entries).

1964   China tested its first nuclear bomb, becoming the world's fifth atomic power.

1978   Cardinal Karol Wojtyla was elected pope (see May 18 entry).

The first non-Italian pope in 465 years was elected by the college of cardinals on this day in 1978. Cardinal Karol Wojtyla had been a professor of moral theology in Poland after his ordination in 1946. Elevated to the post of archbishop and then cardinal in the city of Cracow between 1964 and 1967, Wojtyla took the name Pope John Paul II when he ascended the pontifical throne at the Vatican.

1855   Henry Bessemer patented his steel-making process (see August 13 entry).

1945   Colonel Juan Perón staged a military coup, seizing power in Argentina (see September 23 entry).

1973   Arab oil ministers agreed to an embargo.

1978   U.S. President Jimmy Carter restored Confederate President Jefferson Davis's American citizenship, eighty-nine years after his death.

1979   The Department of Education was created.

1989   A major earthquake struck the San Francisco Bay area (see October 21 entry).

2000   A pig flew first-class across the United States.

The gas crisis in the Western Hemisphere began on this day in 1973. Oil ministers from Arab nations had met in Kuwait and agreed to an oil embargo against Western nations. As a result, the price of fuel oil and gasoline more than doubled. Gasoline was rationed out to stations in both the United States and Europe; huge waiting lines formed to purchase fuel for automobiles and trucks.

Earthquakes aren't a new experience in the San Francisco Bay area. But on this day in 1989, a major tremor rocked the metropolis, destroying segments of the bridge connecting Oakland and San Francisco; the East Bay area's Nimitz Freeway; and numerous houses and businesses along the Presidio waterfront, Chinatown, and downtown, as well as sections of Marin County.

As US Airways spokesperson David Castelveter remarked on this day in 2000, "We can confirm that the pig traveled, and we can confirm that it will never happen again. Let me stress that. It will never happen again." Somehow, two women managed to convince airline personnel that a large pig was a "therapeutic companion" and had to accompany them in the first-class section of a plane headed from Philadelphia, Pennsylvania, to Seattle, Washington. Before the plane even took off on its six-hour flight, the pig began running up and down the aisle while the plane taxied on the runway. Continuing to squeal, it tried to get into the cockpit rather than staying on the floor with its human companions. Its frantic motions didn't stop for six hours, and the squealing didn't stop even when it was escorted through the Seattle airport terminal.

18th.

1898   Lotte Lenya was born.

1919   Anita O'Day was born.

1919   Pierre Trudeau was born.

1925   Melina Mercouri was born.

1945   Paul Robeson won the Spingarn Medal for his singing and acting contributions (see April 9 entry).

1956   Martina Navratilova was born (see September 7, September 9 entries).

1959   The Soviet Union announced that an unmanned space vehicle had photographed the far side of the moon.

1968   Olympic athletes Tommie Smith and John Carlos were suspended for "black power" salutes.

1974   The Soviet Union and Egypt agreed to support the creation of a Palestinian state.

1976   Arab leaders signed a peace plan.

2000   The world's oldest living organism was revived.

Three women whose singing careers were marked by their unusual voices share this birthday. Born in Chicago, Illinois, on this day in 1919, jazz singer Anita O'Day performed her unique brand of improvisational vocalizing with the Stan Kenton and Gene Krupa orchestras during the 1940s, which led to a successful recording career over the next twenty years. Married to Krupa for a number of years, O'Day appeared in the 1958 documentary *Jazz on a Summer Day,* which vaulted her into international jazz stardom. Born in Athens, Greece, on this day in 1925, Melina Mercouri is best remembered for the first film she did with her husband, Jules Dassin, *Never on Sunday.* The raspiness of her voice lent a seductive quality to the songs she performed in the film. Together Dassin and Mercouri made nine films before she turned her attentions to politics, becoming the Greek Minister of Culture and Sciences. In 1990 Mercouri followed in her father's footsteps, becoming mayor of Athens for the next three years. Born in Penzing, Austria, on this day in 1898, Lotte Lenya was often described as having a voice with the qualities of sandpaper. The wife of composer Kurt Weill, Lenya often sang in her husband's musicals, playing the role of Jenny in the *Threepenny Opera* when it premiered in Germany. In 1956, Lenya won a Tony Award for her Broadway reprise of the role. She also produced a number of one-woman shows that featured her husband's songs during the 1960s and 1970s.

One of Canada's most liberal prime ministers was born in Montreal, Quebec, on this day in 1919. Before rising to power during the 1960s, Pierre Trudeau was an active advocate of educational and electoral reforms as well as a public opponent of Prime Minister Maurice Duplessis, becoming a member of the socialist *Rassemblement* movement. In 1965 he joined the Liberal party—after having rejected an invitation to ally himself with the New Democratic party—and was elected to the House of Commons. The next year, this charismatic public figure was appointed as the prime minister's parliamentary secretary. Unlike many of his Francophile contemporaries, Trudeau avidly opposed Quebec's separation from Canada. This was a sentiment he brought with him when he was elected prime minister in 1968. Although he was defeated in the next general election, Trudeau was reelected as Canada's prime minister once again in 1981.

The world's oldest living organism—a 250-million-year-old bacteria—was revived by scientists on this day in 2000, after existing in a state of suspended animation in a salt crystal. Encased in this protective shell and suspended in a brine pocket, the bacteria laid in an underground cavern near Carlsbad, New Mexico. Called *Bacillus permians,* the organism was carefully extracted under sterile conditions and incubated until it grew. As microbiolost Russell Vreeland said, "From a biological standpoint this is extremely significant because quite literally this organism is the next best thing to having been there."

The modern Olympics has always been regarded as an event where nations put their political sentiments aside to participate in the spirit of the games. But on this day in 1968, two members of the U.S. Olympic team crossed that fragile line at the Mexico City Olympiad. Tommie Smith and John Carlos were suspended after they both gestured "black power" salutes from their positions on the victory stand.

The great rivalry between tennis champions Chris Evert and Martina Navratilova filled the sports pages during the 1970s. Born in Prague on this day in 1956, Martina Navratilova had made her name winning the Federation Cup three times before she defected to the United States in 1975. During her impressive career, she won more than a hundred international tournaments, becoming a nine-time Wimbledon champion, four-time U.S. Open winner, three-time Australian Open winner, and two-time French Open champion.

A major cease-fire was called in Lebanon on this day in 1976, after six Arab heads of state met in Saudi Arabia. This august group signed a peace plan that called for 30,000 troops to supervise an organized withdrawal of forces from both battling factions.

19th.

1945   John Lithgow was born.

1960   The United States ordered a trade embargo of all goods to Cuba, with the exception of food and medicine, by American companies.

1983   Grenadan Prime Minister Maurice Bishop was assassinated in a military coup (see October 25 entry).

1987   Black Monday—the New York Stock Exchange lost 508 points.

1989   The U.S. Senate rejected a proposed constitutional amendment banning desecration of the American flag.

For the first time since the 1929 stock market crash, a black day occurred on Wall Street in 1987. Known as "Black Monday," the New York stock market took a record 508-point nose dive, plunging the nation into a deep recession.

Although actor John Lithgow was the son of an actress and a theatrical producer, he didn't follow in the family footsteps until he entered Harvard University on a scholarship. Born in Rochester, New York, on this day in 1945, Lithgow had a gift for acting that earned him two Oscar nominations for his portrayals in the 1982 film *The World According to Garp* and the 1983 film *Terms of Endearment.* His Broadway stage performances have earned him Tony Awards and nominations for his roles in *The Changing Room, Requiem for a Heavyweight,* and *M. Butterfly.* But it's the ability to deliver fresh comedy that has made Lithgow's name a household word, with his portrayal of the mission commander in the television series "3rd Rock from the Sun" for five years.

20th.

1882 Bela Lugosi was born.

1968 Jacqueline Kennedy married Aristotle Onassis (see January 15, July 3, July 28, September 12 entries).

1971 *Jesus Christ Superstar* premiered on Broadway.

1978 The Women's Army Corps was deactivated and troops were integrated into the regular military branches.

The world's most famous vampire was born in Lugos, Hungary, on this day in 1882. Bela Lugosi had tried his hand at acting at a very early age, running away from home when he was only eleven years old to pursue his dream. After serving in the Hungarian Army for two years during the First World War, Lugosi began to land film roles in Hungary. This triggered a desire to move to the United States, which he did in 1921. Billed as a ladies' man in stage and film productions, Lugosi first played Count Dracula on stage in 1929, winning rave reviews. When Universal Studios decided to make the film version, they originally hired Lon Chaney to play the vampiric lead. But when the actor died before production, Lugosi was contracted to reprise his role for $500 a week. The 1931 film *Dracula* made Lugosi's name a household word. Typecast throughout the next twenty years as a horror film star, Lugosi landed only one role that didn't involve monsters or horror: He played Comrade Razinin in the 1939 comedy film *Ninotchka.*

As the horror movie craze waned during the 1950s, Lugosi couldn't find work and ended up playing in two films that are still regarded as the worst ever made: *Glen or Glenda* and *Plan 9 from Outer Space,* both directed by Ed Wood, Jr.

21st.

1959 The Guggenheim Museum, designed by Frank Lloyd Wright, was officially opened to the public in New York City.

1967 An estimated 150,000 antiwar demonstrators marched on the Pentagon, demanding an end to the Vietnam War.

1969 Willy Brandt became West Germany's first socialist chancellor (see May 6, December 18 entries).

1979 Israeli Foreign Minister Moshe Dayan resigned (see May 20, June 24 entries).

1986 The Titanic Maritime Memorial Act was signed (see September 2 entry).

1989 Disaster teams rescued a man from the wreckage of the Nimitz Freeway (see October 17, November 18 entries).

1993 NATO ministers endorsed limited partnerships.

Respect for the dead prompted the signing of a unique bill on this day in 1986. Concern had been made public by descendants of those who went down with the *Titanic* in 1912 after the ship's hull and remains were discovered by a marine archaeological team in 1985. U.S. President Ronald Reagan signed the Titanic Maritime Memorial Act, which made it illegal for any U.S. citizen to scavenge, buy, sell, or own anything that went down with the ill-fated luxury cruise ship.

A miraculous but tragic rescue occurred on this day in 1989, four days after an earthquake destroyed a section of the Nimitz Freeway in the San Francisco Bay area. Disaster teams pulled longshoreman Buck Helm from his car, which had been trapped in the wreckage after a portion of the freeway collapsed. Miraculously, Helm was still alive. But tragically, the man died from his numerous injuries less than a month later.

A limited agreement was made by the North Atlantic Treaty Organization on this day in 1993. NATO ministers endorsed the restricted formation of a partnership between the United States and Russia. They also agreed that limited alliances could be made with other former East Bloc nations. But NATO heads were reticent to offer those nations full membership in the organization, which was dedicated to fight communist aggression in Europe and North America.

1962 The Cuban missile crisis began when U.S. President John F. Kennedy called for a naval blockade around Cuba (see September 2, October 16, October 25 entries).

1994 The Rhinoceros and Tiger Conservation Act went into effect.

On this day in 1994, the Rhinoceros and Tiger Conservation Act went into effect in the United States. This bill was intended to assist in the preservation of rhinoceroses and tigers by supporting and providing financial resources for the conservation programs of nations whose activities directly or indirectly affect rhinoceros and tiger populations.

1910 Blanche Scott became the first female pilot to make a solo flight, rising 12 feet into the air in Fort Wayne, Indiana.

1942 Michael Crichton was born.

1954 Great Britain, France, the United States, and the Soviet Union ended their occupation of Germany.

1956 A rebellion against communist rule in Poland and Hungary was put down by Soviet troops.

1958 Boris Pasternak won the Nobel Prize in Literature.

1973   U.S. President Richard Nixon finally agreed to turn over the Watergate tapes to U.S. District Judge John Sirica (see August 5, September 15, September 19, October 1, November 21 entries).

1987   The U.S. Senate voted against the confirmation of Robert Bork (see March 1 entry).

1992   U.S. President George H. Bush signed the Cuban Democracy Act, to further tighten the thirty-year trade embargo.

Born in Chicago, Illinois, on this day in 1942, Michael Crichton was a visiting anthropology lecturer at Cambridge University in England when he was only twenty-three years old. When he returned to the United States, he paid his way through Harvard's medical school by writing thrillers under a pen name. Even before he had gotten his medical degree, he had written the 1969 best-seller *The Andromeda Strain.* Crichton devoted his career to writing after that, producing eleven novels, including *Jurassic Park, Anaconda, Eaters of the Dead,* and *Congo.* He directed a few films, including *Westworld, Coma,* and *The Great Train Robbery.* He also created the television series "ER. "

24th.

1978   The Airline Deregulation Act was signed.

1989   Jim Bakker was sentenced to 45 years' imprisonment.

1992   The Toronto Blue Jays won the World Series (see October 1 entry).

2000   Secretary of State Madeleine Albright gave her e-mail address to North Korean leader, Kim Jong-Il.

2000   The federal government reported a record budget surplus.

The age of airfare price wars began shortly after a new bill was signed on this day in 1978. U.S. President Jimmy Carter put his signature on the Airline Deregulation Act, which allowed commercial passenger airlines to cut all short routes that didn't turn a profit and allowed for healthy competition among airlines for passengers on key flights between major cities and to popular foreign destinations.

During a state dinner that took place on this day in 2000 in Pyongyang, North Korea, U.S. Secretary of State Madeleine Albright gave North Korean leader Kim Jong-Il a basketball personally autographed by ex-Chicago Bulls basketball great Michael Jordan. As she was getting ready to leave, Albright invited Jong-Il to "pick up the phone any time." Although the North Korean leader is known for his reclusiveness, he was not computer illiterate, replying, "Please give me your e-mail address." She did.

It's not often that the federal government has been able to declare that there is enough money in the treasury from tax revenues to report a surplus. But for the third consecutive year, the Clinton administration announced a surplus of funds. And on this day in 2000, it was recorded as the largest surplus ever—$273 billion. "This is the third surplus in a row—the first time our nation has done that in 51 years, since 1949, when Harry Truman was president," U.S. President Bill Clinton happily announced at a press conference.

For the first time in major league baseball history, a non-United States team won the World Series. On this day in 1992, the Toronto Blue Jays from the Canadian province of Ontario defeated the Atlanta Braves in the eleventh inning of the series' sixth game.

1888   Admiral Richard E. Byrd was born.

1925   John Logie Baird transmitted the first television images from the attic laboratory of his home in London, England.

1954   A U.S. Cabinet session was televised for the first time.

1962   U.S. Ambassador Adlai E. Stevenson III unveiled photographic evidence of Soviet missile bases in Cuba at the United Nations (see October 16, October 22 entries).

1964   The Rolling Stones appeared on "The Ed Sullivan Show" (see January 15, May 10, May 12, June 3, June 14, July 30, December 5, December 6, December 18 entries).

1971   Taiwan was expelled from the United Nations, allowing the People's Republic of China to join (see August 25 entry).

1975   The Soviet Union landed its second spacecraft on the planet Venus, transmitting photographs of a different area than had been previously seen.

1983   U.S. troops invaded Grenada (see October 19 entry).

2000   A new planetoid was discovered.

2000   American Telephone & Telegraph split into four companies.

2000   Ground was broken for the Smithsonian Institution's new Air and Space Museum.

For the second time in less than twenty years, American Telephone & Telegraph split itself into multiple concerns. But unlike the split in 1984, which was prompted by an antitrust suit, falling stock prices forced the telecommunications giant to reorganize its interests. The company allowed each division—consumer, business, broadband, and wireless—to operate as a separate entity so investors could track the progress or slowdown of each segment as a discrete business venture.

Ground was broken at Washington's Dulles International Airport for a new National Air and Space Museum on this day in 2000. The original museum—situated in downtown Washington, D.C.—could barely hold one-tenth of the national museum's collection of aeronautic and aerospace artifacts, which include a F-86A Sabre, Wiley Post's Lockheed Vega, a Chance-Vought F4U Corsair, and a Curtiss JN-4D Jenny. The ten-story structure will be named after Hungarian-born businessman Steven F. Udar-Hazy, who donated $60 million to the project.

A new, minor planet was discovered on this day in 2000. Named 2000 EB173, the planetoid is only one-fourth the size of its neighbor, Pluto. It was spotted with an extremely powerful telescope situated at the CIDA Observatory in Merida, Venezuela. As Yale University's Charles Baltay commented, "Wow! After all these years, we can still find something new in our solar system." It's customary that whoever discovers a new celestial body be allowed to name it after it's circled the sun two times. According to Baltay, it will take 2000 EB173 approximately 243 years to make that journey just once.

26th.

1920   The Lord Mayor of Cork died in prison (see October 27 entry).

1994   Frank Thomas was named the American League's Most Valuable Player for the second consecutive year.

2000   Four new moons were found orbiting the planet Saturn.

A sad moment occurred in the history of Irish-British relations on this day in 1920. In the city of Cork, Ireland's lord mayor died in prison. Mayor Terrence MacSwiney had been imprisoned by British authorities on conspiracy charges stemming from his involvement with Sinn Fein rebels. During his incarceration, he began a seventy-five-day hunger strike in his cell. This nonviolent protest led to his death from starvation.

United States astronomers found four new moons orbiting the planet Saturn on this day in 2000. This makes Saturn the planet with the most moons, surpassing the planet Uranus by one moon. Each of these celestial bodies is less than 30 miles in diameter, according to a Cornell University research team. But the group's leaders, professors Joseph Burns and Philip Nicholson, also planned to confirm the potential existence of additional moons orbiting some 9 million miles away from the ringed planet.

27th.

1904   The New York subway system opened.

1970   Charles Manson's defense lawyers announced that they planned to subpoena the rock band The Beatles to testify as to the meaning of their song "Helter Skelter" (see January 25, March 6, August 9, December 8 entries).

1980   Seven Sinn Fein guerrillas launched a hunger strike (see October 26 entry).

1991   The United States handed an air base over to the Philippines.

A maze of underground mass transit lines had its official beginnings on this day in 1904. Although the New York City subway system weaves an intricate underground web throughout the sprawling metropolis, it began with a single system: the Interborough Rapid Transit line. On this particular day, New York City Mayor George B. McClellan opened the IRT (now known as the 4/5/6 line) for public use, connecting Manhattan's east side from the Brooklyn Bridge to 145th Street.

The fight for freedom by the Sinn Fein continued on this day in Northern Ireland. In 1980 seven Sinn Fein guerrillas who had been incarcerated in a Northern Ireland prison launched a hunger strike. They demanded that Great Britain commute their status to that of political prisoners rather than terrorists before they would give up their protest.

Clark Air Force Base in the Philippines had been severely damaged by the volcanic eruption of Mount Pinatubo. Rather than make repairs on the property, on this day in 1991, the United States handed over the military installation to the Philippine government. Before a month had gone by, the base was stripped of every usable piece of material and supplies by looters and guards.

28th.

1914 Dr. Jonas Salk was born in New York City (see January 10, February 23, August 1 entries).

1955 Bill Gates was born.

1959 Turkey and the United States sign an agreement to put Jupiter missiles in Turkey.

1962 The Soviet Union agreed to remove its nuclear missiles from Cuba (see October 16, October 22, October 25 entries).

1965 Pope Paul VI absolved the Jewish people of their collective guilt for Jesus Christ's crucifixion (see June 21, June 30, July 29, September 26, November 27, December 9 entries).

1974 Arab heads of state officially recognized the Palestine Liberation Organization as the Palestinian people's sole representative.

1985 John Walker pleaded guilty to charges of espionage, selling U.S. Navy secrets to the Soviet Union.

1993 Ousted Haitian President Jean-Bertrand Aristide pleaded for an international trade blockade against Haiti while speaking at the United Nations.

The world's youngest multi-billionaire was born in Seattle, Washington, on this day in 1955. Bill Gates took up computer programming when he was thirteen years old, attending the Lakeside School in north Seattle. He developed a unique version of the BASIC programming language when he was at Harvard University, but he dropped out in 1975 to spend his time on the formation of the Microsoft Corporation. Within less than two decades, Gates built the company into the world's largest software development corporation.

The Cuban missile crisis wasn't the first time one nation placed missiles in another country for defense purposes. On this day in 1959, Turkey and the United States signed a similar agreement. Turkey arranged to accept the placement of fifteen nuclear-tipped Jupiter missiles that had been built in the United States.

29th.

1947 The General Electric Company successfully seeded clouds with dry ice, producing rain in Concord, New Hampshire.

1956 War broke out between Egypt and Israel.

1967 The musical *Hair* opened at the Public Theater in New York's Greenwich Village (see April 28 entry).

1974 Muhammad Ali regained his heavyweight title, knocking out George Foreman in a bout at Kinshasa, Zaire.

1998 Astronaut John Glenn joined the space shuttle *Discovery* crew, participating in a scientific study of the aging process (see April 9 entry).

A heated debate over the use of an international waterway led to the use of force on this day in 1956. Acting in conjunction with Great Britain and France, the state of Israel sent invasion forces to Egypt's Sinai Peninsula. The Egyptian government had refused to allow access to the Suez Canal for Israeli shipping vessels. Since the canal is the sole link between the Mediterranean Sea and all of Asia, this restriction was a direct insult to the relatively new nation.

30th.

1956   Great Britain and France demanded a cease-fire, ordering both Egypt and Israel to end the fight over the Suez Canal.

1975   New York City almost went broke.

1975   Prince Juan Carlos became king of Spain (see July 22, December 4 entries).

1979   A presidential commission finished a study of Three-Mile Island (see March 28, April 13, June 28 entries).

The way nuclear reactors used for commercial purposes are constructed, operated, and regulated changed after this day in 1979. A presidential commission finished its study of the core meltdown at the Three-Mile Island nuclear plant near Harrisburg, Pennsylvania, concluding that a combination of poor construction, lax management, and a lack of federal regulation had contributed to the radioactive accident.

Business almost didn't go on as usual in New York City on this day in 1975. In fact, the hub of American business almost went broke and nearly defaulted on $2 billion in bond obligations. Fortunately, the federal government loaned the city the funds to pay its commitments and reorganize its financial affairs.

31st.

1941   Work ceased on Mount Rushmore's partially completed figures (see March 3, July 2, July 4, August 30, September 17, October 1, December 28 entries).

1968   U.S. President Lyndon B. Johnson announced the end of bombing in North Vietnam.

1994   The California Desert Protection Act went into effect.

2000   ICBMs were offered for sale by Russia.

The desert is a fragile environment. The federal government recognized that fact on this day in 1994, when the California Desert Protection Act went into effect. This bill designated 9.4 million acres of the California desert as either national park or wildlife preserve land, saving its subtle beauty for future generations' appreciation.

The Russian nuclear missile chief, General Vladimir Yakolev, announced an unusual sale on this day in 2000. To raise cash for the military, Russia's Strategic Rocket Forces offered to sell 250 decommissioned intercontinental ballistic missiles (ICBMs) for use by commercial and government agencies to launch satellites into orbit. Since it would be cheaper to cut up the former defense mechanisms than to scrap them or manufacture non-combat versions for use with satellites, the sale made sense. Yakolev commented that "the needs of many countries for launching satellites are constantly growing."

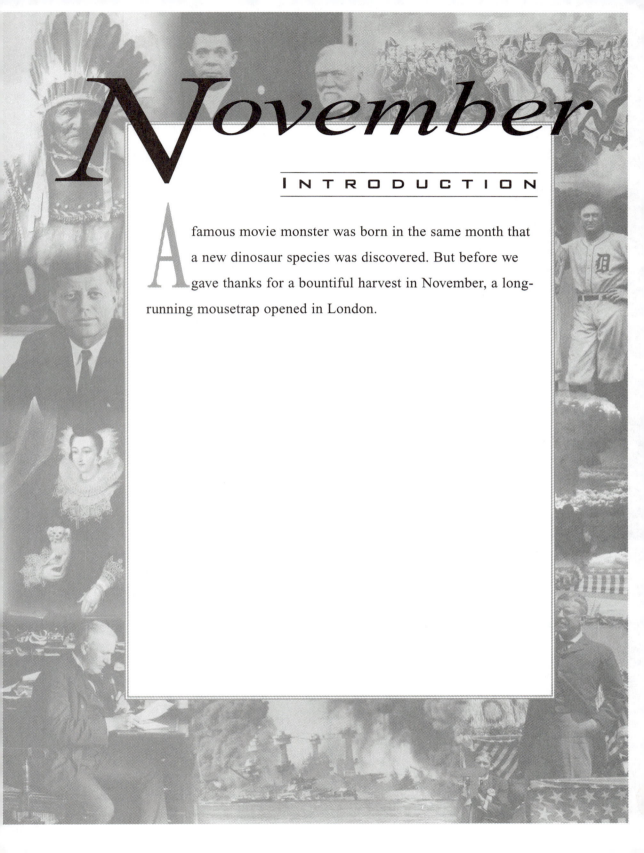

November

A famous movie monster was born in the same month that a new dinosaur species was discovered. But before we gave thanks for a bountiful harvest in November, a long-running mousetrap opened in London.

1st.

1910 W.E.B. DuBois published the first issue of the NAACP magazine, *Crisis* (see February 23, June 13 entries).

1943 Rent control went into effect in New York City.

1945 The first issue of *Ebony* magazine was published.

1950 Two Puerto Rican nationalists attempted to assassinate U.S. President Harry S Truman at Blair House in Washington, D.C.

2000 Yugoslavia reestablished relations with the United States.

2000 The White House celebrated its 200th anniversary.

A unique system was set in place to manage runaway rent hikes in New York City on this day in 1943. Enacted as a wartime measure to ensure that New York tenants could afford shelter in one of the world's most expensive cities, rent controls were imposed on nearly a million houses, tenements, apartments, hotels, and rooming houses within the five boroughs. Rents were frozen at the rates charged on March 1, 1943, and weren't allowed to be raised by the city's landlords or innkeepers. Although incremental increases have been allowed over the past five decades, rent control is still in effect in more than a quarter of the city's residences.

Two very influential African-American magazines were born on this day. In 1910 W.E.B. DuBois published the first issue of the NAACP's monthly magazine, *Crisis,* in New York City. And in 1945 John H. Johnson published the first issue of *Ebony* magazine in Chicago, Illinois. For Johnson, this was only the beginning of a multi-magazine publishing empire, which is now headed by his daughter.

The White House in Washington, D.C., celebrated its 200th birthday on this day in 2000. Home to forty presidents, the house was barely finished when U.S. President John Quincy Adams arrived to take possession. His wife, Abigail, still hadn't arrived. Writing her that night from the freshly whitewashed sandstone mansion, he remarked, "Before I end my letter I pray heaven to bestow the best of blessings on this House, and on all that shall hereafter inhabit it. May none but honest and wise men ever rule under this roof."

2nd.

1903 The U.S. Navy landed at Colon, Panama (see April 18, May 18, August 10, September 7, November 3, December 31 entries).

1983 U.S. President Ronald Reagan signed the bill designating the third Monday in January as a national holiday, Martin Luther King Day.

1988 The Internet Worm was released.

2000 The international space station *Alpha* was officially inhabited by American and Russian personnel.

2000 A scooter manufacturer sued fifteen companies for copying its design.

Fads come and go, and so do the profits in the toy-making industry. Although two-wheeled scooters had been a hot item during the 1920s, Razor USA had improved on the basic design and construction. But rather than wait to receive the patent for the polished aluminum scooter with its skateboard-style wheels and rear-fender friction brake, the manufacturer sold $100 million worth of the new model within three months during the summer season to both children and adults. Naturally, copycat designs followed, taking away significant market share. On this day in 2000, Razor USA filed lawsuits against fifteen of its rivals in a Los Angeles district court, including ski manufacturer K2 Inc. and retailer Children's Place Retail Stores Inc.

A powerful worm was set loose on this day in 1988. Robert Morris, Jr., released the monitoring program known as the Internet Worm, which was used by approximately 6,000 out of the 60,000 existing Internet hosts at that time. Within a year, concerns detected by the worm were handled by the Computer Emergency Response Team (CERT), which was organized specifically for that purpose.

3rd.

1883 The U.S. Supreme Court ruled that Native Americans were not American citizens (see February 8 entry).

1896   The state of Idaho granted women the right to vote (see February 28, July 1 entries).

1903   The United States invaded Panama (see April 18, May 18, August 10, September 7, November 2, December 31 entries).

1954   Godzilla was born.

1957   The Soviet Union launched *Sputnik 2,* which carried the first animal into space: a dog named Laika.

1983   Reverend Jesse Jackson declared his candidacy as a Democratic presidential nominee.

The world's most famous reptilian monster was born in Japan on this day in 1954, when the film *Gojira* premiered in Tokyo. Known as Godzilla in the Western Hemisphere, the monster was said to be from the Angilas family of fire-breathing reptiles that slept underwater. Exposure to radiation from H-bomb tests in the South Pacific mutated Godzilla into a 164-foot creature that breathed atomic rays. A half-century later, the legend continues. Dozens of films, a television series, and numerous spin-offs have kept Godzilla alive. The monster even descended upon New York City in the 1998 American feature film version of the story.

4th.

1979   The 444-day Iran hostage crisis began (see January 20, November 17, November 20, November 22, December 26 entries).

A long, arduous experience began on this day in 1979. The Iranian hostage crisis began when Shiite Muslim militants stormed the U.S. Embassy in Tehran, Iran. The Ayatollah Khomeini ordered the release of all women and African-American captives as well as the release of thirteen other hostages within a few weeks. But for the fifty-two remaining hostages, this was the beginning of a 444-day ordeal.

Citizens of Texas and Wyoming elected two female governors who had a lot in common on this day in 1924. Texas Governor Miriam Ferguson's husband had held the same position before his impeachment in 1917. She held the office twice, winning her second term in 1932. Wyoming Governor Nellie Ross's husband had also held the same position until his death in office. Ross had completed her husband's term in office and was reelected to her own term on this particular day.

5th.

1952 Agatha Christie's *The Mousetrap* premiered in London, England.

1968 Shirley Chisholm became the first black woman elected to the U.S. House of Representatives (see June 4 entry).

2000 A Moroccan runner won the New York Marathon.

Shirley Chisholm made history on this day in 1968. Before she became the first female African-American to run for a presidential nomination, she put her name in the record books for another reason. Chisholm became the first African-American woman to be elected to the U.S. House of Representatives, taking her seat for the Bedford-Stuyvesant congressional district of Brooklyn, New York.

A Moroccan runner won the New York Marathon on this day in 2000. In previous attempts, Abdelkhader El Mouaziz had placed fourth and seventh in this grueling race. At the 13.1-mile marker, El Mouaziz made one of the earliest breaks from the pack in the race's history. Only 1996 Olympic gold medalist Josia Thugwane kept up with his pace during the first half. And at the finish line, only four-time marathon winner Japhet Kosgei of Kenya could be seen in the distance, finishing second at 2 hours, 12 minutes, 29 seconds.

6th.

1814 Adolphe Sax was born in Dinant, Belgium (see January 17, June 21 entries).

1913   Indian nationalist Mohandas K. Gandhi was arrested for organizing and leading a protest march of Indian miners in South Africa.

1926   Negro History Week was initiated by Carter G. Woodson (see December 19 entry).

1990   Fourteen women arrested for driving in Saudi Arabia.

1991   Russian President Boris Yeltsin disbanded the Communist Party (see February 1, March 20, May 29, December 18, December 25 entries).

2000   A judge upheld a $145-billion class-action damage suit awarded to Florida smokers to be paid by five major tobacco companies (see January 2, January 10, April 11, July 17, August 1, August 24, December 1 entries).

A woman's right to publicly drive an automobile is not internationally recognized, as evidenced by a situation that took place on this day in 1990. Fourteen female drivers—who were accompanied by thirty-two passengers—lodged an unusual protest in Riyadh, Saudi Arabia. The women pulled out of a Safeway supermarket parking lot, driving only a short distance before police and devout Muslim men stopped them at a traffic light. While the Muslims beat on the windows, accusing the women of being prostitutes and sinners, the police began the arrest process. They took the protesters to the local police station for interrogation. Then, rather than have them be stoned by men, the authorities released the women into the custody of their male relatives for punishment. Ironically, some of those male relatives supported the women's demonstration.

7th.

1967   Public television was born.

1973   The U.S. Congress passed the War Powers Act.

2000   Presidential candidate Albert Gore refused to concede.

2000   Hillary Rodham Clinton became a U.S. senator.

A monumental leap for educational television programming took place on this day in 1967. U.S. President Lyndon B. Johnson signed a bill that established the Corporation for Public Broadcasting. This organization funds and broadcasts television shows that would not normally receive backing from more commercial venues. "Sesame Street," "Nature," and "Masterpiece Theater" are just a few examples of what this bill has provided the American public.

One of the country's closest presidential elections was undecided on this day in 2000. In order to win the U.S. presidency, a candidate must get 270 votes in the electoral college. And on this particular day, Vice President Albert Gore held 260 votes while Texas Governor George W. Bush held 246 votes. Florida and Oregon remained undecided, which created one of history's great cliffhanger elections. Many people believed that since Bush won by at least 650 popular votes—or less than 1 percent—in Florida, he would win the critical 25 electoral votes from that state. But Florida's election law requires an automatic vote recount if the margin of difference is less than 0.5 percent, unless the losing candidate declines to call for a recount. Gore retracted his concession in a telephone call to Bush, without making any announcement to the press.

For the first time in United States history, a president's wife was elected to a public office. First Lady Hillary Rodham Clinton was elected to the U.S. Senate on this day in 2000, representing the state of New York. She had tough competition: two Republican politicians who were born and raised in the Empire State. Clinton initially ran against New York Mayor Rudolph Giuliani, who bowed out of the race for personal reasons. Still facing harsh criticism that she was not a native New Yorker, Clinton managed an overwhelming victory against her second opponent, U.S. Congressman Rick Lazio.

An unprecedented bill finally made it through the U.S. Congress after nine attempts and a presidential veto. On this day in 1973, Congress passed the War Powers Act, which limited the president's power to send U.S. military troops to fight in foreign nations without first securing congressional approval.

8th.

1956   Lieutenant Commander Malcolm D. Ross and M. Lee Lewis unofficially broke an altitude record (see November 11 entry).

1994   The Republican Party gained control of Congress for first time since 1954.

1994   California's Proposition 187, prohibiting access to public social services, passed.

2000   A new dinosaur species was discovered.

2000   A Picasso painting sold for $55 million.

The fifth-highest price ever paid for an auctioned work of art was handed over on this day in 2000 at Christie's auction house. Pablo Picasso's *Woman with Crossed Arms* was sold to an undisclosed buyer who wanted this "Blue period" masterpiece, which had originally been owned by art collector and author Gertrude Stein.

A highly controversial initiative was passed by popular vote in the state of California on this day in 1994. Proposition 187 was passed, winning 59 percent of the state's votes. In an effort to combat the huge influx of illegal aliens settling in the state, the initiative prohibited access to public social services to anyone who couldn't establish his or her status as a U.S. citizen, a legal permanent resident, or an alien living in California on a student or temporary visa. Those public social services included health care and emergency medical care. The initiative also denied the children of illegal aliens the right to attend California schools. The federal courts put down this state law, citing it as in direct violation of numerous federal laws and the U.S. Constitution, which grant all persons living in the United States the right to basic social services and educational opportunities.

An altitude record set in 1935 by the hot-air balloon *Explorer II* was unofficially broken on this day in 1956. Lieutenant Commander Malcolm D. Ross and M. Lee Lewis ascended to 76,000 feet in their hot-air balloon *Strato-Lab I,* exceeding the 72,395-foot record previously held.

The Republican Party gained control of both houses of Congress on this day in 1994. During the state races for representative and senator posts, more Republican candidates were elected than Democrats—some of whom were running for reelection. It was the first time since 1954 that the Republicans had held a full congressional majority.

Human beings have not found out everything there is to know about prehistoric life, but each century it seems they get a little closer. It was announced on this day in 2000 that a new carnivorous dinosaur species had been discovered in Italy. A team of paleontologists working a northern Italian quarry uncovered fragments of a 26.4-foot-long *Saltriosaurus* that had 2.8-inch-long sharp teeth. Scientists dated the beast as having lived over 200 million years ago, during the early Jurassic era. But unlike its carnivorous cousins of the period, this particular specimen proved that the species evolved more quickly into creatures related to the *Allosaurus* and *Tyrannosaurus rex* than previously believed.

9th.

1961   Record shop owner Brian Epstein saw The Beatles perform for the first time at the Cavern Club in Liverpool, England.

1967   The first issue of *Rolling Stone* was published.

A strong, new voice hit the newsstands on this day in 1967. Until this time, the politically and musically outspoken Baby Boomer generation didn't have a publication that addressed its personal interests in topics ranging from antiwar protests and government corruption to interviews and reviews of the day's top rock and roll, R&B, blues, and soul performers. Published by twenty-one-year-old Jann Wenner in San Francisco, California, *Rolling Stone* magazine grew from a newsprint music magazine to a major four-color publication in less than two decades. The premiere issue featured a photograph of the Beatles' John Lennon on the cover.

10th.

1869   The Suez Canal was officially opened.

1891   Granville T. Woods patented his design for an electric railway (see April 23, November 15 entries).

1895   John Northrop was born.

1951   Coast-to-coast, operator-assisted dial telephone service began in the United States.

1954   The Iwo Jima Memorial was dedicated.

1973   U.S. Secretary of State Henry Kissinger arrived in Beijing, China, to discuss normalization of relations between the United States and China (see March 25, September 21 entries).

1981   The hot-air balloon *Double Eagle V* began a transpacific crossing (see November 13 entry).

1982   The Vietnam Veterans Memorial was dedicated.

1993   The Church of England (Anglican Church) agreed to ordain female priests.

Two war memorials were opened to the public in the Washington metropolitan area on this day. In 1954 the Iwo Jima Memorial was dedicated in Arlington, Virginia. The statue depicts the U.S. Marines raising the flag on the Japanese island during the Second World War. The image was inspired by a photograph taken at the battlefront. And in 1982 the Vietnam Veterans Memorial greeted its first public visitors in Washington, D.C. The memorial is in the form of a monolith engraved with the names of those who died during the Vietnam War. A smaller travel model of the memorial was sent across the United States so that those who couldn't visit the nation's capital could view the sculpture.

Aviation design and manufacture became a fine and profitable art in the hands of John Knuden Northrop, who was born in Newark, New Jersey, on this day in 1895. A project engineer for Douglas Aircraft when he was twenty-one years old, Northrop became chief engineer and vice president of the Lockheed Aircraft Company in 1927 after moving to Burbank, California. He opened his own subsidiary of Douglas Aircraft six years later—Northrop Corporation—which produced a number of famous aircraft, including the world's first all-wing plane, which he called the Flying Wing.

An attempt to cross the Pacific Ocean in a hot-air balloon began on this day in 1981. The owner of the Benihana's restaurant chain, Rocky Aoki, was accompanied by balloonists Ben Abruzzo, Larry Newman, and Ron Clark when he took off from Nagashima, Japan, in the hot-air balloon *Double Eagle V.* They set their destination at a landing site in California.

11th.

1935 Captains Albert W. Stevens and Orvil A. Anderson broke the altitude record at 72,395 feet above the Black Hills of South Dakota in their hot-air balloon *Explorer II* (see November 8 entry).

1965 Rhodesian Prime Minister Ian Smith declared the nation's independence, although Great Britian declared the regime illegal.

1972 The U.S. Army turned over its base at Long Bihn.

1983 The United States deployed missiles to sites throughout Europe.

1989 The first telephone conversation occurred between Helmut Kohl and Egon Krenz at which German reunification was discussed.

An ironic telephone conversation took place on this day in 1989. West German Chancellor Helmut Kohl had called East German leader Egon Krenz to discuss the potential reunification of their two countries. During the conversation, however, Krenz ruled out any possibility of such an event. But by the following year, East and West Germany were again united, with Helmut Kohl as chancellor.

The United States pulled out and potentially instigated military action on two separate occasions on this day. In 1972 the U.S. Army turned over its base at Long Bihn to South Vietnamese military authorities. This action ended the direct involvement of United States military forces in the Vietnam War. And in 1983 the United States shipped 572 intermediate-range cruise missiles to various sites throughout Europe. This action forced the Soviet Union to back out of negotiations aimed at reducing the number of such missiles placed on that continent.

12th.

1866   Dr. Sun Yat-Sen was born.

1946   The world's first drive-in bank service was opened by The Exchange National Bank of Chicago.

1961   Nadia Comaneci was born (see November 28 entry).

Born in Guangdong Province, China, on this day in 1866, Dr. Sun Yat-Sen quickly abandoned medicine for politics in 1895, when he joined a student rebellion in Canton. After living in exile in the United States and Europe for nearly sixteen years, Yat-Sen returned to China in 1911 as the leader of the Kuomintang. He was elected provisional president of the Chinese republic, which only lasted one year. Internal arguments forced him to flee to Japan, where he organized a new party. He was reinstalled as Chinese head of state in 1923, reorganizing the Kuomintang on the model of the Soviet Communist Party within a year. Sun Yat-Sen never saw his political dreams come to fruition: He died the following year.

Nadia Elena Comaneci was the first contestant ever to receive a perfect score in a woman's gymnastic event, when she was only fourteen years old. Born in Gheorghe Gheorghiu-Dej, Romania, on this day in 1961, Comaneci was an international sensation after she achieved this perfect score at the 1976 Olympics, winning seven perfect scores and three gold medals in singles events. In 1989 she defected from Romania, crossing the Hungarian border by foot. And in 1996 she and her husband, Olympic medalist Bart Conner, opened a gymnastics academy in Oklahoma.

13th.

1972   The U.S. Supreme Court refused to hear an appeal requested by the defendants in the Pentagon Papers case (see February 15, June 21, July 12 entries).

1973   The U.S. Senate passed the bill that authorized the construction of the Alaska oil pipeline.

1974   Karen Silkwood was killed in a car crash (see May 18 entry).

1974   Yasser Arafat addressed the United Nations.

1975   The World Health Organization announced that for the first time in history, Asia was free of the smallpox virus.

1981   The hot-air balloon *Double Eagle V* completed the first transpacific crossing in 84 hours, 31 minutes, landing in Covelo, California (see November 10 entry).

1985   The Nevado del Ruiz volcano erupted.

1986   U.S. President Ronald Reagan admitted that the government had been illegally selling arms to Iran.

2000   Philippine President Joseph Estrada was impeached.

Evidence is not always easy to access. On this day in 1972, the U.S. Supreme Court refused to hear an appeal from Daniel Ellsberg and Anthony Russo, who applied to see the transcript of a government wiretap on attorney Russo's home telephone. The two Pentagon Papers trial defendants had hoped to review this evidence before continuing with their defense.

The world's third largest volcanic disaster occurred on this day in 1985. The Nevado del Ruiz volcano in Colombia erupted, killing 25,000 people. The avalanche of ash and mud that spewed from the mountain destroyed fourteen nearby towns in its wake. Only the 1888 eruption of Krakatoa in Indonesia and the 1902 Mount Pelé eruption on the island of Martinique caused more damage to life and property in the past two centuries.

Palestinian Liberation Organization leader Yasser Arafat spoke before the United Nations General Assembly on this day in 1974. During his speech, he told the world's political representatives that the PLO's only goal was to establish an independent state of Palestine that was separate from the state of Israel, which had been formed by the United Nations itself in the late 1940s.

A Philippine president was impeached by the nation's House of Representatives on this day in 2000. The motion came after allegations that President Joseph Estrada had taken illegal bribes from gambling syndicates. The former film actor refused to listen to calls for him to resign; rather, he took the stance that the proceedings were unconstitutional and had yet to be approved by a vote in the Philippine senate.

14th.

1889   Jarwajarlal Nehru was born.

1930   Astronaut Edward H. White, Jr., was born in San Antonio, Texas.

1935   King Hussein of Jordan was born.

1935   The Philippines became a free commonwealth.

1948   Prince Charles of Great Britain was born.

1973   Great Britain's Princess Anne married Captain Mark Phillips.

The start of a gradual independence from United States territorial rule began on this day in 1935, when U.S. President Franklin D. Roosevelt announced that the Philippine Islands was a free commonwealth. The U.S. commonwealth status of the Philippines was adopted as part of the Tydings-McDuffie Act, an American resolution that called for the gradual transition to complete Philippine independence by 1942. The four-year Japanese occupation during the Second World War delayed the independence, which was finally achieved in 1946, after 400 years of rule by other nations.

Both royal and common international figures in politics celebrate their birthday today. India's first prime minister was born in Allahabad, India, on this day in 1889. Educated at Cambridge University in England, Jarwajarlal Nehru returned home after graduating in both natural sciences and law to serve in Allahabad's high court in 1912. Inspired by Mohandas K. Gandhi, Nehru joined the fight for independence from British rule and was imprisoned for a total of eighteen years before his nation won its freedom. Nehru was appointed India's first prime minister in 1947, maintaining his position until his death in 1964. King Hussein ibn Talal of Jordan was also born on this day in 1935. Succeeding his father to the throne in 1952, Hussein maintained his strong pro-Western stance amid political upheaval in both the Near and Middle East throughout his reign, which ended with his death in 1999. Great Britain's Prince Charles was born on this day in 1948. An advocate of organic agricultural methods and a mentor to many architectural projects, this heir apparent to the throne became the first House of Windsor prince to divorce his wife, which he did in the mid 1990s.

15th.

1873   Sara Josephine Baker was born.

1887   Georgia O'Keeffe was born.

1887   Granville T. Woods patented his Synchronous Multiplier Railway Telegraph (see April 23, November 11 entries).

1968   Roman Catholic bishops reached a compromise on the use of birth control by married couples.

1990   The U.S. Senate Ethics Committee opened hearings on the activities of five senators who had interceded on Charles Keating's behalf (see January 6, April 10 entries).

2000   The United States's first bullet train went into service.

The train ride between Washington, D.C., and New York City got thirty minutes faster on this day in 2000. The Acela Express bullet train took its maiden trip, hitting speeds of up to 135 mph. Although Japan's Shinkansen trains and France's TGV trains had been in service since the late 1960s, hitting speeds of up to 186 mph, the United States government had not been willing to subsidize the expense of track adjustments and train purchases until the 1990s. But after a decade of planning, twenty trains were set to compete against the airline shuttles that regularly transport commuters along the nation's busiest corridor, making stops at Boston, New York, Philadelphia, and Washington, D.C.

A reasonable compromise was made on this day in 1968. Roman Catholic bishops in the United States approved a controversial stance on the use of birth control by their followers. The bishops agreed that married couples could use birth control methods other than the natural rhythm method and still remain members of the church.

A woman who saved thousands of infants' lives in the city of New York was born on this day in 1873. Public health worker and doctor Sara Josephine Baker dared to go into the homes of tenement dwellers in the city's Lower East Side to bring health education to the people who needed it most. She taught immigrant and poor mothers proper hygiene and sanitation methods, provided prenatal care and nutrition, and even introduced the concept of baby clothes with front openings to reduce the potential for suffocation, which was a leading cause of infant mortality. With her work, New York City's infant mortality rate became the nation's lowest, dropping from 144 out of 1,000 cases per year in 1908 to 66 out of 1,000 per year by 1923.

16th.

1873   W.C. Handy was born (see September 27 entry).

1984   The space shuttle *Discovery* brought the first two satellites ever salvaged from outer space back to earth.

2000   U.S. President Bill Clinton made a visit to Vietnam.

Born in Florence, Alabama, on this day in 1873, William Christopher Handy became known as the "father of the blues" during his long career. He once said about his music, "Each one of my blues is based on some old Negro song of the South. . . . Something that sticks in my mind, that I hum to myself when I'm not thinking about it." Although Handy had played at the 1893 Columbian Exposition in Chicago and in clubs throughout the South, he really didn't start writing and performing blues until 1902. That's when he and his band were booed off the stage because the audience wanted them to play "their music." He and his band had rehearsed only cakewalks and other marches. Although his first popular song, "The Memphis Blues," didn't become a hit when he first performed it in 1909, it eventually made its way to the ears and hearts of Florenz Ziegfeld as well as dancers Vernon and Irene Castle (who reputedly devised the fox-trot around its unique rhythm). In 1938 Handy became the first blues musician to be given a tribute at New York's Carnegie Hall.

U.S. President Bill Clinton made a historic visit to Vietnam on this day in 2000. It was the first time an American president had made the journey since the fall of South Vietnam and the reunification of North Vietnam with South Vietnam under communist rule. Only two other United States presidents had ever made the journey to this Southeast Asian nation: Lyndon B. Johnson and Richard M. Nixon.

17th.

1855 Dr. David Livingstone became the first European explorer to see the Zambezi River's Victoria Falls.

1933 The United States recognized the Soviet Union and its communist government.

1970 The Soviet robot *Lunokhod 1* landed on the moon on board the *Luna 17* spacecraft and maneuvered on the lunar surface while being steered from earth.

1975 The FBI reported that crime in the United States had risen 18 percent in a single year.

1979 The Ayatollah Ruhollah Khomeini ordered the release of all female and African-American hostages at the U.S. Embassy in Tehran, Iran (see January 20, November 4, November 20, November 22, December 26 entries).

1992 The gopherspace search engine tool Veronica was released by the University of Nevada.

2000 The first biplane flight around the world was completed.

The first person to circumnavigate the world in an open-cockpit biplane completed the 23,000-mile journey on this day in 2000. Robert Ragozzino arrived in his 1942 Stearman biplane at Wiley Post Airport in Oklahoma City, Oklahoma. He had begun his trip from Newfoundland, crossing over Europe and Asia while bundled in a fur-hooded leather flight suit, ski goggles, and earmuffs. The entire trip took five months, since the pilot could only fly five to seven hours per day.

18th.

1923 Astronaut Alan B. Shepard, Jr., was born in East Derry, New Hampshire (see April 9, May 5 entries).

1964 J. Edgar Hoover publicly demanded Martin Luther King (see May 10 entry).

1970 West Germany and Poland agreed to restore relations.

1978 An ambush and a mass suicide took place in Guyana.

Two tragedies occurred in Guyana on this day in 1978. U.S. Representative Leo Ryan of California and four other members of his party were killed in an ambush by People's Temple cult members. Later that same day, in nearby Jonestown, Guyana, approximately 800 People's Temple members committed suicide or were killed on orders from their leader, Jim Jones.

On this day in 1964, FBI director J. Edgar Hoover publicly called civil rights leader Reverend Dr. Martin Luther King, Jr., "the most notorious liar in the country."

19th.

1938 Ted Turner was born.

1990 The Treaty on Conventional Forces in Europe was signed.

1996 The federal government agreed to a settlement.

Founder and former owner of the Cable News Network, the Turner Broadcasting System, and WTBS, as well as the Atlanta Braves and Atlanta Hawks sports teams, Ted Turner is one of the world's richest men. Born in Cincinnati, Ohio, on this day in 1938, the multi-billionaire Turner also won the 1977 America's Cup on board his yacht *Courageous.* In 1986 he unsuccessfully bid to purchase the CBS network. To console himself, he bought MGM/United Artists instead. For a number of years, he was married to an equally public person, actress Jane Fonda.

Activities surrounding the Cold War made the news even after it had ended. On this day in 1990, NATO and Warsaw Pact leaders signed the Treaty on Conventional Forces in Europe. This momentous event marked the end of the Cold War, uniting both communist and non-communist factions for the first time in fifty years. In 1996 the United States government agreed to pay $4.8 million to victims who had filed suit for Cold War-era radiation experiments that had been carried out on unwitting victims.

20th.

1873   The rival Hungarian cities of Buda and Pest united to form a single capital.

1914   The regulation requiring photographs on U.S. passports went into effect.

1920   The first United States municipal airport opened in Tucson, Arizona.

1947   Great Britain's Princess Elizabeth and Lieutenant Philip Mountbatten married in Westminster Abbey.

1967   The United States population passed the 200 million mark.

1970   The United Nations General Assembly failed to win a two-thirds majority to seat the People's Republic of China.

1972   The U.S. Supreme Court ruled that computer programs or software could not be patented under existing laws.

1979   Militants released thirteen hostages being held at the U.S. Embassy in Tehran, Iran (see November 4, November 17, November 22, December 26 entries).

1983   An estimated 100 million viewers watched the controversial ABC-TV movie-of-the-week "The Day After," which depicted American life in the aftermath of a nuclear war.

1993   The Brady Bill regulating handguns was passed (see November 29 entry).

A filibuster ended on this day in 1993 in the U.S. Senate. Despite the use of this effective verbal tactic, the Brady Bill was passed with a vote of 63 to 36 in favor. The law imposed a five-day waiting period for handgun purchases throughout the United States, allowing law enforcement agencies to check the records of buyers to confirm a clean criminal record prior to purchase.

21st.

1877   Thomas Edison announced the phonograph's invention in Menlo Park, New Jersey.

1898   Rene Magritte was born.

1963   The Second Vatican Council authorized the use of languages other than Latin in the administration of Roman Catholic sacraments, including the mass.

1973   U.S. President Richard Nixon's attorney revealed an 18.5-minute gap in a White House tape recording related to the Watergate incident (see August 5, September 15, September 19, October 1, October 23 entries).

A master traveler between the worlds of illusion and reality, Rene Magritte often juxtaposed unrelated objects in realistic surroundings in his surrealistic paintings. Magritte was born in Lessines, Belgium, on this day in 1898, and one of his favorite images portrays a woman with a fish's head. *Le Chant d'Amour* simply twists the common image of a mermaid into a reverse reality. Another painting depicts a man wearing a bowler hat floating in the air while holding an umbrella, as if he is the rain rather than the target of rain. Magritte is frequently regarded as one of the grand masters of surrealism along with Marcel Duchamp and Man Ray.

22nd.

1890   French President Charles de Gaulle was born in Lille, France (see April 28, June 1, December 21 entries).

1930   The Black Muslim movement was initiated in Detroit, Michigan.

1940   Terry Gilliam was born.

1972   U.S. President Richard Nixon lifted the ban on American travel to mainland China that had lasted twenty-two years.

1973   Saudi Arabia threatened to cut oil production.

1979   The thirteen Iran hostages returned to the United States (see January 20, November 4, November 17, November 20, December 26 entries).

1989   Lebanese President Rene Moawad was assassinated less than three weeks after taking office when a bomb exploded next to his motorcade in West Beirut, Lebanon.

1993   Mexico's senate unanimously approved the North American Free Trade Agreement.

1999   Eliàn Gonzalez and his mother left Cuba aboard a motorboat, which capsized, resulting in his mother's death.

A threat to the quality of life in Western civilization occurred on this day in 1973. Saudi Arabia threatened to cut oil production by 80 percent if the United States, Europe, or Japan tried to counter the Arab oil embargo that had been imposed a little over a month earlier.

Born in Minneapolis, Minnesota, on this day in 1940, Terry Gilliam really wanted to be an illustrator, so he graduated in political science. He went to New York, where he became associate editor of *Help!* magazine in 1962, doing freelance illustrations on the side just for fun. Three years later, he bummed around Europe before moving to Los Angeles so he could fail as an illustrator, a copywriter, and an advertising art director. In a brilliant move, he settled in London in 1967, where he worked as a freelance illustrator. He befriended Eric Idle one day and found himself doing animation for the television series "Do Not Adjust Your Set" and "Marty." He began working with "Monty Python's Flying Circus" in 1969. It was the start of a long relationship that led him to direct a non-Python film, *Jabberwocky,* which starred Monty Python's Michael Palin. He and Palin combined their talents again in 1980, writing and directing *Time Bandits.* The film ball kept rolling from there during the 1990s. Gilliam wrote and directed *Brazil, The Adventures of Baron Munchausen, The Fisher King,* and *Twelve Monkeys,* among others.

23*rd.*

1887   Boris Karloff was born.

1899   The first jukebox was installed by the Pacific Phonograph Company at the Paris Royal Hotel in San Francisco, California.

1993 U.S. President Bill Clinton apologized to Native Hawaiians for the overthrow of the Kingdom of Hawaii in the nineteenth century.

Horror film great Boris Karloff was born in London, England, on this day in 1887, as William Henry Pratt. Emigrating to Canada when he was 22, Karloff decided to pursue an acting career, working with a few touring troupes before making his way to Hollywood. He had gotten a number of minor and supporting roles in the silents and then in the talkies. But it wasn't until Bela Lugosi turned down the role of the Frankenstein monster that Karloff got his big break, at the age of 45. During the 1930s and 1940s, he and Lugosi vied for the title of "King of the Horror Flicks." But unlike Lugosi, Karloff found a fresh start for his career during the 1960s, when he hosted the television series "Thriller."

24th.

1941 The U.S. Supreme Court ruled that the Anti-Migrant Law was unconstitutional.

1989 The entire presidium and secretariat of the Czechoslovak Communist Party resigned.

1998 America Online announced its acquisition of Netscape Communications.

The U.S. Supreme Court handed down a ruling that a California state law was unconstitutional on this day in 1941. California's Anti-Migrant Law was declared to be in violation of the U.S. Constitution because its sole purpose was to keep the "Okies"—migrants from Oklahoma, Texas, and other so-called dust bowl states—from settling in California.

A major Internet merger took place on this day in 1998. America Online announced the acquisition of Netscape Communications in a stock transaction that was valued at $4.2 billion.

25th.

1960 John F. Kennedy, Jr., was born (see July 28 entry).

1969 The Beatles' John Lennon returned his MBE to Queen Elizabeth II, protesting Great Britain's involvement in Vietnam and Biafra.

1973 A military coup ousted Greek President George Papadapoulos (see June 1, August 21, August 23 entries).

1973 The United States government declared a speed limit reduction from 70 mph to 55 mph on interstate highways.

1976 The Band's farewell concert—"The Last Waltz"—occurred at Winterland in San Francisco, California.

1980 Sugar Ray Leonard regained his welterweight title, defeating Roberto Duran at New Orleans's Superdome.

1990 Lech Walesa won a popular election in Poland.

The only son of U.S. President John F. Kennedy and Jacqueline Kennedy Onassis was born in Washington, D.C., on this day in 1960. John F. Kennedy, Jr., had a very public life as a baby: The newspapers and national magazines called him "John-John." The world wept when he saluted his father's casket as it rode by before millions of television viewers. He quietly studied law and worked at the New York district attorney's office for a few years before he came before the public eye once again as the publisher of *George* magazine. Tragically, he, his wife, Caroline Bessette, and his sister-in-law died in a flying accident in 1999 on their way to joining the Kennedy clan on Martha's Vineyard, Massachusetts.

26th.

1922 Charles Schulz was born in St. Paul, Minnesota.

1988 Yasser Arafat was denied a United States visa.

1995 Ireland allowed for separation before divorce.

U.S. Secretary of State George Shultz rejected a visa application on this day in 1989. PLO leader Yasser Arafat's visa request was rejected, even though the leader was scheduled to address the United Nations in New York City. Schultz cited the PLO's continued involvement in terrorism against American citizens as his reason for the rejection.

The predominantly Catholic people of Ireland made a monumental decision on this day in 1995. In a general vote, the Irish people agreed that an amendment to their constitution could be added allowing spouses to live apart for four out of five years prior to their application for a divorce.

27th.

1942 Jimi Hendrix was born (see March 31 entry).

1961 The Soviet Union proposed an immediate nuclear testing ban without international controls.

1970 Pope Paul VI escaped injury when a Bolivian painter disguised as a priest tried to stab him during a visit to the Philippines (see June 21, June 30, July 29, September 26, October 28, December 9 entries).

1973 The U.S. Senate unanimously confirmed Gerald Ford as vice president, succeeding Spiro Agnew.

A rock and roll icon was born in Seattle, Washington, on this day in 1942. Jimi Hendrix taught himself to play acoustic guitar by listening to blues records. His father then bought him his first electric guitar, just before Hendrix enlisted in the army. A parachuting accident got him discharged and into the New York recording studios, working as a session musician for Ike and Tina Turner, Sam Cooke, and Little Richard. Jimi met the bass player for the Animals, Chas Chandler, who convinced him to move to London. With Chandler's help, Jimi formed the Jimi Hendrix Experience. Their first single, "Hey Joe," rocketed to the top of the charts in 1967. And their first album, *Are You Experienced?*, did the same. They then appeared at the 1967 Monterey Pop Festival, becoming an overnight sensation in the United States. Hendrix built his own recording studio in New York—Electric Lady—before the group recorded the album *Electric Ladyland* in 1968, and then disbanded. Hendrix then appeared at the 1969 Woodstock Music & Arts Festival, playing his unique version of "The Star Spangled Banner." Sadly, Hendrix's brilliant career ended the next year, when he died of a drug overdose.

28th.

1929   Berry Gordy, Jr., was born.

1963   U.S. President Lyndon B. Johnson announced that Cape Canaveral, Florida, was renamed Cape Kennedy.

1989   Romanian gymnast Nadia Comaneci arrived in New York after her defection (see November 11 entry).

1995   The 55 mph speed limit on interstate highways was repealed.

Born in Detroit, Michigan, on this day in 1929, Motown Records founder Berry Gordy, Jr., had pursued a career as a boxer before he decided to take off his gloves and open a record store. He also produced a few of his own songs before founding Motown Records in 1959. His first gold record was Smokey Robinson's 1960 hit "Shop Around." The hits didn't stop there. Gordy signed Motown greats like the Supremes, the Four Tops, the Temptations, Martha and the Vandellas, Marvin Gaye, Stevie Wonder, and the Jackson Five. His repertoire of the Motown sound made him an icon in the music industry during the 1960s through the 1980s.

29th.

1864   The Sand Creek Massacre occurred.

1908   Thurgood Marshall was born.

1944   The Federal Highway Act was passed.

1945   Yugoslavia's monarchy was abolished.

1947   The United Nations voted to grant the Jewish people a homeland, which was to be established in Palestine.

1962   U Thant was elected United Nations secretary general.

1963   U.S. President Lyndon B. Johnson appointed Supreme Court Chief Justice Earl Warren to investigate President John F. Kennedy's assassination.

1993   U.S. President Bill Clinton signed the Brady Bill (see November 21 entry).

The interstate highway system was born on this day in 1944. Although it took additional funding, the Federal Highway Act—passed by the U.S. Congress—established the plans and funds to create the national system of interstate highways that connects the four corners of the United States.

A massacre took place at Sand Creek, Colorado, on this day in 1864. A Colorado civilian militia of 1,200 men was led by Colonel John M. Chivington, and the group murdered approximately 400 Cheyenne men, women, and children. Ironically, their chief, Black Kettle, held a United States flag and a white surrender flag in full view before the assault took place.

30th.

1929   Dick Clark was born.

1961   U.S. President John F. Kennedy instigated Operation Mongoose (see August 13, September 5, October 5, October 11, December 2 entries).

2000   El Salvador adopted United States currency.

Not every nation in the world prefers to develop and use its own currency. And on this day in 2000, El Salvador became the third Latin American nation to adopt the United States dollar as its national currency. To thwart further inflation of its own colon-based monetary system, the country chose to convert its existing reserves at 8.75 colons to the U.S. dollar. Ecuador had made a similar decision in September 2000, and Panama had been using the U.S. standard for many years.

A new covert action was instigated on this day in 1961. U.S. President John F. Kennedy authorized Operation Mongoose, which was aimed at overthrowing Fidel Castro's communist government. Involving approximately 400 CIA agents and 2,000 Cubans as well as a private fleet of speedboats and an annual budget of $50 million, actions such as the contamination of Cuban sugar shipments and sabotage of industrial imports commenced.

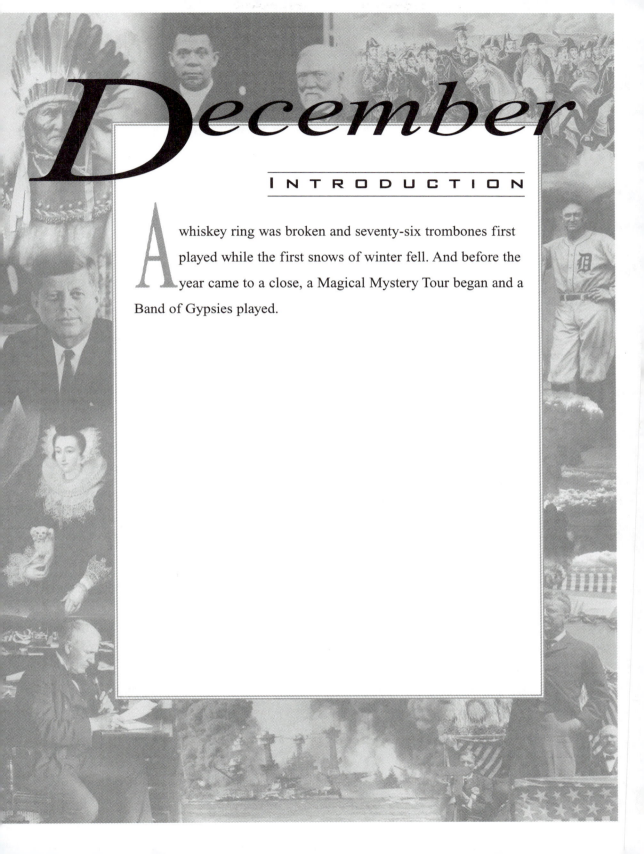

December

A whiskey ring was broken and seventy-six trombones first played while the first snows of winter fell. And before the year came to a close, a Magical Mystery Tour began and a Band of Gypsies played.

1st.

1878   NAACP co-founder Arthur Spingarn was born in New York City.

1934   Soviet leader Sergei Kirov was assassinated.

1957   The New York City Ballet debuted the production *Agon,* which was a collaboration between composer Igor Stravinsky and choreographer George Balanchine (see March 19 entry).

1966   Soviet Premier Alexei Kosygin went to Paris, France.

1974   A TWA jetliner crashed in a rainstorm.

1975   U.S. President Gerald Ford went to China.

1980   The U.S. Surgeon General reported that cigarettes are bad for human health, especially for women (see January 2, January 10, April 11, July 17, August 1, August 24, September 28 entries).

1981   A Yugoslav DC-9 charter flight slammed into a mountain.

1984   A remote-controlled jetliner crashed.

1989   Soviet Premier Mikhail Gorbachev went to the Vatican.

1990   British and French workers knocked out a passage in the tunnel under the English Channel and met for the first time (see January 7, January 18, July 25, August 6, August 25, September 10 entries).

1993   A Northwest Airlink commuter plane crashed.

This particular day in history was marked by numerous airline disasters, including one that was intentional. In 1974 a TWA jetliner crashed during a rainstorm as it flew over Virginia, killing ninety-two people. In 1981 a Yugoslav DC-9 charter plane slammed into a mountain while making its approach toward Ajaccio Airport on the Mediterranean island of Corsica. The crash killed 180 passengers and crew. And in 1993 a Northwest Airlink commuter plane crashed in flight over Minnesota, killing eighteen passengers. But on this same day in 1984, a remote-controlled jetliner was purposefully crashed in California's Mojave Desert. The unmanned plane—which only briefly burst into flames—was downed in order to test an antiflame fuel additive.

The Soviet Union was the focus of attention more than once on this day. In 1934 Soviet leader Sergei Kirov was assassinated, which led to a purge of the Communist Party by Josef Stalin. In 1966 Soviet Premier Alexei Kosygin went to Paris, France, where he was the guest of French President Charles de Gaulle. In 1989 Soviet Premier Mikhail Gorbachev went to Vatican City, where he had an audience with Pope John Paul II. And in 1975 the Soviet Union was the center of discussions between U.S. President Gerald Ford and Chinese Deputy Prime Minister Deng Xiaoping. While the leaders were meeting in Beijing, China, they discussed the United States's détente policy toward the Soviet Union.

2nd.

1886	Josephine Roche was born.
1901	King C. Gillette patented his safety razor.
1956	Fidel Castro and his guerrillas landed in Cuba to begin their takeover (see September 5, October 5, October 11, November 30 entries).
1965	The USS *Enterprise* launched its first air strikes.
1970	The U.S. Environmental Protection Agency was established.
1977	A South African magistrate absolved security police of the death of Steven Biko (see January 28 entry).
1988	Benazir Bhutto was sworn in as Pakistan's new prime minister (see April 4, June 21 entries).
1991	American hostage Joseph Cicippio was freed after being held by Lebanese terrorists for five years (see January 20 entry).

Safety was the key word in business on this day. In 1901 King C. Gillette patented the first safety razor that employed disposable blades. In 1886 Josephine Roche, industrialist and director of the National Consumers League, was born. Her father forbade her as a child from going to the family coal mines because it was too dangerous. She then asked the question: "Then why is it safe enough for the miners?"

A South African magistrate absolved security police on this day in 1975. The officers had been held responsible for the death of black South African student Steven Biko, who died of injuries sustained while in their custody.

The first nuclear-powered military vessel entered combat on this day in 1965. The aircraft carrier USS *Enterprise* launched its first air strikes over Vietnam.

3rd.

1842   Ellen Henrietta Richards was born.

1910   The first neon sign was installed.

1956   *The Million Dollar Quartet* was recorded (see March 5, March 24, June 26, July 30, August 2, August 15, August 22, September 25 entries).

1967   Dr. Christiaan Barnard performed the first human heart transplant in South Africa on patient Louis Washkansky.

1970   The National Air Quality Control Act was signed.

Automobiles were highlighted on this day. In 1910 George Claude designed and installed the world's first neon sign, at the Paris Motor Show. Sixty years later, U.S. President Richard M. Nixon signed the National Air Quality Control Act, which mandated a 90-percent reduction in pollution caused by car exhaust within five years.

A landmark album was recorded on this day in 1956, but it was never released. Taped at Sam Phillips's legendary Sun Studios, *The Million Dollar Quartet* documented the songs and singing talents of country and rock and roll music greats Elvis Presley, Jerry Lee Lewis, Johnny Cash, and Carl Perkins.

Homemaking was crafted into a science thanks to the female chemist who was born on this day in 1842. Ellen Henrietta Richards started the home economics movement by demonstrating that the need for balanced nutrition, sanitation, and hygiene practices in the home required a basic understanding of simple scientific methods. As an added result, she created a unique profession—dietitian—and discovered the naphtha-based dry cleaning process.

4th.

1586 Queen Elizabeth I confirmed the execution of Mary, Queen of Scots (see December 14 entry).

1843 Manila paper was patented.

1892 Spanish dictator General Francisco Franco was born in El Ferrol, Spain (see July 22, October 30 entries).

1906 The first African-American fraternity, Alpha Phi Alpha, was founded.

1915 Henry Ford sailed to Europe.

1918 U.S. President Woodrow Wilson sailed to Europe.

1945 The U.S. Congress approved the United States's participation in the United Nations.

1978 City Supervisor Dianne Feinstein became San Francisco's first female mayor (see June 22 entry).

Recycled products weren't an invention of the late twentieth century. One of the first products to be made from recycled goods was patented on this day in 1843, by John Mark and Lyman Hollingsworth. This pair of inventors from South Braintree, Massachusetts, had developed an inexpensive paper-manufacturing process that employed used ship sails made from hemp fiber combined with used canvas and rope. Manila paper is a recycled product that's still in demand today.

Two influential Americans set sail for Europe on this day during the First World War. Both men had the same purpose in mind: the search for international peace. In 1915 automotive magnate Henry Ford hosted a private peace expedition that set sail from Hoboken, New Jersey, toward war-torn Europe. Dedicated to the negotiation of a peaceful end to the fighting in Europe, the group and its purpose dissolved before they landed. Disagreements among its members had caused too much dissension. And in 1918 U.S. President Woodrow Wilson set sail from Washington, D.C., for France in hopes of negotiating a peaceful end to the same war. When he landed, he became the first U.S. president to visit a European nation while still in office.

5th.

1492	Christopher Columbus discovered the island of Santo Domingo (see March 31, April 16, May 3, May 9, May 13, May 20, June 13, July 31, August 23 entries).
1934	Anti-Stalinist conspirators were executed.
1955	A bus boycott began in Montgomery, Alabama (see February 4 entry).
1955	The American Federation of Labor and the Congress of Industrial Organizations merged, forming the AFL-CIO.
1968	The Beatles opened the Apple Boutique in London, England.
1968	The Rolling Stones released their album *Beggars Banquet* (see January 15, May 10, May 12, June 3, June 14, July 30, October 25, December 6, December 18 entries).
1969	The U.S. Congress passed the Endangered Species Conservation Act.
1975	Great Britain ended its detention-without-trial policy.
1977	Egypt broke diplomatic relations with five Arab nations.
1979	Sonia Johnson was formally excommunicated by the Mormon Church for her public support of the Equal Rights Amendment.
1980	The United States suspended aid to El Salvador.
1989	East German leaders were placed under house arrest.
1993	A Palestinian terrorist boarded an Israeli bus.

Every nation has its own way of dealing with terrorism. The most drastic measure took place on this day, in 1934, when sixty-six people who were charged with involvement in an alleged plot against Josef Stalin's government were executed in the Soviet Union. Lenience was handed down, in 1975, when Great Britain announced the end of its detention-without-trial policy toward suspected terrorists in Northern Ireland. And in 1980 a firm but reasonable hand was used when the United States suspended aid to El Salvador, pending an investigation. According to allegations, El Salvadoran government security forces were responsible for the killing of four American churchwomen.

Both of Great Britain's greatest pop icons made headlines on this day in 1968. The Beatles opened their Apple Boutique in London, England, which sold clothes, boots, accessories, and other vestiges of Swinging Sixties style. A hot item on the racks were brightly colored satin military jackets. The Rolling Stones wore attire that looked like it came off the Apple Boutique's racks on the cover of their album *Beggars Banquet,* which was released in London on the exact same day.

Peace in the Near East was fragile throughout the last half of the twentieth century, as evidenced on this day. In 1977 Egypt broke diplomatic relations with five Arab nations. The leaders of those countries objected to Egyptian President Anwar Sadat's overtures toward peace with Israel. In 1993 a Palestinian terrorist boarded a bus and opened fire with an assault weapon. An Israeli reservist was mortally wounded before the terrorist was gunned down. It was the first major attack in Israel since the signing of a peace pact with the Palestinian Liberation Organization.

6th.

1877   Thomas Alva Edison made the first audio recording in his laboratory at Menlo Park, New Jersey.

1921   The Anglo-Irish Treaty was signed.

1957   The AFL-CIO voted to expel the International Brotherhood of Teamsters.

1969   A concertgoer was beaten to death by Hells Angels members.

1970   *Gimme Shelter* premiered in New York City (see January 15, May 10, May 12, June 3, June 14, July 30, October 25, December 5, December 18 entries).

1971   Pakistan severed relations with India.

1972   The United States's last manned mission to the Moon, *Apollo 17,* was launched from Cape Canaveral, Florida.

1977   The Foreign Corrupt Practices Act was passed.

1982   The Irish National Liberation Army exploded a bomb.

2000   A pair of giant pandas arrived at the National Zoo.

The way in which American corporations do business in foreign countries was placed under partial control on this day in 1977. The U.S. Congress passed the Foreign Corrupt Practices Act. This bill mandated that if a U.S. corporation is found to have paid a bribe to a foreign government, the company could be fined up to $1 million.

Music doesn't always bring out the best in people. On this day in 1969, a fan was beaten to death by Hells Angels who had been employed as security guards during a Rolling Stones concert held at the Altamont Speedway in Altamont, California. Exactly one year later, *Gimme Shelter* premiered in New York City. The film documented the tragedy that occurred at the Altamont Speedway.

A rare species that's only found in the wilds of China, giant pandas are beloved by people the world over. On this day in 2000, the National Zoo in Washington, D.C., welcomed two of these gentle and very rare creatures to their new multi-million-dollar home. Mei Xiang and Tian Tian had been flown in direct from China on a seventeen-hour flight. Not known for their sociability among themselves or their ability to handle stress, the pandas surprised their keepers when they raced over to the fresh bamboo plants in their new environment and began to eat. What's more, the male and female pandas ate nose to nose and spent time playing together before settling down for a much-needed rest.

An uneasy peace began on this day in 1921. Great Britain and Ireland signed the Anglo-Irish Treaty. In exchange for the establishment of the Irish Free State, Northern Ireland was partitioned as a British possession in order to settle the long-standing dispute between the two nations. But that peace didn't last, as was evidenced sixty years later. On this same day in 1982, members of the Irish National Liberation Army exploded a bomb in a pub in Ballykelly, Northern Ireland, killing eleven soldiers and six civilians.

7th.

1977   Egypt closed its cultural centers in the Soviet Union.

1982   Charles Brooks, Jr., was executed (see June 26, July 2, December 18 entries).

1993   U.S. Energy Department Secretary Hazel O'Leary made a disclosure.

Capital punishment became a reality once again in the United States on this day in 1982. Convicted murderer Charles Brooks, Jr., was executed by lethal injection in a penitentiary located near Huntsville, Texas. It was the first time this particular method of execution was used.

The road to peace is sometimes bumpy, as was proven on this day in 1977. The Egypt government closed cultural centers in the Soviet Union and other East European countries because of their public criticisms of Egyptian President Anwar Sadat's drive for peace negotiations with the state of Israel.

On this day in 1993, U.S. Energy Department Secretary Hazel O'Leary made a shocking public admission: She disclosed that the federal government had conducted more than 200 secret nuclear weapons tests despite agreements made with the Soviet Union banning such activities.

8th.

1914 Irving Berlin's first musical, *Watch Your Step,* opened on Broadway.

1969 Charles Manson and five of his followers were indicted for the murders of actress Sharon Tate and six other victims (see January 25, March 6, August 9, October 27 entries).

1975 Bob Dylan performed a benefit concert at Madison Square Garden, campaigning for the release of Rubin "Hurricane" Carter (see May 1, May 12, May 24, June 7, July 25, July 31, August 9, August 17, September 11 entries).

1977 The U.S. Congress officially banned the manufacture of aerosol products containing chlorofluorocarbons (CFCs) within the United States.

1980 The Beatles' John Lennon was mortally wounded in New York City (see August 24 entry).

1987 U.S. President Ronald Reagan and Soviet Premier Mikhail Gorbachev signed a treaty eliminating medium-range intermediate nuclear weapons in both nations.

1991 The Union of Soviet Socialist Republics was dissolved.

1993 U.S. President Bill Clinton signed the North American Free Trade Agreement.

1998 The U.S. Supreme Court decided that the police do not have blanket authority to search suspects.

On this day in 1998, the U.S. Supreme Court handed down a critical decision limiting police authority. In the case of *Knowles v. State of Iowa,* the court ruled that police do not have blanket authority to search suspects and their cars. If a suspect is stopped and ticketed for a regular traffic violation, the officer must obtain consent from the suspect before a search of person or property can take place.

The Union of Soviet Socialist Republics was dissolved on this day in 1991. After three-quarters of a century, Russia, Byelorussia, and the Ukraine forged a new alliance under a non-communist government. Eventually the new partnership was named the Commonwealth of Independent States.

9th.

1875   The Whiskey Ring was broken.

1971   Pope Paul VI reaffirmed the Roman Catholic Church's ban on marriage for its priests (see June 21, June 30, July 29, September 26, October 28, November 27 entries).

1973   Arab oil ministers ordered a production cutback of approximately 750,000 barrels of oil per day.

1987   The Christmas Virus attacked the Internet.

1992   Great Britain's Prince Charles and Princess Diana announced their separation (see February 24, July 1, July 29 entries).

The first viral attack of the Internet took place not in the 1990s but on this day in 1987. The Christmas Virus caused numerous educational, scientific, and government e-mail servers to overload and crash. To stop the spread of this malicious program, most of the existing Internet had to be temporarily shut down.

Corruption in campaign funding policies was not unique to the twentieth century. On this day in 1875, the Whiskey Ring was broken up by U.S. Secretary of the Treasury Benjamin H. Bristow. In order to fund the reelection campaign of President Ulysses S. Grant, a number of businessmen and federal tax officials had skimmed taxes procured from the manufacture and sale of whiskey to sweeten the campaign coffers.

10th.

1898   The Spanish-American War ended.

1961   The first direct U.S. military support arrived in South Vietnam.

1964   Reverend Dr. Martin Luther King, Jr., won the Nobel Peace Prize.

1966   The first asbestos lawsuit was filed.

1973   The U.S. Supreme Court handed police more authority.

1977   The Sex Pistols released their album *Never Mind the Bollocks* (see October 8 entry).

1985   General Electric announced its intention to purchase RCA.

The cancer-causing effect of asbestos in human beings had been recognized by the medical profession, but on this day in 1966 the legal profession confirmed its reality. Attorney Ward Stephenson filed the first asbestos products lawsuit on behalf of Claude Tomplait in Beaumont, Texas.

History's largest non-oil company business merger took place on this day in 1985. The General Electric Corporation announced its intention to purchase RCA, which included the acquisition of the NBC television network.

The U.S. Supreme Court gave police added authority on this day in 1973. The court handed down a decision that police officers in the field could search a suspect without first obtaining a search warrant.

The Spanish-American War ended on this day in 1898, when representatives from the United States and Spain met in Paris, France, and signed a peace treaty. This agreement produced one other result: The United States gained possession of Cuba, Puerto Rico, Guam, the Philippines, and other Spanish-held islands in the West Indies.

The first direct military support given by the United States during the Vietnam War arrived on this day in 1961. Two U.S. helicopter companies were delivered by aircraft carrier to troops stationed in Saigon, South Vietnam.

11th.

1939	Wiretapped evidence was outlawed.
1980	The Hazardous Waste Containment Act went into effect.
1997	The Kyoto Climate Accord was signed.

The effect of certain forms of waste was deemed hazardous to the environment on more than one occasion on this day. In 1980 the Hazardous Waste Containment Act went into effect, mandating that dangerous chemicals and radioactive materials had to be properly rendered inactive and disposed of under strictly controlled conditions within the United States. And in 1997 150 representatives signed the Kyoto Climate Accord, which mandated that the world's industrialized nations drastically cut the emission of toxic waste gases cited as the cause of global warming.

Limitations were placed on a valuable new source of evidence on this day in 1939. The U.S. Supreme Court handed down a decision that evidence taken from telephone conversations through the use of wiretap equipment was illegal. In order to lawfully utilize wiretapped conversations, authorities needed to obtain a warrant before installing the equipment.

12th.

1900	The African-American anthem, "Lift Every Voice and Sing," was published by James Weldon and J. Rosamond Johnson (see August 11 entry).
1925	The world's first motor hotel opened.
1975	Former Manson Family member Sara Jane Moore pleaded guilty for attempting to assassinate U.S. President Gerald R. Ford (see September 22 entry).
1981	The Polish government imposed martial law to thwart the Solidarity movement.
1989	Leona Helmsley was sentenced for tax evasion.

The hospitality industry made headlines twice on this day. Automobile travel had not yet blossomed and the interstate highway network hadn't even been built in 1925, when the world's first motor hotel—the Motel Inn—opened in San Luis Obispo, California. And in 1989 one of the world's most famous female hoteliers was sentenced to four years in prison for tax evasion. Leona Helmsley ended up serving eighteen months in prison, a month in a halfway house, and two months under house arrest for her white-collar crime.

13th.

1956   The U.S. Supreme Court negated an Alabama state law.

1989   South African President F.W. de Klerk met African National Congress leader Nelson Mandela (see February 10, March 18, July 18 entries.

1993   The European Community ratified the creation of the European Economic Area.

1993   The space shuttle *Endeavour* landed after the crew repaired the Hubble Space Telescope while in outer space.

An Alabama state law that had been on the books for a number of years was deemed unconstitutional on this day in 1956. The U.S. Supreme Court handed down a decision that a law requiring African-Americans to take seats only in the back of public transit buses was contrary to all federal regulations and guarantees made by the U.S. Constitution.

Although South African President F.W. de Klerk had outlawed the African National Congress and arrested its leader, Nelson Mandela, in 1960, he had never met with the charismatic activist during the twenty-nine years he was imprisoned. On this day in 1989, the two men met for the first time in de Klerk's office in Cape Town, South Africa. It took another five years before apartheid was abolished and Mandela was released from prison, but this day marked the beginning of a change in the relationship between the nation's two most powerful factions.

14th.

1542	Six-day-old Mary Stuart ascended the Scottish throne (see December 4 entry).
1895	King George VI of England was born in Sandringham, England (see February 6, May 12, August 4 entries).
1918	Women voted for the first time in a general election in Great Britain.
1946	The UN General Assembly established its headquarters in New York City.
1962	The U.S. space probe *Mariner 2* approached Venus and began atmospheric and temperature data transmission.
1972	*Apollo 17* left the moon after three days of research on its surface.
1980	Yoko Ono asked the world to observe ten minutes of silence in memory of her late husband John Lennon (see December 8 entry).
1981	Polish workers mounted protest strikes against martial law.
1994	The World Wide Web Consortium held its first meeting (see August 6, December 16 entries).
1995	Yugoslavian leaders signed a peace treaty.

The World Wide Web was officially organized on this day in 1994. The first meeting of the World Wide Web Consortium (W3C) took place at the Massachusetts Institute of Technology Laboratory for Computer Science in Cambridge. Created by Internet founder Tim Berners-Lee and Al Vezza, the group met to discuss programming standards to be used in Web development in collaboration with CERN—the European Organization for Nuclear Research.

During the 1990s, Bosnia-Herzegovina had been the center of Europe's bloodiest and most tragic conflict since the Second World War. But on this day in 1995, former Yugoslavian leaders signed a peace treaty to settle disputes between Bosnian Serbs and Croats over religious, political, and cultural differences.

15th.

1832   Alexander Eiffel was born.

1890   Chief Sitting Bull died.

1978   U.S. President Jimmy Carter announced the establishment of diplomatic relations with China and the end of relations with Taiwan (see October 1 entry).

1989   A revolt began in Romania (see December 22, December 23 entries).

Design and politics are not always the best collaborators, as engineer Alexander Eiffel learned during his lifetime. Born in Dijon, France, on this day in 1832, Eiffel had gained international fame for the construction of the world's tallest building. Standing 985 feet high, the Eiffel Tower was erected in Paris for the 1889 World Exhibition at a cost of nearly $1 million—a monument to the engineer's genius and inability to contain construction expenses. Four years later, Eiffel found himself sentenced to two years' imprisonment and a stiff fine for breach of trust. Eiffel had been associated with the horribly mismanaged Panama Canal project, which was aborted and handed to the United States government by France for completion and management.

The most famous of the Sioux Nation's leaders died at a U.S. Army post in Grand River, South Dakota, on this day in 1890. Chief Sitting Bull had been arrested during a skirmish with U.S. troops. After arriving at the post, he was mortally wounded by Native American guards when he attempted to escape.

This day marked the beginning of a revolt that eventually led to the overthrow of Romanian dictator Nicolae Ceausescu. Demonstrators gathered on this day in 1989 in Timisoara, Romania, to protest and prevent the arrest of a priest who had spoken out against Ceausescu's government.

16th.

1904   Usherettes were first hired at Broadway's Majestic Theater in New York City.

1907   The Great White Fleet set sail.

1972   The construction of a waterway linking the Tennessee Valley and the Gulf of Mexico commenced.

1976   The federal swine flu vaccination program was canceled.

1990   Jean-Bertrand Aristide was elected as Haiti's president.

1994   CERN discontinued the World Wide Web (see August 6, December 14 entries).

The construction of a major water link in the United States began on this day in 1972. The $2 billion Tennessee-Tombigbee waterway was intended to connect the lower Tennessee Valley and the Gulf of Mexico, offering inland businesses alternative transportation of their goods. The project took twelve years to complete.

Although it had been involved in the establishment of the Internet and the World Wide Web, CERN—the European Organization for Nuclear Research—decided to discontinue its work on the development of the Web's programming standards on this day in 1994. The computer think-tank group had received funds to construct the Large Hadron Collider, refocusing its attention on particle physics rather than computer science. Management handed the Web project over to an associate organization, INRIA.

Broadway's Majestic Theater in New York City caused quite a stir among its patrons on this day in 1904. The theater's management hired its first female ushers to direct ticket holders to their seats and hand them programs, which was traditionally a man's job. Protesters demonstrated outside the doors, demanding that the young women be sent home where they belonged.

The U.S. Navy set sail on this day in 1907. But rather than setting out to win a war, the fleet of sixteen battleships—known as the Great White Fleet—set out to circumnavigate the world.

The national swine flu vaccination program was discontinued by the federal government on this day in 1976. Although fears about the disease had spread across the country, so did the stories about the vaccination's serious side effects. Fifty-one reports of paralysis linked to the influenza vaccine had sounded the alarm by both authorities and the public.

17th.

1908 William Frank Libby was born.

1943 The Chinese Exclusion Act was repealed (see February 2, May 6, September 2 entries).

1998 The U.S. House of Representatives delayed impeachment proceedings against U.S. President Bill Clinton.

Chinese immigration to the United States was opened for the first time in sixty-one years on this day in 1943. U.S. President Franklin Delano Roosevelt repealed the 1882 Chinese Exclusion Act, which had closed the nation to an influx of workers looking to find their fortunes in railroad construction and gold prospecting.

The best means to determine the age of an object was developed by the American chemist who was born in Grand Valley, Colorado, on this day in 1908. Willard Frank Libby had worked on the separation of uranium isotopes with the Manhattan Project at Columbia University during the 1940s. A member of the U.S. Atomic Energy Commission during the 1950s, Libby invented the carbon-14 dating method used by archaeologists, paleontologists, and other scientists to date the age of solid objects. He received the 1960 Nobel Prize in Chemistry for his invention.

18th.

1886 Ty Cobb was born in Narrows, Georgia (see July 18 entry).

1913 Willy Brandt was born in Lübeck, Germany (see October 21 entry).

1915 U.S. President Woodrow Wilson got married.

1917 The U.S. government nationalized the railroads.

1943 Keith Richards was born in Dartford, England (see January 15, May 10, May 12, June 3, June 14, July 26, July 30, October 25, December 5, December 6 entries).

1969 Great Britain abolished the death penalty (see June 26, July 2, entries).

1970   The Italian divorce law went into effect.

1978   NASA abandoned the rescue of the *Skylab* space station.

1981   The United States suspended a strategic pact with Israel in protest over annexation of the Golan Heights.

1993   U.S. Vice President Albert Gore and Chancellor Helmut Kohl met in Germany (see February 1, March 20, December 25 entries).

1996   Ethanol producers were given tax breaks by the U.S. Congress.

1997   Drugs sent to Bosnia and Herzegovina were deemed useless.

1998   Impeachment proceedings began against U.S. President Bill Clinton.

To guarantee that business kept its shipments in motion during the First World War, the federal government interceded on this day in 1917. The U.S. government nationalized most of the nation's railroads in order to avert rate hikes and ensure continuous operation. Authorities paid individual railway owners a rent rate equal to their average earnings based on their respective incomes during the previous three years.

Marriage and divorce entered the political arena on this day. In 1915 U.S. President Woodrow Wilson married Edith Bolling Gale. A widower, the president married this jeweler's widow in the bride's Washington, D.C., home. And in 1970 Italy's first divorce law went into effect, even though the Roman Catholic Church objected to this strict legislation.

A cooperative meeting took place in Oggersheim, Germany, on this day in 1993. U.S. Vice President Albert Gore and German Chancellor Helmut Kohl made a pledge to provide Russia with a cooperative aid package. In light of Russia's political and economic crises in the aftermath of the Soviet Union's dissolution, the two leaders chose to offer a helping hand to Boris Yeltsin, putting aside past political differences.

Not all supplies and aid donated by the U.S. government and businesses have been without strings or hitches. On this day in 1981, the United States suspended a strategic pact and arms agreement with Israel in protest over the recent annexation of the Golan Heights by Israeli forces. And in 1997 the *New England Journal of Medicine* reported that of the seventeen tons of drugs and medical supplies donated by American pharmaceutical firms and distributed by the World Health Organization to war-torn Bosnia and Herzegovina, at least half was spoiled, out of date, or inappropriate to the needs of the recipients.

19th.

1875   Carter G. Woodson was born in New Canton, Virginia (see November 6 entry).

1946   War broke out in Indochina.

1957   *The Music Man* premiered on Broadway.

1972   The *Apollo 17* spacecraft splashed down in the Pacific Ocean.

1974   U.S. Vice President Nelson Rockefeller took the oath of office.

1978   The Coca-Cola Company began selling its products in the People's Republic of China.

1985   Mary Lund became the world's first female artificial-heart recipient.

1986   The Soviet Union released Andrei Sakharov and pardoned his wife, Yelena Bonner (see October 9 entry).

1995   The Lobbying Disclosure Act was passed.

Lobbying activities in the nation's capital had reached an all-time high in 1995 and the amounts spent by various concerns on lobbying the federal government had also escalated without a strict monitoring of costs or the extent of activities. On this day of that year, the U.S. Congress passed the Lobbying Disclosure Act, which mandated the disclosure of lobbying activities and expenses paid by companies and institutions.

Guerrillas led by Ho Chi Minh began a series of attacks on the French in Indochina on this day in 1946. This was the start of the original Vietnam War.

20th.

1928   Ethel Barrymore had a theater named after her.

1954   France ordered 20,000 troops to Algeria to stop a rebellion.

1963   The Berlin Wall opened for the first time to West Berliners.

1970 Polish Communist Party leader Wladyslaw Gomulka resigned.

1981 Israeli Prime Minister Menachem Begin accused U.S. President Ronald Reagan.

1984 Thirty-three unknown compositions by Johann Sebastian Bach were found in the Yale Library at Hartford, Connecticut.

1989 U.S. President George H. Bush sent troops into Panama (see January 3, September 5 entries).

A new theater opened in New York City on this day in 1928, named after an American actress with an illustrious lineage. Ethel Barrymore became the first living American actress to have a theater named after her.

East Bloc nations made the headlines on this day in 1963. For the first time since it was built, the Berlin Wall was opened to West Berlin citizens. The temporary opening allowed families single-day passes to visit their East Berlin relatives for Christmas and New Year celebrations. And in 1970 Communist Party leader Wladyslaw Gomulka resigned in Poland, after a week of riots over food prices.

Relations between the state of Israel and the United States became slightly strained on this day in 1981. Israeli Prime Minister Menachem Begin publicly accused U.S. President Ronald Reagan of treating his nation as if it were a satellite of the United States.

Operation Just Cause began on this day in 1989, when U.S. President George H. Bush sent army and marine units into Panama. During this planned assault—which also included the enlistment of airborne forces—Panamanian leader General Manuel Noriega was captured.

21st.

1879 Josef Stalin was born in Gori, Georgia, USSR.

1913 The first crossword puzzle appeared.

1919 A series of raids took place.

1954 Tennis player Chris Evert was born in Fort Lauderdale, Florida.

1958 Charles de Gaulle won France's presidential election (see April 28, June 1, November 22 entries).

1959 Track star Florence Griffith-Joyner was born in Los Angeles, California.

1968 *Apollo 8* was launched, resulting in the first lunar orbit.

1973 The first Arab-Israeli peace conference opened in Geneva, Switzerland.

1988 Bomb causes Pan Am Flight 103 to crash.

A series of raids took place in the United States on this day in 1919. U.S. Attorney General A. Mitchell Palmer ordered the arrest of more than a dozen people suspected of being communists and organized their deportation back to Europe.

One of the saddest terrorist attacks took place on this day in 1988, when Pan Am Flight 103 crashed near Lockerbie, Scotland. Caused by an explosion on board the aircraft, the catastrophe killed 259 passengers as well as 11 people on the ground.

The Sunday newspaper crossword puzzle has become a tradition for many people. On this day in 1913, the first crossword puzzle—written by Arthur Wynne—appeared in the *New York World*'s Sunday supplement section.

22nd.

1894 French army officer Alfred Dreyfus was convicted of espionage.

1921 The Russian Famine Relief Act was passed.

1976 U.S. Attorney General Griffin Bell announced his resignation from restrictive clubs.

1989 Romanian President Nicolae Ceausescu was overthrown (see December 15, December 23 entries).

1997 The American Registry for Internet Numbers began operations.

U.S. Attorney General Griffin Bell stood by his convictions on this day in 1976. He publicly announced his resignation from all private clubs, including two organizations in Atlanta, Georgia, that had no African-Americans or Jews on its membership rosters.

The U.S. Congress authorized a generous donation of aid to Russia on this day in 1921. The Russian Famine Relief Act was passed, resulting in the purchase of $20 million in food for citizens of the newly formed Soviet Union, which was headed by Vladimir Lenin.

23rd.

1805 Joseph Smith, founder of the Mormon church, was born in Sharon, Vermont (see May 2, August 8, August 29, October 6 entries).

1978 Rod Stewart donated his royalties to UNICEF.

1986 The first non-refueled, nonstop flight around the world was completed.

1989 Nicolae Ceausescu and his wife, Elena, were captured as they attempted to flee Romania (see December 15, December 22 entries).

The first non-refueled, nonstop air circumnavigation ended on this day in 1986. The experimental plane *Voyager,* which was piloted by Dick Rutan and Jeana Yeager, safely landed at Edwards Air Force Base in California.

Pop singer Rod Stewart made a very generous donation on this day in 1978. The Scottish performer transferred his royalties from the song "Do Ya Think I'm Sexy" as a contribution to UNICEF. Ironically, the song became Stewart's biggest-selling hit.

24th.

1908 Motion picture censorship began.

1948 The first solar-heated house was occupied.

1992 U.S. President George H. Bush pardoned six people involved in the Iran-Contra affair.

On this day in 1948, residents moved into the world's first solar-heated home, situated in Dover, Massachusetts. Designed by Eleanor Raymond, the project was funded by

Amelia Peabody. The building's unique solar-based heating system was designed and developed by Dr. Maria Telkes.

In 1908 motion pictures were still in their infancy as a public form of entertainment. To assure the viewing public that the content of this new medium abided by general social mores and morals, the Society for the Prevention of Vice in New York City established a new panel on this day. This small group of concerned citizens inaugurated the first motion picture censorship system, rating feature films as well as shorts for the decency of their content and presentation.

U.S. President George H. Bush pardoned six criminals on this day in 1992. Among those people were former U.S. Secretary of Defense Caspar W. Weinberger as well as five Reagan administration officials who had been indicted or convicted of lying before Congress about incidents surrounding the Iran-Contra affair.

25th.

1918   Anwar Sadat was born in the Tala district of Egypt.

1924   Rod Serling was born.

1971   Reverend Jesse Jackson organized Operation PUSH (People United to Save Humanity) in Chicago, Illinois.

1991   Mikhail Gorbachev resigned as Soviet premier, transferring power to Russian President Boris Yeltsin (see February 1, March 20, May 29, November 6, December 18 entries).

A man who changed our perceptions of fantasy and terror was born in Syracuse, New York, on this day in 1924. Rod Serling had won an award for a television script he wrote while still in college. This encouraged him to pursue a full-time career as a scriptwriter during the 1950s. Starting out with investigative dramas such as "Patterns" for NBC-TV, Serling expanded his repertoire to classic television dramas like the award-winning "Requiem for a Heavyweight." His liberal attitude toward his subjects caused some strain, so he turned to fantasy as his next outlet. As he once said, "I found that it was all right to have Martians saying things Democrats and Republicans could never say." The result was "The Twilight Zone," which won three Emmy awards and millions of loyal fans even though the show lasted only five seasons. Serling also cowrote a film classic, the 1968 sci-fi feature *Planet of the Apes*.

26th.

1908   Jack Johnson was born.

1962   Eight East German citizens escaped to West Berlin by crashing a bus through a border checkpoint.

1966   Kwanzaa, the African-American cultural festival, was first observed.

1967   The Beatles' television movie "Magical Mystery Tour" premiered on BBC-TV.

1971   Fifteen Vietnam War veterans seized control of the Statue of Liberty to protest U.S. involvement in Vietnam.

1980   American hostages offered holiday greetings (see January 20, November 4, November 17, November 20, November 22 entries).

Holiday greetings were sent by more than a dozen of the fifty-two American hostages held in Iran on this day in 1980. Families and friends in the United States were able to see their captive loved ones in a televised broadcast that was delayed by Iranian officials for one full day.

The world's first African-American heavyweight boxing champion was born in Galveston, Texas, on this day in 1908. Jack Johnson won the title when he knocked out Canada's Tommy Burns in a match held in Sydney, Australia. His success, however, triggered much racial prejudice in the United States and elsewhere. Things didn't improve when he knocked out the "great white hope" James L. Jeffries two years later. Johnson was finally defeated in a controversial match with Jess Willard in the twenty-sixth round. His relationship with a white woman eventually led to Johnson's arrest and conviction under the Mann Act. Johnson's tragic life was the subject of the 1968 Broadway hit *The Great White Hope,* which starred James Earl Jones.

27th.

1904   The play *Peter Pan* opened in London, England (see February 11 entry).

1927   The musical *Showboat* opened on Broadway.

1932   Radio City Music Hall opened to the public in New York City.

1968 The *Apollo 8* spacecraft splashed down in the Pacific Ocean.

1978 King Juan Carlos ratified Spain's first democratic constitution.

1984 Four Polish secret police officers went on trial.

1985 Arab terrorists attacked two airline ticket offices.

1985 Dian Fossey was found hacked to death in her cabin (see January 16 entry).

1989 Egypt and Syria resumed full diplomatic relations.

The world was in a state of unrest on this day during the 1980s. Four secret police officers went on trial in Poland on this day in 1984. They were accused of the kidnapping and murder of Reverend Jerzy Popielszko, who supported the Solidarity movement. They were eventually convicted. And in 1985 Arab terrorists launched attacks on two El Al Airline ticket counters. Situated in Rome, Italy, and Vienna, Austria, the attacks resulted in the deaths of 16 people as well as severe injuries to more than 115 tourists who were in those offices at the time.

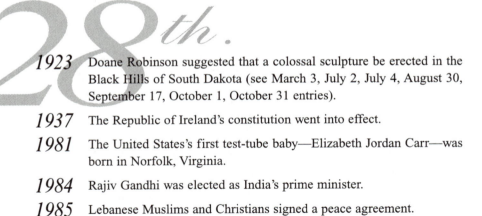

1923 Doane Robinson suggested that a colossal sculpture be erected in the Black Hills of South Dakota (see March 3, July 2, July 4, August 30, September 17, October 1, October 31 entries).

1937 The Republic of Ireland's constitution went into effect.

1981 The United States's first test-tube baby—Elizabeth Jordan Carr—was born in Norfolk, Virginia.

1984 Rajiv Gandhi was elected as India's prime minister.

1985 Lebanese Muslims and Christians signed a peace agreement.

1993 The Vatican and Israel officially recognized each other.

Religion has caused more rifts than unions throughout history. But on this particular day, two separate peace pacts were made. In 1985 Muslim and Christian leaders in Lebanon signed a peace agreement, which was also backed by the Syrian government.

And in 1993 the Vatican and the state of Israel officially recognized each other when they exchanged letters documenting this historic moment.

29th.

1835 The Treaty of New Echota was signed with the Cherokee Nation, after which the Cherokee were forcibly moved to the Oklahoma Territory along the Trail of Tears (see May 20, May 23, July 20, September 16 entries).

1970 The Poison Prevention Packaging Act was passed.

There was a time when both prescription and nonprescription drug containers were easier to open and household chemicals were simpler to use. But on this day in 1970, those days ended. The U.S. Congress passed the Poison Prevention Packaging Act, requiring safety caps to be used with all medicines and chemicals to prevent access by children.

30th.

1936 The United Auto Workers union staged its first sit-down strike, at the Fisher Body plant in Flint, Michigan.

1944 King George of Greece renounced his throne.

1947 King Michael of Romania abdicated his throne.

1968 The federal Bureau of Prisons made an announcement.

1969 At the Paris Peace Accord the United States gave North Vietnam the names of over 1,400 American soldiers who were missing in action.

1970 Spain's General Francisco Franco commuted the death sentence imposed on six Basque guerrillas.

1978 The House Select Committee on Assassinations concluded that U.S. President John F. Kennedy "probably was assassinated as a result of a conspiracy."

1984   The Madhya Pradesh state government in India announced it would sue Union Carbide (see February 14, April 8 entries).

A major international lawsuit was filed on this day in 1984. India's Madhya Pradesh state government announced its intentions to file a suit in U.S. courts against the Union Carbide Corporation. The government sought reparations after a poisonous gas leak at one of the American company's plants in Bhopal resulted in the deaths of thousands of people.

An amazing announcement was made on this day in 1968. The federal government's Bureau of Prisons announced that no one had been executed in the United States that year. It marked the first time in thirty-eight years since the bureau had kept records of executions.

Two European monarchs left their thrones on this day. In 1944 King George of Greece renounced his throne, proclaiming that a regency would rule in the future. And in 1947 King Michael of Romania abdicated his throne, but declared that he was coerced by the Communist Party.

31st.

1961   Carl and the Passions performed under their new name, the Beach Boys.

1969   Jimi Hendrix and the Band of Gypsies performed at the Fillmore East.

1971   The Band recorded a double album during a live concert.

1974   U.S. citizens were allowed to privately purchase and own gold bullion (see April 5, April 19, June 5, August 14 entries).

1982   Steve Van Zandt married Maureen Santoro in New York City.

1999   The United States handed over operation of the Panama Canal to Panama (see April 18, May 18, August 10, September 7, November 2, November 3 entries).

The music world had much to celebrate as the old year ended and the new year began. In 1961 the surfer band Carl and the Passions performed under their new name, the

Beach Boys. In 1969 Jimi Hendrix and the Band of Gypsies performed at the Fillmore East in New York City. Hendrix's new band included Buddy Miles and Billy Cox. Their show was recorded live and later released as an album. In 1971 The Band recorded a live concert that included an encore featuring folk great Bob Dylan. They eventually released as the double album *Rock of Ages*. And in 1982 Steve Van Zandt married Maureen Santoro in New York City. The nuptials were performed by rock-and-roll preacher Little Richard. Bruce Springsteen was the best man. Little Milton and Gary U.S. Bonds performed at the couple's reception.

Index

Brady, James, 102
Bramlett, Delaney, 161
Branch Davidian, 69
Brand, Stewart, 106
Brandt, Willy, 147, 324, 377
Braniff, 153
Branson, Richard, 20, 225
Breitling Orbiter 3, 74, 87, 92-3
Bremer, Arthur, 155
Brezhnev, Leonid, 97-8, 193-4, 195, 317
Brice, Fanny, 94
Bridge: Brooklyn, 186, 236; Golden Gate, 170
Brilliant, Larry, 106
Brisco-Hooks, Valeria, 284
Bristow, Benjamin H., 370
British Association for the Advancement of Science, 254, 278-9
Brock, Lou, 283-4
Brontë, Emily, 260
Brooks: Jr., Charles, 368; Mel, 204
Brown: Dave, 61; Helen Gurley, 61; Ron, 50-1
Bruce, James, 151
Bruno, Giordano, 60
Bruzzo, Ben, 254
Bryant, Anita, 97
Buchanan: Buck, 282-3; James McGill, 304-5
Buddha, 115-6, 215. See Siddhartha, Prince Gautama
Buis, Dale R., 217
bull, 279
Bull, Chief, Sitting, 227-8, 375
Bunche, Ralph J., 246-7
Bunker, Archie, 17
Bureau: of Alcohol Tobacco and Firearms (BATF), 75-76, 210; of Fisheries, 170; of Immigration, 259; of Indian Affairs (BIA), 84-5, 155
Burgess, Anthony, 67
Burnell, Dr. Jocelyn Bell, 71
Burns: Joseph, 329; Ken, 236; Tommy, 384
Burroughs, William, 44
Burton: Richard, 69 Sir Richard, 91-92; Tim, 266, 268
Bush: George H., 6, 16, 23, 44, 88, 95-6, 118, 186, 197, 203, 233, 249-50, 263, 299, 326, 380, 382-3; George W., 23, 58-9, 341
Buthelezi, Chief Mangosuthu, 268
Buy.com, 56
Byrd, Richard E., 327
Byrds, 108
Byron, Red, 56

C

Cable & Wireless, 60, 82
Cable News Network (CNN), 56, 122, 160, 176, 351

Cagney, James, 196
Calculus, Professor, 15
Calhoun, John C., 85
Calley, William, 103
Calloway, Cab, 207
Camargo, Maria, 112-3
Cambodia, 155
camels, 78-9
Cameroons, 262
Camp David, 277, 292
Campaneris, Bert, 280
Campbell Soup Company, 288
Campbell, Joseph, 98
Canada, 57, 200
Canter, Lawrence, 122
Cantor, Eddie, 94
Cape Hatteras Lighthouse, 192-3
Capitol Cities Communications Inc., 90-1
Capra, Frank, 158
carbon-14, 377
Carew, James, 69
Carlin, George, 314
Carlos: John, 320, 322; Juan, 229, 332, 382
Carmichael, Stokely, 182
Carnegie, Andrew, 34
Carnegie: Hall, 349; Institution, 34
Carpenter, M. Scott, 119, 165
Carpentier, George, 212
Carr, Elizabeth Jordan, 385
Carroll, James, 268
Carson Pirie Scott & Company, 300
Carson: Johnny, 163; Rachel Louise, 169-70
Carter: Billy, 300; Jimmy (James Earl), 10-11, 26-7, 63, 103, 109, 122, 193, 210, 223, 277, 279-280, 300, 304, 311, 319, 326, 375; Rubin "Hurricane," 93, 369
Cartland, Barbara, 211, 217
Carver, George Washington, 165-6
Cash, Johnny, 118, 142, 183, 241, 362
Cassidy, Cardinal Edward, 86
Castelveter, David, 320
Castle, Vernon and Irene, 349
Castro, Fidel, 21, 189, 254, 264, 277-8, 308, 314, 359, 363
Cats, 181
Catwoman, 32, 137
Cavern Club, 343
Cayun, Sun, 50-1
CBS: 160, 184, 241; *Evening News,* 80; *Sunday Morning Show,* 13 *Weekend News,* 13
Ceausescu: Elena, 382; Nicholae, 375, 381-2
censorship, 382
Center for the Study of Southern Culture, 27
Center, Karisoke Research, 22
Centers for Disease Control, 41-2

F

Faisal I, King, 222
Falkland: Islands, 107-8, 136, 150, 155-6, 196; War,
  138
Farmer, Fannie, 94-5
Farouk, King, 20
Faubus, Orval, 276
Faulkner, Shannon, 26,257
Federal: Aviation Administration, 221, 245; Bureau
  of Investigation (FBI), 135, 144-5, 163-4;
  Council on Environmental Quality, 247-8;
  debt, 96; Emergency Management Agency
  (FEMA), 227-8; Farm Bureau, 82;
  Housing Adminstration, 203; Theatre
  Project, 232; Trade Commission, 106, 298
Fedje, Daryl, 157
Feinstein, Dianne, 197, 365
Fenian Society, 71
Ferdinand of Spain, King, 102-3, 125
Ferguson, Miriam, 339
ferret, black-footed, 318
Fetch, Tom, 262
Fiat (Fabrrica Italiano Automobili Torino), 86
Fields, W.C., 94
Fiennes, Ranulph, 270
"Fight of the Century," 23
Finland, 2
Finnbogadottir, Vigdis, 125, 207
Firestone Tire Company, 112-3
Fisher, Eddie, 69
Fixx, Jim, 227
Flaherty, Robert, 58-9
Fleetwood Mac, 36
Fleming: Ian, 287; Victor, 65
Flipper, Henry O., 62, 190
Florida Citrus Growers Association, 97
Flower, Roswell P., 84
Flying Wing, 344
Flynn, Errol, 195
Follies Bergere, 94
Fonda: Henry, 65; Jane, 65, 351; Peter, 65
Fonteyn, Dame Margot, 89, 158
food stamp, 156, 180
football: Chicago Bears, 188; New York Giants, 171
Ford Motor Company, 85-86, 154, 191, 276
Ford: Betty, 116-117; Gerald R., 114, 123, 165-6,
  214, 280, 290, 295, 315, 357, 362-3;
  Harrison, 221; Henry, 166, 191, 365
Foreman, George, 15, 331
Forest, Bandelier National, 145
Fort: Chafee Relocation Center, 177; Megis Treaty,
  301
Fortensky, Larry, 69
Fortune, 189
Fosdick, Henry Emerson, 78-9

Fosse, Bob, 198
Fossett, Steve, 19, 26, 64, 247, 257
Fossey, Dian, 21, 385
Foucault, Jean, 292
Four: Noble Truths, 116; Tops, 358
Fox, 223
Franco, Francisco, 229, 365, 386
Frank, Anne, 186, 190
Franklin Mint, 13
Franklin, Aretha, 4, 6, 82, 97
Fraser, Dawn, 276-7
Frazier, Joe, 22-3, 82
Frederick of Denmark, King, 204
Freemen, 188
French, George Arthur, 164
Friedman, Milton, 237-8
Friends of the Everglades, 116
Frontier Airlines, 187
Fuller: Ida May, 37; Robert Buckminster, 220
Fundamentalism, 79
fundamentalist, 80-1, 125, 200

G

Gagarin, Yuri, 83, 122
Galabert Astronautical Prize, 83
Gale, Edith Boling, 378
Galloping Ghost, 188
Galtieri, Leopoldo, 108, 192
Gandhi: Mohandas K., 90-1, 189, 269, 340, 348;
  Rajiv, 385
Garagiola, Joe, 153
Garcia, Jerry, 240-1, 250-1
Garvey, Marcus, 241, 258
gasoline, 78, 121
Gaspar, Matej, 220
Gates, Bill, 330-1
Gaye, Marvin, 107-8, 358
Gehrig, Lou, 117
Geisel, Dr. Theodore (Teddy), 21, 75-6. *See also*
  Dr. Seuss
Gemini: 4, 179; *8,* 245; *9,* 181 *III,* 110
gender gap, 154
General Electric Company, 331, 371
General Motors Corporation, 43, 152, 242
genocide, 62
Genovese, Kitty, 86-87
geodesic, 220
George: of Greece, King, 386-7; VI of England,
  King, 45, 151, 178-9, 244, 374
Geronimo, 276
Gershwin, George, 53, 274
Getz, Stan, 41-2
Ghadafi, Moammar, 274
Giamatti, A. Bartlett, 288
Giannini, Giancarlo, 255

Gibson: Althea, 215, 218, 256; William, 61
Gielgud, Sir Arthur John, 123-4
Gilbert, William 167
Gilberto, Astrid, 42
Gilbreth: Frank Bunker, 165; Millian Moller, 165
Gillespie, Dizzy, 9
Gillette, King C., 363
Gilliam, Terry, 353-4
Ginsburg, Ruth Bader, 189
ginseng, 64
Gipsy Moth: 291; *III,* 291; *IV,* 291
Giuliani, Rudolph, 341
Givens, Robin, 208
glaucoma, 121
Glenn, John, 83, 119, 331
global warming, 198-9
Gnadenhutten, 82
Goddard, Robert, 222
Godwin, William, 69
Godzilla, 338
gold, 12-3, 22, 83, 112-4, 128, 181, 255-6, 307, 377, 387
Gomulka, Wladyslaw, 380
Gonzalez, Elián, 8, 132, 354
gonzo, 226
Goodall, Jane, 108, 110
Goodman: Andrew, 244; Benny, 216; Jr., Robert O., 4-5
Goolagong, Evonne, 216
gopherspace, 350
Gorbachev: Mikhail, 32-4, 75-6, 84-5, 155, 162, 218, 236, 362-3, 369, 383; Raisa, 76
Gordy, Jr., Berry, 358
Gore, Albert, 93, 102, 341, 378
gorilla, mountain, 21-2
Graf, Steffi, 190, 281
Graham, Katharine, 132, 191
Grahame, Kenneth, 82
Grand Funk Railroad, 198
Grand Ole Opry, 139, 297, 314, 317,
Grange, Harold "Red," 188
Grant, Ulysses S., 370
Grappelli, Stephane, 30
Grateful Dead, 241, 251, 290
Gray, L. Patrick, 135
Great: Depression, 96, 171-2, 232, 235; White Fleet, 376
Greene, Graham, 304-5
Greenglass, David, 113
Greenspan, Alan, 79-80
Greer, Germaine, 36
Gregory, Frederick, 137
Grenada, 328
Gretzky, Wayne "The Great One," 32
Greyhound, 94

Griffith: D.W. (David Wark), 28; Melanie, 25
Grissom, Virgil "Gus," 108, 110, 119
Gromyko, Andrei, 57
Grossinger, Jennie, 191
Guam, 195-6
Guantanamo, 9, 66, 79, 259
guerillas, 89, 203, 255, 261, 274, 386
Guest, Judith, 101
Guevara, Ernesto Ché, 189, 312, 314
Guggenheim Museum, 324
Guillaume, Marcel, 54
Guinness, Sir Alec, 107-8
Gullickson, Bill, 283-4
gun control, 154, 240
Gunyashev, Alexander, 176-7
Guofeng, Hua, 312-3
Gustav, King, 180
Gutenberg, Beno, 135
Guthrie, Woody, 166, 240
Guy, Buddy, 237
Gyatso, Tenzin, 215
gyroscopes, 316

H

H.M.S. Pinafore, 167
Haakon VII of Norway, 242-3
Haddock, Captain, 15
Haganah, 161
Haggard, Merle, 114-5
Haig, Alexander, 96
Haile-Mariam, Mangista, 52
Hair, 136
HAL, 17
Haldeman, H.R., 63
Haley, Bill, 260-1
Hall & Oates, 198
Halliburton, Richard, 14
Hammarskjöld, Dag, 292
Hanafi Muslims, 84-5
Handy, W.C. (William Christopher), 298, 349
Hansberry, Lorraine, 159
Hansen, James E., 199
Harding, Warren B., 96, 243
Hari, Mata, 246, 248, 317
Harlem Renaissance, 40
Harlow, Jean, 77
Harper's Bazaar, 149
Harpo Productions, 36
Harris, Eric, 129
Harrison, George, 46-7, 118, 166, 234, 238, 270, 278, 293
Harryhausen, Ray, 205-6
Harvard Political Review, 109
Havel, Vaclav, 308-9
Hawaii, 246

Hawkins, Screamin' Jay (Jalacy J.), 225-6
Hawthorne, Alice, 234
Hayes, Isaac, 314
Hayton, Lenny, 207
Hearst, Patricia, 92-3
Heckle and Jeckle, 6
Hedin, Sven A., 62
Hedren, Tippi, 25
Heifetz, Jascha, 41-2
Heller, Joseph, 142
Hells Angels, 367
Helm, Buck, 324, 351
Helms, Jesse, 137
Helmsley, Leona, 372-3
Hendrix, Jimi, 103, 108, 112, 237, 357, 387
Henson: Jim, 296; Matthew, 249
heparin, 69
Herbert, Victor, 40
Hergé, 15
Herman, Pee Wee, 266, 268
Herndon, Jr., Hugh, 308
heroin, 156
Herrera, Omar, 224, 238, 279-80
Hershey Hotel, 19
Hershey, Milton, 19
Hewson, Paul, 150; *see also* Vox, Bono
Heyerdahl, Thor, 135, 309-10
hijakc, 142
Hiller, Dame Wendy, 256
Hilton: James, 281; Nicky, 69
Hinckley, Jr., John W., 102, 265
Hines, James, 282-3
histaminase, 69
Hitchcock, Alfred, 25
hockey: Chicago Blackhawks, 176-7; Edmonton
      Oilers, 33; Pittsburgh Penguins, 176-7
Hogmanay, 387
Holiday, Billie, 207, 215
Holinwin, Jack 216
Holland: John, 70-1, 121; Robert, 123
Hollies, 42
Hollingsworth, Lyman, 365
Holly, Buddy, 32, 42, 279
Holmes, Julia Archibald, 244-5
Hoover: Herbert, 30, 96, 235; J. Edgar, 113, 149,
      351
Hopkins: Lightnin', 219; Sheila Christine, 136;
      see also Scott, Sheila
Horne, Lena, 167, 206-7
Hoskins, Tom, 213
hostage, 26, 133-4, 203-4, 207, 338, 352, 354, 363,
      384
hotel: strike, 203-4; motor, 372-3

House: of Commons, 68, 135; Select Committee on
      Assassinations, 386; Un-American
      Activities Committee, 169
Houseman, John, 232
Houston Symphony Orchestra, 128
Houston, Whitney, 251
Howard, Moe, 194
Howell, Emily, 187
Hoyo, José Azcona, 33-4
Hubble Space Telescope, 134, 373
Hughes: Howard, 77, 217; Langston, 40
Hunley, H.L. 249
Hunter: Alberta, 110-1; Ivory Joe, 313; Jim
      "Catfish," 116-7
Hunza, 281
hurricane, 100
Hurt, Mississippi John, 212
Husar, Archbishop Lubomyr, 64
Hussein: ibn Talal of Jordan, King, 307, 347, 348;
      Saddam, 18
Huxley, Aldous, 232-3
Hyde: Chryssie, 36; Henry, 137
hydrogen bomb, 23, 162, 265; 307

I

I Love Lucy, 317
ICBM, 169, 333
Iceland, 192
Ida, Don, 203
Idle, Eric, 354
immigrants, Chinese, 41
Immigration and Naturalization Service, 259
immigration, 68, 169
Imperial Ballet School, 70
Impi, 17
India, 48, 158, 293
Indiana Jones, 48, 221
Indochina, 379
Ingalls, Laura, 313
Inquisition, 60, 86, 102-3, 223
insole, 17
Institute: for Sex Research, 199; of Experimental
      Medicine, 298
insulin, 68
Interborough Rapid Transit (IRT), 330
International: Association for Management
      Education, 11; Institute of Education, 134;
      Telecommunications Union, 93;
      Brotherhood of Teamsters, 367
Internet: iv, 2, 11, 28, 55, 93, 99, 106, 122, 126, 187,
      224, 279, 295, 355, 370; Protocol (IP), 2;
      Worm, 337
Inventional Factory Bulletin Board, 126
Iran-Contra, 58, 145, 383

Irish: National Liberation Army, 367-8; Nationalists, 134; Republican Army (IRA), 16, 49, 90, 263. *See also* Sinn Fein
iron lung, 315
Irvine, Andrew, 182, 184
Irving: John, 75-6; Leslie, 136
Isherwood, Christopher, 267
Islamic Revolution, 157
Israel, 188, 269
Issigonis, Alec, 307
Ivanov, Igor, 13
Ivashov, Captain Leonid, 59
Ivins, Marsha, 53
Iwo Jima memorial, 343-4

J

Jackson: Andrew, 100-1, 170, 250; Reverend Jesse, 5, 338, 383; Thomas Penfield, 109
Jacobs-Bond, Carrie, 252-3
Jagger, Mick, 152-3, 232-3, 238
JAH, 230
James: Elmore, 33; Rick, 40
Jan and Dean, 108
Japanese Americans, 66, 243, 251-2
Jarvik VII, 115
Jarvis, Howard, 182
Jaworski, Leon, 292
jazz: 236; Gumbo French, 103
Jefferson: Blind Lemon, 219; Thomas, 114, 270
Jeffersons, The, 24
Jeffrey, Millie, 250
Jeffries, James L., 384
Jelderks, John, 132
Jesus Christ Superstar, 323
Jewell, Richard, 234
Jewish Theological Seminary of America, 56
Jews, 103
Jimi Hendrix Experience, 357
Jobim, Antonio Carlos, 31, 42
Jobs, Steve, 253
John Hopkins University Applied Physics Laboratory, 53
John, Robert, 33
Johnson: Amy, 145; Andrew, 66; Floyd, 235; J. Rosamond, 252-3, 372; Jack, 384; John H., 336; Lady Bird, 24, 32; Lyndon Baynes, 182, 198, 240, 245, 271, 275, 301, 332, 341, 350, 358; Magic, 114; Sonia, 366
Joliot: Jean, 286; -Curie, Irene, 286
Jones: Brian, 74, 91; George, 314; Grace, 159-60; James Earl, 384; Jim, 351; Thomas, 52; Tom, 183
Jong-Il, Kim, 327
Joplin: Janis, 25, 185, 220, 232, 253; Scott, 106

Jordan: Elizabeth Garver, 149; Michael, 327
Joseph, Chief, 3067
Joyce, James, 246
Joyner, Florence Griffith, 381
Juilliard School, 228
jukebox, 354
Julian, Dr. Percy Lavon, 121, 129
Justice Policy Institute, 57

K

K2, 128
Kaczynski, Theodore, 109
Kahl, Gordon, 54, 178
Kaifu, Toshiki, 211-2
Kai-shek, Chiang, 27
Kaminsky, Mel, 205; *see also* Brooks, Mel
Kane, Carol, 193
Karloff, Boris, 354-5
Karnicar: Andre, 311; David, 311
Karup, Marcus, 262
Kasparov, Gary, 50
Kauffman, Murray,2 52
Kaufmann, Andy, 193
Kaye, Danny, 23-4
Keating: III, Charles H., 9; Jr., Charles H., 9, 120, 348
Kelley, Beverly, 178
Kelly: Grace, 127; Oakley, 143
Kennedy: Caroline, 235; Edward, 74; John F., 31, 81, 87, 167, 198, 203, 235, 286, 293, 295, 299, 300-1, 302, 310-1, 319, 325, 356, 358-9, 386; Jr., John F., 235, 356
Kennewick Man, 132, 234-5
Kenobi, Obi Wan, 108
Kenton, Stan, 312
Kentucky Derby, 47
Kepner, William E., 235
Kermit the Frog, 297
Kern, Jerome, 94
Kerr-McGee Corporation, 158
Key, Francis Scott, 240
Khan: Ali, 319; Ayub, 97-8; Chaka, 183; Ehsan Ulla, 126
Khatami, Mohammad, 296
Khomeini, Ayatollah Ruhollah, 40, 156-7, 194, 338, 350
Khrushchev, Nikita, 62, 81, 83, 99, 317
Kilgore, Evelyn Pickett, 316
Killy, Jean-Claude, 271
King: Albert, 211; B.B., 27, 219, 290; Jr., Reverend Dr. Martin Luther, 129, 154, 182, 250, 351, 371; Rodney, 77, 138, 244; Stephen, 294
Kingsley, Gregory, 297
Kinks, 36

Louis, Joe (Joe Louis Barrow), 153, 190, 296
Louvre Museum, 263
Lovecraft, H.P., 260
Lowell, Percival, 86
Lower East Side, 349
LST, 21-2
Lucas, George, 98, 221
Ludwig, Karl, 311
Lugosi, Bela, 323, 355
Luna: 17, 350; *21,* 12-3; *I,* 3-4
lunar rover, 130
Lund, Mary, 379
Lunik 2, 288
Lunokhod I, 350
Lynn, Loretta, 317
Lynne, Jeff, 166

M

MacArthur: Douglas, 235; John Donald, 79-80
Macbeth, 231-2
Macdonald, Jeanette, 193
MacDonald, Sir John A., 164
MacKenzie, Kevin, 122
Mackenzie, William Lyon, 85-6
MacReady, John, 143
MacSwiney, Terrence, 329
Magritte, Rene, 353
Mahre: Phil, 150; Steve, 150
Maigret, Jules, 54
Makonnen, Ras Tafari, 230
Malenchenko, Yuri, 287
Malenkov, George Maksimillianovich, 79, 81
Mallory, George Leigh, 142, 182, 184
Man of the Year, 110
Man, Mr. Question, 29
Mandela, Nelson, 50-1, 90, 212, 225-6, 373
Manhattan Project, 377
Mankiller, Wilma, 276
Manley, Dwight, 246
Manson: Charles, 31, 80-1, 329, 369; Family 372
Mantle, Mickey, 117, 282, 284
Maori, 46
Marcos, Ferdinand, 31, 65, 284-5
Mardian, Robert, 63
Mariam, Menghistu Haile, 230
Mariner 2, 374
Maris, Roger, 282-3
Mark, John, 365
Marley, Bob (Robert Nesta), 45-6
Marshall, Thurgood, 358
Martian, 271
Martin: George, 4, 182; Judith, 287
Martini, 17
Maryinski Theatre, 70

Masekela, Hugh, 111
Masih, Iqbal, 126
Mason, Monck, 123
Massine, Leonide, 92
Mastroianni, Marcello, 293
Mathison, Melissa, 221
Matlock, Glen, 177
maximum highway speed, 3
Mayfield, Curtis, 178-9
Mays, Willie, 147
McAuliffe, Christa, 35, 274-5
McCandless II, Bruce, 46
McCarrick, Archbishop Theodore, 64
McCarthy: John, 250; Joseph P. 134
McCartney, Paul, 270
McClellan, George B., 330
McClintock, Barbara, 191-2
McClure, Matthew, 106
McClure's Magazine, 114
McDaniel, Hattie, 185
McEnroe, John 183
McJohn, Goldie, 40
McLuhan, Herbert Marshall, 228
McMurdo Station, 3, 52
McNamara, Robert, 125
McVeigh, Timothy, 129
Meatloaf, 198
Medal of Honor, 196
Meer, Johnny Vander, 190
Mei Xiang, 368
Mellon, Andrew W., 95-96
Memphis Minnie, 178
Mendelssohn, Felix, 42
Mercouri, Melina, 320-1
Mercury: IV, 110; 155; *Redstone,* 38
Meredith, James, 250, 301-2
message in a bottle, 313
Metcalfe, Robert, 163
Métis, 164
Metropolitan Opera, 167
Mexico, 5
Miami: 302; *Herald,* 229; *News,* 229
Michael of Romania, King, 386-7
Mickey Mouse, 128
Microsoft Corporation, 109, 331
MIDI interface, 164
Mifune, Toshiro, 106-7
Miles: Buddy, 388; Lizzie, 102-3; Nelson, 276
Milk, Harvey, 197
millennium, 2-3
Milli Vanilli, 66
Million Dollar Quartet, The, 364
Million Mom March, 154
Milne, A.A. (Alan Alexander), 23-24
Milosevic, Slobodan, 61, 308-9

Oswald, Lee Harvey, 87, 299
Otis, Elisha Graves, 94
Ovington, Mary White, 121
Ovnand, Chester M., 217
Owen, Jesse, 211
ozone layer, 281-2

P

Pacelli, Eugenio, 75-6
Pacific: *Clipper,* 9; *Flyer,* 20, 22; Phonograph
    Company, 354
Pahlavi, Shah Mohammed Reza, 21, 157
Paige, Leroy Robert "Satchel," 48, 215-6
Palace, Buckingham, 137-8, 247
Palestinian: 158-9; Liberation Organization (PLO),
    144, 261, 268, 276, 281, 330, 347, 357,
    367
Palin, Michael, 354
Palmer: A. Mitchell, 381; Bruce, 40
Panama Canal, 128, 158-9, 251, 279, 375, 387
panda, 262-3, 367-8
Panghorn, Clude, 308
Papadapoulos, George, 176, 261, 264, 356
Papandreou: Andreas, 44; George, 44
parachute, 136, 257
Park: Grand Canyon National, 67; Lafayette
    National, 67; Yellowstone National, 261
Parker: Charlie, 9; Colonel Tom, 201, 256
Parks: Bert, 282-3; Rosa, 43
Parliament, South African, 296
Parliament-Funkadelic, 229
Parton, Dolly, 25, 317
passenger elevator, 94
passport, 352
Pasternak, Boris, 325
patent, 11-2, 20-1, 91, 222, 319, 343, 365
Patrick, St., 89-90
Patterson, Floyd, 148
Patton, George S., 235
Pavlov, Ivan, 298
Paye, Rufus, 291
PCB, 315
Peabody Fund, 46
Peabody, Amelia, 383
Peanuts, 8, 305
Peary, Robert E., 146-7, 224
Peller, Clara, 14
pen, fountain, 10-1
Penguin Books, 294
Penitentiary: Louisiana State, 27; New Mexico
    State, 41
Pentagon: 18, 30, 171-2, 324; Papers, 57-8, 191, 346
Penthouse, 227
Penwick, Harvey, 299
People's Temple, 351

Pepperidge Farm, 288
Pepsi Cola, 191
Peres, Shimon, 256-7
perestroika, 41, 85
Perkins, Carl, 117-8, 364
permanent wave, 311
Permian extinction, 59
Perón: Eva De Duarte ("Evita"), 147; Isabel. *See
    also* Peron, Maria Estela "Isabel"
    Martinez; Juan, 43, 148, 296, 319; Maria
    Estela "Isabel" Martinez, 43, 95-6, 160
Perry, Antoinette, 203-4
Peter Pan, 52, 384
Petit, Phillippe, 247
Petrochilos, George P. 274
petroleum, 90
Petty, Tom, 166
Pfeiffer, Michelle, 137
Philippines, 213, 214, 296, 329, 347, 357
Philips, Mark, 347
Phillips, Sam, 118, 202, Sam, 364
Picasso, Pablo, 92, 342
Piccard: Auguste, 34-5, 74, 169, 258; Bertrand, 74,
    91; Jean, 34-35, 74
Pickett, Bobby, 108
pig, 319-20
Pikes Peak, 244-5
Pink Floyd, 152-3
Pinochet, Augusto, 286
Pinto, 86
Pioneer I, 314
Place, Martha M., 93
Planck, Max Karl Ernst, 132-3
planetoid, 328
Planinc, Milka, 156
planned parenthood, 145. *See also* birth control
Playboy: Bunny, 97; Club, 97
Plessy, Homer A., 184
Pluto, 44, 86, 328
Poe, Edgar Allan, 122-3
Poindexter, John, 58
Point Foundation, 106
polio, 65-66
Politburo, 83
Polk, James K., 253
polygamy, 126-7, 298, 309
polygraph, 23-4
Pompidou, George Jean Raymond, 214
Ponti, Carlo, 293
Pop, Iggy, 131
Pope: John Paul II, 63-4, 85-6, 152-3, 177, 229, 300,
    306, 310, 311,, 319, 363; Paul VI, 64, 95,
    207, 236, 298, 330, 357, 370; Pius XI,
    172-3; Pius XII, 76-7
Popeye the Sailorman, 22

Richter, Charles, 135
Richtoven's Flying Circus, 143
Rickenbacker, Eddie, 311-2
Rickey, Branch, 153
Ride, Dr. Sally, 168-9
right: to refuse, 268; to vote, 69, 109, 110, 210, 338
Riis, Jacob A., 143-4
Rimsky-Korsakov, 133
riot, 217
Ripper, Jack the, 246-7
Ritchie: Dennis, 318; Simon, 150. *See also* Vicious,
    Sid
Roberts, Joseph Jenkins, 233
Robertson, Robbie, 82
Robeson, Paul, 117-8, 207, Paul, 320
Robin, Christopher, 24
Robinson: Bill "Bojangles," 167; Doane, 385; Frank,
    305; Jackie, 30, 37-8, 318; Smokey, 358;
    Sugar Ray, 97; Tony, 50-1
robot, 350
Roche, Josephine, 363
Rock and Roll Hall of Fame, 4, 6, 229
Rock, Dr. John, 145
Rockefeller, Nelson, 120, 379
Rockwell, Rick, 57
Rodriguez, pete, 224
Roe v. Wade, 28, 120
Roebling, John A., 185-6
Rogers: Will, 94, 263
Rolling Stones, The 9, 19-20, 93, 108, 112, 142, 150,
    152-3, 178, 189, 211, 233, 237-8, 327,
    366-7, 368
Rolls, Charles Stewart, 100
Rolls-Royce Limited, 100
Romania, 375
Romanov: Anastasia, 193; Tsar Nicholas II, 178-9;
    Tsar Peter the Great, 277; Tsarina
    Alexandra Fyodorovna, 179, 182
Romero, Archbishop Oscar Arnulfo, 102
Roosevelt: Eleanor, 119; Franklin Delano, 23, 43,
    62, 68, 80, 94, 112, 113, 114, 347, 377;
    Theodore, 3, 40, 144, 211, 246, 317
Rose: Fred, 291; Pete, 123-4, 225, 283, 284; Tokyo,
    213-4
Rosenberg: Ethel, 101, 112-3, 194; Julius, 101,
    112-3, 151, 194
Rosie O'Grady, 288, 292
Ross: Malcolm D., 144-5, 3412; Nellie, 339
Rossellini: Isabella, 193; Robert, 193
Rostenkowski, Dan, 120, 227, 231
Rowan & Martin's Laugh-In, 28
Rowl, F. Sherwood, 314-5
Royal Geographic Society, 92
Royce Limited, 99
Royce, Sir Henry, 99

roziere, 64
Ruby, Jack, 87
Rudkin, Margaret Fogarty, 288
Rudolph, Wilma, 198-9
Rules Committee, 154
Rundgren, Todd, 197-8
Rush, Otis, 237
Rushdie, Salman, 157, 194
Russell, Leon, 107-8, 161, 238
Russia, 231
Russian Revolution, 83, 179
Rust, Mathias, 242, 276
Ruth, Babe, 117, 146-7, 302
Rutna, Dick, 382
Ryan: Leo, 351; Nolan, 37-38

S

Sacagawea, 246, 315
Sadat, Anwar, 81, 109, 125, 256, 277, 292, 308, 313,
    367, 369, 383
Sakharov: Andrei, 161-2, 312, 379
Sakigake, 13
Sales: Hunt, 198; Tony, 198
Salk, Dr. Jonas P., 66, 240, 330
Sallé, Marie, 113
SALT: I, 168-9; II, 149, 193
Salyut: 6, 16; *I,* 128-9
Sam, Magic, 237
samurai, 106
San Francisco News, The, 191
Sanchez, Arancha, 190
Sandinista, 183
Sanger, Margaret, 318
Santoro, Maureen, 387-8
Saperstein, Abe, 12
satellite, 305-6
Satie, Eric, 92
Satre, Jean-Paul, 113
Saturday: *Evening Post,* 172; *Night Live,* 314
Saturn, 329
Saudi Arabia, 353
Sauve, Jeanne, 135
Savoid, Lee, 190
Sax: Adolph, 339; Antoine-Joseph, 196
Saxe-Coburg: 179; Prince Edward, 55-6. *See also*
    Windsor
saxophone, 196-7
Schirra, Wally, 119, 305-6
Schliemann, Heinrich, 8, 10
Schmeling, Max, 154
Schroeder, William J., 114-5
Schultz, George, 201-2, 285, 357
Schulz: Charles M., 9; Charles, 305, 356
Schwarz, Hans, 314
Schwermer, Michael A., 244

Specter, Arlen, 278
Spector: Phil, 252; Ronnie, 251
Spencer, Lady Diana Frances, 66, 210-1, 236. *See also* Windsor, Princess Diana
Spielberg, Steven, 45
Spingarn Medal, 284-5, 320
Spingarn, Arthur, 362
Spirfire, 100
Spitz, Mark, 276-7
Springsteen, Bruce, 184, 284-5, 388
Spruce, Tabitha, 294-5
Sputnik 2, 338
Squalus, 164
Sri Lanka, 162
St. Lawrence Seaway, 134
Stafford, Thomas P., 159
Stalin, Josef, 81, 133, 366, 380
stamp, 113
Standard & Poor's, 124
Stanford University, 15
Stanislavski, Konstantin, 22-3
Stanley Cup, 99, 100, 177
Stanley: Albert, 71; Sir Henry Morton, 34-5, 92
Stapleton Airport, 70
Star of India, 12-3
Star Wars, 48, 98, 108, 221
"Star Wars," 95
Stardust, 47
Starliner Coup, 94
Starr Report, 285
Starr: Kenneth, 281-2; Ringo, 135-6, 215, 238, 257, 284, 307
State Farm Insurance Company, 137
Statue of Liberty, 107, 236, 384
stealth bomber, 224
Stearman biplane, 350
Steel, Danielle, 255
Steffens, Joseph Lincoln, 114
Stein, Gertrude, 342
Steinbrenner, George, 117
Steinem, Gloria, 97, 275-6
Steiner, Peter, 214
Stephens, Cynthia, 161
Stephenson, Ward, 371
Stern, Howard, 16-7
Stevens: Albert W., 235, 344; Siaka, 129; Thomas, 6-7
Stevenson III, Adlai E., 327
Stewart: Mike, 213; Robert L., 46; Rod, 382
Stimson, Henry L., 312
Stochastic Neural-Analog Reinforcement Computer (SNARC), 250
Stockholm, 232
Stokowski, Leopold, 127-8
Stooges, 194
Strategic: Defense Initiative, 95; Rocket Forces, 333
Strato Lab: V, 144-5; *I,* 342
Stravinsky, Igor, 92, 108, 362
Stray Cats, 118
Strijdom, J.G., 91
Strummer, Joe, 261-2

Stuart, Mary, 374
Studebaker Corporation, 94
Student Nonviolent Coordinating Committee (SNCC), 182
submarine, 71, 120-1, 164, 169, 248-9, 309-10
subway, 329
Suddhodana, 116
Sue, 154-5
Suez Canal, 343
suicide: 351; assisted, 161
Sullivan: Arthur, 167; Kathy, 314
Sumac, Yma, 282-3
sumo, 51
Sun: Records, 118; Studios, 264
Superman, The Adventures of, 8-9, 53
Supremes, 358
Surveyor VII, 14
Susann, Jacqueline, 260
Sweden, 2
swine flu, 376
Symposium on Operating Systems Principles, 318
Synchronous Multiplex Railway Telegraph, 133, 348
Szold, Henrietta, 56

T

Tabram, Martha, 247
tabulating machine, 12
Taft, Helen Herron, 100
Taglioni, Marie, 132
Taiwan, 327
Tanzania, 17
Tarbell, Ida, 115
Tate, Sharon, 31, 249, 369
Taylor: Elizabeth, 68-9; Koko, 237; Zachary, 253
Tecumseh, 302
telecast, 317
telephone, 11, 95, 343
television, 106
televisor, 34
Telkes, Dr., Maria, 383
Telstar, 217, 225
Temple, Shirley, 167
Temptations, The, 150, 358
Tennessee-Tombigbee, 376
Tensquatawa, 302
Tereshkova, Valentina, 191-2, 194
term limits, 101, 163
terrorism, 204, 206, 234
terrorist, 84-5, 88, 102, 125, 146, 310, 315, 363, 366-7, 381, 385
Terry: Ellen, 68-9, 124; Luther, 16
Thant, U, 358
Tharp, Twyla, 33
Thatcher, Margaret, 315
Thayer, Helen, 129-30
Theosophy, 254
therbligs, 165
Thible, Marie Elisabeth, 180

Thomas: Frank, 329; Lowell, 114-5
Thompson: Hunter S., 225-6; Ken, 318; Tina, 50;
    Uncle Jimmy, 317
Thorpe, Jim, 170-1
Three Mile Island, 100-1, 123, 157, 204-5, 332
3Com Corporation, 163
Thuan, Archbishop Francois Xavier Nguyen Van, 64
Thugwane, Josia, 339
Thurman, Uma, 137-8
Thurmond, Strom, 269
Tian Tian, 368
Tiananmen Square, 180
Tibet, 162
Tigris, 310
Tintin, 15
Tiny Grimes & His Rocking Highlanders, 226
Titanic, 274, 324
tobacco, 70, 106, 195, 225, 262, 266, 340
Today Show, 297
Todd, Michael, 69
Toguri, Iva Ikoku, 214
Toho Films, 106
Tolstoy, Count Leo, 269
Tombaugh, Clyde W., 43-4
Tomplait, Claude, 371
Tonight Show, 29, 163, 220
Tonto, 169
Tontons Macoutes, 124
Topkapi, 13
Torch Song Trilogy, 181
tornadoes, 101-1
Toronto Star, 21
Tosh, Peter, 46
Tour de France, 13, 232, 234
Townshend, Pete, 159-160, Pete, 264
Trail of Tears, 164, 386
train: Acela Express, 348; bullet, 348; Shinkansen,
    348; TGV, 348
transcontinental, 143, 261-2, 265, 312-3
Transmission Control Protocol (TCP), 2
Traveling Wilburys, 166
treaty: 62, 95-6, 160, 230, 253, 292; of Fort Finney,
    37-8; of Fort Jackson, 249-50; of Fort
    Wayne, 302; of Long island, 228; of New
    Echota, 386; of Rome, 97-8; on
    Conventional Forces in Europe, 351-2;
    Anglo-Irish, 367-8; Japanese Peace,
    280-1; Lateran, 173
Trenton Times The, 21
Treschkova, Valentia, 169
Trieste, 29
Tripp, Linda, 18
Triton project, 313
Troy, 10
Trudeau, Pierre, 61, 320-1

Truffaut, François, 45
Truman: Harry S, 150, 248, 264, 296, 327, 336;
    Margaret, 264
Truth and Reconciliation Commission, 35
Tubb, Ernest, 285, 317
Tubman, Harriet, 129-30
Tunney, Gene, 200, 295
Turkish Council of Ministries, 133
Turner Broadcasting System (TBS), 351
Turner: Ike, 108, 357; Ted, 351; Tina, 108, Tina, 357
Turtles, The, 150
Tuskegee Institute, 166
tutu, 132
Tuvalu, 277-8
TWO2001: A Space Odyssey, 17
Tyrannosaurus rex, 154-5, 342
Tyson, Mike, 50-51, 207

U

Udar-Hazy, Steven F., 328
Unabomber, 108
Underground Railroad, 129-30
unemployment, 10-1
UNICEF, 24, 382
Union Carbide Corporation, 55, 116, 387
Union of Soviet Socialist Republics, 369-70
United: Airlines, 80, 165; Auto Workers, 210, 386
United Nations, 248, 293, 314, 327, 347, 358, 365;
    General Assembly, 352, 374; Security
    Council, 181
United States (U.S.) Army Yellow Fever
    Commission, 268; Bureau of Immigration,
    258; Cabinet, 327; Census Bureau, 306;
    Civil Rights Commission, 4; Congress, 3,
    7, 43-4, 47-8, 49, 51, 66-7,
    77-8, 81-2, 91, 101, 119, 133-4, 146-7,
    163, 168-9, 170, 184-5, 194-5, 201, 203,
    210, 223, 229-30, 243, 259, 267, 275, 298,
    307, 340, 365-6, 379, 386; Constitution,
    88; Court of Appeals, 11; Department of
    Agriculture, 180; Department of Justice,
    182; Embassy, 100; Fish and Wildlife
    Service, 318; Forest Service, 40; House of
    Representatives, 74, 101, 113-4, 120, 155,
    311; Immigration and Naturalization
    Service, 8; Information Agency, 134;
    Justice Department, 5, 242-3; Marine
    Corps, 99-100; Military Academy, 242;
    Naval Observatory, 2; *News and World*
    Report, 271; Post Office, 90; Rabbinical
    Assembly of Conservative Judaism, 55-56;
    Senate Committee on Energy and Natural
    Resources, 198-9; Senate Ethics
    Committee, 348; Senate, 62, 81, 92, 96,
    100-101, 128, 220, 230, 300, 311, 322,